CRE▲TIVE
HOMEOWNER®
CreativeHomeowner.com

ULTIMATE
BOOK OF Home Plans

COMPLETELY UPDATED & REVISED 4TH EDITION

OVER
680
HOME PLANS IN FULL COLOR

CONTENTS

What's The Right Plan For You?   4

10 Steps To Building Your Dream Home   5-6

Ultimate Book Of Home Plans Introduction   7

Style Seeker: The Top Architectural Styles Of Today   66-69

Creating Curb Appeal:
Making Your Home Stand Out From The Crowd   114-119

What Home Buyers Want: Wide Open Spaces   196-200

Bonus Rooms & Basements: Finding Flexibility Within Your Home   282-287

Looking Inside Today's Best Smart Homes   370-377

The Wow Factor: The "It" Features Home Buyers Want   456-463

Home Plans Index   515-519

Why Buy Stock Plans?   520-521

How Can I Find Out If I Can Afford To Build A Home?   522

What Kind Of Plan Package Do I Need?   523

Our Plan Packages Include...   524

Do You Want To Make Changes To Your Plan?   525

Helpful Building Aids   526

Before You Order   527

Home Plan Order Form   528

Top to bottom: Plan #F10-101D-0122 on page 128; Plan #F10-007D-0207 on page 106; Plan #F10-051D-0886 on page 64; Plan #F10-128D-0108 on page 159; Plan #F10-051D-0977 on page 39; Plan #F10-024S-0011 on page 121.

what's the right PLAN for you?

Choosing a house design is exciting, but can be a difficult task. Many factors play a role in what home plan is best for you and your family. To help you get started, we have pinpointed some of the major factors to consider when searching for your dream home. Take the time to evaluate your family's needs and you will have an easier time sorting through all of the house designs offered in this book.

BUDGET is the first thing to consider. Many items take part in this budget, from ordering the blueprints to the last doorknob purchased. When you find the perfect house plan, visit houseplansandmore.com and get a cost-to-build estimate to ensure that the finished home will be within your cost range. A cost-to-build report is a detailed summary that gives you the total cost to build a specific home in the zip code where you're wanting to build. It is interactive allowing you to adjust labor and material costs, and it's created on

demand when ordered so all pricing is up-to-date. This valuable tool will help you know how much your dream home will cost before you buy plans (see page 522 for more information).

FAMILY LIFESTYLE After your budget is deciphered, you need to assess you and your family's lifestyle needs. Think about the stage of life you are in now, and what stages you will be going through in the future. Ask yourself questions to figure out how much room you need now and if you will need room for expansion. Are you married? Do you have children? How many children do you plan on having? Are you an empty-nester? How long do you plan to live in this home?

Incorporate into your planning any frequent guests you may have, including elderly parents, grandchildren or adult children who may live with you.

Does your family entertain a lot? If so, think about the rooms you will need to do so. Will you need both formal and informal spaces? Do you need a gourmet kitchen? Do you need a game room and/or a wet bar?

FLOOR PLAN LAYOUTS When looking through these home plans, imagine yourself walking through the house. Consider the flow from the entry to the living, sleeping and gathering areas. Does the layout ensure privacy for the master bedroom? Does the garage enter near the kitchen for easy unloading? Does the placement of the windows provide enough privacy from any neigh-

boring properties? Do you plan on using furniture you already have? Will this furniture fit in the appropriate rooms? When you find a plan you want to purchase, be sure to picture yourself actually living in it.

EXTERIOR SPACES With many different home styles throughout ranging from Traditional to Contemporary, flip through these pages and find which home design appeals to you the most and think about the neighborhood in which you plan to build. Also, think about how the house will fit on your site. Picture the landscaping you want to add to the lot. Using your imagination is key when choosing a home plan.

Choosing a house design can be an intimidating experience. Asking yourself these questions before you get started on the search will help you through the process. With our large selection of sizes and styles, we are certain you will find your dream home in this book.

MAKE A LIST!

Experts in the field suggest that the best way to determine your needs is to begin by listing everything you like or dislike about your current home.

---

10 steps to BUILDING your dream home

1 talk to a lender

If you plan to obtain a loan in order to build your new home, then it's best to find out first how much you can get approved for before selecting a home design. Knowing the financial information before you start looking for land or a home will keep you from selecting something out of your budget and turning a great experience into a major disappointment. Financing the home you plan to build is somewhat different than financing the purchase of an existing house. You're going to need thousands of dollars for land, labor, and materials. Chances are, you're going to have to borrow most of it. Therefore, you will probably need to obtain a construction loan. This is a short-term loan to pay for building your house. When the house is completed, the loan is paid off in full, usually out of the proceeds from your long-term mortgage loan.

2 determine needs

Selecting the right home plan for your needs and lifestyle requires a lot of thought. Your new home is an investment, so you should consider not only your current needs, but also your future requirements. Versatility and the potential for converting certain areas to other uses could be an important factor later on. So, although a home office may seem unnecessary now, in years to come, the idea may seem ideal. Home plans that include flex spaces or bonus rooms can really adapt to your needs in the future.

3 choose a home site

The site for your new home will have a definite impact on the design you select. It's a good idea to select a home that will complement your site. This will save you time and money when building. Or, you can then modify a design to specifically accommodate your site. However, it will most likely make your home construction more costly than selecting a home plan suited for your lot right from the start. For example, if your land slopes, a walk-out basement works perfectly. If it's wooded, or has a lake in the back, an atrium ranch home is a perfect style to take advantage of surrounding backyard views.

> **SOME IMPORTANT CRITERIA TO CONSIDER WHEN SELECTING A SITE:**
>
> - Improvements will have to be made including utilities, walks and driveways
> - Convenience of the lot to work, school, shops, etc.
> - Zoning requirements and property tax amounts
> - Soil conditions at your future site
> - Make sure the person or firm that sells you the land owns it free and clear

4 select a home design

We've chosen the "best of the best" of the home plans found at houseplansandmore.com to be featured in this book. With over 20,000 home plans from the best architects and designers across the country, this book includes the best variety of styles and sizes to suit the needs and tastes of a broad spectrum of homeowners.

5 get the cost to build

If you feel you have found "the" home, then before taking the step of purchasing house plans, order an estimated cost-to-build report for the exact zip code where you plan to build. Requesting this custom cost report created specifically for you will help educate you on all costs associated with building your new home. Simply order this report and gain knowledge of the material and labor cost associated with the home you love. Not only does the report allow you to choose the quality of the materials, you can also select options in every aspect of the project from lot condition to contractor fees. This report will allow you to successfully manage your construction budget in all areas, clearly see where the majority of the costs lie, and save you money from start to finish.

A COST-TO-BUILD REPORT WILL DETERMINE THE OVERALL COST OF YOUR NEW HOME INCLUDING THESE 5 MAJOR EXPENSE CATEGORIES:

- Land
- Foundation
- Materials
- General Contractor's fee - Some rules-of-thumb that you may find useful are: (a) the total labor cost will generally run a little higher than your total material cost, but it's not unusual for a builder or general contractor to charge 15-20% of the combined cost for managing the overall project.
- Site improvements - don't forget to add in the cost of your site improvements such as utilities, driveway, sidewalks, landscaping, etc.

6 hire a contractor

If you're inexperienced in construction, you'll probably want to hire a general contractor to manage the project. If you do not know a reputable general contractor, begin your search by contacting your local Home Builders Association to get references. Many states require building contractors to be licensed. If this is the case in your state, its licensing board is another referral source. Finding a reputable, quality-minded contractor is a key factor in ensuring that your new home is well constructed and is finished on time and within budget. It can be a smart decision to discuss the plan you like with your builder prior to ordering plans. They can guide you into choosing the right type of plan package option especially if you intend on doing some customizing to the design.

7 customizing

Sometimes your general contractor may want to be the one who makes the mod-

ifications you want to the home you've selected. But, sometimes they want to receive the plans ready to build. That is why we offer home plan modification services. Please see page 525 for specific information on the customizing process and how to get a free quote on the changes you want to make to a home before you buy the plans.

8 order plans

If you've found the home and are ready to order blueprints, we recommend ordering the PDF file format, which offers the most flexibility. A PDF file format will be emailed to you when you order, and it includes a copyright release from the designer, meaning you have the legal right to make changes to the plan if necessary as well as print out as many copies of the plan as you need for building the home one-time. You will be happy to have your blueprints saved electronically so they can easily be shared with your

contractor, subcontractors, lender and local building officials. We do, however, offer several different types of plan package depending on your needs, so please refer to page 523 for all plan options available and choose the best one for your particular situation.

Another helpful component in the building process that is available for many of the house plans in this book is a material list. A material list includes not only a detailed list of materials, but it also indicates where various cuts of lumber and other building components are to be used. This will save your general contractor significant time and money since they won't have to create this list before building begins. Visit houseplansandmore.com to see if a material list is available for a home featured in this book.

9 order materials

You can order materials yourself, or have your contractor do it. Nevertheless, in order to thoroughly enjoy your new home you will want to personally select many of the materials that go into its construction. Today, home improvement stores offer a wide variety of quality building products. Only you can decide what specific types of windows, cabinets, bath fixtures, etc. will make your new home yours. Spend time early on in the construction process looking at the materials and products available.

10 move in

With careful planning and organization, your new home will be built on schedule and ready for your move-in date. Be sure to have all of your important documents in place for the closing of your new home and then you'll be ready to move in and start living your dream.

Browse the pages of the Ultimate Book of Home Plans and discover over 680 home designs offered in a huge variety of sizes and styles to suit many tastes. From Craftsman and Country, to Modern and Traditional, there is a home here for everyone with all of the amenities and features homeowners are looking for in a house today. Start your search right now for the perfect home!

Top, left: Plan #F10-076D-0220 on page 56; top, right: Plan #F10-170D-0006 on page 110;
bottom, left: Plan #F10-036D-0242 on page 14; bottom, right: Plan #F10-101D-0123, on page 61.

Plan #F10-101D-0057

Dimensions:	58' W x 90' D
Heated Sq. Ft.:	2,037
Bonus Sq. Ft.:	1,330
Bedrooms: 1	Bathrooms: 1½
Exterior Walls:	2" x 6"
Foundation:	Walk-out basement

See index for more information

Images provided by designer/architect

Features

- The entry hall is flanked by the formal dining room and a staircase to the lower level
- The U-shaped kitchen has dining space and a wet bar
- The private master bedroom has a stepped ceiling, a luxury bath, and a large walk-in closet
- The optional lower level has an additional 1,330 square feet of living area and offers two bedrooms with baths, an office, an rec area, and safe room
- 3-car side entry garage

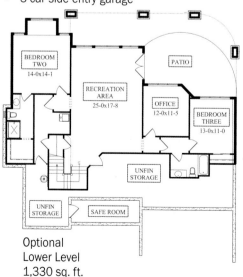

Optional
Lower Level
1,330 sq. ft.

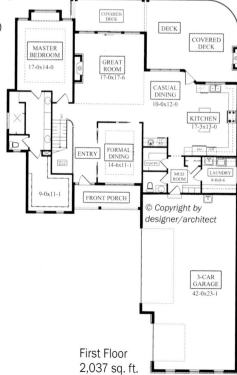

© Copyright by
designer/architect

First Floor
2,037 sq. ft.

Plan #F10-011D-0417

Dimensions:	63' W x 89' D
Heated Sq. Ft.:	3,084
Bedrooms: 4	**Bathrooms:** 3½
Exterior Walls:	2" x 6"

Foundation: Crawl space or slab standard; basement for an additional fee

See index for more information

Images provided by designer/architect

Features

- A Contemporary take on Craftsman style, this home no doubt will stand out from the rest

- The great room has an amazing window wall that will be a focal point, while also providing views of the lovely vaulted outdoor covered porch

- The master suite has a convenient first floor location and includes outdoor access, a sensible bath and walk-in closet

- A second master suite is on the opposite side of the first floor with the same amenities

- The second floor offers a full bath, a bedroom, as well as a game room or additional bedroom

- 3-car side entry garage

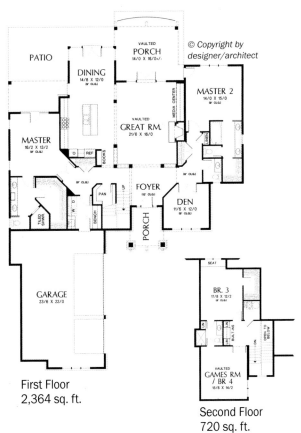

© Copyright by designer/architect

First Floor
2,364 sq. ft.

Second Floor
720 sq. ft.

Plan #F10-164D-0031

Dimensions:	80' W x 81'6" D
Heated Sq. Ft.:	4,522
Bedrooms:	3
Bathrooms:	3 full, 2 half
Foundation:	Slab

See index for more information

Images provided by designer/architect

Features

- Grand European architectural details create a luxurious home waiting to be explored
- There are two master suites; one on the first floor and one on the second floor
- The first floor has a formal dining room for entertaining, or dine in the nook for everyday meals
- Double doors off the foyer lead to the library, a perfect escape or home office
- 2-car front entry garage, and a 1-car rear entry garage

© Copyright by
designer/architect

First Floor
2,726 sq. ft.

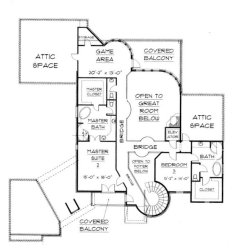

Second Floor
1,796 sq. ft.

Plan #F10-082D-0066

Dimensions:	49'5" W x 40'10" D
Heated Sq. Ft.:	1,833
Bonus Sq. Ft.:	1,009
Bedrooms: 3	**Bathrooms:** 3
Foundation:	Walk-out basement

See index for more information

Images provided by designer/architect

Features

- The family room enjoys a cozy stone fireplace and is brightened by a wall of windows
- The eating room, that is adjacent to the kitchen and family room, is surrounded by casement windows and has a sloped ceiling that adds volume
- The master bedroom has a unique sloped tray ceiling, a wall of windows, and a walk-in closet
- The optional lower level has an additional 1,009 square feet of living area and would be perfect as an apartment

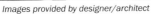

Second Floor
618 sq. ft.

© Copyright by designer/architect

Optional
Lower Level
1,009 sq. ft.

First Floor
1,215 sq. ft.

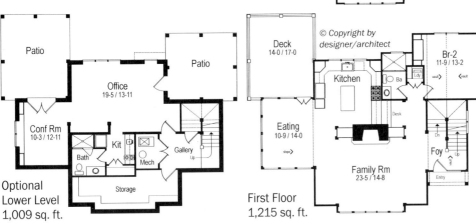

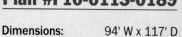

Plan #F10-011S-0189

Dimensions:	94' W x 117' D
Heated Sq. Ft.:	4,903
Bonus Sq. Ft.:	394
Bedrooms:	4
Bathrooms:	4 full, 2 half
Exterior Walls:	2" x 6"

Foundation: Crawl space or slab standard; basement for an additional fee

See index for more information

Images provided by designer/architect

Features

- This stunning home has five amazing double French doors across the front allowing virtually every room in the home to access the outdoors easily
- The welcoming great room has a large fireplace and to the right is the open kitchen with an oversized island
- The hobby/mud room is a great place for a variety of tasks
- The spacious vaulted master suite enjoys vaulted porch access, his and hers walk-in closets, and a luxurious bath
- Around the corner from the kitchen and near the hobby/mud room is a wine cellar and a walk-in pantry
- The cozy den has two sets of French doors adding plenty of natural sunlight and makes a great home office
- The second floor laundry room makes this chore an easy one
- The optional bonus room on the second floor has an additional 394 square feet of living area
- 4-car side entry garage

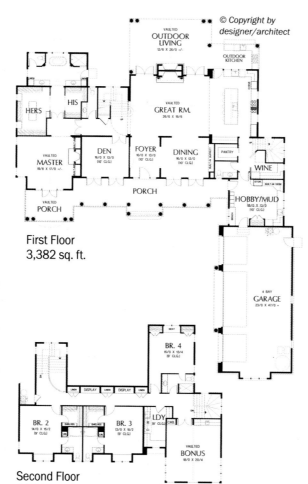

© Copyright by designer/architect

First Floor
3,382 sq. ft.

Second Floor
1,521 sq. ft.

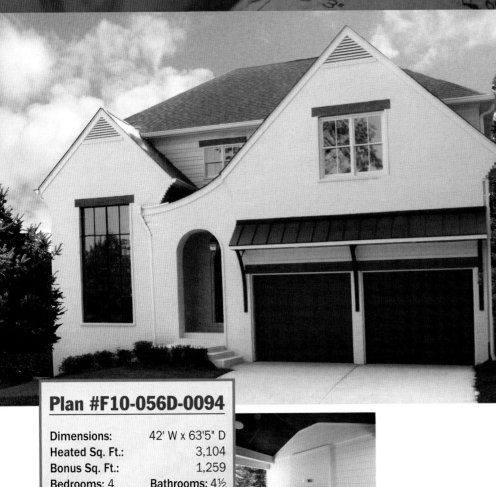

Plan #F10-056D-0094

Dimensions: 42' W x 63'5" D
Heated Sq. Ft.: 3,104
Bonus Sq. Ft.: 1,259
Bedrooms: 4 **Bathrooms:** 4½
Foundation: Basement standard; crawl space or slab for an additional fee

See index for more information

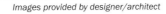

Images provided by designer/architect

Features

- This charming European inspired two-story home has a sleek facade loaded with curb appeal
- A social room has French doors that access a covered porch and is steps from the kitchen and breakfast area
- The second floor features a large media room, great for movie nights
- The optional lower has an additional 1,259 square feet of living area and includes a party room, billiards, a wet bar, a bedroom and a full bath
- 2-car front entry garage

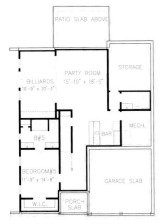

Optional Lower Level
1,259 sq. ft.

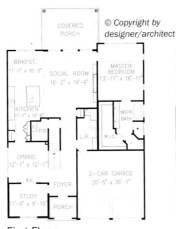

© Copyright by designer/architect

First Floor
1,675 sq. ft.

Second Floor
1,429 sq. ft.

Second Floor
637 sq. ft.

© Copyright by
designer/architect

Plan #F10-036D-0242

Images provided by
designer/architect

Dimensions:	80' W x 83'4" D
Heated Sq. Ft.:	3,341
Bedrooms: 4	Bathrooms: 3½
Foundation:	Slab

See index for more information

First Floor
2,704 sq. ft.

Optional
Second Floor
332 sq. ft.

© Copyright by designer/architect

Plan #F10-170D-0015

Images provided by
designer/architect

Dimensions:	90'8" W x 59' D
Heated Sq. Ft.:	2,694
Bonus Sq. Ft.:	332
Bedrooms: 4	Bathrooms: 3

Foundation: Monolithic slab
or slab standard; crawl space,
basement or daylight basement for
an additional fee

See index for more information

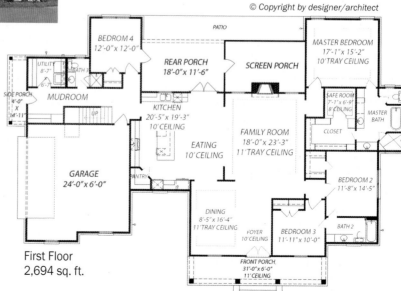

First Floor
2,694 sq. ft.

Plan #F10-056D-0098

Dimensions: 84'10" W x 61' D
Heated Sq. Ft.: 3,123
Bedrooms: 4   **Bathrooms:** 3
Foundation: Basement standard; crawl space or slab for an additional fee

See index for more information

Images provided by designer/architect

© Copyright by designer/architect

Lower Level
1,247 sq. ft.

SOCIAL ROOM 21'-5"X27'-2"
PATIO SLAB
STORAGE#1
STORAGE#2
BAR
SHOP AREA 16'-6"x19'-8"
BEDROOM#4 13'-0"x11'-1"
B#3
SPA
BEDROOM#3 13'-0"x11'-2"

First Floor
1,876 sq. ft.

LAKE ROOM 21'-5"x16'-3" VAULTED
SCREENED PORCH 21'-3"x16'-3" VAULTED
VAULT VAULT
OFFICE 11'-6"x6'-0"
LAUN. 11'-6"x6'3"
12' CEILING
KITCHEN 15'-2"x14'-2"
DINING 15'-1"x1'-6"
MASTER BEDROOM 13'-0"x18'-2" VAULTED
STORAGE 7'-0"x13'6"
PAN.
W.I.C.
B#2
W.I.C.
2-CAR GARAGE 23'-9" x 23'-5"
BEDROOM#2 STUDY 11'-6"x10'-9" 10' CEILING
FOYER
M.BATH
PORCH

Plan #F10-170D-0003

Dimensions: 70'9" W x 91' D
Heated Sq. Ft.: 2,672
Bedrooms: 4   **Bathrooms:** 3½
Foundation: Slab or monolithic slab standard; crawl space, basement or daylight basement for an additional fee

See index for more information

Images provided by designer/architect

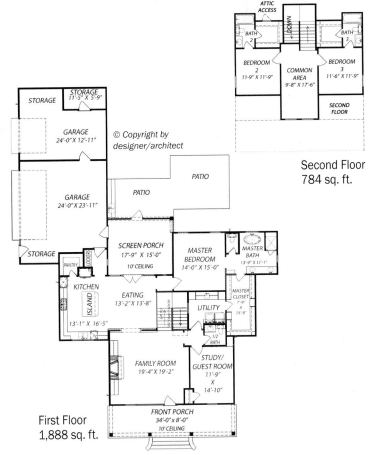

ATTIC ACCESS
DOWN
BATH 2
BATH 3
BEDROOM 2 11'-9" X 11'-9"
COMMON AREA 9'-8" X 17'-6"
BEDROOM 3 11'-6" X 11'-9"
SECOND FLOOR

© Copyright by designer/architect

Second Floor
784 sq. ft.

STORAGE
STORAGE 11'-5" X 5'-9"
GARAGE 24'-0" X 12'-11"
GARAGE 24'-0" X 23'-11"
STORAGE
PATIO
PATIO
PATIO
SCREEN PORCH 17'-9" X 15'-0" 10'CEILING
MASTER BEDROOM 14'-0" X 15'-0"
MASTER BATH 13'-9" X 11'-1"
PANTRY
KITCHEN
ISLAND 13'-1" X 16'-5"
EATING 13'-2" X 13'-8"
MASTER CLOSET 7'-9" X 15'-9"
UTILITY
1/2 BATH
FAMILY ROOM 19'-4"X 19'-2"
STUDY/ GUEST ROOM 11'-9" X 14'-10"
FRONT PORCH 34'-0" X 8'-0" 10'CEILING

First Floor
1,888 sq. ft.

Plan #F10-101D-0050

Dimensions:	110'6" W x 84' D
Heated Sq. Ft.:	4,784
Bonus Sq. Ft.:	1,926
Bedrooms: 5	Bathrooms: 4½
Exterior Walls:	2" x 6"
Foundation:	Basement

See index for more information

Features

- Rustic beams above the entry give this home a lodge feel
- The first floor enjoys an open floor plan that has the kitchen in the center of activity surrounded by the great room and casual dining area with a fireplace
- The private master bedroom and bath enjoy covered deck access and his and hers walk-in closets
- A quiet home office is hidden behind the kitchen
- The second floor loft is a nice place to hang-out, and the laundry room is located near the second floor bedrooms for ease with this ongoing chore
- The optional lower level has an additional 1,926 square feet and has a wet bar, a family room for entertaining, and for hobbies there's a climbing room and craft room
- 2-car side entry garage, and a 1-car front entry garage

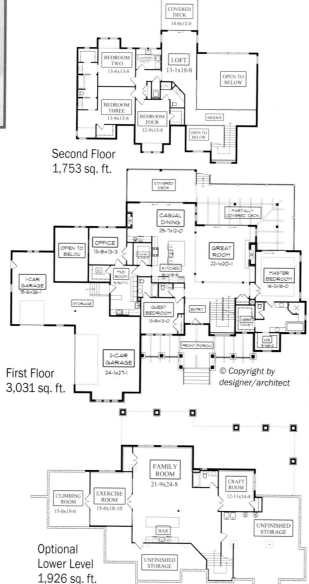

Second Floor
1,753 sq. ft.

First Floor
3,031 sq. ft.

© Copyright by designer/architect

Optional
Lower Level
1,926 sq. ft.

Images provided by designer/architect

Plan #F10-144D-0023

Dimensions:	58' W x 32' D
Heated Sq. Ft.:	928
Bedrooms: 2	Bathrooms: 2
Exterior Walls:	2" x 6"

Foundation: Crawl space or slab, please specify when ordering

See index for more information

Features

- This Modern Craftsman home has an inviting entry with space for outdoor relaxation
- Enter the home and discover an open living room with a kitchen behind it
- The kitchen features a large breakfast bar with space for up to four people to dine comfortably
- To the right of the entry is the master bedroom with a large wheelchair accessible bath and walk-in closet
- A highly functional mud room/laundry area offers storage and convenience to the garage
- 2-car front entry garage

Images provided by designer/architect

houseplansandmore.com

Plan #F10-011S-0088

Dimensions:	100'6" W x 97' D
Heated Sq. Ft.:	4,352
Bedrooms: 3	**Bathrooms:** 3½
Exterior Walls:	2" x 6"

Foundation: Crawl space or slab standard; basement for an additional fee

See index for more information

Images provided by designer/architect

Features

- This home exudes Old World charm with its French Country style
- The beams in the kitchen complete the impression of a rustic, yet richly appointed villa
- The spacious covered deck extends living to the outdoors especially with the cozy fireplace
- The private master suite offers a spa style bath and two walk-in closets
- The laundry room is something to envy with its folding counter, bench, and sink
- The second floor bonus room is included in the square footage
- 3-car side entry garage

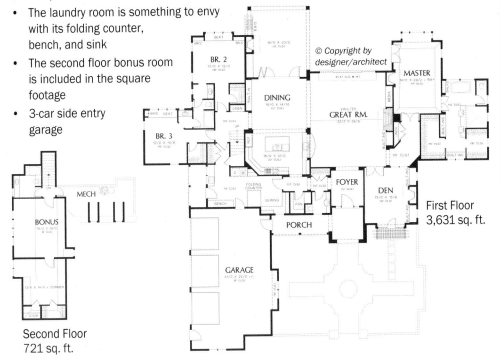

© Copyright by designer/architect

First Floor
3,631 sq. ft.

Second Floor
721 sq. ft.

call 1-800-373-2646

Plan #F10-126D-0832

Dimensions:	50' W x 48' D
Heated Sq. Ft.:	2,453
Bedrooms: 3	Bathrooms: 2½
Exterior Walls:	2" x 6"
Foundation:	Basement

See index for more information

Images provided by designer/architect

Features

- Two-story home takes Prairie style into the future with its sleek, uncluttered interior and asymmetrical exterior
- Enter to discover an amazing openness that makes this home feel much larger than its true size
- The living area, dining area, and kitchen are designed to be one large space, great for entertaining
- There is also a casual dining space near a covered rear porch and the kitchen
- The second floor enjoys privacy and houses all of the bedrooms
- The second floor flex space has a handy laundry room attached
- 2-car front entry garage

Second Floor
1,267 sq. ft.

14'-0"x13'-4"
4,27x4,06

16'-6"x5'-0"
5,03x1,52

16'-6"x13'-2"
5,03x4,01

12'-0"x11'-0"
3,66x3,35

10'-6"x11'-0"
3,20x3,35

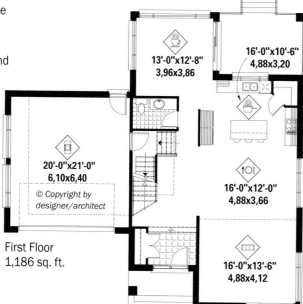

First Floor
1,186 sq. ft.

13'-0"x12'-8"
3,96x3,86

16'-0"x10'-6"
4,88x3,20

20'-0"x21'-0"
6,10x6,40

16'-0"x12'-0"
4,88x3,66

16'-0"x13'-6"
4,88x4,12

© Copyright by designer/architect

houseplansandmore.com

Plan #F10-091D-0449

Dimensions:	98' W x 79'10" D
Heated Sq. Ft.:	3,207
Bedrooms: 3	**Bathrooms:** 2½
Exterior Walls:	2" x 6"
Foundation:	Daylight basement

See index for more information

Images provided by designer/architect

© Copyright by designer/architect

Second Floor
1,506 sq. ft.

First Floor
1,701 sq. ft.

Features

- The spacious foyer greets guests and impresses with a view of the elegant dining room and quiet study
- The two-story family room is an enchanting space to relax with family or entertain guests, and it's also convenient to the kitchen that features a large island
- The screen porch is a tranquil outdoor retreat that has a cozy outdoor fireplace
- The mud room is designed for great family function and features cubbies, a bench, a walk-in closet, and a stacked washer and dryer
- All of the bedrooms are located on the second floor including the amazing owner's suite with a private balcony, bath and walk-in closet
- 3-car side entry garage

Plan #F10-137D-0065

Dimensions:	62' W x 67'10" D
Heated Sq. Ft.:	2,361
Bedrooms: 3	**Bathrooms:** 3
Foundation:	Slab

See index for more information

Images provided by designer/architect

© Copyright by designer/architect

Plan #F10-076D-0230

Dimensions:	66'10" W x 67'7" D
Heated Sq. Ft.:	2,298
Bonus Sq. Ft.:	439
Bedrooms: 3	**Bathrooms:** 2½
Foundation: Crawl space or slab, please specify when ordering	

See index for more information

Optional Second Floor 439 sq. ft.

First Floor 2,298 sq. ft.

Images provided by designer/architect

© Copyright by designer/architect

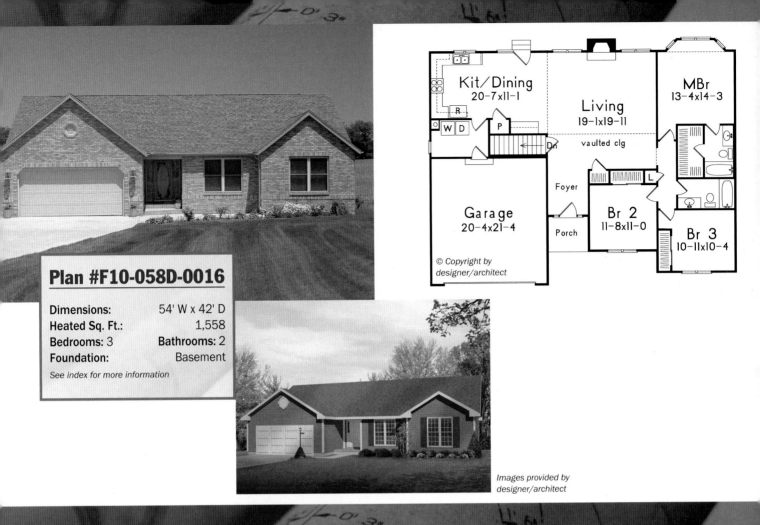

Plan #F10-058D-0016

Dimensions:	54' W x 42' D
Heated Sq. Ft.:	1,558
Bedrooms: 3	Bathrooms: 2
Foundation:	Basement

See index for more information

Images provided by designer/architect

Plan #F10-022D-0026

Dimensions:	60' W x 48' D
Heated Sq. Ft.:	1,993
Bedrooms: 3	Bathrooms: 2
Foundation:	Basement

See index for more information

Images provided by designer/architect

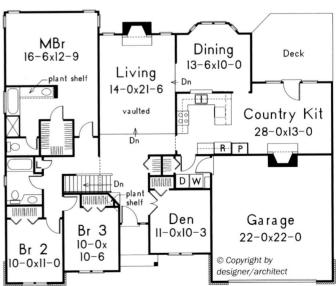

Plan #F10-082S-0001

Dimensions: 121'4" W x 78'4" D
Heated Sq. Ft.: 6,816
Bedrooms: 4 **Bathrooms:** 7½
Foundation: Walk-out basement or basement, please specify when ordering

See index for more information

Images provided by designer/architect

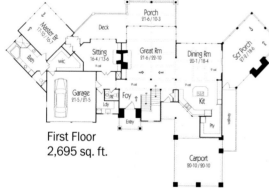

First Floor
2,695 sq. ft.

Second Floor
2,179 sq. ft.

© Copyright by designer/architect

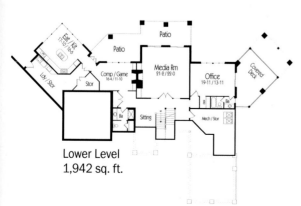

Lower Level
1,942 sq. ft.

Features

- The first floor features an abundance of amenities including a two-story great room, and an enchanting sun porch
- Three additional bedroom suites and a studio for guests are offered on the second floor
- The lower level includes an amazing media room, computer/game room, office and a second kitchen
- 2-car front entry garage, and a 2-car side entry carport

Plan #F10-084D-0091

Dimensions: 59' W x 68'2" D
Heated Sq. Ft.: 1,936
Bedrooms: 3   **Bathrooms:** 2
Foundation: Slab standard; crawl space for an additional fee

See index for more information

Features

- The perfect stylish ranch home with a split bedroom layout
- Enter the dining/foyer and find a beamed ceiling for added interest and it opens to the vaulted living area with centered fireplace
- The kitchen enjoys an open feel and has an island and a mud room entrance from the garage
- The vaulted master bedroom has a built-in bench for added character plus a walk-in closet, and a private bath with an oversized tub and a walk-in shower with seat
- Two additional bedrooms share a full bath
- 2-car side entry garage

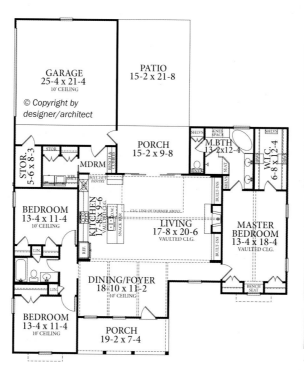

Images provided by designer/architect

Plan #F10-011D-0627

Dimensions:	52' W x 61' D
Heated Sq. Ft.:	1,878
Bedrooms: 3	Bathrooms: 2
Exterior Walls:	2" x 6"

Foundation: Crawl space or slab standard; basement for an additional fee

See index for more information

Features

- Upon entering the foyer that is flanked by benches, there is a soaring 16' ceiling allowing for plenty of natural light to enter the space
- Beautiful family-friendly design with a centrally located great room, dining room and kitchen combination and the sleeping quarters in a private wing
- The master suite is complete with the amenities of a walk-in closet, a double-bowl vanity and separate tub and shower units in the private bath
- Enjoy outdoor living on the covered rear patio that has a built-in barbecue grill and cabinets for ease when cooking outdoors
- 2-car front entry garage

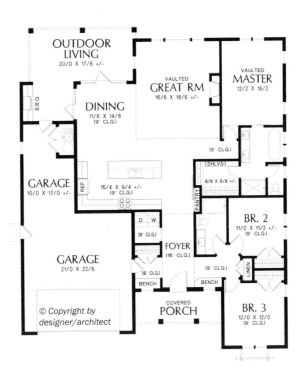

Images provided by designer/architect

Plan #F10-011S-0196

Dimensions:	144'6" W x 86' D
Heated Sq. Ft.:	7,149
Bedrooms: 4	**Bathrooms:** 4½
Exterior Walls:	2" x 6"

Foundation: Crawl space or slab standard; basement for an additional fee

See index for more information

Images provided by designer/architect

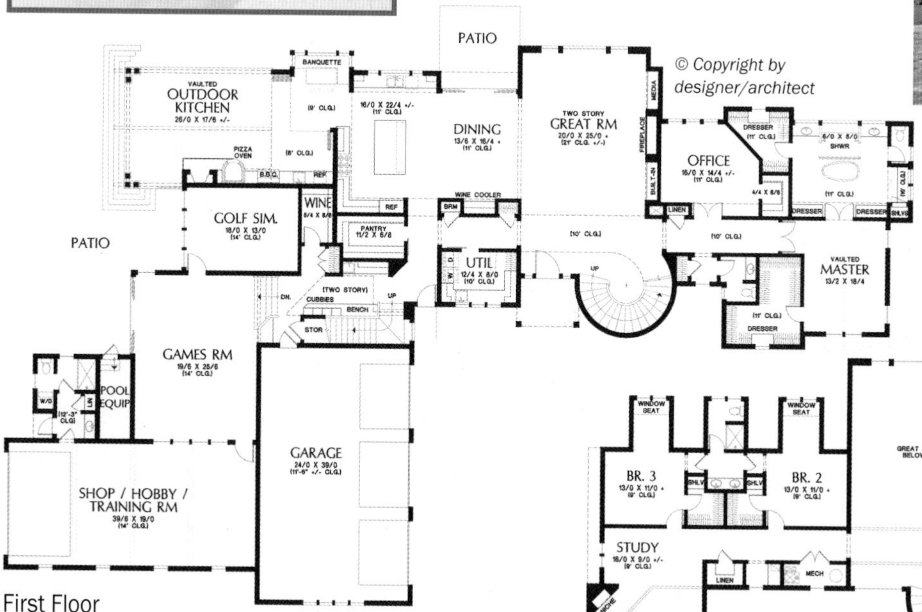

© Copyright by designer/architect

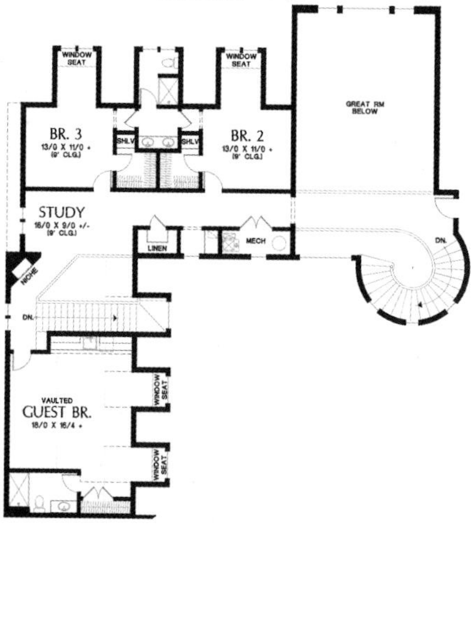

First Floor
5,355 sq. ft.

Second Floor
1,794 sq. ft.

First Floor plan labels:
VAULTED OUTDOOR KITCHEN 26/0 X 17/6 +/-
PIZZA OVEN
B.B.Q.
BANQUETTE
PATIO
WINE 8/4 X 8/8
GOLF SIM. 18/0 X 13/0 (14' CLG.)
REF
PANTRY 11/2 X 8/8
PATIO
GAMES RM 19/6 X 25/6 (14' CLG.)
DN.
CUBBIES BENCH
STOR
(TWO STORY)
POOL EQUIP
W/D
SHOP / HOBBY / TRAINING RM 39/6 X 19/0 (14' CLG.)
GARAGE 24/0 X 39/0 (11'-6" +/- CLG.)
DINING 13/6 X 16/4 (11' CLG.)
WINE COOLER
UTIL 12/4 X 8/0 (10' CLG.)
UP
TWO STORY GREAT RM 20/0 X 25/0 (2Y CLG. +/-)
FIREPLACE
OFFICE 15/0 X 14/4 (11' CLG.)
MEDIA
LINEN
DRESSER
SHWR
DRESSER
VAULTED MASTER 13/3 X 18/4
DRESSER

Second Floor plan labels:
WINDOW SEAT
WINDOW SEAT
BR. 3 13/0 X 11/0 (9' CLG.)
BR. 2 13/0 X 11/0 (9' CLG.)
GREAT RM BELOW
STUDY 15/0 X 9/0 (9' CLG.)
LINEN
MECH
DN.
VAULTED GUEST BR. 13/0 X 16/4

Features

- The elegant entrance of this luxury home opens into a magnificent two-story great room
- Gain access to the second floor via one of two staircases - one has rear access to the guest bedroom, and the other is a dramatic curved stairway that opens into the balcony overlooking the great room
- The master suite is in a private wing to itself and has a space to pamper yourself in comfort and relax in style
- Ample space to enjoy unwinding after a long day is provided by not only an outdoor kitchen but a golf simulator, game room, shop/hobby/training room and private pool bath
- 3-car side entry garage

Plan #F10-055D-0194

Dimensions: 38'4" W x 68'6" D
Heated Sq. Ft.: 1,379
Bedrooms: 3   **Bathrooms:** 2
Foundation: Crawl space or slab, please specify when ordering
See index for more information

Images provided by designer/architect

© Copyright by designer/architect

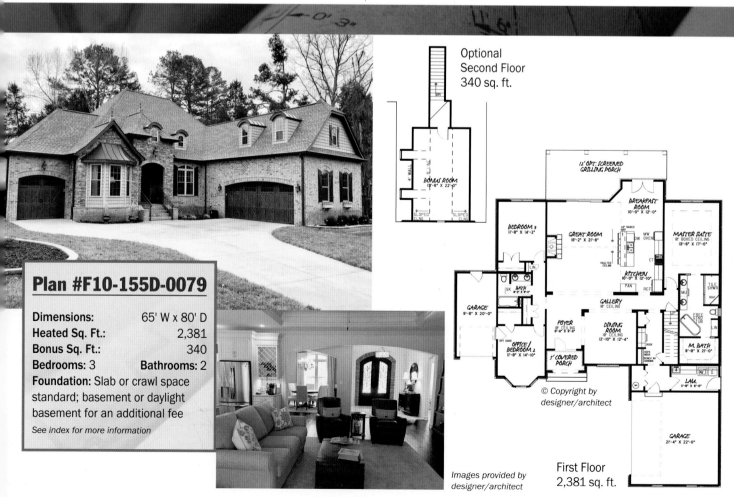

Plan #F10-155D-0079

Dimensions: 65' W x 80' D
Heated Sq. Ft.: 2,381
Bonus Sq. Ft.: 340
Bedrooms: 3   **Bathrooms:** 2
Foundation: Slab or crawl space standard; basement or daylight basement for an additional fee
See index for more information

Optional
Second Floor
340 sq. ft.

© Copyright by designer/architect

First Floor
2,381 sq. ft.

Images provided by designer/architect

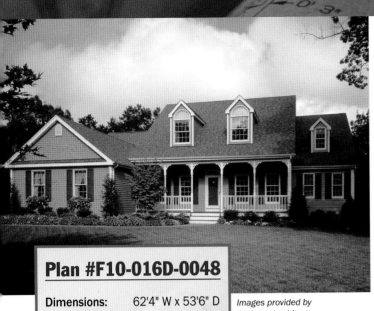

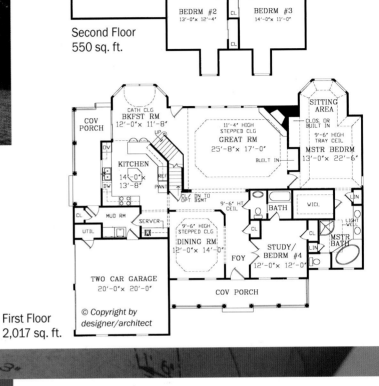

Second Floor
550 sq. ft.

BKFST RM
PLANT LEDGE
ATTIC SPACE
(ALTERNATE VAULTED
CLG FOR GREAT RM)
STORAGE
FUTURE SPACE
20'-0" X 18'-10"
DN
HALL
BATH #3
BEDRM #2
13'-0" X 12'-4"
BEDRM #3
14'-0" X 11'-0"

First Floor
2,017 sq. ft.

COV PORCH
CATH CLG
BKFST RM
12'-0" X 11'-8"
11'-4" HIGH
STEPPED CLG
GREAT RM
25'-8" X 17'-0"
BUILT IN
SITTING AREA
CLOS. OR BUILT IN
9'-6" HIGH
TRAY CEIL
MSTR BEDRM
13'-0" X 22'-6"
KITCHEN
14'-0" X 13'-8"
REF.
PANT
UP
BUILT IN
DN TO BSMT
OPT
9'-6" HT CEIL
BATH
WICL
MUD RM
SERVER
UTIL
CL
9'-6" HIGH
STEPPED CLG
DINING RM
12'-0" X 14'-0"
FOY
STUDY/
BEDRM #4
12'-0" X 12'-0"
LIGHT WELL
MSTR BATH
TWO CAR GARAGE
20'-0" X 20'-0"
COV PORCH

© Copyright by
designer/architect

Plan #F10-016D-0048

Images provided by
designer/architect

Dimensions: 62'4" W x 53'6" D
Heated Sq. Ft.: 2,567
Bonus Sq. Ft.: 300
Bedrooms: 4   **Bathrooms:** 3
Foundation: Crawl space or slab,
please specify when ordering

See index for more information

Second Floor
1,012 sq. ft.

SLOPE CLG
BEDROOM 3
13'4 X 12'10
W.I.C.
OPEN TO BELOW
ATTIC
SLOPE CEILING
BONUS ROOM
14'8 X 13'2
BATH 3
BALCONY
SLOPE CLG
BEDROOM 2
15'0 X 11'10
ATTIC
LINEN
BATH 2
W.I.C.
BEDROOM 4
13'3 X 13'3
OPEN TO BELOW
OPEN TO BELOW
SLOPE CLG
PLATFORM

© Copyright by
designer/architect

First Floor
2,150 sq. ft.

PATIO
PATIO
BREAKFAST
12'0 X 10'4
UTIL.
LIVING
19'3 X 15'6
FIREPLACE
MASTER SUITE
17'1 X 15'8
3-CAR GARAGE
23'2 X 31'0
KITCHEN
12'0 X 14'2
PANTRY
LOGGIA
CLOS.
PWDR
MSTR. BATH
STOR.
W.I.C.
DINING
12'0 X 14'0
FOYER
PLANT SHELF
LIBRARY
12'0 X 17'6
W.I.C.
PORCH

Plan #F10-111D-0029

Images provided by
designer/architect

Dimensions: 81' W x 47'10" D
Heated Sq. Ft.: 3,162
Bonus Sq. Ft.: 208
Bedrooms: 4   **Bathrooms:** 3½
Foundation: Slab standard; crawl
space or basement for an
additional fee

See index for more information

Plan #F10-019S-0004

Dimensions: 81'3" W x 101'4" D
Heated Sq. Ft.: 3,381
Bedrooms: 3   **Bathrooms:** 4
Foundation: Slab standard; crawl space or basement for an additional fee

See index for more information

Features

- This luxury one-story home offers ultra private bedrooms and plenty of spaces for entertaining in style
- As you enter the foyer you are greeted by a wine bar to the left
- The spacious great room enjoys covered porch views and a cozy corner fireplace
- The open kitchen has an island with a breakfast bar extension, a drop zone from the garage and a walk-in pantry
- A friend's entry off the side of the home has the office steps away creating an easy way for clients or business partners to access the office space
- The master suite enjoys an oversized bath with all of the amenities, a huge walk-in closet with utility room reach and a nearby exercise room
- A fun game room is near the secondary bedrooms and offers plenty of space for billiards, a gaming area or a card table
- 3-car side entry garage

© Copyright by designer/architect

Images provided by designer/architect

houseplansandmore.com

Plan #F10-011S-0187

Dimensions:	65'6" W x 113'2" D
Heated Sq. Ft.:	4,142
Bedrooms: 3	**Bathrooms:** 3½
Exterior Walls:	2" x 6"

Foundation: Crawl space or slab standard; basement for an additional fee

See index for more information

Images provided by designer/architect

First Floor 3,099 sq. ft.

© Copyright by designer/architect

Second Floor 1,043 sq. ft.

Features

- Luxury European home offers spacious rooms and extra amenities conducive to easier living
- An open kitchen connects to a vaulted great room with views of the cozy outdoor fireplace in the outdoor living area
- The master suite has its own wing with a huge closet, and a posh bath with a skylight
- A private den with built-ins is the perfect office
- A cozy second floor library is a great study
- 3-car side entry garage

Plan #F10-101D-0107

Dimensions: 90' W x 72'6" D
Heated Sq. Ft.: 2,861
Bonus Sq. Ft.: 1,176
Bedrooms: 2 **Bathrooms:** 2½
Exterior Walls: 2" x 6"
Foundation: Basement, daylight basement or walk-out basement, please specify when ordering

See index for more information

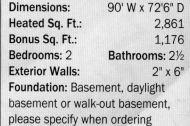

Images provided by designer/architect

Features

- Stunning rustic Craftsman luxury home is a wonderfully inviting home that has all of the amenities homeowners love including an open-concept floor plan
- The kitchen features a massive island and a dining nook surrounded in windows
- There is both a mud room filled with storage as well as a laundry room with a sink
- The first floor guest bedroom has its own full bath and walk-in closet
- The optional lower level has an additional 1,176 square feet of living area and includes a rec room with a wet bar, and a spacious bedroom with direct bath access and a huge walk-in closet
- 2-car front entry garage, and a 2-car front entry tandem garage

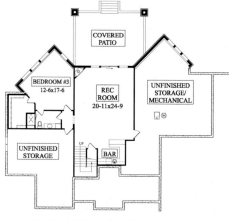

Optional Lower Level
1,176 sq. ft.

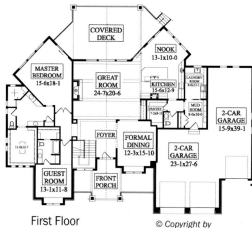

First Floor
2,861 sq. ft.

© Copyright by designer/architect

houseplansandmore.com

Plan #F10-011S-0087

Dimensions:	68'6" W x 102' D
Heated Sq. Ft.:	4,372
Bonus Sq. Ft.:	254
Bedrooms: 4	Bathrooms: 4½
Exterior Walls:	2" x 6"

Foundation: Crawl space or slab standard; basement for an additional fee

See index for more information

Images provided by designer/architect

© Copyright by designer/architect

First Floor
2,833 sq. ft.

Second Floor
1,539 sq. ft.

Features

- Craftsman details add charm to this two-story with room to grow
- The kitchen is surrounded with both casual and formal dining options
- The vaulted outdoor living space has a fireplace to enjoy year-round
- The office has a cozy fireplace with built-in bookcases
- The second floor includes a built-in desk and a bonus space that could adapt to a guest room, or a playroom
- The bonus room has an additional 254 square feet of living area
- 3-car side entry garage

Plan #F10-076D-0223

Dimensions:	91'9" W x 81'6" D
Heated Sq. Ft.:	2,818
Bonus Sq. Ft.:	3,188
Bedrooms: 3	**Bathrooms:** 2½

Foundation: Walk-out basement, crawl space or slab, please specify when ordering

See index for more information

First Floor
2,818 sq. ft.

© Copyright by designer/architect

Optional
Second Floor
468 sq. ft.

Features

- The vaulted foyer creates a grand entrance into this amazing home
- The open kitchen is a chef's dream and a large walk-in pantry
- The rear covered terrace is great for enjoying the outdoors in comfort
- The master suite features a stunning vaulted master bath
- The optional lower level has an additional 2,720 square feet of living area, while the optional second floor has an additional 468 square feet of living area
- 2-car side entry garage

Optional
Lower Level
2,720 sq. ft.

Images provided by designer/architect

houseplansandmore.com

Plan #F10-101D-0131

Dimensions:	99' W x 87' D
Heated Sq. Ft.:	2,889
Bonus Sq. Ft.:	2,561
Bedrooms: 2	Bathrooms: 2½
Exterior Walls:	2" x 6"
Foundation:	Walk-out basement

See index for more information

Images provided by designer/architect

Features

- This charming Craftsman combines casual rustic style and beautiful architectural details creating tons of personality
- The beamed living and dining rooms surround the huge T-shaped kitchen island
- The private master suite enjoys a huge walk-in shower and walk-in closet
- The enormous mud room includes plenty of closetspace
- The optional lower level has an additional 2,561 square feet of living area and includes a media area, a billiards area, a wet bar, a laundry room, a bunk room, a bedroom and a full bath
- 3-car side entry garage

First Floor 2,889 sq. ft.

© Copyright by designer/architect

Optional Lower Level 2,561 sq. ft.

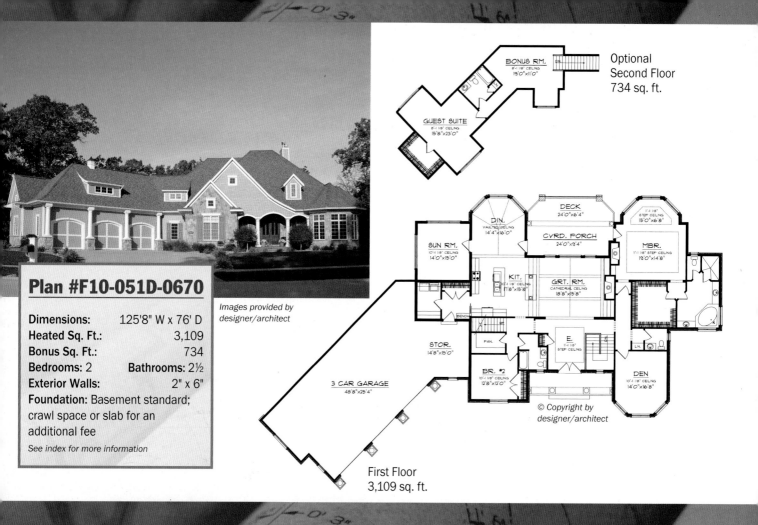

Plan #F10-051D-0670

Dimensions: 125'8" W x 76' D
Heated Sq. Ft.: 3,109
Bonus Sq. Ft.: 734
Bedrooms: 2 **Bathrooms:** 2½
Exterior Walls: 2" x 6"
Foundation: Basement standard; crawl space or slab for an additional fee

See index for more information

Images provided by designer/architect

Optional Second Floor 734 sq. ft.

BONUS RM.
8'-1 1/8" CEILING
19'0"x11'0"

GUEST SUITE
8'-1 1/8" CEILING
15'8"x23'0"

DIN.
VAULTED CEILING
14'4"x16'0"

DECK
24'0"x6'4"

CVRD. PORCH
24'0"x9'4"

MBR.
17'-1 1/8" STEP CEILING
19'0"x14'8"

SUN RM.
10'-1 1/8" CEILING
14'0"x15'0"

KIT.
10'-1 1/8" CEILING
18'8"x15'8"

GRT. RM.
CATHEDRAL CEILING
18'8"x15'8"

STOR.
14'8"x15'0"

PAN.

E.
17'-1 1/8" STEP CEILING

BR. #2
10'-1 1/8" CEILING
12'8"x12'0"

DEN
10'-1 1/8" CEILING
14'0"x16'8"

3 CAR GARAGE
48'8"x25'4"

© Copyright by designer/architect

First Floor 3,109 sq. ft.

Plan #F10-028D-0097

Dimensions: 60' W x 53' D
Heated Sq. Ft.: 1,908
Bedrooms: 3 **Bathrooms:** 2
Exterior Walls: 2" x 6"
Foundation: Floating slab standard; monolithic slab, crawl space, basement or walk-out basement for an additional fee

See index for more information

Images provided by designer/architect

© Copyright by designer/architect

MASTER BEDROOM
18'-0" X 14'-0"

GREAT ROOM
18'-0" X 18'-4"

MASTER BATH
13'-6" x 9'6"

WIC

DINING AREA
14'-0" X 12'-0"

DOUBLE GARAGE
24'X20'

BEDROOM 2
12'-6" X 12'-0"

BATH 2

FOYER

KITCHEN
16'-0" X 16'6"

BEDROOM 3
12'-6" X 12'-0"

PANTRY

6 FT. DEEP COVERED PORCH

Plan #F10-051D-0977

Dimensions:	58' W x 64'4" D
Heated Sq. Ft.:	1,837
Bedrooms: 3	Bathrooms: 2
Exterior Walls:	2" x 6"

Foundation: Basement standard; crawl space or slab for an additional fee

See index for more information

Images provided by designer/architect

© Copyright by designer/architect

Plan #F10-016D-0005

Dimensions:	81' W x 68' D
Heated Sq. Ft.:	2,347
Bonus Sq. Ft.:	823
Bedrooms: 4	Bathrooms: 2½

Foundation: Crawl space or slab standard; basement for an additional fee

See index for more information

Images provided by designer/architect

© Copyright by designer/architect

First Floor
2,347 sq. ft.

Optional
Second Floor
823 sq. ft.

Second Floor
1,190 sq. ft.

Br.4
12⁰ x 11⁰

Br.3
12⁰ x 11⁰

Master
17⁰ x 14⁰
9'-0" CEILING

DN

OPEN TO BELOW

Br.2
11⁴ x 11⁴

WIC

First Floor
1,065 sq. ft.

Dining
11⁴ x 11⁴

Family
18⁰ x 14⁰

Kit.
11⁸ x 14⁰

PAN

DROP ZONE

STOR

Flex
15⁰ x 12⁰

UP

HUTCH

2 Car Garage
23⁴ x 23⁰

COVERED PORCH

© Copyright by designer/architect

Plan #F10-026D-1870

Dimensions:	48' W x 40' D
Heated Sq. Ft.:	2,255
Bedrooms: 4	Bathrooms: 2½

Foundation: Slab standard; crawl space, basement or walk-out basement for an additional fee

See index for more information

Images provided by designer/architect

Second Floor
982 sq. ft.

LEDGE

2-STORY FAMILY ROOM
18' CH

W.I.C.

OPEN TO LIVING ROOM BELOW
13' - 16' CH

BEDROOM 2
12'-2" x 14'-0"
8'-9'-6" CH

BATH 2

W.I.C.

W.I.C.

BALCONY
8' CH

BATH

BEDROOM 3
12'-0" x 15'-6"
8'-9'6" CH

PORCH

BEDROOM 4
11'-0" x 14'-4"
8'-9'6" CH

First Floor
2,112 sq. ft.

F.P.
T.V. ABOVE

FAMILY ROOM
18'-0" x 16'-0"
18' CH

PORCH
12' CH

BREAKFAST
9' CH

KITCHEN
9' CH

PANTRY

LIVING ROOM
13'-6" x 13'-6"
13' - 16' CH

MASTER BEDROOM
17'-0" x 13'-0"
11'-13' CH

ENTRY
18' CH

F.P.

HIS CLO.

UTILITY

W

D

COAT CLO.

PWDR

MASTER BATH
ARCH CLG.

DINING ROOM
12'-0" x 15'-0"
9' CH

PORCH
6' CH

STUDY
11'-0" x 13'-0"
9' CH

HER CLO.

3-CAR GARAGE
9' CH

© Copyright by designer/architect

Plan #F10-026D-0175

Dimensions:	67'1" W x 65'10" D
Heated Sq. Ft.:	3,094
Bedrooms: 4	Bathrooms: 3½

Foundation: Slab standard; basement or walk-out basement for an additional fee

See index for more information

Images provided by designer/architect

Plan #F10-032D-0040

Dimensions:	32' W x 40' D
Heated Sq. Ft.:	1,480
Bedrooms: 2	Bathrooms: 2
Exterior Walls:	2" x 6"

Foundation: Walk-out basement standard; crawl space, floating slab or monolithic slab for an additional fee

See index for more information

Images provided by designer/architect

Second Floor
456 sq. ft.

© Copyright by designer/architect

First Floor
1,024 sq. ft.

Plan #F10-024D-0062

Dimensions:	85'10" W x 88'10" D
Heated Sq. Ft.:	4,257
Bedrooms: 4	Bathrooms: 5
Foundation:	Slab

See index for more information

Second Floor
1,398 sq. ft.

© Copyright by designer/architect

First Floor
2,859 sq. ft.

Images provided by designer/architect

Plan #F10-032D-1135

Dimensions:	65' W x 50' D
Heated Sq. Ft.:	1,788
Bonus Sq. Ft.:	1,788
Bedrooms: 2	**Bathrooms:** 2
Exterior Walls:	2" x 6"

Foundation: Basement standard; crawl space, floating slab or monolithic slab for an additional fee

See index for more information

Images provided by designer/architect

Features

- Stylish one-level living offering an open modern feel that is easy to come home to
- Directly off the foyer is the office/den, perfect for easy access if business associates arrive
- The master suite enjoys his and hers walk-in closets that lead to a posh private bath
- The kitchen has an open feel to the nearby dining room and beyond to the living room featuring a cozy fireplace
- A handy mud room connects the garage to the rest of the home
- The optional lower level has an additional 1,788 square feet of living area
- 2-car front entry garage

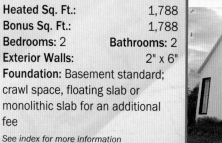

© Copyright by designer/architect

Optional Lower Level
1,788 sq. ft.

First Floor
1,788 sq. ft.

© Copyright by designer/architect

Plan #F10-011S-0085

Dimensions:	168'8" W x 77'6" D
Heated Sq. Ft.:	6,658
Bedrooms:	4
Bathrooms:	3 full, 3 half
Exterior Walls:	2" x 6"

Foundation: Crawl space or slab standard; basement for an additional fee

See index for more information

Images provided by designer/architect

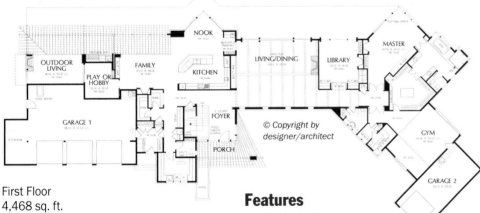

© Copyright by designer/architect

First Floor
4,468 sq. ft.

Second Floor
2,190 sq. ft.

Features

- Prairie and modern influence combine creating a luxury home that has no bounds when it comes to style

- The secluded master suite has a posh bath with a walk-in shower and a spa tub

- The vaulted living/dining area is topped with beams for a rustic feel

- Some fun family areas include: a play or hobby room, an activities room, a home theater, and an outdoor area with fireplace

- 3-car front entry garage, and a 1-car front entry garage

call 1-800-373-2646

Plan #F10-011S-0090

Dimensions:	159'4" W x 93'10" D
Heated Sq. Ft.:	4,887
Bedrooms:	4
Bathrooms:	4 full, 2 half
Exterior Walls:	2" x 6"
Foundation:	Crawl space or slab standard; basement for an additional fee

See index for more information

Images provided by designer/architect

ROOF DECK

Second Floor
1,380 sq. ft.

LOFT
BR. 2

OPEN TO GREAT ROOM

BR. 4
BR. 3

OPEN TO
FOYER
BELOW

Third Floor
231 sq. ft.

CROWS NEST

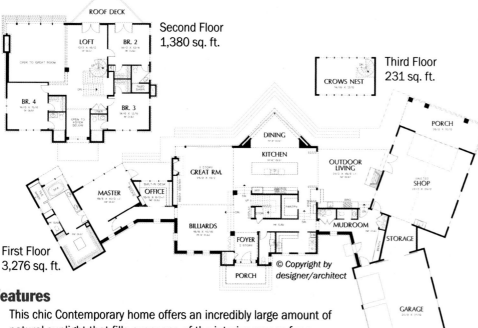

DINING
KITCHEN

GREAT RM.
OUTDOOR LIVING

PORCH

MASTER
OFFICE
MEDIA CENTER

SHOP

BILLIARDS

MUDROOM

STORAGE

FOYER

© Copyright by
designer/architect

First Floor
3,276 sq. ft.

PORCH

GARAGE

Features

- This chic Contemporary home offers an incredibly large amount of natural sunlight that fills every one of the interior spaces for a cheerful feeling
- The popular open floor plan is what families want today with the kitchen, great room, dining and outdoor living spaces merging together
- The kitchen has a massive island with an amazing viewpoint that overlooks the dining space that's completely opens to the outdoors
- Other great features include: a billiards area, a covered outdoor living area with a fireplace, an efficient office with built-ins, and a third floor crow's nest hideaway
- The first floor master suite enjoys a wall of windows, and a tranquil bath with a spa tub
- 3-car front entry garage, and a 2-car rear entry garage

Plan #F10-020D-0348

Dimensions: 70' W x 64' D
Heated Sq. Ft.: 2,342
Bedrooms: 4   **Bathrooms:** 3½
Foundation: Slab standard; crawl space for an additional fee
See index for more information

Images provided by designer/architect

Features

- Rustic Craftsman appeal makes this home feel inviting and casual
- Portions of the front covered porch are large creating outdoor living space
- The formal dining room can easily be reached by the kitchen
- Straight ahead you'll find a living room with a corner fireplace, covered porch access, and an open layout to the kitchen
- The split bedroom floor plan is the most popular and has the master suite in a private location away from the other bedrooms
- A swing room offers flexibility families need and could be turned into a nursery, an in-law suite, a home office, or playroom
- 2-car side entry garage

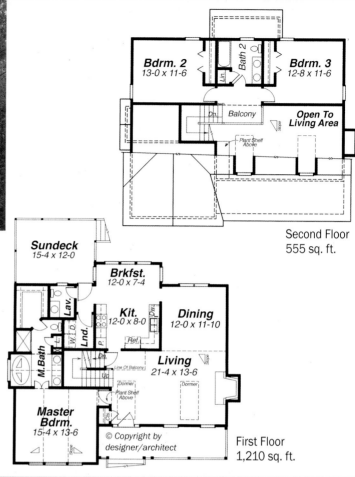

Second Floor
555 sq. ft.

Bdrm. 2
13-0 x 11-6

Bath 2

Bdrm. 3
12-8 x 11-6

Lin.

Dn. Balcony

Open To
Living Area

Plant Shelf
Above

Sundeck
15-4 x 12-0

Brkfst.
12-0 x 7-4

Lav.

Kit.
12-0 x 8-0

Dining
12-0 x 11-10

W.I.D.

Lnd.

P.

Ref.

Dn.

M.Bath

Line Of Balcony

Living
21-4 x 13-6

Up.

Dormer

Dormer

Plant Shelf
Above

Cls.

Master
Bdrm.
15-4 x 13-6

© Copyright by
designer/architect

First Floor
1,210 sq. ft.

Plan #F10-140D-0006

*Images provided by
designer/architect*

Dimensions:	43'4" W x 37' D
Heated Sq. Ft.:	1,765
Bonus Sq. Ft.:	416
Bedrooms: 3	Bathrooms: 2½
Foundation:	Walk-out basement

See index for more information

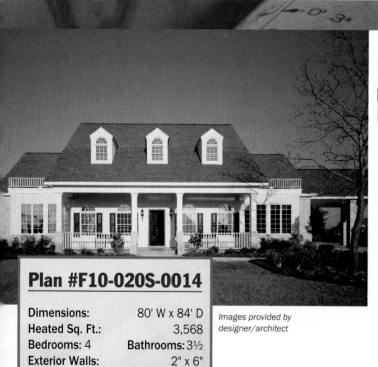

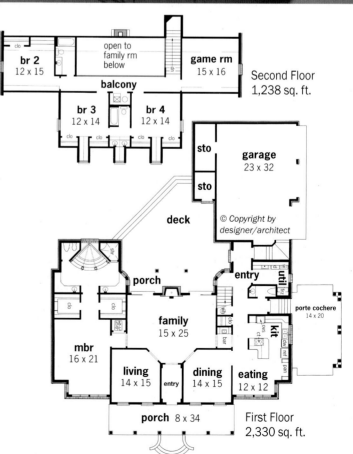

br 2
12 x 15

open to
family rm
below

game rm
15 x 16

Second Floor
1,238 sq. ft.

balcony

clo

br 3
12 x 14

br 4
12 x 14

clo clo clo clo

sto

garage
23 x 32

sto

deck

© Copyright by
designer/architect

porch

entry

util

clo

family
15 x 25

porte cochere
14 x 20

kit

mbr
16 x 21

bar

living
14 x 15

entry

dining
14 x 15

eating
12 x 12

porch 8 x 34

First Floor
2,330 sq. ft.

Plan #F10-020S-0014

*Images provided by
designer/architect*

Dimensions:	80' W x 84' D
Heated Sq. Ft.:	3,568
Bedrooms: 4	Bathrooms: 3½
Exterior Walls:	2" x 6"
Foundation:	Crawl space standard;

basement or pilings for an
additional fee

See index for more information

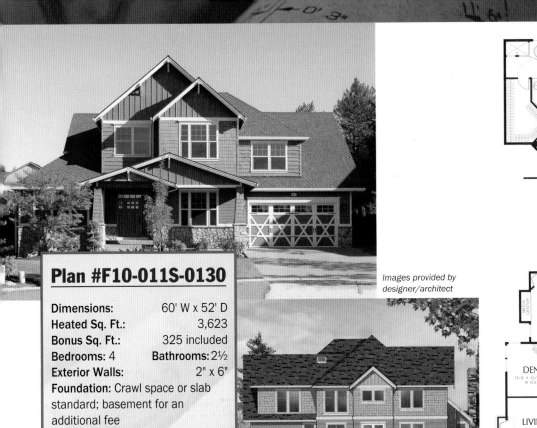

Plan #F10-011S-0130

Dimensions:	60' W x 52' D
Heated Sq. Ft.:	3,623
Bonus Sq. Ft.:	325 included
Bedrooms: 4	Bathrooms: 2½
Exterior Walls:	2" x 6"

Foundation: Crawl space or slab standard; basement for an additional fee

See index for more information

Images provided by designer/architect

Second Floor
1,788 sq. ft.

© Copyright by designer/architect

First Floor
1,835 sq. ft.

Plan #F10-020D-0250

Dimensions:	34' W x 52' D
Heated Sq. Ft.:	2,020
Bedrooms: 4	Bathrooms: 3
Exterior Walls:	2" x 6"
Foundation:	Pier

See index for more information

Images provided by designer/architect

© Copyright by designer/architect

Second Floor
838 sq. ft.

First Floor
1,182 sq. ft.

Second Floor
1,322 sq. ft.

Plan #F10-052D-0073

Dimensions: 48' W x 44' D
Heated Sq. Ft.: 2,389
Bedrooms: 4   Bathrooms: 2½
Foundation: Walk-out basement

See index for more information

Images provided by designer/architect

First Floor
1,067 sq. ft.

© Copyright by
designer/architect

Plan #F10-082D-0030

Dimensions: 62'11" W x 62'10" D
Heated Sq. Ft.: 3,962
Bedrooms: 3   Bathrooms: 3½
Foundation: Walk-out basement

See index for more information

*Images provided by
designer/architect*

Second Floor
1,155 sq. ft.

First Floor
2,807 sq. ft.

© Copyright by
designer/architect

First Floor
1,793 sq. ft.

9'-4" HIGH CLG
BONUS SPACE
46'-2" x 16'-4" / 15'-0"

Optional
Second Floor
779 sq. ft.

© Copyright by designer/architect

COVERED PORCH
26'-0" x 10'-0"

SITTING AREA
8' x 5'

11'-0" HIGH TRAY CEIL
MSTR BEDRM
18'-0" x 12'-0"

11'-0" HIGH STEPPED CEIL
GREAT RM
22'-0" x 16'-0"

9'-4" HIGH CLG

MSTR BATH

LAUN RM

BATH

9'-4" HIGH CLG
BEDRM #3
11'-0" x 13'-0"

VAULTED
BEDRM #2
10'-6" x 12'-0"

FOY

9'-4" HIGH STEPPED CEIL
DINING RM
11'-0" x 13'-0"

KITCHEN
15'-6" x 13'-0"

BKFST AREA

TWO CAR GARAGE
21'-4" x 21'-0"

LOC. OF ALT BSMT STAIR

UTIL

COVERED PORCH

Images provided by designer/architect

Plan #F10-016D-0049

Dimensions: 69'10" W x 51'8" D
Heated Sq. Ft.: 1,793
Bonus Sq. Ft.: 779
Bedrooms: 3   **Bathrooms:** 2
Foundation: Slab or crawl space standard; basement for an additional fee

See index for more information

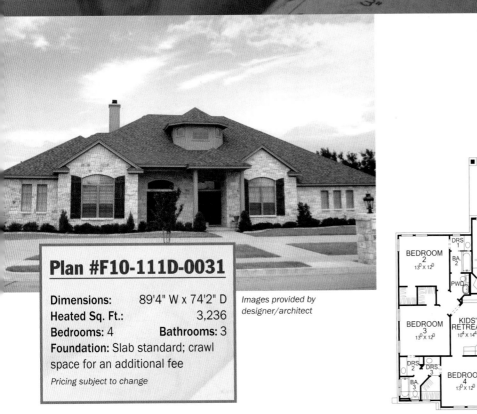

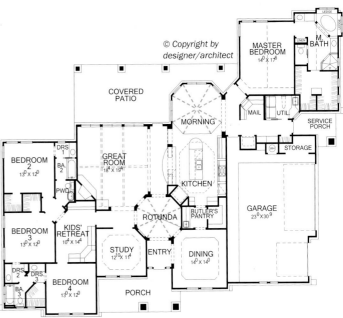

© Copyright by designer/architect

COVERED PATIO

MORNING

MASTER BEDROOM
14'0 x 17'0

M. BATH

MAIL   UTIL

SERVICE PORCH

BEDROOM 2
13'0 x 12'0

BA 2

PWD

GREAT ROOM
18'0 x 19'0

KITCHEN

STORAGE

GARAGE
23'0 x 30'9

BEDROOM 3
13'0 x 12'0

KIDS' RETREAT
10'4 x 14'4

ROTUNDA

BUTLER'S PANTRY

DRS 2   DRS

BA 3

BEDROOM 4
13'0 x 12'0

STUDY
12'10 x 11'0

ENTRY

DINING
14'0 x 14'0

PORCH

Plan #F10-111D-0031

Dimensions: 89'4" W x 74'2" D
Heated Sq. Ft.: 3,236
Bedrooms: 4   **Bathrooms:** 3
Foundation: Slab standard; crawl space for an additional fee

Pricing subject to change

Images provided by designer/architect

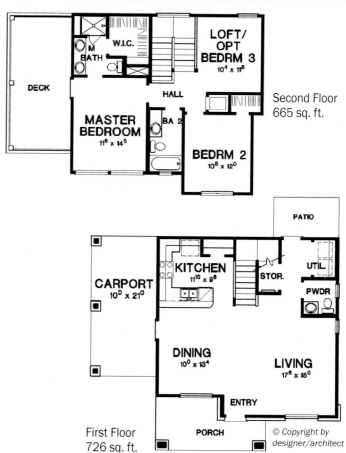

Plan #F10-111D-0036

Dimensions: 38'6" W x 32' D
Heated Sq. Ft.: 1,391
Bedrooms: 3 **Bathrooms:** 2½
Foundation: Slab standard; crawl space for an additional fee

See index for more information

Images provided by designer/architect

Second Floor
665 sq. ft.

First Floor
726 sq. ft.

© Copyright by designer/architect

Plan #F10-047D-0022

Dimensions: 40' W x 60' D
Heated Sq. Ft.: 1,768
Bedrooms: 3 **Bathrooms:** 2
Foundation: Slab

See index for more information

Images provided by designer/architect

© Copyright by designer/architect

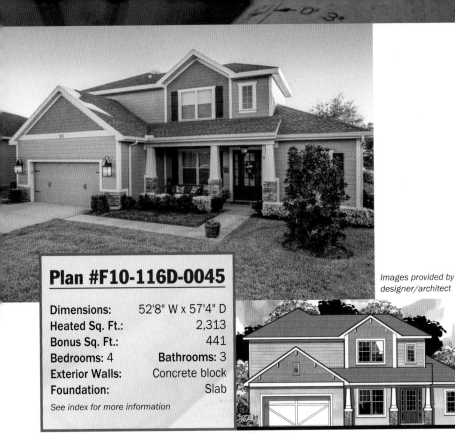

BONUS
20'-2" X 18'-0"
9'-0" CEILING

Second Floor
524 sq. ft.

BR4
13'-0" X 12'-3"
9'-0" CEILING

BR3
13'-0" X 12'-3"
9'-0" CEILING

OPEN

Plan #F10-116D-0045

Dimensions:	52'8" W x 57'4" D
Heated Sq. Ft.:	2,313
Bonus Sq. Ft.:	441
Bedrooms: 4	Bathrooms: 3
Exterior Walls:	Concrete block
Foundation:	Slab

See index for more information

Images provided by designer/architect

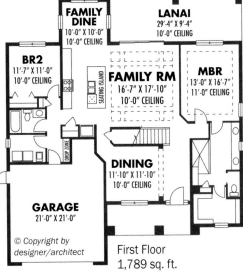

FAMILY DINE
10'-0" X 10'-0"
10'-0" CEILING

LANAI
29'-4" X 9'-4"
10'-0" CEILING

BR2
11'-7" X 11'-0"
10'-0" CEILING

FAMILY RM
16'-7" X 17'-10"
10'-0" CEILING

SEATING ISLAND

MBR
13'-0" X 16'-7"
11'-0" CEILING

DROP ZONE

DINING
11'-10" X 11'-10"
10'-0" CEILING

GARAGE
21'-0" X 21'-0"

© Copyright by designer/architect

First Floor
1,789 sq. ft.

Plan #F10-141D-0037

Dimensions:	75' W x 72' D
Heated Sq. Ft.:	2,697
Bedrooms: 4	Bathrooms: 3½

Foundation: Slab standard; crawl space, basement or walk-out basement for an additional fee

See index for more information

Images provided by designer/architect

REAR PORCH 16 x 14

SITTING AREA 14 x 10

BREAKFAST 10 x 13

BEDROOM #3 13 x 12

BEDROOM #4 13 x 12

CLOSET

MASTER BEDROOM 14 x 15

FAMILY ROOM 16 x 20

KITCHEN 13 x 16

HALL

BATH #3

LINEN

1/2 BATH

VAULTED MASTER BATH

SHOWER

BATH #2

DOUBLE GARAGE 21 x 20

FOYER

DINING 11 x 14

UTILITY

BEDROOM #2 12 x 12

CLOSET

FRONT PORCH 17 x 8

DOUBLE GARAGE 21 x 20

STORAGE

© Copyright by designer/architect

Plan #F10-172D-0024

Dimensions:	42' W x 83'6" D
Heated Sq. Ft.:	3,054
Bonus Sq. Ft.:	2,613
Bedrooms: 4	**Bathrooms:** 2½
Exterior Walls:	2" x 6"

Foundation: Walk-out basement standard; basement, daylight basement, crawl space, monolithic slab or stem wall slab for an additional fee

See index for more information

Features

- This country Farmhouse style home has tons of personality and curb appeal
- The first floor features an open layout that includes a kitchen with a large island with enough seating for four people to dine comfortably
- The second floor contains all of the bedrooms, two full baths, and a second floor laundry room
- The optional bonus room on the second floor has an additional 767 square feet of living area
- The optional lower level has an additional 1,846 square feet of living area and includes another kitchen, two bedrooms, a living room and a full bath
- 3-car side entry garage

Images provided by designer/architect

Optional Lower Level
1,846 sq. ft.

First Floor
1,548 sq. ft.

Second Floor
1,506 sq. ft.

houseplansandmore.com

Plan #F10-101D-0061

Dimensions:	146' W x 88'3" D
Heated Sq. Ft.:	6,563
Bonus Sq. Ft.:	1,940
Bedrooms:	5
Bathrooms:	4 full, 3 half
Exterior Walls:	2" x 6"
Foundation:	Walk-out basement

See index for more information

Images provided by designer/architect

Features

- Luxury on three levels makes this home comfortable for everyone including all guests
- There are several outdoor living areas including a courtyard, a patio, a covered patio, and a deck
- The first floor has both casual and formal spaces including: a formal dining room, a library, and a great room; with casual spaces including a dining area, the kitchen, and mud and craft rooms
- The second floor is comprised of private bedrooms with ample organization space
- The optional lower level has an additional 1,940 square feet of living area and is ideal for entertaining with a media area, a centered wet bar, billiards, a recreation area, and a guest room with a full bath
- One 2-car side entry garage, one 2-car front entry garage, and a 1-car rear entry toy garage

Second Floor
3,685 sq. ft.

First Floor
2,878 sq. ft.

© Copyright by designer/architect

Optional
Lower Level
1,940 sq. ft.

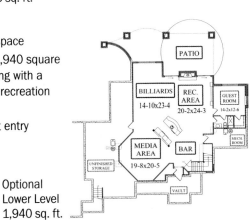

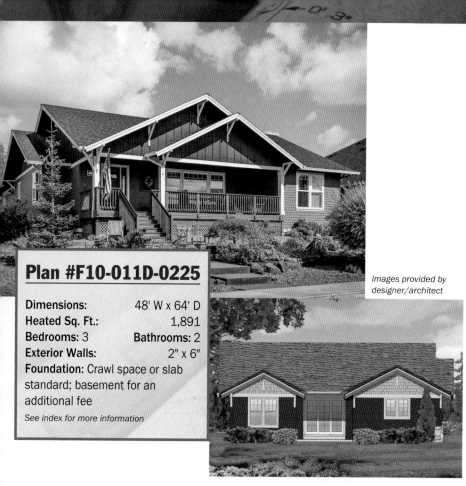

Images provided by designer/architect

© Copyright by designer/architect

Plan #F10-011D-0225

Dimensions: 48' W x 64' D
Heated Sq. Ft.: 1,891
Bedrooms: 3 **Bathrooms:** 2
Exterior Walls: 2" x 6"
Foundation: Crawl space or slab standard; basement for an additional fee

See index for more information

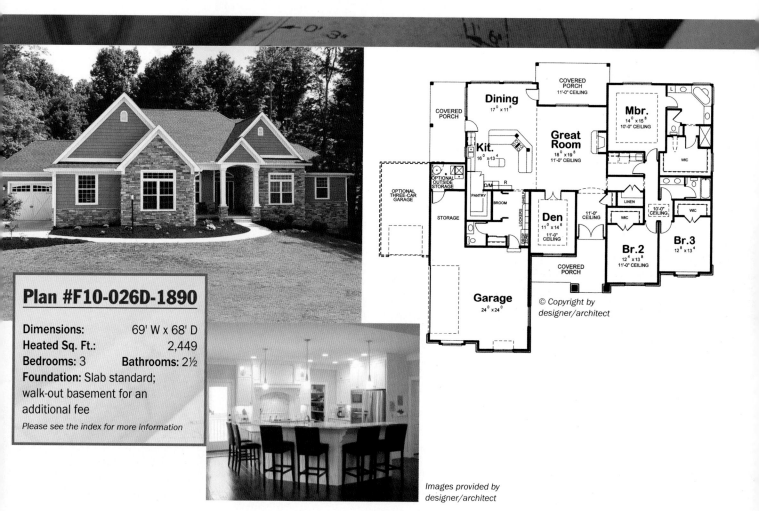

Plan #F10-026D-1890

Dimensions: 69' W x 68' D
Heated Sq. Ft.: 2,449
Bedrooms: 3 **Bathrooms:** 2½
Foundation: Slab standard; walk-out basement for an additional fee

Please see the index for more information

© Copyright by designer/architect

Images provided by designer/architect

Second Floor
636 sq. ft.

OPEN TO BELOW

SLOPE   SLOPE
DOWN
A/C
LOFT   BATH 2   LINEN

BEDRM 2   GAME
11⁰x12⁰   ROOM   BEDRM 3
OPT. BR 4   12⁸x11⁰
11⁶x12⁰
SLOPE CLG.   SLOPE   SLOPE   SLOPE CLG.
SLOPE   SLOPE

OPTIONAL FIREPLACE
SLOPE   SLOPE

COVERED
PATIO   FAMILY
14⁸x15³   MASTER
BEDROOM
WINDOW SEAT   SLOPE   SLOPE   12⁰x16⁰
UP
BRKFST.   STOR
8²x12⁸
KITCHEN
9⁶x10⁸   M. BATH
PANTRY
PWDR
SHELF
DINING   LINEN
OPT. STUDY   FOYER   UTILITY   W.I.C.
12⁸x11¹

© Copyright by
designer/architect   PORCH

First Floor
1,304 sq. ft.

Plan #F10-111D-0005

Dimensions: 40'4" W x 46'10" D
Heated Sq. Ft.:   1,940
Bedrooms: 3   Bathrooms: 2½
Foundation: Slab standard; crawl space or basement for an additional fee

See index for more information

Images provided by designer/architect

First Floor
1,122 sq. ft.

Porch
12'x 9'5"
Kitchen
8'8"x 18'
Dining   Bedroom
11'6"x 18'   13'x 10'11"

Living   Bath
16'6"x 14'5"
Bedroom
13'x 10'9"
Porch
20'6"x 5'
Deck
34'x 10'

© Copyright by
designer/architect

Second Floor
528 sq. ft.

Bedroom   Ma.
14'x 11'2"   Ba.

Open to   Master
Below   Bedroom
13'x 13'6"

Images provided by designer/architect

Plan #F10-024D-0008

Dimensions: 36'6" W x 47'5" D
Heated Sq. Ft.:   1,650
Bedrooms: 4   Bathrooms: 2
Foundation: Pilings or slab, please specify when ordering

See index for more information

Plan #F10-076D-0220

Dimensions:	97'2" W x 87'7" D
Heated Sq. Ft.:	3,061
Bonus Sq. Ft.:	3,644
Bedrooms: 3	**Bathrooms:** 3½

Foundation: Basement, crawl space or slab, please specify when ordering

See index for more information

Features

- Luxury Craftsman home is loaded with curb appeal thanks to multiple gables, and a covered porch adding that undeniable charm
- The first floor is open and airy with the main gathering spaces combining perfectly
- The kitchen is open to the family room with a grilling terrace nearby
- The optional lower level has an additional 2,975 square feet of living area including a hobby room, theater, office, and rec area with bar
- The optional second floor has an additional 669 square feet of living area with 277 square feet in the bedroom and 392 square feet in the rec area
- 3-car front entry garage

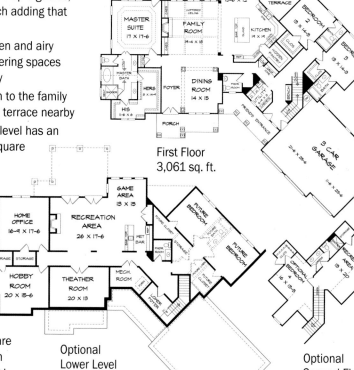

© Copyright by designer/architect

First Floor
3,061 sq. ft.

Optional
Lower Level
2,975 sq. ft.

Optional
Second Floor
669 sq. ft.

Images provided by designer/architect

call 1-800-373-2646   houseplansandmore.com

Plan #F10-019D-0046

Dimensions: 125'5" W x 76'1" D
Heated Sq. Ft.: 2,413
Bedrooms: 3   **Bathrooms:** 2½
Foundation: Slab standard; crawl space or basement for an additional fee

See index for more information

Images provided by designer/architect

Features

- This stunning Southwestern inspired home combines stone and stucco to create a home with tons of style and curb appeal
- The courtyard front entry offers a private escape for enjoying morning coffee or a cocktail at happy hour
- The grand great room is the main focal point as you enter the home thanks to its centered fireplace and tall ceiling with beams
- Off the kitchen is a handy flex room that could become a great home office, formal dining room or kid's play space
- The private master bedroom offers a luxurious environment for relaxing at the end of the day
- 3-car rear entry garage

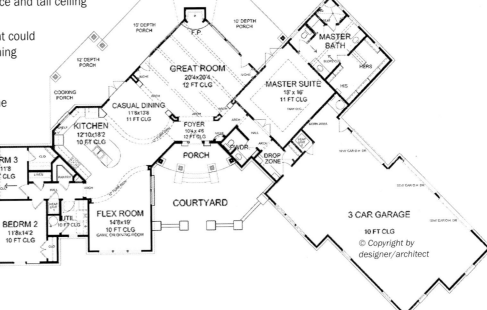

Plan #F10-161D-0001

Dimensions:	145'9" W x 93' D
Heated Sq. Ft.:	4,036
Bedrooms: 3	**Bathrooms:** 3½
Exterior Walls:	2" x 8"

Foundation: Crawl space or slab, please specify when ordering

See index for more information

Images provided by designer/architect

Features

- Craftsman and modern style collide with this stunning rustic one-story home
- The open floor plan is ideal for maximizing square footage
- The master suite can be found in its own wing and it features a huge bath and two walk-in closets
- Built-ins and a walk-in pantry keep the kitchen sleek and clutter-free
- There is a flex space perfect as a kid's playroom
- 3-car side entry garage

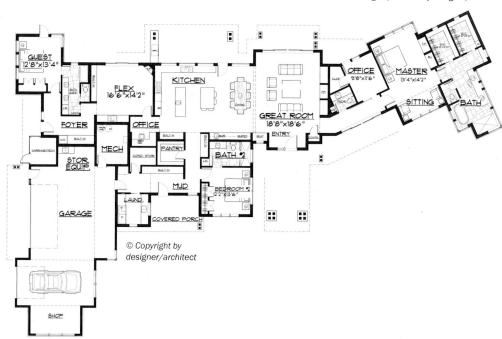

© Copyright by designer/architect

Plan #F10-026D-1891

Dimensions:	56' W x 72' D
Heated Sq. Ft.:	2,407
Bedrooms: 3	Bathrooms: 2½
Exterior Walls:	2" x 6"

Foundation: Basement standard; slab, crawl space or walk-out basement for an additional fee

See index for more information

Images provided by designer/architect

Features

- This Craftsman style bungalow home has all the charm of homes from the past, but with all of the amenities and the layout homeowners want in a home today
- The vaulted open great room merges with the kitchen and dining room to form a central gathering place where dining, relaxing and cooking can all take place in comfort
- The kitchen features a large island that overlooks the activity in the great room
- The owner's suite has a private location and includes a bath with a walk-in shower and an oversized closet
- The flex room offers many possibilities including space for formal dining, a home office, a media room, or a nursery
- 2-car front entry garage

Plan #F10-101D-0123

Dimensions:	96' W x 102' D
Heated Sq. Ft.:	3,456
Bonus Sq. Ft.:	1,754
Bedrooms: 2	Bathrooms: 3½
Exterior Walls:	2" x 6"

Foundation: Basement, daylight basement or walk-out basement, please specify when ordering

See index for more information

Images provided by designer/architect

Features

- This stunning Craftsman masterpiece has uncompromisable rustic style and details both inside and out
- Six fireplaces make this home cozy in every possible place from the master bedroom and screened porch to the home office and media area
- The laundry room, mud room, and walk-in pantry all provide great possibilities for maintaining an organized home
- The optional lower level has an additional 1,754 square feet of living area with a wet bar, media area, billiards space, two bedrooms and baths
- 3-car side entry garage, and a 1-car front entry garage

Second Floor
484 sq. ft.

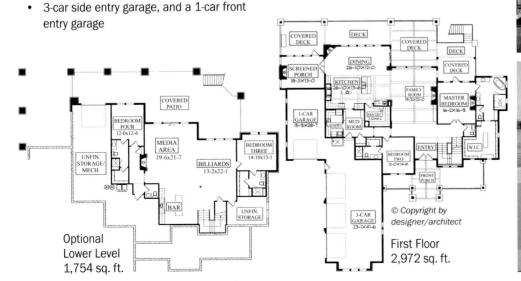

Optional
Lower Level
1,754 sq. ft.

© Copyright by
designer/architect

First Floor
2,972 sq. ft.

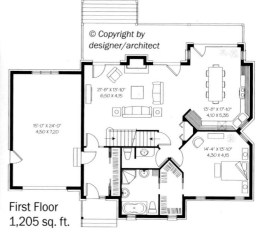

Second Floor
611 sq. ft.

Plan #F10-032D-1068

Dimensions: 59'4" W x 37'4" D
Heated Sq. Ft.: 1,816
Bedrooms: 3   **Bathrooms:** 2½
Exterior Walls: 2" x 6"
Foundation: Basement standard; crawl space, floating slab or monolithic slab for an additional fee

See index for more information

Images provided by designer/architect

© Copyright by designer/architect

First Floor
1,205 sq. ft.

Plan #F10-170D-0010

Dimensions: 58'6" W x 77'10" D
Heated Sq. Ft.: 1,824
Bedrooms: 3   **Bathrooms:** 2
Foundation: Monolithic slab or slab standard; crawl space, basement or daylight basement for an additional fee

See index for more information

Images provided by designer/architect

© Copyright by designer/architect

Bath 2

Bedroom 2
11-5x10-10

Master Rm.
12-2x10-10

L

Hall

W/D

Dine/Living
19-1x10-10

Kitch.

Bath 1

Images provided by
designer/architect

Plan #F10-169D-0005

Dimensions:	34' W x 25' D
Heated Sq. Ft.:	809
Bedrooms: 2	Bathrooms: 2

Foundation: Slab standard; crawl
space for an additional fee

See index for more information

Images provided by
designer/architect

Plan #F10-170D-0005

Dimensions:	54' W x 53' D
Heated Sq. Ft.:	1,422
Bedrooms: 3	Bathrooms: 2

Foundation: Slab or monolithic slab
standard; crawl space, basement
or daylight basement for an
additional fee

See index for more information

GARAGE
22'-6" X 22'-5"

REAR PORCH
17'-6" X 8'-0"

BEDROOM 2
11'-3" X 10'-4"

KITCHEN
17'-3" X 10'-10"
10' CEILING

MASTER CLOSET
8'-8" X 11'-0"

UTILITY
8'-9" X 6'-9"

BATH 2

PANTRY
8'-9" X 4'-0"

MASTER BATH

MASTER BEDROOM
13'-0" X 12'-5"

FAMILY ROOM
17'-3" X 16'-8"
10' CEILING

BEDROOM 3
11'-3" X 10'-4"

FRONT PORCH
28'-6" X 6'-0"
10' CEILING

© Copyright by
designer/architect

Plan #F10-051D-0886

Images provided by designer/architect

Dimensions:	112'4" W x 81' D
Heated Sq. Ft.:	4,540
Bonus Sq. Ft.:	612
Bedrooms: 4	Bathrooms: 3½
Exterior Walls:	2" x 6"

Foundation: Basement standard; crawl space or slab for an additional fee

See index for more information

Features

- This Craftsman home has effortless style and an uncomplicated open floor plan
- The entry has a curved staircase ascending to a second floor balcony with views overlooking the great room below
- The kitchen is designed to feel a part of the breakfast nook and sun room with its angled island overlooking both spaces
- A covered porch extends off the sun room creating a covered place for a grill not far from the kitchen
- The private master bedroom has a pampering bath and large walk-in closet
- The bonus room on the second floor has an additional 612 square feet of living area
- 2-car front entry garage, and a 1-car side entry

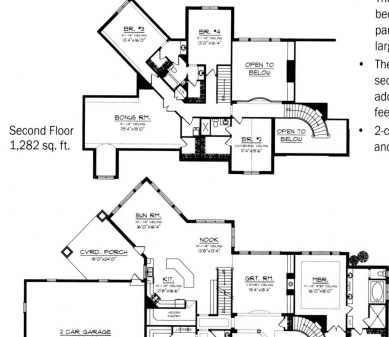

Second Floor
1,282 sq. ft.

© Copyright by designer/architect

First Floor
3,258 sq. ft.

Plan #F10-101D-0230

Dimensions:	67' W x 70'6" D
Heated Sq. Ft.:	2,439
Bonus Sq. Ft.:	1,843
Bedrooms: 2	Bathrooms: 2½
Exterior Walls:	2" x 6"
Foundation:	Basement

See index for more information

Features

- This home's stone and modern style create tremendous curb appeal
- The spacious great room enjoys a stylish free-standing fireplace and gorgeous views of the rear covered patio
- A large island in the efficient kitchen offers additional seating and sufficient workspace
- A large den with double doors will make the perfect secluded home office
- The optional lower level has an additional 1,843 square feet of living area and includes a living room with a fireplace and wet bar, two bedrooms, and two full baths
- 3-car front entry garage

Images provided by designer/architect

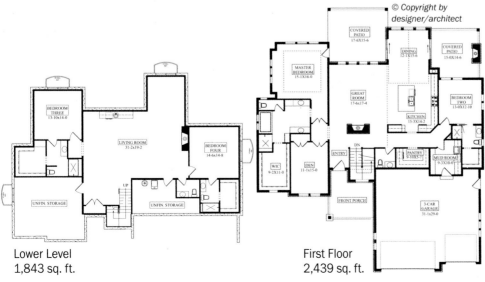

© Copyright by designer/architect

Lower Level
1,843 sq. ft.

First Floor
2,439 sq. ft.

Style Seeker
the top architectural styles of today

New homeowners love the look and feel of many architectural styles somewhat new to them. Perhaps the Traditional homes of their past remind them of their parent's homes, but in reality, the interior layouts and finish preferences being demanded by new homeowners most likely are dictating the exterior style changes that are occurring, too. Homeowners want sleek interiors with modern furnishings, and the architectural styles being designed on the exterior today reflect that simpler interior style. These streamlined, less-cluttered, and informal interior spaces being requested by homeowners are definitely changing the style and feel of home exteriors. However, there is also no less of a desire for homes that feature front facades covered in stone and brick, so basically there's still something being built for everyone.

Here are some of the top architectural styles being designed today. Many you will see throughout the pages of this book. Some are timeless, some a little more trendy, but all display tons of personality and style.

mid-century modern

The Mid-Century Modern home features a steel structure that allows large floor-to-ceiling windows and doors to be supported. This style blurs the lines between indoor and outdoor spaces perfectly, which is a popular trend.

international modern

Stripped of any ornamentation on the exterior, this boxy, typically stucco home has a precise almost machine-like sleek style.

industrial modern

Using Industrial style, this style includes more texture and uses varied materials on the exterior such as corrugated metal, concrete, and exposed wood. It's becoming quite popular in urban developments.

Unless noted, copyright by designer/architect; Page 66, left, top to bottom: Plan #F10-11S-0018 on page 167, Bob Greenspan, photographer; Plan #F10-013S-0011 on page 235; Plan #F10-011D-0351 on page 84; middle, top: Plan #F10-101D-0145; middle, bottom: Plan #032D-0927; right, top: Plan #F10-011D-0588 on page 76; Plan #026D-1913 on page 290. See additional photos and purchase plans at houseplansandmore.com.

american farmhouse & modern farmhouse

This style ranges from small and simple to industrial or Traditional Victorian, but some newer versions have more streamlined exteriors.

cape cod

This distinctly American style was a result of the harsh weather conditions of the Northeast coast, but its classic look remains a mainstay throughout America.

georgian and federal

A Traditional symmetrical two-story style that is seen in every neighborhood across the country. It's a classic two-story that never seems to go out of style.

french eclectic and european

These European styles evoke a vision of cottages and Chateaus often seen across the French and European countryside. Country French is another term associated with this style of home.

tudor

Based loosely off early English tradition, the distinctive features of Tudor style include exposed timber mixed with stucco. Many similar details have spread to Prairie and Craftsman style.

mission revival

Inspired by Spanish mission churches that appeared in California around the late 1800s, this style features stucco walls, and clay tile roofs with large arched openings.

spanish colonial

Seen throughout Florida and California in the early 1900s, there were several bathhouses and exhibit halls being designed in this style helping to spread the design across the country and especially the sunbelt region.

prairie

Popularized by Frank Lloyd Wright, Prairie Style homes embrace the belief that homes should appear as if they have grown from nature. They use horizontal bands of windows and trim to evoke a prairie landscape.

craftsman bungalow

Shallow roofs, exposed rafters, a mixture of brick, stone, shingles and siding give this style tons of personality. The addition of the term Bungalow means it's a 1 1/2 story Craftsman home with a deep covered front porch.

queen anne

This residential style, also referred to as Victorian displays an eclectic amount of details often with various colors and textures. Turrets, bay windows, and gables all contribute to their heavy ornamentation.

shingle

Shingle style homes were adopted as a way to move away from the heavily ornate Victorian and Queen Anne style. They feature shingle siding and are often seen in the rugged coastal towns of the Northeast and the Northwest.

ranch

Typically long and narrow one-story structures that spread out on their lot, ranch style homes can adopt any of the other styles mentioned previously for added character.

The exterior design of homes today is clearly changing from the past decades. As homeowners want less maintenance, they have shifted to yearning for a dwelling that requires little or no maintenance and fits their "paired down," less is more attitude and lifestyle. However, some architectural styles are always popular simply because their beauty can't be overlooked, so no matter what the trend may be certain styles will always remain popular even if they are deemed opulent for the times. The most popular styles of architecture remind us of our country's rich history, its diversity of cultures, and how they've collided to create the neighborhoods and landscapes full of history we're lucky enough to call "home."

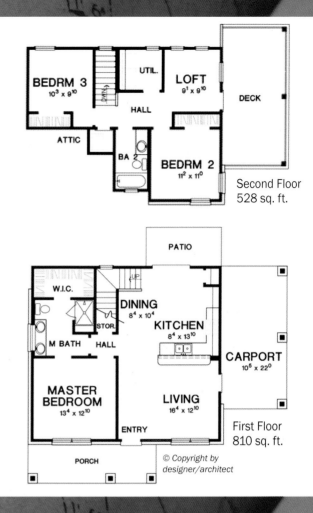

Second Floor
528 sq. ft.

Plan #F10-111D-0035

Dimensions: 40'11" W x 33'6" D
Heated Sq. Ft.: 1,338
Bedrooms: 3   **Bathrooms:** 2
Foundation: Slab standard; crawl space or basement for an additional fee

See index for more information

Images provided by designer/architect

First Floor
810 sq. ft.

© *Copyright by designer/architect*

Second Floor
471 sq. ft.

© *Copyright by designer/architect*

Plan #F10-011D-0507

Dimensions: 50' W x 56' D
Heated Sq. Ft.: 2,074
Bedrooms: 3   **Bathrooms:** 2½
Exterior Walls: 2" x 6"
Foundation: Crawl space or slab standard; basement for an additional fee

See index for more information

Images provided by designer/architect

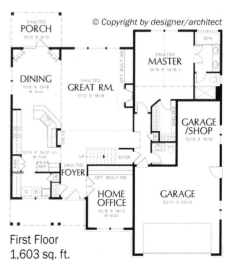

First Floor
1,603 sq. ft.

© Copyright by designer/architect

Images provided by designer/architect

Plan #F10-007D-0049

Dimensions: 68' W x 48'4" D
Heated Sq. Ft.:   1,791
Bedrooms: 4   Bathrooms: 2
Foundation: Basement standard;
crawl space or slab for an
additional fee

See index for more information

© Copyright by designer/architect

*Images provided by
designer/architect*

Plan #F10-013D-0025

Dimensions: 70'2" W x 59' D
Heated Sq. Ft.:   2,097
Bonus Sq. Ft.:   452
Bedrooms: 3   Bathrooms: 3
Foundation: Slab standard; crawl
space or basement for an
additional fee

See index for more information

Plan #F10-051D-0993

Dimensions: 83'4" W x 59' D
Heated Sq. Ft.: 4,210
Bedrooms: 5   **Bathrooms:** 3
Exterior Walls: 2" x 6"
Foundation: Walk-out basement standard; crawl space or slab for an additional fee

See index for more information

Features

- This Craftsman style ranch home is adorned with wood columns, shingle and stone siding, and corbels in the peaks of the roof creating great curb appeal

- A gracious great room with fireplace leads to the dining area and kitchen through stylish columns

- The master bedroom features a tray ceiling, walk-in closet, and a private bath with a spa style tub

- Two additional bedrooms share the full bath off the hall

- The finished walk-out basement has two bedrooms, a family room, an exercise room, and a garden room accessible from the outdoors

- 3-car front entry garage

© Copyright by designer/architect

First Floor
2,105 sq. ft.

Lower Level
2,105 sq. ft.

Images provided by designer/architect

Plan #F10-091D-0485

Dimensions:	77' W x 65' D
Heated Sq. Ft.:	1,918
Bedrooms: 1	Bathrooms: 1½
Exterior Walls:	2" x 6"
Foundation:	Walk-out basement

See index for more information

Features

- The great room, kitchen and dinette all combine for an open living atmosphere and are topped with 9' ceilings and warmed by a grand fireplace
- An enchanting screened porch features a corner fireplace and connects to the rear deck
- The vaulted study has double doors off the foyer and could easily be converted to a second bedroom
- 3-car front entry garage

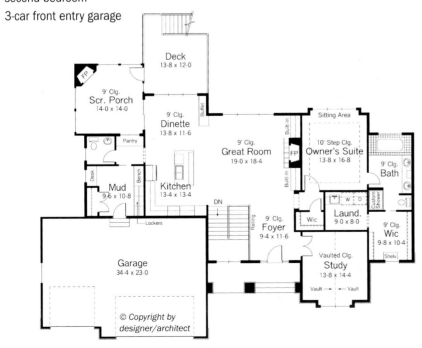

Images provided by designer/architect

Second Floor
1,062 sq. ft.

SUITE 2
13'-0" X 14'-10"

SUITE 3
13'-0" X 15'-0"

BALCONY

LOFT
15'-2" X 10'-4"

BATH

BONUS
ROOM
14'-0" X 19'-6"

© Copyright by
designer/architect

COVERED LANAI

MASTER SUITE
18'-6" X 16'-6"

OWNER'S STUDY

FAMILY ROOM
19'-0" X 15'-0"

W.I.C.

MASTER BATH

DINING ROOM
19'-0" X 13'-10"

W.I.C.

LAUNDRY

KITCHEN
19'-0" X 14'-2"

FOYER

PDR

PORTICO

2 CAR GARAGE
21'-6" X 22'-8"

First Floor
2,297 sq. ft.

Plan #F10-129S-0021

Dimensions:	55' W x 71'5" D
Heated Sq. Ft.:	3,359
Bonus Sq. Ft.:	322
Bedrooms: 3	Bathrooms: 4½
Foundation:	Crawl space

See index for more information

Images provided by designer/architect

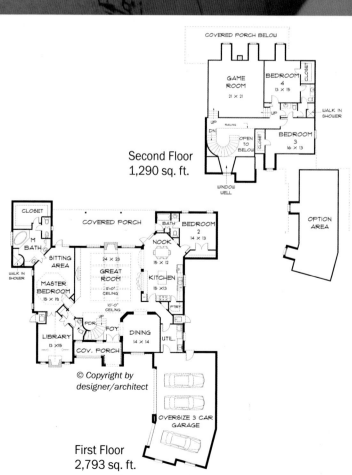

COVERED PORCH BELOW

GAME ROOM
21 x 21

BEDROOM 4
13 x 15

CLOSET

WALK IN SHOWER

OPEN TO BELOW

BEDROOM 3
16 x 13

Second Floor
1,290 sq. ft.

WINDOW WELL

OPTION AREA

CLOSET

M BATH

SITTING AREA

COVERED PORCH
24 x 23

BATH

BEDROOM 2
14 x 13

WALK IN SHOWER

MASTER BEDROOM
15 x 19

GREAT ROOM
18'-0" CEILING

NOOK
15 x 12

KITCHEN
15 x13

10'-0" CEILING

PDR

LIBRARY
13 x15

FOY

DINING
14 x 14

UTIL.

COV. PORCH

© Copyright by
designer/architect

OVERSIZE 3 CAR GARAGE

First Floor
2,793 sq. ft.

Plan #F10-164D-0037

Images provided by designer/architect

Dimensions:	76'9" W x 96'9" D
Heated Sq. Ft.:	4,083
Bonus Sq. Ft.:	614
Bedrooms: 4	Bathrooms: 3½
Foundation:	Slab

See index for more information

Plan #F10-060D-0233

Dimensions:	50'1" W x 69'3" D
Heated Sq. Ft.:	1,962
Bonus Sq. Ft.:	541
Bedrooms: 3	Bathrooms: 2
Foundation:	Slab

See index for more information

Images provided by designer/architect

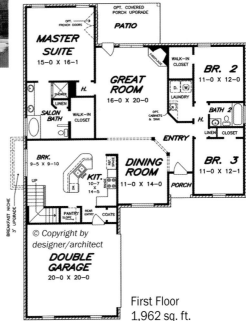

First Floor
1,962 sq. ft.

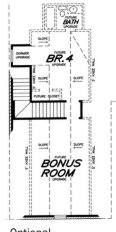

Optional
Second Floor
541 sq. ft.

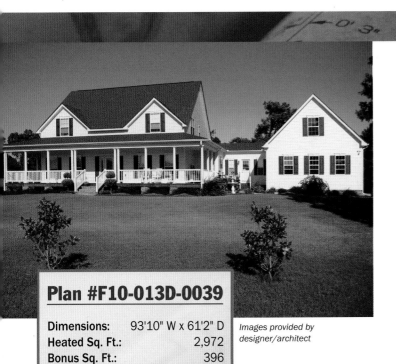

Plan #F10-013D-0039

Dimensions:	93'10" W x 61'2" D
Heated Sq. Ft.:	2,972
Bonus Sq. Ft.:	396
Bedrooms: 4	Bathrooms: 3½

Foundation: Slab standard; basement or crawl space for an additional fee

See index for more information

Images provided by designer/architect

Second Floor
986 sq. ft.

Optional
Bonus Room
396 sq. ft.

First Floor
1,986 sq. ft.

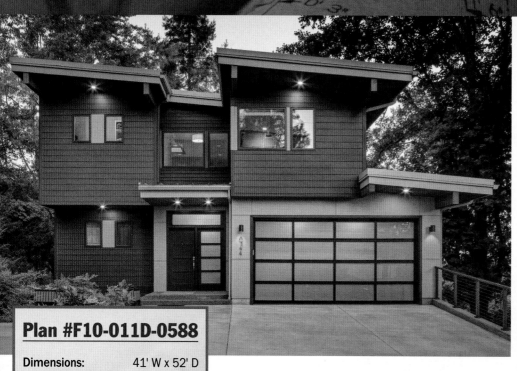

Plan #F10-011D-0588

Dimensions:	41' W x 52' D
Heated Sq. Ft.:	3,026
Bedrooms: 4	**Bathrooms:** 3½
Exterior Walls:	2" x 6"
Foundation:	Walk-out basement

See index for more information

Features

- Make a bold statement in any neighborhood with this cutting-edge modern home floor plan
- An elevator makes this floor plan highly accessible for all
- The open floor plan has the kitchen overlooking all gathering and dining spaces
- A flexible office/guest room adapts to your needs
- The second floor has a sizable master suite with its own bath and walk-in closet
- The lower level has a roomy laundry/mud room combo space, a media room and direct patio access
- 2-car front entry garage

Lower Level
900 sq. ft.

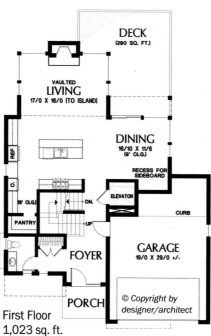

First Floor
1,023 sq. ft.

Second Floor
1,103 sq. ft.

Images provided by designer/architect

Plan #F10-011D-0542

Dimensions:	24' W x 43' D
Heated Sq. Ft.:	2,217
Bonus Sq. Ft.:	Included
Bedrooms: 3	**Bathrooms:** 3½
Exterior Walls:	2" x 6"

Foundation: Crawl space or slab standard; basement for an additional fee

See index for more information

Features

- A home that brings the old style of row housing to a new modern dimension
- The first floor features the living, or main gathering spaces, the second floor has the sleeping quarters, and the third floor allows design flexibility for whatever suits the homeowner's needs
- When standing at the kitchen island one can see-through the dining and living rooms and onto the front covered porch
- Conveniently located off the kitchen is a large walk-in pantry, a laundry room, a half bath, a built-in bench, and a rear covered porch
- The bonus area on the third floor is included in the square footage

First Floor
941 sq. ft.

Second Floor
801 sq. ft.

Third Floor
475 sq. ft.

Images provided by designer/architect

First Floor
1,736 sq. ft.

Second Floor
516 sq. ft.

Images provided by designer/architect

© Copyright by designer/architect

Plan #F10-130D-0135

Dimensions:	80' W x 59' D
Heated Sq. Ft.:	2,252
Bonus Sq. Ft.:	272
Bedrooms: 4	Bathrooms: 3

Foundation: Slab standard; crawl space or basement for an additional fee

See index for more information

© Copyright by designer/architect

Images provided by designer/architect

Optional Second Floor
602 sq. ft.

First Floor
2,470 sq. ft.

Plan #F10-055D-1049

Dimensions:	85'6" W x 61'3" D
Heated Sq. Ft.:	2,470
Bonus Sq. Ft.:	602
Bedrooms: 4	Bathrooms: 2½

Foundation: Crawl space or slab standard; basement or daylight basement for an additional fee

See index for more information

Plan #F10-141D-0027

Dimensions:	46'11" W x 52'10" D
Heated Sq. Ft.:	2,272
Bonus Sq. Ft.:	350
Bedrooms: 3	**Bathrooms:** 2½

Foundation: Slab standard; crawl space, basement or walk-out basement for an additional fee

See index for more information

Images provided by designer/architect

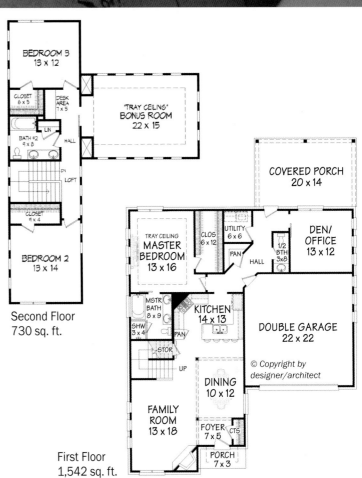

Second Floor
730 sq. ft.

First Floor
1,542 sq. ft.

© Copyright by designer/architect

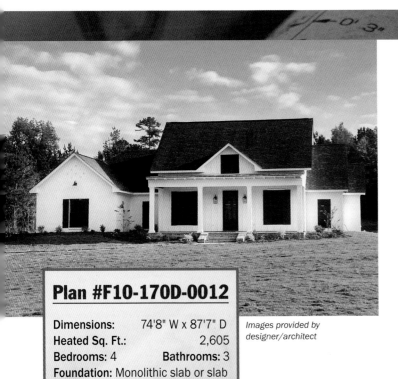

Plan #F10-170D-0012

Dimensions:	74'8" W x 87'7" D
Heated Sq. Ft.:	2,605
Bedrooms: 4	**Bathrooms:** 3

Foundation: Monolithic slab or slab standard; crawl space, basement or daylight basement for an additional fee

See index for more information

Images provided by designer/architect

© Copyright by designer/architect

Plan #F10-091D-0525

Dimensions: 50' W x 56'2" D
Heated Sq. Ft.: 2,453
Bedrooms: 3   **Bathrooms:** 3½
Exterior Walls: 2" x 6"
Foundation: Crawl space standard; slab, basement, daylight basement or walk-out basement for an additional fee

See index for more information

Images provided by designer/architect

© Copyright by designer/architect

First Floor
1,522 sq. ft.

Second Floor
931 sq. ft.

Plan #F10-013D-0154

Dimensions: 36' W x 42'4" D
Heated Sq. Ft.: 953
Bedrooms: 2   **Bathrooms:** 1½
Foundation: Crawl space standard; slab or basement for an additional fee

See index for more information

Images provided by designer/architect

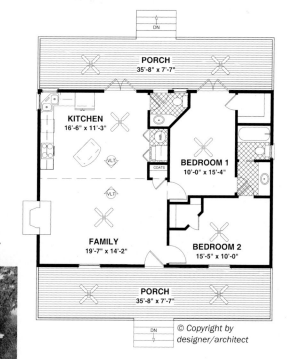

© Copyright by designer/architect

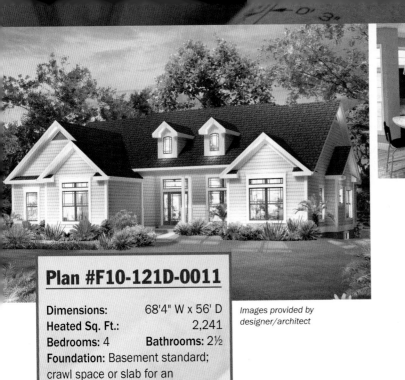

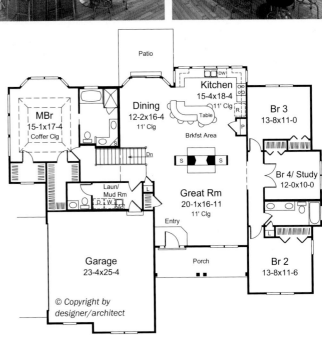

Plan #F10-121D-0011

Dimensions:	68'4" W x 56' D
Heated Sq. Ft.:	2,241
Bedrooms: 4	Bathrooms: 2½

Foundation: Basement standard; crawl space or slab for an additional fee

See index for more information

Images provided by designer/architect

Patio

MBr
15-1x17-4
Coffer Clg

Dining
12-2x16-4
11' Clg

Kitchen
15-4x18-4
11' Clg
Table
Brkfst Area

Br 3
13-8x11-0

Br 4/ Study
12-0x10-0

Laun/
Mud Rm

Great Rm
20-1x16-11
11' Clg

Entry

Br 2
13-8x11-6

Garage
23-4x25-4

Porch

© Copyright by designer/architect

Plan #F10-155D-0170

Dimensions:	60'6" W x 64'8" D
Heated Sq. Ft.:	1,897
Bedrooms: 4	Bathrooms: 2

Foundation: Crawl space or slab standard; basement or daylight basement for an additional fee

See index for more information

Images provided by designer/architect

BEDROOM 4
11'-0"X11'-2"

GRILLING PORCH
20'-0"X9'-4"

DINING
12'-0"X9'-6"

MASTER SUITE
13'-0"X15'-0"

VAULTED CEILING

BATH

GREAT ROOM
18'-8"X15'-10"

ISLAND

M.BATH
16'-4"X15'-0"

GLASS SHOWR

FREE STND TUB

BEDROOM 3
11'-0"X12'-0"

FALSE BEAMS

VAULTED CEILING

PANTRY

LAU
9'-4"X8'-4"

STRG
7'-0"X5'-0"

OPT. BARN DOOR

FOYER
7'-4"X6'-2"

KID'S NOOK

BEDROOM/OFFICE
11'-4"X12'-0"

GARAGE
25'-4"X21'-8"

8' COVERED PORCH

© Copyright by designer/architect

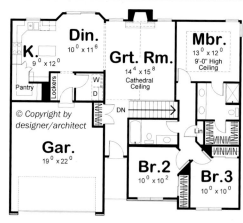

Images provided by designer/architect

Plan #F10-123D-0006

Dimensions: 47'8" W x 41' D
Heated Sq. Ft.:   1,343
Bedrooms: 3   Bathrooms: 2
Foundation: Basement standard;
crawl space, slab or walk-out
basement for an additional fee

See index for more information

Plan #F10-077D-0002

Dimensions: 72'8" W x 51' D
Heated Sq. Ft.:   1,855
Bonus Sq. Ft.:   416
Bedrooms: 3   Bathrooms: 2½
Foundation: Basement, crawl
space or slab, please specify when
ordering

See index for more information

Images provided by designer/architect

Optional
Second Floor
416 sq. ft.

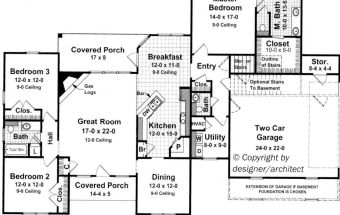

First Floor
1,855 sq. ft.

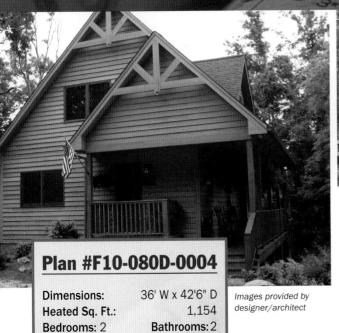

© Copyright by designer/architect

Plan #F10-080D-0004

Dimensions:	36' W x 42'6" D
Heated Sq. Ft.:	1,154
Bedrooms: 2	Bathrooms: 2
Exterior Walls:	2" x 6"
Foundation:	Crawl space

See index for more information

Images provided by designer/architect

First Floor
672 sq. ft.

Second Floor
482 sq. ft.

Plan #F10-032D-0513

Dimensions:	38' W x 40' D
Heated Sq. Ft.:	1,832
Bedrooms: 3	Bathrooms: 2
Exterior Walls:	2" x 6"

Foundation: Walk-out basement standard; crawl space, floating slab or monolithic slab for an additional fee

See index for more information

Images provided by designer/architect

First Floor
1,212 sq. ft.

© Copyright by designer/architect

Second Floor
620 sq. ft.

Plan #F10-011D-0351

Dimensions:	50' W x 58'8" D
Heated Sq. Ft.:	3,242
Bedrooms: 4	**Bathrooms:** 4
Exterior Walls:	2" x 6"
Foundation:	Walk-out basement

See index for more information

Features

- Angled roof lines and an open floor plan make this Modern home an architectural masterpiece, perfect for a sloping lot
- The great room has a sleek and modern feel with its vaulted ceiling and clerestory windows
- The open kitchen has the island surveying an open space ideal for dining with a view
- 2-car front entry garage

Lower Level
1,349 sq. ft.

First Floor
1,893 sq. ft.

Images provided by designer/architect

Plan #F10-170D-0004

Dimensions:	48'4" W x 66'4" D
Heated Sq. Ft.:	1,581
Bedrooms: 3	**Bathrooms:** 2

Foundation: Slab or monolithic slab standard; crawl space, basement or daylight basement for an additional fee

See index for more information

Features

- This modest sized one-story home offers many great features for today's family
- A side entry garage gives the exterior added curb appeal
- When entering from the garage you'll find lockers on the right and a utility room on the left
- The kitchen has a very open feel and includes an island with dining space
- The family room enjoys a cozy corner fireplace and an entire wall of windows that overlook the rear covered porch and beyond onto the patio
- The master bedroom and bath include a large walk-in closet
- Two secondary bedrooms share the full bath between them
- 2-car side entry garage

© Copyright by designer/architect

Images provided by designer/architect

Plan #F10-076D-0238

Dimensions: 91'5" W x 79' D
Heated Sq. Ft.: 2,925
Bonus Sq. Ft.: 3,361
Bedrooms: 4 **Bathrooms:** 3½
Foundation: Slab or crawl space standard; basement for an additional fee

See index for more information

Images provided by designer/architect

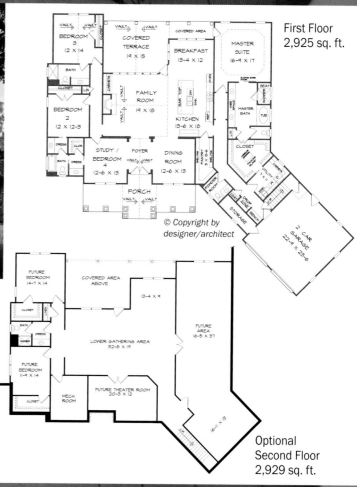

First Floor
2,925 sq. ft.

© Copyright by designer/architect

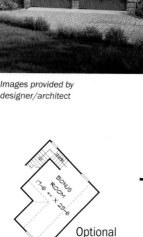

Optional
Second Floor
432 sq. ft.

Optional
Second Floor
2,929 sq. ft.

Plan #F10-149D-0004

Dimensions: 33' W x 74'6" D
Heated Sq. Ft.: 2,234
Bedrooms: 3 **Bathrooms:** 2½
Foundation: Slab standard; crawl space or basement for an additional fee

See index for more information

Images provided by designer/architect

© Copyright by designer/architect

Second Floor
618 sq. ft.

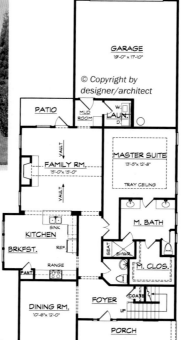

First Floor
1,616 sq. ft.

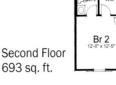

Second Floor
693 sq. ft.

Br 2
12'-0" x 12'-5"

Br 3
12'-0" x 12'-5"

First Floor
1,443 sq. ft.

© Copyright by
designer/architect

*Images provided by
designer/architect*

Plan #F10-147D-0008

Dimensions: 73'8" W x 50'8" D
Heated Sq. Ft.: 2,136
Bedrooms: 3   **Bathrooms:** 3½
Foundation: Basement standard;
crawl space or slab for an
additional fee

See index for more information

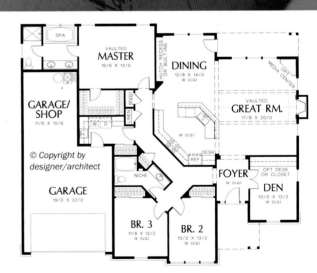

Images provided by designer/architect

Plan #F10-011D-0013

Dimensions: 60' W x 50' D
Heated Sq. Ft.: 2,001
Bedrooms: 3   **Bathrooms:** 2
Exterior Walls: 2" x 6"
Foundation: Crawl space or slab
standard; basement for an
additional fee

See index for more information

Plan #F10-011S-0191

Dimensions: 110'10" W x 98'7" D
Heated Sq. Ft.: 6,349
Bedrooms: 5   **Bathrooms:** 5½
Exterior Walls: 2" x 6"
Foundation: Crawl space or slab standard; basement for an additional fee
See index for more information

Features

- Symmetrically pleasing Craftsman luxury home offers a floor plan designed perfectly for today's active families
- The first floor is comprised primarily of the two-story great room, breakfast nook, and kitchen with an enormous island
- A secluded office and guest suite are also found on the first floor as well as an organized mud room space with cubbies
- The second floor enjoys a spacious master suite with huge walk-in closets, an additional three bedrooms, as well as fun extras like an exercise room, and a game room
- There is also outdoor living space for dining and grilling when the weather permits
- Two 2-car front entry garages

Second Floor
3,269 sq. ft.

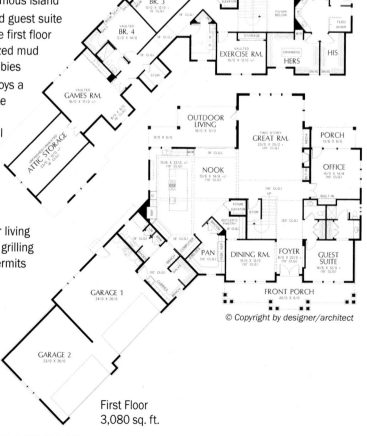

First Floor
3,080 sq. ft.

© Copyright by designer/architect

Images provided by designer/architect

Plan #F10-091D-0017

Dimensions:	80' W x 49'8" D
Heated Sq. Ft.:	2,982
Bedrooms: 4	**Bathrooms:** 2½
Exterior Walls:	2" x 6"
Foundation:	Walk-out basement

See index for more information

Features

- French doors lead into a private study, perfect for a home office

- An extra-large kitchen island offers space for quick meals, or buffet style dinners and opens to the enchanting sun room

- A double-door entry leads into the elegant master suite that features a vaulted ceiling and a plush bath with a sizable walk-in closet

- 3-car front entry garage

Second Floor
1,419 sq. ft.

Master Suite
22-2 x 13-0
11' Vault Clg

Built-In

Master Bath

KS

WIC

Bedroom 4
11-8 x 13-6

DN

Linen

Desk

Books

Bedroom 2
12-4 x 14-4

Bedroom 3
11-8 x 15-0

First Floor
1,563 sq. ft.

DN

Deck
16-0 x 12-0

Sun Rm
11-0 x 11-6
12' Vault Clg

Slp

Slp

Kitchen
16-4 x 14-4
9' Clg

Ref
D
W

Bench

Lockers

Bench

Pantry

Ref

DW

Family Rm
19-8 x 14-4
9' Clg

Built-In

FP

Built-In

UP

DN

© Copyright by
designer/architect

Garage
35-0 x 26-4

Books

Built-In

Dining Rm
12-2 x 12-4
9' Clg

Foyer
7-6 x 12-4
9' Clg

Study
12-10 x 12-4
9' Clg

Porch
35-0 x 8-0

Images provided by designer/architect

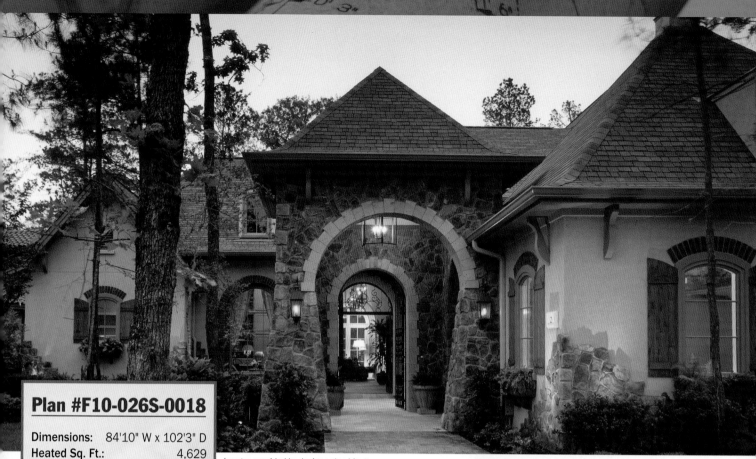

Plan #F10-026S-0018

Dimensions: 84'10" W x 102'3" D
Heated Sq. Ft.: 4,629
Bedrooms: 4 **Bathrooms:** 4½
Foundation: Slab standard; basement or walk-out basement for an additional fee
See index for more information

Images provided by designer/architect

Features

- Enter an amazing foyer with a curved staircase
- A beautiful courtyard has a popular outdoor fireplace that is a stunning focal point
- Three sets of double-doors line one wall of the family room that features a cathedral ceiling and a large fireplace
- The second floor has a wonderful game room with a barrel vaulted ceiling and an octagon-shaped covered porch attached
- The unbelievable master suite offers two walk-in closets, and a bath with two vanities, a spa style tub and a walk-in shower
- 2-car side entry garage, 2-car front entry garage

First Floor
3,337 sq. ft.

Second Floor
1,292 sq. ft.

Plan #F10-060D-0229

Images provided by designer/architect

Dimensions:	47'10" W x 62' D
Heated Sq. Ft.:	1,944
Bonus Sq. Ft.:	342
Bedrooms: 3	Bathrooms: 2
Foundation:	Slab

See index for more information

First Floor
1,944 sq. ft.

© Copyright by designer/architect

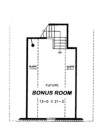

Optional
Second Floor
342 sq. ft.

Plan #F10-149D-0005

Images provided by designer/architect

Dimensions:	42' W x 70'6" D
Heated Sq. Ft.:	2,885
Bonus Sq. Ft.:	312
Bedrooms: 4	Bathrooms: 3½
Foundation: Slab standard; crawl space or basement for an additional fee	

See index for more information

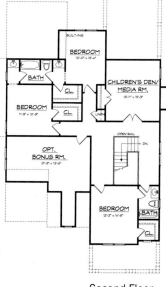

Second Floor
1,289 sq. ft.

© Copyright by designer/architect

First Floor
1,596 sq. ft.

Plan #F10-024S-0024

Dimensions:	52' W x 62' D
Heated Sq. Ft.:	3,610
Bedrooms: 5	Bathrooms: 4
Foundation:	Slab

See index for more information

Second Floor
1,286 sq. ft.

BONUS ROOM/
BEDR'M. #5
14'-0"X19'-6"

SITTING
17'-0"X15'-1"

BA. #4

BEDR'M #4
18'-0"X17'-6"

BEDR'M #3
12'-8"X15'-8"

DRESS

BA. #3

DRESS

W.C.

Images provided by designer/architect

PATIO
© Copyright by designer/architect

MA. BEDR'M.
17'-10" X
19'-1"

SUNROOM/
BRK'FST.
12'-1"X
11'-8"

COVERED
PORCH
22'-5"X 12'-0"

MA. BA.

UTIL.
6'-5"X
7'-10"

KITCHEN
16'-10 1/2"X
16'-3"

DINING
15'-9"X16'-3"

WALK IN CLOSET

SHELVES

LIVING
18'-0"X20'-6"

BA. #2

BEDR'M #2
15'-10"X
13'-2"

FOYER
8'-1"X
5'-0"

PORCH
26'-5"X8'-0"

First Floor
2,324 sq. ft.

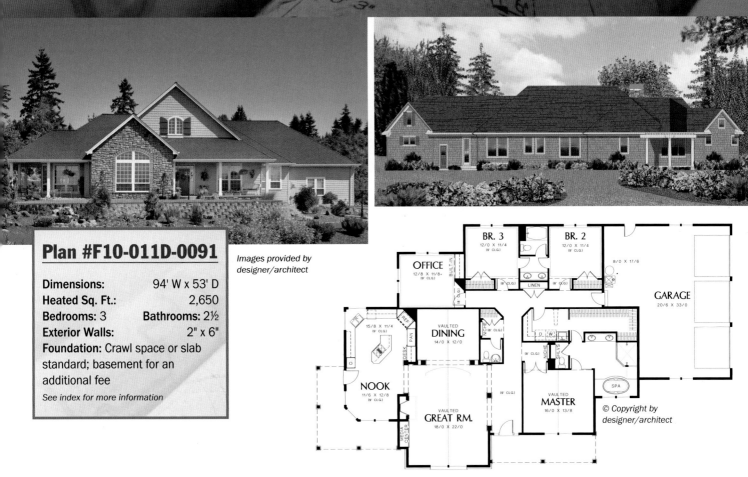

Plan #F10-011D-0091

Images provided by designer/architect

Dimensions:	94' W x 53' D
Heated Sq. Ft.:	2,650
Bedrooms: 3	Bathrooms: 2½
Exterior Walls:	2" x 6"
Foundation: Crawl space or slab standard; basement for an additional fee	

See index for more information

BR. 3
12/0 X 11/4
(9' CLG.)

BR. 2
12/0 X 11/4
(9' CLG.)

8/0 X 17/6

OFFICE
12/8 X 11/8+
(9' CLG.)

BUILT-IN

LINEN

GARAGE
20/6 X 33/0

15/8 X 11/4
(9' CLG.)

DINING
14/0 X 12/0

NICHE

NICHE

D W

REF.

PAN.

DESK

NOOK
11/6 X 12/8
(9' CLG.)

(9' CLG.)

SPA

MASTER
16/0 X 13/8

VAULTED

MEDIA CENTER

GREAT RM.
18/0 X 22/0

VAULTED

© Copyright by designer/architect

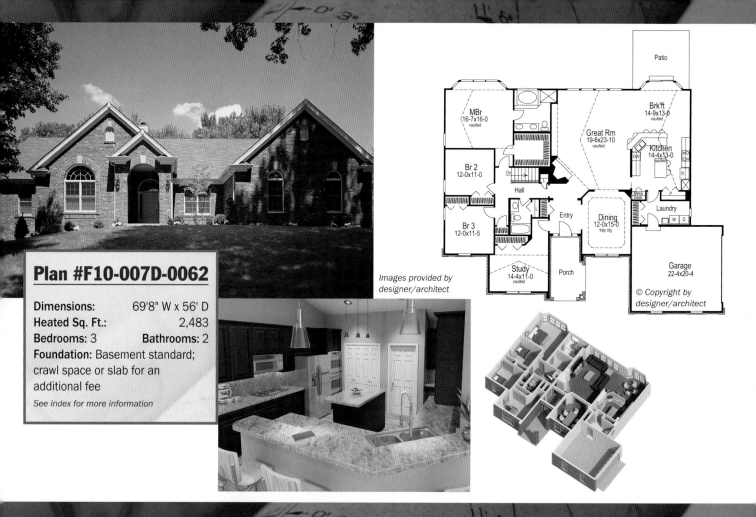

Plan #F10-007D-0062

Dimensions: 69'8" W x 56' D
Heated Sq. Ft.: 2,483
Bedrooms: 3   Bathrooms: 2
Foundation: Basement standard; crawl space or slab for an additional fee

See index for more information

Images provided by designer/architect

© Copyright by designer/architect

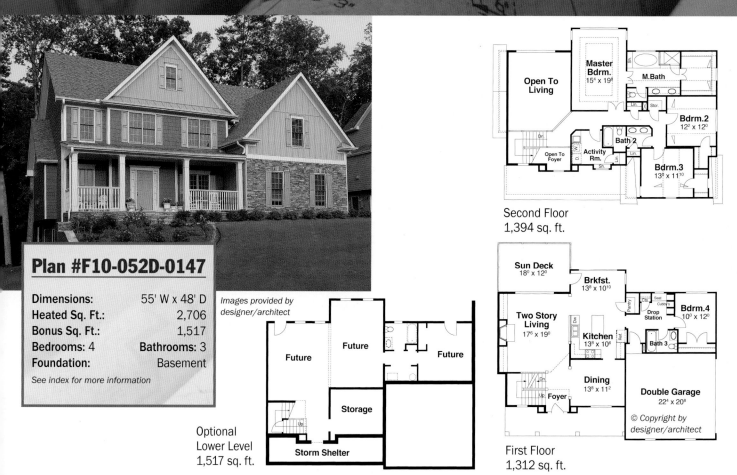

Plan #F10-052D-0147

Dimensions: 55' W x 48' D
Heated Sq. Ft.: 2,706
Bonus Sq. Ft.: 1,517
Bedrooms: 4   Bathrooms: 3
Foundation: Basement

See index for more information

Images provided by designer/architect

Second Floor
1,394 sq. ft.

Optional
Lower Level
1,517 sq. ft.

First Floor
1,312 sq. ft.

© Copyright by designer/architect

Plan #F10-055D-0192

Dimensions: 69'2" W x 74'10" D
Heated Sq. Ft.: 2,096
Bedrooms: 3   **Bathrooms:** 2½
Foundation: Slab or crawl space
standard; basement or daylight
basement for an additional fee

See index for more information

Images provided by designer/architect

© Copyright by designer/architect

WORK SHOP / GARAGE
23'-0" X 20'-0"

COVERED GRILLING PORCH
30'-6" X 12'-6"

STRG.

GARAGE
23'-0" X 22'-4"

BRKFAST RM.
12'-4" X 9'-6"

M. BATH
15'-2" X 18'-0"

GREAT RM.
17'-0" X 22'-8"
9' BOXED CEILING

WHP TUB

LIN

OPT ISLAND

LAU.

BEDROOM 3
17'-8" X 14'-8"

BOOK SHELVES

KITCHEN
12'-4" X 12'-0"

GALLERY

BOOK SHELVES

FOYER
9' CEILING

MASTER SUITE
15'-2" X 16'-0"
9' BOXED CEILING

COVERED PORCH
17'-0" X 8'-0"
9' CEILING

DINING RM.
12'-4" X 12'-0"
9' BOXED CEILING

BEDROOM 2
13'-4" X 10'-8"

Plan #F10-065D-0166

Dimensions: 57' W x 36'4" D
Heated Sq. Ft.: 1,698
Bonus Sq. Ft.: 269
Bedrooms: 3   **Bathrooms:** 2½
Foundation: Basement standard;
walk-out basement or crawl space
for an additional fee

See index for more information

Images provided by designer/architect

Bonus Room
17'5" x 10'7"

Bedroom
12' x 10'6"

Bath

Bath

Hall

Bedroom
13'7" x 11'6"

Master Bedroom
14'10" x 14'10"

Second Floor
830 sq. ft.

Breakfast
9'6" x 14'6"

Two-car Garage
20' x 20'

Kitchen
8'4" x 11'4"

Great Room
14'6" x 25'4"

Laun.

© Copyright by
designer/architect

Foyer

First Floor
868 sq. ft.

Porch

Plan #F10-101D-0027

Dimensions:	107' W x 97'9" D
Heated Sq. Ft.:	5,002
Bonus Sq. Ft.:	2,557
Bedrooms: 4	Bathrooms: 3½
Exterior Walls:	2" x 6"
Foundation:	Walk-out basement

See index for more information

Features

- This rustic masterpiece offers amazing beamed ceilings throughout adding character
- The circular staircase offers high drama on every floor
- There are plenty of great spaces for entertaining in comfort
- The optional lower level has an additional 2,557 square feet of living area and features a gym, a sauna, guest room, rec area with a wet bar, and a media area
- One 2-car side entry garage, and one 2-car front entry garage

Second Floor
1,311 sq. ft.

© Copyright by designer/architect

First Floor
3,691 sq. ft.

Optional
Lower Level
2,557 sq. ft.

Images provided by designer/architect

Plan #F10-055D-1039

Dimensions:	91'6" W x 61'3" D
Heated Sq. Ft.:	2,661
Bonus Sq. Ft.:	602
Bedrooms: 4	**Bathrooms:** 3½

Foundation: Crawl space or slab standard; basement or daylight basement for an additional fee

See index for more information

Features

- The stunning great room has a attention-grabbing fireplace with rustic beams above
- Relax in the outdoor living/grilling porch and discover a cozy fireplace and built-in grill area
- The kitchen enjoys a massive island that overlooks the great room and offers seating for several people
- The optional second floor has an additional 602 square feet of living area
- 2-car side entry garage, and 1-car front entry garage

Images provided by designer/architect

Optional
Second Floor
602 sq. ft.

First Floor
2,661 sq. ft.

© Copyright by designer/architect

Plan #F10-055D-0790

Dimensions:	66' W x 52' D
Heated Sq. Ft.:	2,075
Bedrooms: 4	**Bathrooms:** 3

Foundation: Slab or crawl space standard; basement or daylight basement for an additional fee

See index for more information

Images provided by designer/architect

© Copyright by designer/architect

Plan #F10-013D-0053

Dimensions:	71'4" W x 74'8" D
Heated Sq. Ft.:	2,461
Bonus Sq. Ft.:	518
Bedrooms: 3	**Bathrooms:** 3½

Foundation: Basement standard; crawl space or slab for an additional fee

See index for more information

Images provided by designer/architect

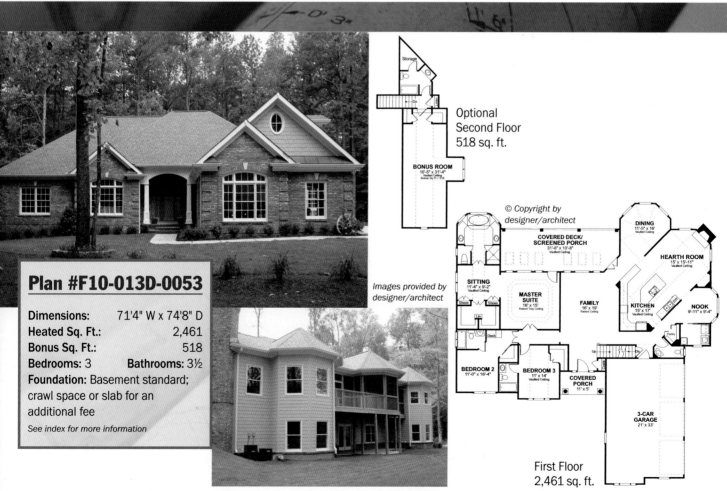

Optional Second Floor 518 sq. ft.

© Copyright by designer/architect

First Floor 2,461 sq. ft.

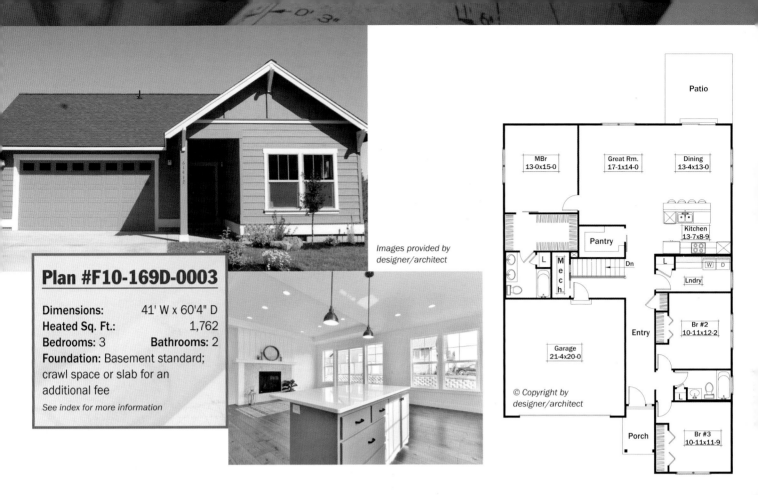

Images provided by
designer/architect

Plan #F10-169D-0003

Dimensions: 41' W x 60'4" D
Heated Sq. Ft.: 1,762
Bedrooms: 3 Bathrooms: 2
Foundation: Basement standard;
crawl space or slab for an
additional fee

See index for more information

© Copyright by
designer/architect

Plan #F10-055D-0199

Dimensions: 73'6" W x 80'6" D
Heated Sq. Ft.: 2,951
Bedrooms: 4 Bathrooms: 3
Foundation: Slab or crawl space
standard; basement or daylight
basement for an additional fee

See index for more information

Images provided by designer/architect

Plan #F10-051D-0964

Dimensions: 103'8" W x 68'4" D
Heated Sq. Ft.: 4,206
Bedrooms: 5 **Bathrooms:** 4½
Exterior Walls: 2" x 6"
Foundation: Basement standard; crawl space or slab for an additional fee

See index for more information

Images provided by designer/architect

Features

- The kitchen has an island perfect for casual dining
- The mother-in-law suite is located on the first floor and has its own private bath and sizable walk-in closet
- The master bath is equipped with a large walk-in closet, a relaxing shower, and a spa style tub
- The cozy hearth room will be a favorite gathering spot with its stone fireplace towering above
- The kids will love the second floor play room
- 2-car front entry garage, and a 1-car side entry garage

Second Floor
1,259 sq. ft.

BR. #4
5'-1 1/8" CEILING
15'0"x11'8"

BR. #3
5'-1 1/8" CEILING
23'0"x11'6"

PLAY RM.
5'-1 1/8" CEILING
12'8"x11'0"

BR. #2
5'-1 1/8" CEILING
11'8"x13'4"

OPEN TO BELOW

First Floor
2,947 sq. ft.

CVRD. PORCH
CATHEDRAL CEILING
16'0"x14'0"

HRTH. RM.
CATHEDRAL CEILING
18'0"x13'4"

MOTHER-IN-LAW SUITE
5'-1 1/8" CEILING
11'8"x11'8"

DIN. RM.
5'-1 1/8" CEILING
15'4"x13'0"

GRT. RM.
CATHEDRAL CEILING
18'4"x19'4"

MBR.
5'-1 1/8" STEP CEILING
15'0"x16'0"

KIT.
5'-1 1/8" CEILING
15'4"x12'0"

2 CAR GARAGE
29'8"x24'4"

PAN.

DEN
5'-1 1/8" CEILING
11'8"x13'4"

E.
2 STORY CEILING

© Copyright by designer/architect

1 CAR GARAGE
23'4"x17'8"

Plan #F10-072D-1108

Dimensions:	64' W x 60' D
Heated Sq. Ft.:	2,445
Bonus Sq. Ft.:	1,381
Bedrooms: 2	Bathrooms: 2
Exterior Walls:	2" x 6"
Foundation:	Walk-out basement

See index for more information

Images provided by designer/architect

Features

- Enjoy the spacious great room featuring a beautiful fireplace that creates a dramatic ambiance while adding character to this home
- The efficient kitchen is quite charming and contains a breakfast island and generous walk-in pantry
- The attractive sunroom provides a lovely space for relaxing
- The theater on the lower level is 336 square feet and is included in the total square footage
- The future finished space on the lower level has an additional 1,381 square feet of living area
- 3-car front entry garage

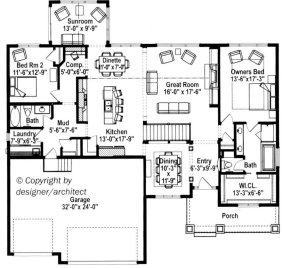

First Floor
2,109 sq. ft.

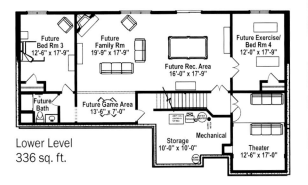

Lower Level
336 sq. ft.

Plan #F10-111D-0066

Dimensions: 38'11" W x 74'2" D
Heated Sq. Ft.: 1,933
Bedrooms: 4   **Bathrooms:** 2
Foundation: Slab standard; crawl space for an additional fee

See index for more information

Images provided by designer/architect

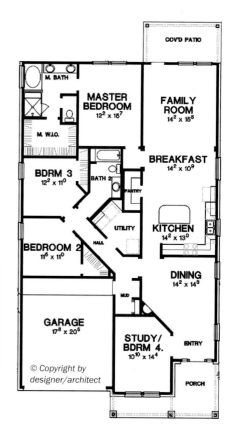

COV'D PATIO

MASTER BEDROOM 12² x 16⁷

FAMILY ROOM 14² x 16⁵

BDRM 3 12² x 11⁰

BATH 2

BREAKFAST 14² x 10⁹

BEDROOM 2 11⁶ x 11⁰

UTILITY

KITCHEN 14² x 13⁰

HALL

DINING 14² x 14⁹

GARAGE 17⁸ x 20⁵

MUD

STUDY/ BDRM 4. 10¹⁰ x 14⁴

ENTRY

PORCH

© Copyright by designer/architect

Images provided by designer/architect

Plan #F10-020D-0305

Dimensions: 84' W x 54' D
Heated Sq. Ft.: 2,791
Bedrooms: 4   **Bathrooms:** 2
Exterior Walls: 2" x 6"
Foundation: Slab standard; crawl space or basement for an additional fee

See index for more information

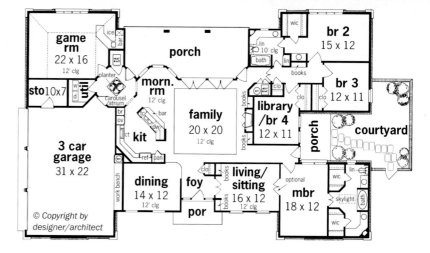

game rm 22 x 16 12' clg

porch

wic

br 2 15 x 12

bath

books

br 3 12 x 11

sto 10x7

morn. rm 12' clg

library /br 4 12 x 11

clo

courtyard

3 car garage 31 x 22

kit

family 20 x 20 12' clg

porch

work bench

dining 14 x 12 12' clg

foy

living/ sitting 16 x 12 12' clg

optional

mbr 18 x 12

skylight

bath

wic

por

© Copyright by designer/architect

Plan #F10-028D-0054

Dimensions:	60' W x 76' D
Heated Sq. Ft.:	2,123
Bedrooms: 3	**Bathrooms:** 2½
Foundation: Floating slab standard; monolithic slab, crawl space, basement or walk-out basement for an additional fee	

See index for more information

Images provided by designer/architect

© Copyright by designer/architect

Plan #F10-155D-0027

Dimensions:	72'2" W x 71'6" D
Heated Sq. Ft.:	2,513
Bedrooms: 5	**Bathrooms:** 3½
Foundation: Crawl space or slab, please specify when ordering	

See index for more information

Images provided by designer/architect

© Copyright by designer/architect

Plan #F10-101D-0062

Dimensions:	87' W x 79'6" D
Heated Sq. Ft.:	2,648
Bonus Sq. Ft.:	1,799
Bedrooms: 3	**Bathrooms:** 3½
Exterior Walls:	2" x 6"

Foundation: Basement, daylight basement or walk-out basement, please specify when ordering

See index for more information

Images provided by designer/architect

Features

- The first floor includes a variety of both formal and informal spaces that are comfortable and spacious for entertaining, or everyday living
- The great room, kitchen and dining area form the main gathering space
- A private office is hidden off the landing of the staircase
- The optional lower level has an additional 1,799 square feet of living area including a rec area, gym, two bedrooms and a bath
- 2-car side entry garage, and a 1-car front entry garage

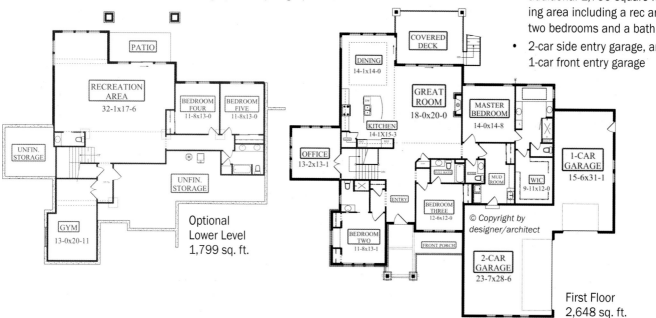

Optional
Lower Level
1,799 sq. ft.

First Floor
2,648 sq. ft.

© Copyright by designer/architect

houseplansandmore.com

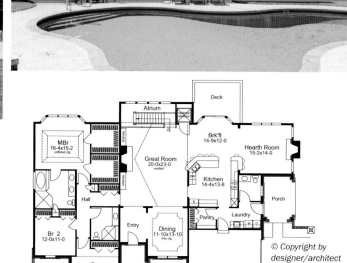

Plan #F10-007D-0207

Dimensions:	79'4" W x 61'4" D
Heated Sq. Ft.:	2,884
Bedrooms: 3	Bathrooms: 2½
Exterior Walls:	2" x 6"
Foundation:	Walk-out basement

See index for more information

Images provided by designer/architect

© Copyright by designer/architect

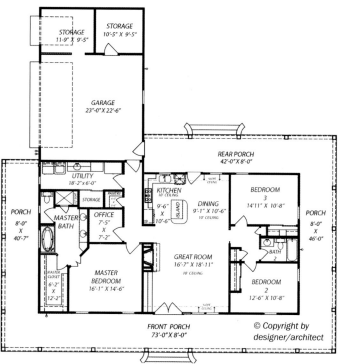

Plan #F10-170D-0001

Dimensions:	73' W x 73' D
Heated Sq. Ft.:	1,768
Bedrooms: 3	Bathrooms: 2

Foundation: Slab or monolithic slab standard; crawl space, basement or daylight basement for an additional fee

See index for more information

Images provided by designer/architect

© Copyright by designer/architect

First Floor
1,655 sq. ft.

© Copyright by designer/architect

Optional
Lower Level
1,219 sq. ft.

Plan #F10-159D-0004

Dimensions:	73' W x 44' D
Heated Sq. Ft.:	1,655
Bonus Sq. Ft.:	1,219
Exterior Walls:	2" x 6"
Bedrooms: 3	Bathrooms: 2
Foundation:	Walk-out basement

See index for more information

Images provided by designer/architect

Plan #F10-111D-0060

Dimensions:	38'11" W x 84' D
Heated Sq. Ft.:	1,768
Bedrooms: 3	Bathrooms: 2
Foundation:	Slab standard; crawl space for an additional fee

See index for more information

Images provided by designer/architect

© Copyright by designer/architect

Plan #F10-185S-0002

Dimensions: 155'8" W x 112'2" D
Heated Sq. Ft.: 7,519
Bedrooms: 5   **Bathrooms:** 6½
Exterior Walls: 2" x 6"
Foundation: Crawl space or slab standard; basement or daylight basement for an additional fee
See index for more information

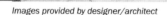

Images provided by designer/architect

Features

- This magnificent home spares no expense with so many incredible extra amenities including a home theater with its own lobby
- The massive master suite has a cozy fireplace, a private covered porch, two enormous walk-in closets and a posh bath
- There's a covered outdoor living area perfect for entertaining
- The hearth room extends off the kitchen
- 4-car side entry garage, and a 1-car rear entry garage

Second Floor
2,477 sq. ft.

First Floor
5,042 sq. ft.

© Copyright by designer/architect

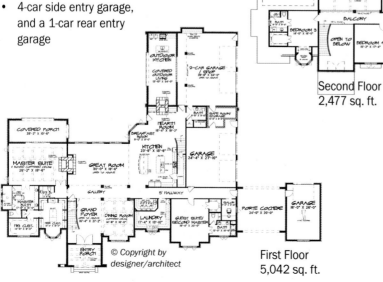

houseplansandmore.com

Plan #F10-055D-0748

Dimensions: 67'2" W x 55'10" D
Heated Sq. Ft.: 2,525
Bedrooms: 4   **Bathrooms:** 3
Foundation: Crawl space or slab standard; basement or daylight basement for an additional fee

See index for more information

Features

- This expansive one-story design has the split-bedroom floor plan everyone loves
- Stunning columns frame the foyer that leads into the open great room with fireplace
- The formal dining room, casual breakfast room, and large grilling porch with fireplace provide an abundance of locations for dining opportunities
- Three bedrooms and two baths occupy one side of this home, while the master suite is secluded on the other
- 2-car front entry garage

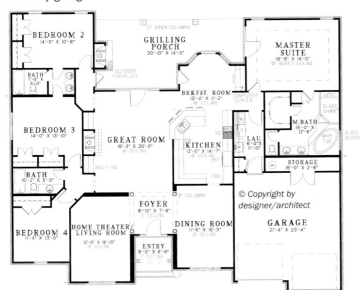

Images provided by designer/architect

Plan #F10-170D-0006

Dimensions:	73'3" W x 84'8" D
Heated Sq. Ft.:	2,176
Bonus Sq. Ft.:	488
Bedrooms: 3	**Bathrooms:** 2

Foundation: Slab or monolithic slab standard; crawl space, basement or daylight basement for an additional fee

See index for more information

Images provided by designer/architect

BONUS ROOM 14'-7" X 27'-0"

5' KNEE WALL

ATTIC ACCESS

DOWN

Optional Second Floor 488 sq. ft.

STORAGE 14'-0" X 6'-0"
STORAGE 14'-0" X 6'-0"

GARAGE 26'-0" X 26'-0"

STORAGE 14'-0" X 6'-0"

UP TO BONUS

© Copyright by designer/architect

REAR PORCH 26'-6" X 16'-0"

11'-2" x 7'-9" UTILITY

MASTER CLOSET 11'-2" X 8'-0"

KITCHEN 9'-4" X 21'-3"

FAMILY ROOM 23'-7" X 18'-11" 10' CEILING

BEDROOM 3 11'-7" X 12'-10"

MASTER BATH

10' CEILING

BATH 2

MASTER BEDROOM 15'-5" X 16'-0" 10' CEILING

DINING 11'-2" X 11'-6" 10' CEILING

FOYER 10' CEILING

BEDROOM 2 11'-5" X 11'-9"

FRONT PORCH 12' CEILING

First Floor 2,176 sq. ft.

Plan #F10-013D-0022

Dimensions:	66'2" W x 62' D
Heated Sq. Ft.:	1,992
Bonus Sq. Ft.:	299
Bedrooms: 4	**Bathrooms:** 3

Foundation: Basement standard; crawl space or slab for an additional fee

See index for more information

© Copyright by designer/architect

BONUS ROOM 10'-7" x 22'-6"

DECK 24'-8" x 15'-5"

GARAGE 22'-0" x 22'-6"

HIS

COVERED PORCH 24'-10" x 12'-0"

6' SPA

MECH.

OPTIONAL STAIRS TO BASEMENT

TV NICHE ABOVE VENTLESS GAS FIREPLACE

HERS

SITTING

MASTER BEDROOM 19'-0" x 15'-0"

CLERESTORY WINDOW ABOVE

19'-9" HIGH CEILING

FAMILY ROOM 16'-0" x 21'-10"

BREAKFAST 8'-6" x 11'-0"

KITCHEN 17'-3" x 12'-6"

OPTIONAL OPENING FOR LIVING

LINE OF 9' HIGH CEILING

BEDROOM 2 11'-0" x 14'-0"

LIVING / BEDROOM 3 11'-0" x 12'-0"

OPEN TO DORMER ABOVE

DINING 13'-8" x 12'-0"

MEDIA / GUEST ROOM 13'-8" x 11'-0"

PORCH 33'-4" x 6'-0"

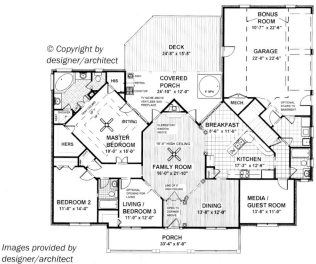

Images provided by designer/architect

houseplansandmore.com

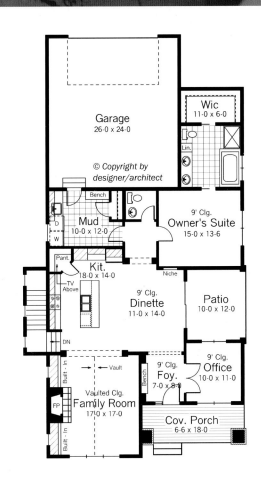

Plan #F10-091D-0478

Dimensions:	39' W x 72' D
Heated Sq. Ft.:	1,598
Bedrooms: 1	Bathrooms: 1½
Exterior Walls:	2" x 6"
Foundation:	Basement

See index for more information

Images provided by designer/architect

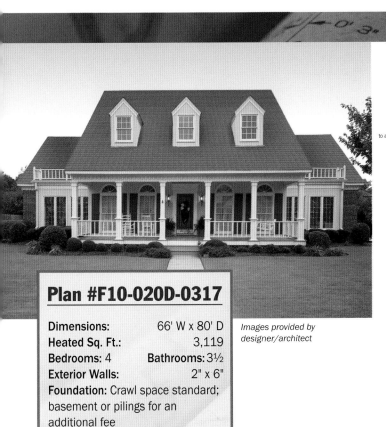

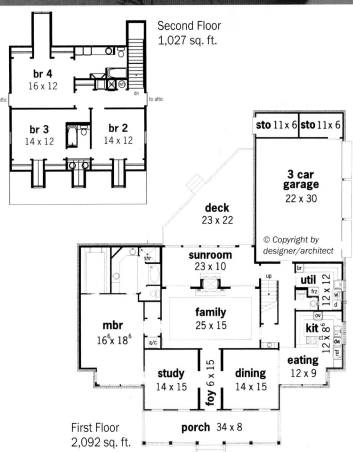

Plan #F10-020D-0317

Dimensions:	66' W x 80' D
Heated Sq. Ft.:	3,119
Bedrooms: 4	Bathrooms: 3½
Exterior Walls:	2" x 6"

Foundation: Crawl space standard; basement or pilings for an additional fee

See index for more information

Images provided by designer/architect

Plan #F10-011D-0664

Dimensions:	64' W x 67'6" D
Heated Sq. Ft.:	2,576
Bonus Sq. Ft.:	374
Bedrooms: 3	**Bathrooms:** 2½
Exterior Walls:	2" x 6"

Foundation: Crawl space or slab standard; basement for an additional fee

See index for more information

Images provided by designer/architect

Features

- This one--story home has all of the curb appeal and style a homeowner wants plus great interior features
- The open living area merges with the kitchen featuring a large island with dining space
- The vaulted dining area has porch access and a cheerful atmosphere
- A quiet home office is found behind the kitchen near the laundry room
- Three bedrooms can be found on the opposite side of the home
- The optional second floor has an additional 374 square feet of living area
- 3-car front entry garage

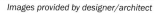

Optional
Second Floor
374 sq. ft.

First Floor
2,576 sq. ft.

© Copyright by designer/architect

houseplansandmore.com

Plan #F10-172D-0040

Dimensions:	59' W x 45'6" D
Heated Sq. Ft.:	2,438
Bonus Sq. Ft.:	1,433
Bedrooms: 3	Bathrooms: 2½
Exterior Walls:	2" x 6"

Foundation: Basement standard; crawl space, daylight basement, monolithic slab, stem wall slab or walk-out basement for an additional fee

See index for more information

Images provided by designer/architect

Features

- This country farmhouse is inviting inside and out
- The sunny living room would make an excellent home office
- All bedrooms are located on the second floor making this an easy layout for families
- The corner fireplace is the focal point of the large family room
- The optional lower level has an additional 1,433 square feet of living area and a family room, two bedrooms and a full bath
- 3-car front entry garage

Second Floor
1,158 sq. ft.

Optional Lower Level
1,433 sq. ft.

First Floor
1,280 sq. ft.

© Copyright by designer/architect

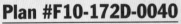

Creating Curb Appeal
making your home stand-out from the crowd

Everyone wants to own that home on the street that stops people in their tracks. No, that doesn't mean it has to be a huge mansion with jaw-dropping over-the-top features, it means it just has that "thing" called curb appeal that makes it feel warm and inviting, and seems to beg neighbors and friends to come on in. Below are some of the most popular ways to create that home "eye-candy" we all dream of.

exciting entries

Gone are the days of cookie-cutter front porch entries. Today's homeowners love showing off their personality and making front porches a precursor to what guests will find inside. These grand entrances often include statement lighting, custom doors, unique surrounding windows, luxurious plant holders and even furniture. Homeowners are really trying to pull you in and they are making these spaces comfortable for outdoor relaxation, too. Front doors that are mostly glass, or that feature iron and glass are becoming more popular. Fun, playful colors are also being introduced. If you're building a European style home, then ornate iron and glass style doors are a beautiful option. For those building a Craftsman home, many front doors include glass windows in a variety of shapes and sizes traditional to the Arts & Crafts style movement. Another playful option is the Dutch door. A Dutch door allows half of the door to be open at anytime, whether it's the top, or the bottom. It's a great way to get some fresh air moving through your home on a nice day.

little extras = big impact

Just like it's being seen in the interior with statement lighting, there is a current statement being made on the exterior, too. Statement house numbers are all the rage and people are getting super creative in how they're displaying their home's address numbers. Adhered or added to modern planters, custom painted in a unique font on the front door, or positioned in a clever place on the front facade, house numbers are actually adding style to a home's exterior whatever its architectural style. No longer a necessity or eyesore, these numbers are enhancing the front of a home and are carefully taking homage to the home's architectural style. A thoughtfully selected style and finish can greatly enhance the authenticity of your home's architecture. Have fun, and be playful with it. It definitely allows you show off you and your home's personality and style.

bright is alright

Bright colors on home exteriors if they fit with the architectural style are still being seen. But, some styles like Craftsman, are still utilizing more neutral tones. Darker paint colors are also making a comeback on the exterior, and in complete contrast, off-white and white exteriors are also growing in popularity just like white has made a major comeback in interior home décor.

custom doors, need we say more?

What used to be a pretty basic element to a home's front facade, the front door was often just a plain solid door meant for security purposes only. The doors homeowners are selecting today are thoughtful, well planned exterior ornamentation. Once again, they carry through with the home's architecture and often include many windows in unusual shapes, which add plenty of extra light to the interior. Take it one step further and paint the door (inside and out) in a vibrant color and add unique house numbers for the perfect expression that's friendly and inviting.

the vintage advantage

Vintage flair hasn't waned, either. Offering a casual and inviting element to a covered front porch, fun vintage pieces like re-purposed benches, antique watering cans, or planters offer a kitschy element that's fun, playful, and asks you to sit down and stay awhile.

nostalgic for front porches

Years ago, the front porch was the gathering place where people would mingle and socialize with neighbors. It was one of the only ways to stay connected with those around them and it provided a space for enjoying the outdoors. This trend is reappearing as lot sizes are becoming smaller and homeowners are interested more than ever in outdoor living spaces. Often, the covered front porch is one of the only outdoor spaces and because of this, people are using this space to the fullest by adding furniture, lighting, and other elements that make it feel comfortable and warm.

sidewalk talk

With all of the thought that goes into every little detail of your home's design, you would think by the time the landscaping and hardscapes have to be determined you can finally relax and not worry so much about the aesthetics of these elements. But, that truly isn't so! Sidewalk design is being carried through with a home's architectural style and color palette as it offers the initial welcome to guests. Don't get lazy when it comes to your sidewalk. You will see that a carefully designed walkway will pave the way for a major curb appeal moment. Today's homeowners are opting for pavers, stone, or other materials for their home's main entrance. And, due to the efficiency and affordability of LED light bulbs lining those paths and walkways with light add curb appeal at night for a very low cost.

sensing a pattern

Driveways, much like sidewalks can offer little or no added style to a home if you choose not to take them into account. But, homeowners today love the look of patterned driveways that either match the sidewalk or complement it. Have fun using textures and materials that complement your home's exterior and it will positively impact curb appeal.

flora forever

Flowers and plants are more popular than ever for surrounding your home's facade and adding softness. Landscape designers of today are thoughtful in their plant choices. Native landscaping is the way to go. Selecting plants that naturally grow in your region allows for less watering and fertilization, which is better for the environment. Choosing native plants also goes in line with the trend that homeowners are pairing down their ecological footprint. Native plants require less water than what is already received in rainfall. Plus, less sprinkler time means lower water bills, less water waste, and all around happier plants.

lighter landscaping

Being paired down to reflect the less cluttered style of homes being designed today, landscaping especially in the front of a home is much less fussy than in previous years. Today, new homeowners are choosing not to over plant shrubs and trees. Think clean, well-manicured lawns, carefully selected bushes, and tree options that are well suited with the home's architecture. By reducing the amount of landscaping a yard has, homeowners are staying eco-friendly creating less erosion issues, too.

So, by using less, your choices are now more important in order to make an impact. Choose plants that complement the color scheme of your home. If your home is gray, then offset it with pinks and reds. Or, if you've chosen a dark blue or slate, then white and yellow can provide that pop of color, or brighten the exterior. Another fun option is to select edible landscape such as colorful pepper plants and herbs and suddenly your landscaping is working twice as hard as your own organic garden, too. This is especially a great idea if you lack backyard space, or the position of the front of your home has more sunlight, making it more suitable to successful gardening.

more than just a pretty pot

The planters on the market today have really come a long way. These vessels that used to just hold flowers can now often upstage their contents. Uniquely shaped, and often in a style that complements a home's architecture, a well chosen and placed planter can add immense curb appeal.

let there be light

Transom windows are being added to the front exterior and around the entire perimeter of a home for several reasons. First, they add character to the facade in a clean, uncomplicated way, that is in line with Craftsman and Mid-Century modern style that is quite popular right now. They have a less formal feel, than an arched window design. And, they are adding additional light to the interior, which is a feature currently popular in interior home design. Open airy interiors are dictating home design, so the addition of larger windows makes an interior feel more open especially in homes with smaller square footages. Also, large picture windows are being seen in every style of home from Craftsman to Mid-Century Modern, and everything in between.

Exterior lighting adds drama once the sky goes dark. Even a solar light placed strategically on a unique ornamental tree can enhance your exterior and draw eyes to want to see more. Or, take it a step further and create a facade lit with soffit lighting, or light the bottom corners of the home for intensified drama. Many of these lighting systems can now be controlled right from your smart phone making it easy to use and creating added security when you're away.

the finish line

Depending on how luxurious the home is, those with larger budgets are using copper gutters to add curb appeal and style that truly stands out. Another interesting addition can be a unique fence that features an artistic pattern that basically becomes a work of art. Choosing a fence style with a similar architectural feel will make your home seem thoughtfully planned.

As homeowners tastes change, so do their ideas of what the ideal architectural style truly is. As their need for less complicated living, free of clutter and visual distractions becomes more important, the popular architectural styles reflect that. If they're craving a need to feel one with nature, then their desired style of home will turn to architecture that allows nature to be honored and respected. These constant shifts in tastes and trends in society are what make the landscape around us so colorful and interesting with glimpses of the past, present and future found all around us in any given city or neighborhood. Whatever style of architecture you choose, remember these curb appeal tips for optimizing the exterior style to the fullest and making your personality and home shine wherever it is that you live.

Unless noted, copyright by designer/architect; Page 118, top, left: Light up the night, Plan #F10-013S-0014 on page 464; top, middle: Easy to maintain native plants stay greener, Plan #F10-106S-0070 on page 378; top, right: Great use of native plants, Plan #011S-0003; middle: Less is more landscaping, Plan #F10-106D-0051 on page 430, Warren Diggles Photography; bottom, left: Planters that make an impact, Plan #101D-0059, Warren Diggles Photography; bottom, right: These planters steal the show, Plan #072S-0002; Page 119, bottom, left: Big windows and glass doors are in, Plan #091D-0028; top, left: Great door details, Plan #111D-0018; top, right: Unique large transom, Plan #011S-0003; bottom, right: Carefully determined decor, Plan #F10-101D-0052 on page 231, Damon Searles, photographer. See additional photos and purchase plans at houseplansandmore.com.

Second Floor
1,770 sq. ft.

© Copyright by designer/architect

First Floor
1,948 sq. ft.

Plan #F10-072D-1121

Dimensions:	66' W x 50' D
Heated Sq. Ft.:	3,718
Bedrooms: 5	Bathrooms: 3½
Exterior Walls:	2" x 6"
Foundation:	Walk-out basement

See index for more information

Images provided by designer/architect

Second Floor
766 sq. ft.

© Copyright by
designer/architect

First Floor
846 sq. ft.

Plan #F10-101D-0002

Dimensions:	43'6" W x 43' D
Heated Sq. Ft.:	1,612
Bedrooms: 3	Bathrooms: 2½
Foundation:	Basement

See index for more information

Images provided by designer/architect

Plan #F10-055D-0677

Images provided by designer/architect

Dimensions: 67'3" W x 68'6" D
Heated Sq. Ft.: 3,167
Bonus Sq. Ft.: 474
Bedrooms: 4 **Bathrooms:** 3
Foundation: Crawl space or slab standard; basement or daylight basement for an additional fee

See index for more information

Second Floor
681 sq. ft.

BATH 5'-8" x 14'-4"
BEDROOM 4 14'-0" x 12'-0"
SLOPED CEILING
UPPER FLOOR CEILING LINE
OPEN TO BELOW
Theater BALCONIES
ATTIC STORAGE
BEDROOM 3 14'-0" x 11'-2"
OPEN TO BELOW
SLOPED CEILING
PLANT LEDGE
COMPUTER CENTER
BONUS ROOM 12'-0" x 34'-8"

First Floor
2,486 sq. ft.

MASTER SUITE 14'-6" x 16'-8" 10' BOXED CEILING
GRILLING PORCH 24'-6" x 8'-0"
BREAKFAST ROOM 12'-0" x 10'-0"
GUEST ROOM / BEDROOM 2 12'-10" x 14'-4"
MEDIA CENTER
M.BATH 10'-8" x 17'-8"
GLASS SHWR
WHP TUB
GREAT ROOM 22'-6" x 17'-8" OPEN TO ABOVE
BUILT-INS
KITCHEN 13'-0" x 13'-6"
DW
REF
BATH 9'-0" x 8'-0"
LIN
OPEN TO ABOVE
OPTIONAL BASEMENT STAIRS
UP
FOYER 7'-6" x 10'-6"
COLUMNS
DINING ROOM 11'-6" x 15'-0"
BENCH W/ HANGING
KID'S NOOK
LAU 11'-6" x 5'-10"
LIN
DEN / OFFICE / NURSERY 14'-6" x 13'-0"
VAULTED CEILING
COVERED PORCH 20'-6" x 8'-0"
3-CAR GARAGE 21'-4" x 33'-4"

© Copyright by designer/architect

Plan #F10-024S-0011

Images provided by designer/architect

Dimensions: 48' W x 71' D
Heated Sq. Ft.: 3,493
Bedrooms: 4 **Bathrooms:** 3½
Foundation: Pier

See index for more information

Second Floor
1,166 sq. ft.

Media Room 13'10" x 14'10"
Bath
Bath
Bedroom 13'10" x 14'10"
WIC
WIC
Bedroom 11'6" x 13'2"
Sitting
Bedroom 11'6" x 13'2"
Balcony 46'x 8'

First Floor
2,327 sq. ft.

Porch 25'6"x 10'
Master Bedroom 20'2"x 16'10"
Family 24'6"x 17'2"
Breakfast 15'6"x 9'8"
Utility
Master Bath
Kitchen 15'6"x 14'2"
1/2 Bath
Walk-In Closet
Dining 11'x 13'8"
Foyer
Living 11'6" x 13'8"
Porch 46'x 8'

© Copyright by designer/architect

Plan #F10-053D-0002

Dimensions:	56' W x 40' D
Heated Sq. Ft.:	1,668
Bonus Sq. Ft.:	780
Bedrooms: 3	Bathrooms: 2
Foundation:	Walk-out basement

See index for more information

Images provided by designer/architect

First Floor
1,668 sq. ft.

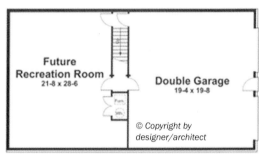

Optional Lower Level
780 sq. ft.

Plan #F10-011D-0008

Dimensions:	55' W x 48' D
Heated Sq. Ft.:	1,728
Bedrooms: 2	Bathrooms: 2
Exterior Walls:	2" x 6"

Foundation: Crawl space or slab standard; basement for an additional fee

See index for more information

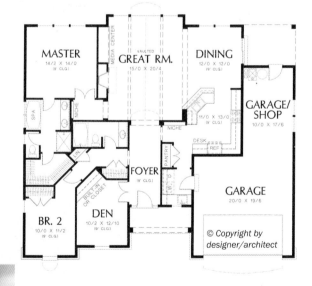

Images provided by designer/architect

Plan #F10-060D-0400

Dimensions:	69'6" W x 69'6" D
Heated Sq. Ft.:	2,871
Bonus Sq. Ft.:	599
Bedrooms: 3	Bathrooms: 3
Foundation:	Slab

See index for more information

Images provided by designer/architect

Optional Second Floor 599 sq. ft.

© Copyright by designer/architect

First Floor 2,871 sq. ft.

Plan #F10-111D-0009

Dimensions:	68'1" W x 74' D
Heated Sq. Ft.:	2,112
Bonus Sq. Ft.:	304
Bedrooms: 3	Bathrooms: 2½

Foundation: Slab standard; crawl space or basement for an additional fee

See index for more information

Images provided by designer/architect

© Copyright by designer/architect

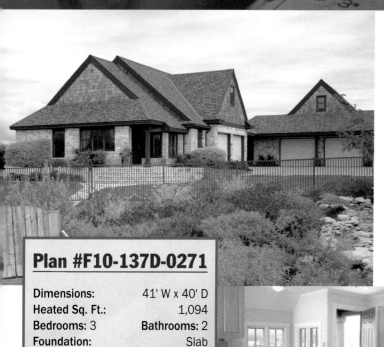

First Floor
646 sq. ft.

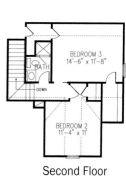

Second Floor
448 sq. ft.

Images provided by designer/architect

Plan #F10-137D-0271

Dimensions:	41' W x 40' D
Heated Sq. Ft.:	1,094
Bedrooms: 3	Bathrooms: 2
Foundation:	Slab

See index for more information

Plan #F10-065D-0002

Dimensions:	59'4" W x 58'10" D
Heated Sq. Ft.:	2,101
Bedrooms: 3	Bathrooms: 2½
Foundation:	Basement standard;

crawl space for slab or an
additional fee

See index for more information

Images provided by designer/architect

Second Floor
475 sq. ft.

First Floor
1,626 sq. ft.

© Copyright by designer/architect

Plan #F10-032D-0825

Dimensions:	70' W x 38'4" D
Heated Sq. Ft.:	1,313
Bedrooms: 2	**Bathrooms:** 1
Exterior Walls:	2" x 6"

Foundation: Basement standard; crawl space, floating slab or monolithic slab for an additional fee

See index for more information

© Copyright by designer/architect

Images provided by designer/architect

Plan #F10-091D-0023

Dimensions:	67' W x 60' D
Heated Sq. Ft.:	3,253
Bonus Sq. Ft.:	384
Bedrooms: 3	**Bathrooms:** 2½
Exterior Walls:	2" x 6"
Foundation:	Walk-out basement

See index for more information

Images provided by designer/architect

Second Floor
1,456 sq. ft.

First Floor
1,797 sq. ft.

© Copyright by designer/architect

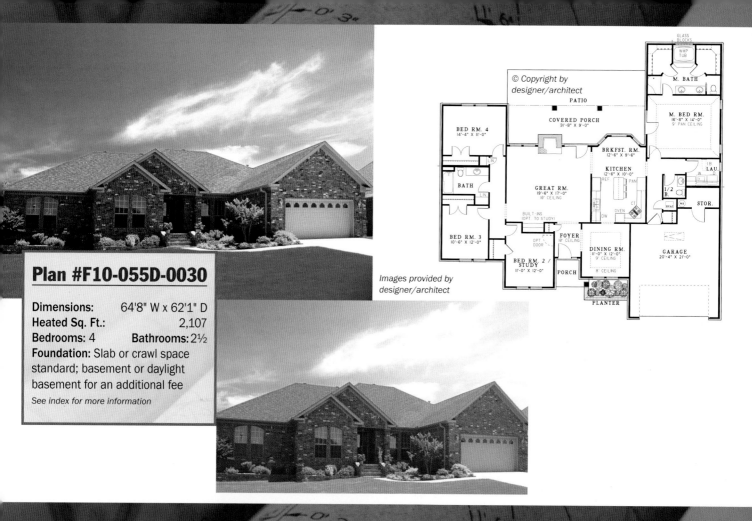

Plan #F10-055D-0030

Dimensions: 64'8" W x 62'1" D
Heated Sq. Ft.: 2,107
Bedrooms: 4   **Bathrooms:** 2½
Foundation: Slab or crawl space standard; basement or daylight basement for an additional fee
See index for more information

Images provided by designer/architect

Plan #F10-141D-0088

Dimensions: 60'3" W x 53'9" D
Heated Sq. Ft.: 3,036
Bedrooms: 4   **Bathrooms:** 3
Foundation: Slab standard; crawl space, basement or walk-out basement for an additional fee
See index for more information

Images provided by designer/architect

Second Floor
1,104 sq. ft.

First Floor
1,932 sq. ft.

Plan #F10-181D-0001

Dimensions: 40' W x 28' D
Heated Sq. Ft.: 1,020
Bedrooms: 2   Bathrooms: 1
Exterior Walls: 2" x 6"
Foundation: Slab standard; crawl space or basement for an additional fee

See index for more information

Images provided by designer/architect

© Copyright by designer/architect

Plan #F10-024D-0011

Dimensions: 43' W x 47' D
Heated Sq. Ft.: 1,819
Bedrooms: 3   Bathrooms: 2½
Foundation: Crawl space or slab, please specify when ordering

See index for more information

Images provided by designer/architect

© Copyright by designer/architect

Second Floor
2,168 sq. ft.

Plan #F10-101D-0122

Dimensions:	82' W x 101'9" D
Heated Sq. Ft.:	4,966
Bonus Sq. Ft.:	1,200
Bedrooms:	6
Bathrooms:	4 full, 2 half
Exterior Walls:	2" x 6"
Foundation:	Crawl space

See index for more information

Images provided by designer/architect

© Copyright by
designer/architect

First Floor
2,798 sq. ft.

Plan #F10-180D-0022

Dimensions:	24' W x 40' D
Heated Sq. Ft.:	897
Bedrooms: 2	Bathrooms: 2
Exterior Walls:	2" x 6"

Foundation: Crawl space or slab,
please specify when ordering

See index for more information

Images provided by designer/architect

© Copyright by
designer/architect

Plan #F10-028D-0001

Dimensions:	33' W x 36' D
Heated Sq. Ft.:	864
Bedrooms: 2	Bathrooms: 1

Foundation: Floating slab standard; monolithic slab, crawl space, basement or walk-out basement for an additional fee

See index for more information

Images provided by designer/architect

LAUNDRY 12' X 6'

BEDROOM 2 13' X 10'

KITCHEN 12' X 10'

BEDROOM 1 13' X 10'

GREAT ROOM 20' X 14'

© Copyright by designer/architect

PORCH - 6' DEEP

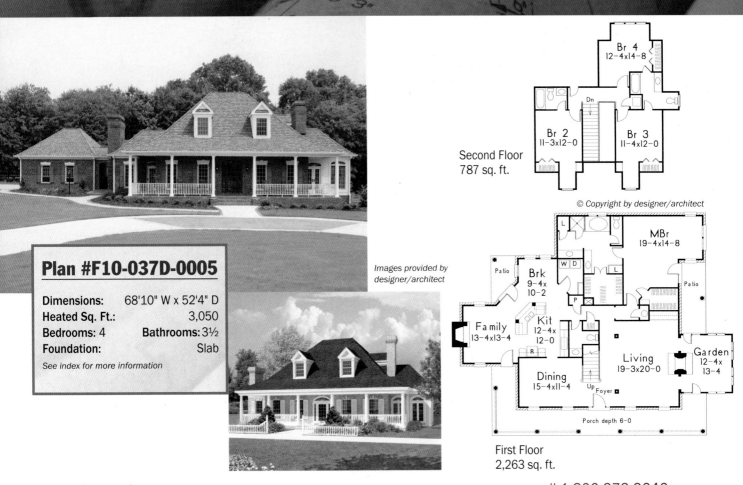

Plan #F10-037D-0005

Dimensions:	68'10" W x 52'4" D
Heated Sq. Ft.:	3,050
Bedrooms: 4	Bathrooms: 3½
Foundation:	Slab

See index for more information

Images provided by designer/architect

Br 4 12-4x14-8

Br 2 11-3x12-0

Br 3 11-4x12-0

Dn

Second Floor 787 sq. ft.

© Copyright by designer/architect

MBr 19-4x14-8

Patio

Brk 9-4x 10-2

W D

L

Patio

Family 13-4x13-4

Kit 12-4x 12-0

R

Living 19-3x20-0

Garden 12-4x 13-4

Dining 15-4x11-4

Up Foyer

Porch depth 6-0

First Floor 2,263 sq. ft.

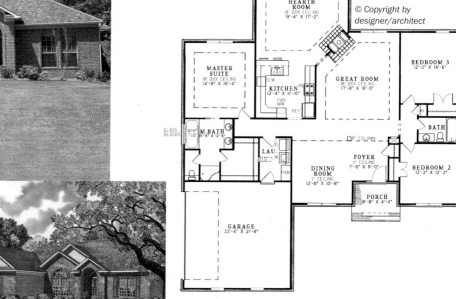

© Copyright by designer/architect

Plan #F10-055D-0031

Dimensions: 58'6" W x 64'6" D
Heated Sq. Ft.: 2,133
Bedrooms: 3   Bathrooms: 2
Foundation: Slab or crawl space
standard; basement or daylight
basement for an additional fee

See index for more information

Images provided by designer/architect

Images provided by designer/architect

Plan #F10-163D-0008

Dimensions: 75'6" W x 77' D
Heated Sq. Ft.: 3,480
Bedrooms: 3   Bathrooms: 3½
Exterior Walls: 2" x 6"
Foundation: Basement

See index for more information

© Copyright by designer/architect

Lower Level
1,414 sq. ft.

First Floor
2,066 sq. ft.

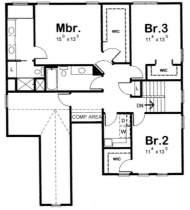

Second Floor
1,080 sq. ft.

Plan #F10-026D-2102

Dimensions:	40' W x 44' D
Heated Sq. Ft.:	2,155
Bonus Sq. Ft.:	250
Bedrooms: 3	**Bathrooms:** 2½

Foundation: Slab standard; crawl space, basement or walk-out basement for an additional fee

See index for more information

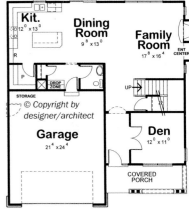

First Floor
1,075 sq. ft.

Plan #F10-051D-0972

Dimensions:	38' W x 74' D
Heated Sq. Ft.:	1,490
Bedrooms: 2	**Bathrooms:** 2
Exterior Walls:	2" x 6"

Foundation: Basement standard; crawl space or slab for an additional fee

See index for more information

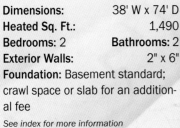

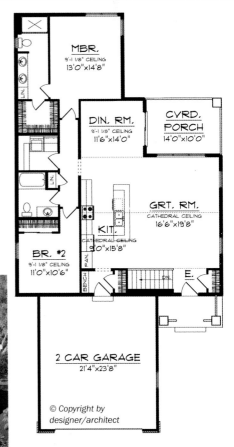

Plan #F10-141D-0011

Dimensions:	23'9" W x 52' D
Heated Sq. Ft.:	1,843
Bedrooms: 3	**Bathrooms:** 2

Foundation: Slab standard; crawl space, basement or walk-out basement for an additional fee

See index for more information

Images provided by designer/architect

Features

- Industrial modern style makes living carefree and easy in this sleek two-story home, perfect for a narrow lot

- The family room enjoys a cozy corner fireplace

- The dining room is only designated by corner columns allowing it to flow freely into the surrounding spaces and making it seem quite large

- The kitchen is spacious and features a breakfast bar large enough for four people to dine comfortably, plus there's plenty of other counterspace for serving

- The first floor master bedroom has a private bath with a space saving pocket door

- 2-car garage attached via a breezeway

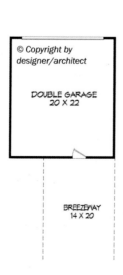

First Floor
1,186 sq. ft.

Second Floor
657 sq. ft.

Plan #F10-032D-1112

Dimensions:	66'4" W x 35'4" D
Heated Sq. Ft.:	2,380
Bonus Sq. Ft.:	1,280
Bedrooms: 4	**Bathrooms:** 2½
Exterior Walls:	2" x 6"

Foundation: Basement standard; crawl space, floating slab or monolithic slab for an additional fee

See index for more information

Features

- This stunning two-story has all of the style a new homeowner could ever want with its Modern Farmhouse facade
- The open first floor layout is ideal for entertaining
- The den/office is a great little nook when working from home
- A handy mud room keeps things organized when entering the home from the garage
- The optional lower level has an additional 1,280 square feet of living area
- 2-car front entry garage

Images provided by designer/architect

Second Floor
1,100 sq. ft.

First Floor
1,280 sq. ft.

© Copyright by designer/architect

Optional
Lower Level
1,280 sq. ft.

houseplansandmore.com

Plan #F10-011D-0657

Dimensions:	26' W x 34' D
Heated Sq. Ft.:	1,394
Bedrooms: 3	**Bathrooms:** 2½
Exterior Walls:	2" x 6"

Foundation: Crawl space or slab standard; basement or finished basement for an additional fee

See index for more information

Images provided by designer/architect

Features

- Stylish Modern Farmhouse design is a great size open floor plan, perfect for today's family
- The living room and dining area are open to one another as well as the kitchen with island
- All three bedrooms are on the second floor for convenience and privacy
- The laundry room is centrally located on the first floor

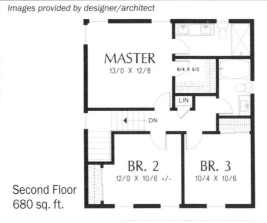

Second Floor
680 sq. ft.

MASTER
13/0 X 12/8

BR. 2
12/0 X 10/6 +/-

BR. 3
10/4 X 10/6

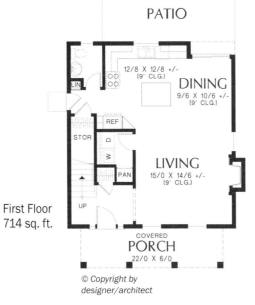

PATIO

12/8 X 12/8 +/-
(9' CLG.)

DINING
9/6 X 10/6 +/-
(9' CLG.)

LIVING
15/0 X 14/6 +/-
(9' CLG.)

First Floor
714 sq. ft.

COVERED
PORCH
22/0 X 6/0

© Copyright by
designer/architect

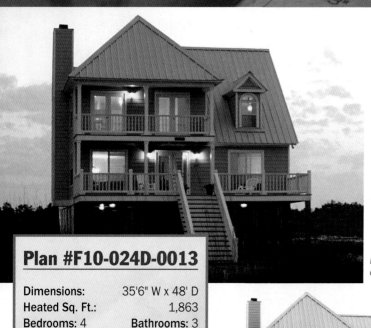

Plan #F10-024D-0013

Dimensions:	35'6" W x 48' D
Heated Sq. Ft.:	1,863
Bedrooms: 4	**Bathrooms:** 3
Foundation:	Pier

See index for more information

Second Floor
807 sq. ft.

Ma. Bath

Bath

Bedroom
13'x 13'

Master Bedroom
16'6"x 19'

Balcony
20'2"x 6'

Images provided by designer/architect

© Copyright by designer/architect

Porch

Kitchen
8'8"x 10'5"

Dining
11'x 11'

Bedroom
13'x 11'

Bath

Living
16'6"x 21'

Bedroom
13'x 11'

Porch
20'2"x 6'

First Floor
1,056 sq. ft.

Deck
33'x 12'

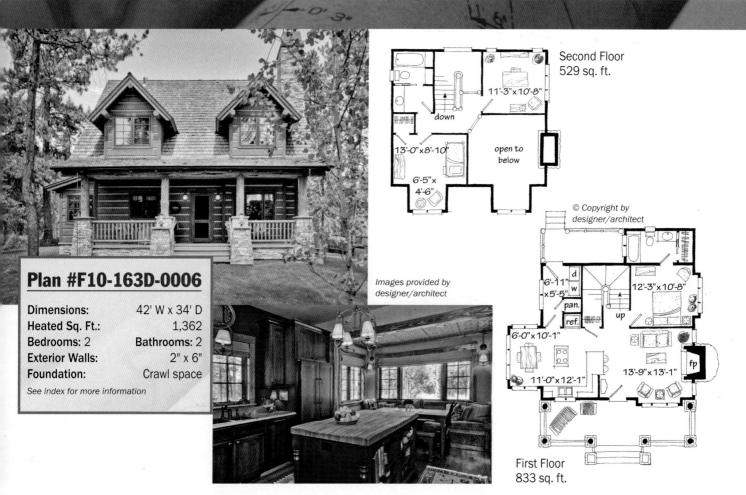

Plan #F10-163D-0006

Dimensions:	42' W x 34' D
Heated Sq. Ft.:	1,362
Bedrooms: 2	**Bathrooms:** 2
Exterior Walls:	2" x 6"
Foundation:	Crawl space

See index for more information

Second Floor
529 sq. ft.

down

11'-3"x 10'-8"

13'-0"x8'-10"

open to below

6'-5"x 4'-6"

Images provided by designer/architect

© Copyright by designer/architect

6'-11"x 5'-5"

pan.

ref.

d/w

12'-3"x 10'-8"

up

6'-0"x 10'-1"

11'-0"x 12'-1"

13'-9"x 13'-1"

fp

First Floor
833 sq. ft.

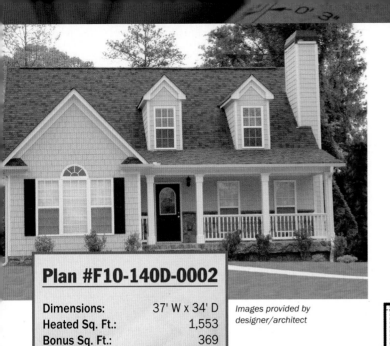

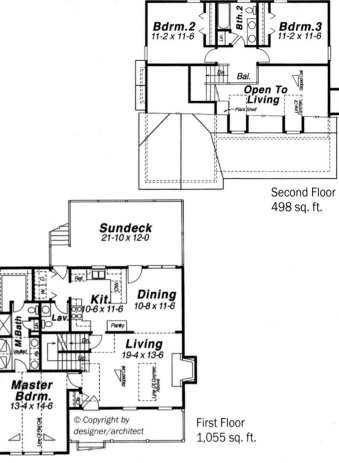

Second Floor
498 sq. ft.

Plan #F10-140D-0002

Dimensions:	37' W x 34' D
Heated Sq. Ft.:	1,553
Bonus Sq. Ft.:	369
Bedrooms: 3	Bathrooms: 2½
Foundation:	Walk-out basement

See index for more information

Images provided by designer/architect

First Floor
1,055 sq. ft.

© Copyright by designer/architect

Plan #F10-013D-0015

Dimensions:	55'8" W x 56'6" D
Heated Sq. Ft.:	1,787
Bonus Sq. Ft.:	263
Bedrooms: 3	Bathrooms: 2
Foundation:	Slab standard; crawl space or basement for an additional fee

See index for more information

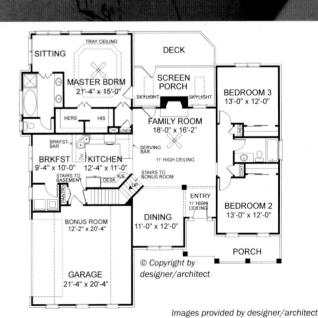

© Copyright by designer/architect

Images provided by designer/architect

Plan #F10-051D-0970

Dimensions:	37' W x 68' D
Heated Sq. Ft.:	1,354
Bedrooms: 2	**Bathrooms:** 2
Exterior Walls:	2" x 6"

Foundation: Basement standard; crawl space or slab for an additional fee

See index for more information

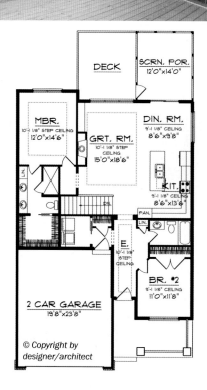

Features

- Small and stylish, this home offers the layout everyone loves in an easy-to-maintain size
- The covered front porch is large enough for relaxing, while the rear has a screened porch with access onto an open deck, perfect when grilling
- The private master bedroom has a private bath with an oversized walk-in shower, a double-bowl vanity, and a spacious walk-in closet
- Bedroom 2 is just steps away from a full bath
- 2-car front entry garage

DECK

SCRN. POR.
12'0"x14'0"

MBR.
10'-1 1/8" STEP CEILING
12'0"x14'6"

GRT. RM.
10'-1 1/8" STEP CEILING
15'0"x18'6"

DIN. RM.
9'-1 1/8" CEILING
8'6"x9'8"

KIT.
9'-1 1/8" CEILING
8'6"x13'6"

PAN.

LIN.

E.
10'-1 1/8" STEP CEILING

BR. #2
9'-1 1/8" CEILING
11'0"x11'8"

2 CAR GARAGE
19'8"x23'8"

© Copyright by designer/architect

Images provided by designer/architect

houseplansandmore.com

Plan #F10-011D-0527

Dimensions:	70' W x 59' D
Heated Sq. Ft.:	2,373
Bonus Sq. Ft.:	226
Bedrooms: 3	Bathrooms: 2½
Exterior Walls:	2" x 6"

Foundation: Crawl space or slab
standard; basement for an
additional fee

See index for more information

Features

- The split bedroom layout places the master suite and secondary bedrooms on opposite sides of the home from each other allowing privacy and separation for older children and guests
- The vaulted great room and covered porch feel seamless as you move from the indoor space
- The office is tucked near the foyer so if your have visitors it's an easy transition
- The kitchen is centrally located between both casual and formal dining options
- The optional second floor has an additional 226 square feet of living area
- 3-car front entry garage

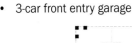

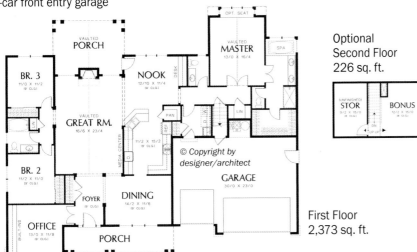

Optional
Second Floor
226 sq. ft.

© Copyright by
designer/architect

First Floor
2,373 sq. ft.

Images provided by designer/architect

Plan #F10-101D-0056

Dimensions:	72' W x 77' D
Heated Sq. Ft.:	2,593
Bonus Sq. Ft.:	1,892
Bedrooms: 2	**Bathrooms:** 2½
Exterior Walls:	2" x 6"
Foundation:	Walk-out basement

See index for more information

Images provided by designer/architect

Features

- This stunning home has the look and feel homeowners love with its sleek interior and wide, open floor plan
- The great room, kitchen and dining area combine maximizing the square footage and making these spaces functional and comfortable
- The master bedroom enjoys a first floor private location adding convenience for the homeowners and it includes an oversized walk-in closet, and a private bath with a walk-in shower, a free-standing tub, and a double-bowl vanity
- The optional lower level has an additional 1,892 square feet of living area and adds extra amenities like a media area, a billiards room, a rec room, and an exercise room in addition to two additional bedrooms and two full baths
- 3-car front entry garage

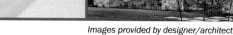

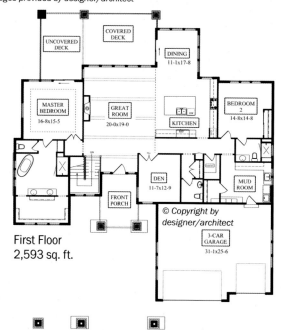

© Copyright by designer/architect

First Floor
2,593 sq. ft.

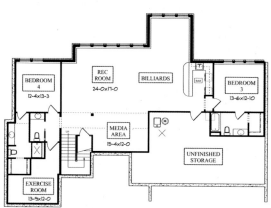

Optional
Lower Level
1,892 sq. ft.

houseplansandmore.com

Plan #F10-065S-0034

Dimensions:	100' W x 93'6" D
Heated Sq. Ft.:	6,465
Bonus Sq. Ft.:	1,568
Bedrooms:	4
Bathrooms:	4 full, 2 half
Foundation:	Basement

See index for more information

Images provided by designer/architect

Features

- Refined Country French home gives way to a gorgeous interior filled with every amenity
- Enter the foyer and discover a variety of living spaces including a cozy hunt room, a pub, and a cheerful conservatory secluded off the hearth room
- Double French doors in the great room blur the lines between the indoor and the outdoor spaces by connecting the great room and the covered porch that has an outdoor fireplace
- The optional lower level has an additional 1,568 square feet of living area
- 2-car side entry garage, and a 1-car front entry garage

Second Floor
1,676 sq. ft.

© Copyright by designer/architect

Optional Lower Level
1,568 sq. ft.

First Floor
4,789 sq. ft.

Plan #F10-137D-0082

Dimensions:	45' W x 36' D
Heated Sq. Ft.:	1,442
Bedrooms: 3	Bathrooms: 2
Foundation:	Slab

See index for more information

Images provided by designer/architect

Second Floor
464 sq. ft.

First Floor
978 sq. ft.

© Copyright by designer/architect

Plan #F10-024D-0624

Dimensions:	62' W x 67' D
Heated Sq. Ft.:	3,223
Bedrooms: 4	Bathrooms: 4
Foundation:	Pier

See index for more information

Images provided by designer/architect

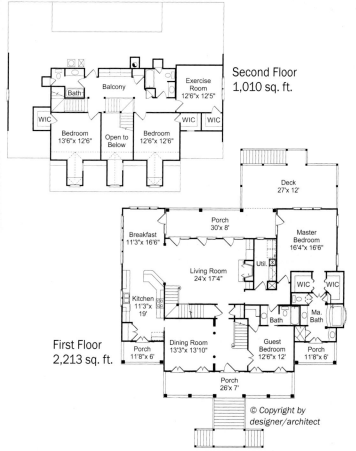

Second Floor
1,010 sq. ft.

First Floor
2,213 sq. ft.

© Copyright by designer/architect

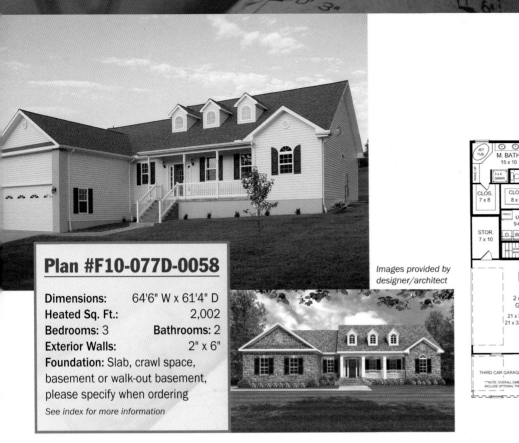

Images provided by designer/architect

© Copyright by designer/architect

Plan #F10-077D-0058

Dimensions:	64'6" W x 61'4" D
Heated Sq. Ft.:	2,002
Bedrooms: 3	Bathrooms: 2
Exterior Walls:	2" x 6"

Foundation: Slab, crawl space, basement or walk-out basement, please specify when ordering

See index for more information

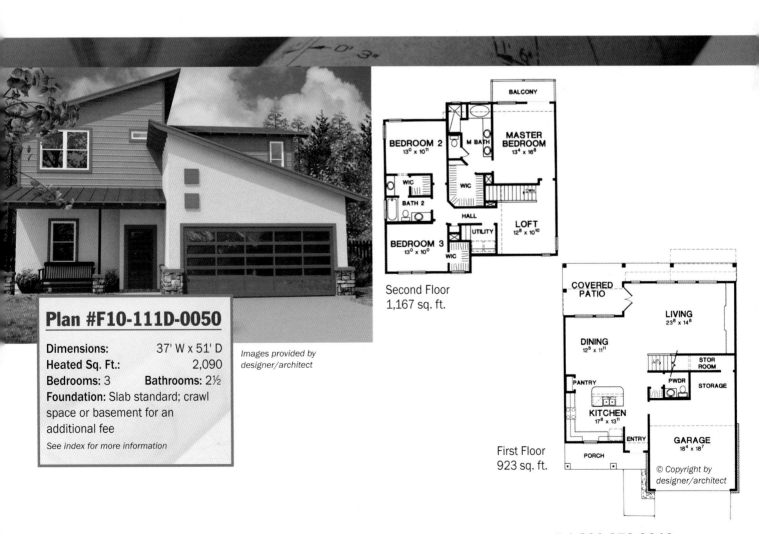

Second Floor
1,167 sq. ft.

First Floor
923 sq. ft.

Images provided by designer/architect

© Copyright by designer/architect

Plan #F10-111D-0050

Dimensions:	37' W x 51' D
Heated Sq. Ft.:	2,090
Bedrooms: 3	Bathrooms: 2½

Foundation: Slab standard; crawl space or basement for an additional fee

See index for more information

Plan #F10-051D-0960

Dimensions:	117' W x 50'8" D
Heated Sq. Ft.:	2,784
Bedrooms: 3	Bathrooms: 2
Exterior Walls:	2" x 6"

Foundation: Basement standard; crawl or slab for an additional fee

See index for more information

Images provided by designer/architect

Features

- The wide open floor plan creates an unimaginable amount of spaciousness
- A massive screened porch is a wonderful outdoor retreat that lends itself to year-round enjoyment
- An elegant dining room is surrounded by windows creating a cheerful backdrop when entertaining
- The walk-in pantry adds much needed kitchen appliance space
- The private master bedroom has a posh bath with a walk-in shower and a spa style tub, plus a huge walk-in closet
- 3-car front entry garage

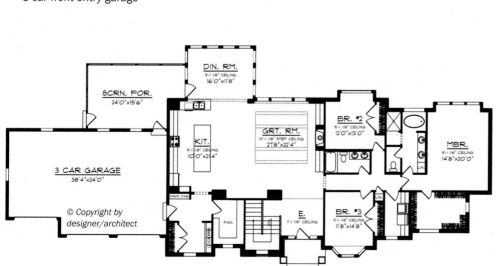

Plan #F10-011D-0246

Images provided by designer/architect

Dimensions:	45' W x 53' D
Heated Sq. Ft.:	2,080
Bedrooms: 3	**Bathrooms:** 2½
Exterior Walls:	2" x 6"

Foundation: Crawl space or slab standard; basement for an additional fee

See index for more information

Features

- This charming Craftsman has an inviting interior thanks to the open floor plan that greets you the minute you walk in
- The large kitchen island spans the entire length of the great room allowing those in the kitchen never to miss any action in the great room
- A beautiful vaulted dining space is flooded in natural sunlight for a pleasant dining experience
- The master suite has a private, yet convenient first floor location and enjoys its own bath and walk-in closet
- 2-car front entry garage

First Floor
1,601 sq. ft.

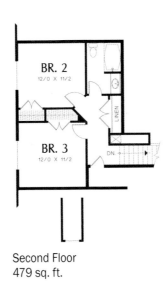

Second Floor
479 sq. ft.

© Copyright by designer/architect

Plan #F10-026D-1939

Dimensions:	60' W x 48' D
Heated Sq. Ft.:	1,635
Bedrooms: 3	Bathrooms: 2½

Foundation: Basement standard; crawl space, slab or walk-out basement for an additional fee

See index for more information

Features

- You can find great style and layout in a manageable sized home that still includes all of those extras with this ranch design
- Discover a handy drop zone featuring storage, a bench and lockers near the garage entry
- An open family room is next to the dining room, which extends further into the kitchen
- The kitchen has plenty of floor space and includes a center island, and a large walk-in pantry
- 3-car front entry garage

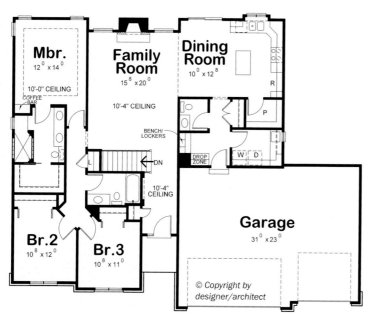

Images provided by designer/architect

Plan #F10-051D-0963

Dimensions:	80' W x 60'8" D
Heated Sq. Ft.:	3,485
Bedrooms: 4	Bathrooms: 3½
Exterior Walls:	2" x 6"

Foundation: Basement standard; crawl space or slab for an additional fee

See index for more information

Images provided by designer/architect

Features

- A hobby room off the mud room would make an ideal play room, or even a quiet home office
- The dining room connects to the outdoor covered porch, perfect when grilling and entertaining
- The open great room flows into the kitchen for a seamless feel
- A second floor loft is a great space for a computer or study spot
- The private master bedroom has a large posh bath and a huge walk-in closet
- 4-car side entry garage

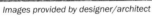

Second Floor
1,272 sq. ft.

BR. #3
12'6"x15'4"
9'-1 1/8" CEILING

LOFT
10'0"x24'4"
9'-1 1/8" CEILING

BR. #4
12'4"x15'4"
9'-1 1/8" CEILING

BR. #2
11'4"x12'4"
9'-1 1/8" CEILING

First Floor
2,213 sq. ft.

DIN. RM.
17'0"x13'6"
10'-1 1/8" CEILING

CVRD. PORCH
20'0"x14'0"

MBR.
14'4"x16'0"
10'-1 1/8" CEILING

4 CAR GARAGE
26'4"x50'4"

GRT. RM.
26'8"x22'4"
10'-1 1/8" CEILING

KIT.
11'0"x22'4"
10'-1 1/8" CEILING

HOBBY RM.
10'0"x10'4"
10'-1 1/8" CEILING

© Copyright by designer/architect

Plan #F10-101D-0094

Dimensions:	72' W x 72'9" D
Heated Sq. Ft.:	2,650
Bonus Sq. Ft.:	1,821
Bedrooms: 3	Bathrooms: 2½
Exterior Walls:	2" x 6"
Foundation:	Basement

See index for more information

Images provided by designer/architect

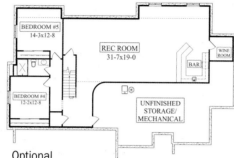

Optional
Lower Level
1,821 sq. ft.

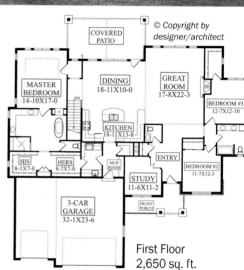

© Copyright by
designer/architect

First Floor
2,650 sq. ft.

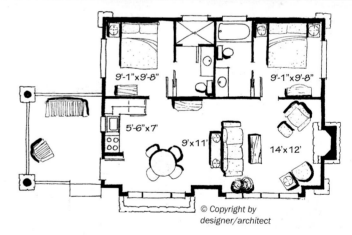

© Copyright by
designer/architect

Images provided by designer/architect

Plan #F10-163D-0004

Dimensions:	40' W x 22' D
Heated Sq. Ft.:	681
Bedrooms: 2	Bathrooms: 2
Exterior Walls:	2" x 6"
Foundation: Crawl space or slab, please specify when ordering	

See index for more information

Second Floor
1,401 sq. ft.

OPEN TO GREAT ROOM BELOW

BEDROOM 5
13'-6" X 15'-0"

OVERLOOK

BRIDGE

OPEN TO BELOW

BEDROOM 3
13'-10" X 13'-4"

CLO

CLO

BATH

BRIDGE

BRIDGE

BEDROOM 4
14'-4" X 12'-0"

CLO

OPEN TO BELOW

GAME ROOM
15'-5" X 18'-3"

1ST FLOOR WALLS BELOW

BALCONY

© Copyright by designer/architect

BEDROOM 2
13'-10" X 13'-6"

OUTDOOR KITCHEN

COVERED PORCH

NOOK
13'-2" X 14'-3"

GREAT ROOM
22'-5" X 23'-6"
VAULTED BEAMED CEILING

MASTER BEDROOM
TRAY CEILING 10' TO 14'
17'-5" X 18'-4"

KITCHEN

2 STORY CEILING BRIDGE ABOVE

OVERLOOK ABOVE

WALK IN SHOWER

M. BATH

14'-2" X 20'-0"

POWDER ROOM

PAN

2 STORY CEILING

FOYER

LIBRARY
14'-6" X 17'-6"

CLOSET

UTILITY

DINING
13'-2" X 15'-6"

COVERED PORCH

First Floor
3,186 sq. ft.

Plan #F10-164D-0028

Images provided by designer/architect

Dimensions: 81'3" W x 82'8" D
Heated Sq. Ft.: 4,587
Bedrooms: 5   Bathrooms: 4½
Foundation: Slab

See index for more information

Plan #F10-055D-1070

Dimensions: 62' W x 69'8" D
Heated Sq. Ft.: 2,498
Bedrooms: 3   Bathrooms: 3
Foundation: Crawl space or slab, please specify when ordering

See index for more information

Images provided designer/archite

3-CAR GARAGE
22'-8" X 35'-0"

OPTIONAL ATTIC STAIRS

SAFE ROOM
8'-0" X 10'-0"

COVERED PORCH
27'-10" X 11'-0"

GAS CT.

REF. DESK

UNDER COUNTER MW

DOUBLE OVEN

DW

BREAKFAST ROOM
9'-8" X 11'-10"

SUN ROOM
12'-4" X 11'-10"

KITCHEN
14'-6" X 12'-8"

GAS FIREPLACE

BATH

PANTRY

VAULTED CEILING

GREAT ROOM
30'-0" X 18'-0"

BEDROOM 3
13'-0" X 13'-8"

LAUNDRY
13'-0" X 6'-2"

MASTER SUITE 2
15'-0" X 17'-4"
11' TRAY CEILING

BATH
8'-10" X 12'-0"

SHWR

FOYER

PORCH

BATH
8'-10" X 12'-0"

SHWR

MASTER SUITE 1
15'-0" X 17'-4"
11' TRAY CEILING

© Copyright by designer/architect

Plan #F10-028D-0141

Dimensions:	46' W x 43' D
Heated Sq. Ft.:	1,334
Bedrooms: 3	Bathrooms: 2
Exterior Walls:	2" x 6"

Foundation: Floating slab standard; monolithic slab, crawl space, basement or walk-out basement for an additional fee

See index for more information

Images provided by designer/architect

Features

- This gorgeous, country style home consists of a great room, kitchen and dining area that create a large open floor plan
- The kitchen features a large island with a microwave, an additional sink, and seating
- Upper and lower cabinets provide plenty of kitchen storage
- The spacious laundry room has cabinets for storage and a closet conveniently located by the door
- The master bedroom has a large walk-in closet and a bath with double sinks, a linen closet, and an oversized shower
- The two secondary bedrooms are on the opposite side of the home with a bath between them

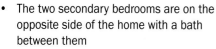

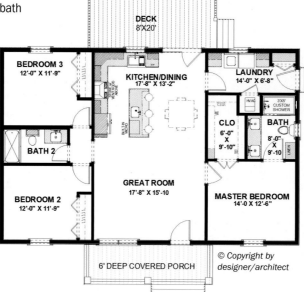

houseplansandmore.com

Plan #F10-084D-0086

Dimensions:	45'4" W x 76' D
Heated Sq. Ft.:	1,725
Bedrooms: 3	Bathrooms: 2
Foundation:	Slab standard; crawl space for an additional fee

See index for more information

Images provided by designer/architect

Features

- This stylish ranch home offers a great split bedroom layout for a more narrow lot
- The open living area enjoys beautiful views of the outdoor living space that features an outdoor fireplace
- The kitchen enjoys a snack bar, a center work island, tons of storage floor-to-ceiling and even a built-in desk
- A cheerful dining area is surrounded in windows
- The private master bedroom features a luxury bath with two walk-in closets, a double-bowl vanity, an oversized tub and walk-in easy access shower
- 2-car front entry garage

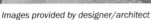
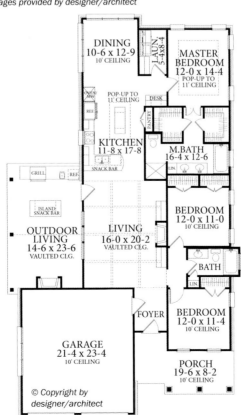

Plan #F10-041D-0006

Dimensions:	36' W x 35'8" D
Heated Sq. Ft.:	1,189
Bedrooms: 3	**Bathrooms:** 2½
Foundation:	Basement

See index for more information

Images provided by designer/architect

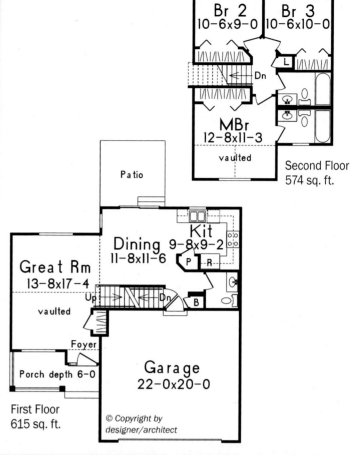

Br 2
10-6x9-0

Br 3
10-6x10-0

Dn

L

MBr
12-8x11-3

vaulted

Second Floor
574 sq. ft.

Patio

Kit
9-8x9-2

Dining
11-8x11-6

P   R

B

Great Rm
13-8x17-4

Up   Dn

vaulted

Foyer

Porch depth 6-0

Garage
22-0x20-0

First Floor
615 sq. ft.

© Copyright by
designer/architect

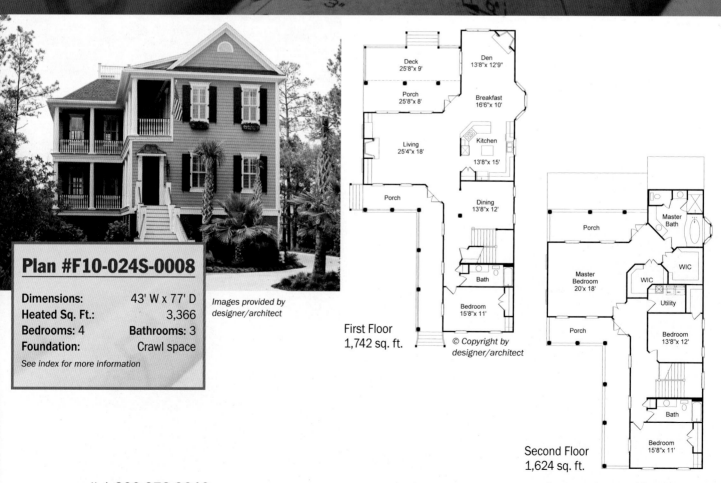

Plan #F10-024S-0008

Dimensions:	43' W x 77' D
Heated Sq. Ft.:	3,366
Bedrooms: 4	**Bathrooms:** 3
Foundation:	Crawl space

See index for more information

Images provided by designer/architect

Deck
25'8"x 9'

Den
13'8"x 12'9"

Porch
25'8"x 8'

Breakfast
16'6"x 10'

Living
25'4"x 18'

Kitchen
13'8"x 15'

Porch

Dining
13'8"x 12'

Bath

Bedroom
15'8"x 11'

First Floor
1,742 sq. ft.

© Copyright by
designer/architect

Porch

Master
Bath

WIC

Master
Bedroom
20'x 18'

WIC

Utility

Porch

Bedroom
13'8"x 12'

Bath

Bedroom
15'8"x 11'

Second Floor
1,624 sq. ft.

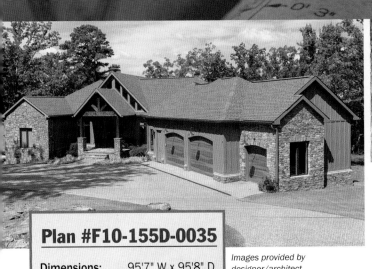

Plan #F10-155D-0035

Dimensions: 95'7" W x 95'8" D
Heated Sq. Ft.: 5,054
Bedrooms: 4   **Bathrooms:** 4½
Foundation: Daylight basement

See index for more information

Images provided by designer/architect

© Copyright by designer/architect

Lower Level
2,165 sq. ft.

First Floor
2,889 sq. ft.

Plan #F10-020D-0365

Dimensions: 57' W x 88'6" D
Heated Sq. Ft.: 1,976
Bonus Sq. Ft.: 333
Bedrooms: 3   **Bathrooms:** 2
Exterior Walls: 2" x 6"
Foundation: Crawl space standard; basement or slab for an additional fee

See index for more information

Images provided by designer/architect

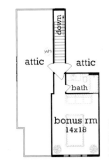

Optional
Second Floor
333 sq. ft.

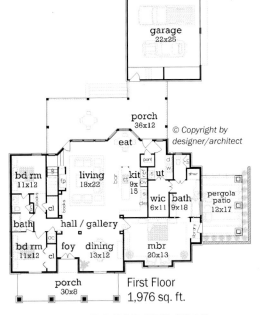

© Copyright by designer/architect

First Floor
1,976 sq. ft.

Plan #F10-032D-1067

Dimensions:	66' W x 50' D
Heated Sq. Ft.:	3,599
Bedrooms: 3	Bathrooms: 3
Exterior Walls:	2" x 6"

Foundation: Basement standard; crawl space, monolithic slab or floating slab for an additional fee

See index for more information

Features

- Symmetrically pleasing to the eye, this Modern Farmhouse design is truly a stunner
- The front entry has a large laundry room to the left and a quiet study/office/den to the right
- The vaulted dining and living rooms are open to one another with the kitchen a mere steps away
- The kitchen is graced with a large island and a walk-in pantry
- The second floor enjoys a huge game room over the garage
- The master suite is special with a unique walk-in closet that leads to a private bath and there's also a private second floor balcony only accessible from the master suite
- 1-car front entry garage

Second Floor
1,852 sq. ft.

© Copyright by designer/architect

First Floor
1,747 sq. ft.

Images provided by designer/architect

Plan #F10-051D-0991

Dimensions: 67'10" W x 63'8" D
Heated Sq. Ft.: 3,583
Bedrooms: 4   **Bathrooms:** 3
Exterior Walls: 2" x 6"
Foundation: Walk-out basement standard; crawl space or slab for an additional fee

See index for more information

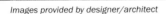

Images provided by designer/architect

Features

- An open floor plan has a spacious kitchen overlooking the great room so the chef can keep an eye on the kids while preparing dinner
- The master suite lies behind the kitchen and garage away from the other bedrooms for maximum privacy and it includes double walk-in closets, dual sinks and a tray ceiling
- The remaining two bedrooms are off the entry to the left with a shared full bath nearby
- A bench with lockers can be found near the garage door
- The lower level has a family room, a game room, an additional bedroom with a full bath, and a theater room
- 3-car front entry garage

Lower Level
1,392 sq. ft.

First Floor
2,191 sq. ft.

© Copyright by designer/architect

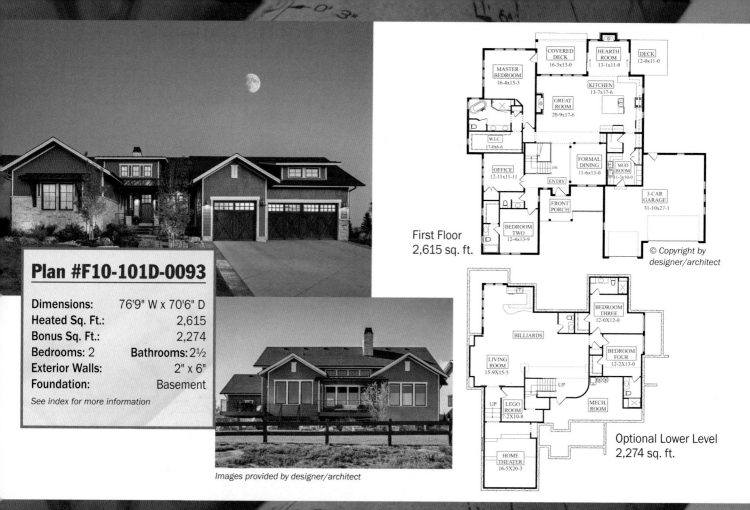

First Floor
2,615 sq. ft.

© Copyright by designer/architect

Optional Lower Level
2,274 sq. ft.

Plan #F10-101D-0093

Dimensions:	76'9" W x 70'6" D
Heated Sq. Ft.:	2,615
Bonus Sq. Ft.:	2,274
Bedrooms: 2	Bathrooms: 2½
Exterior Walls:	2" x 6"
Foundation:	Basement

See index for more information

Images provided by designer/architect

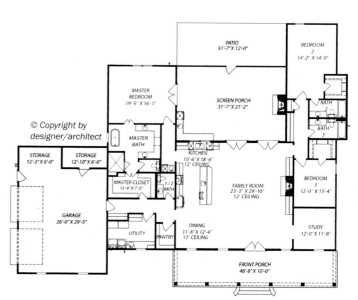

© Copyright by designer/architect

Plan #F10-170D-0016

Dimensions:	95' W x 74' D
Heated Sq. Ft.:	3,013
Bedrooms: 3	Bathrooms: 3½

Foundation: Slab or monolithic slab standard; crawl space, basement, or daylight basement for an additional fee

See index for more information

Images provided by designer/architect

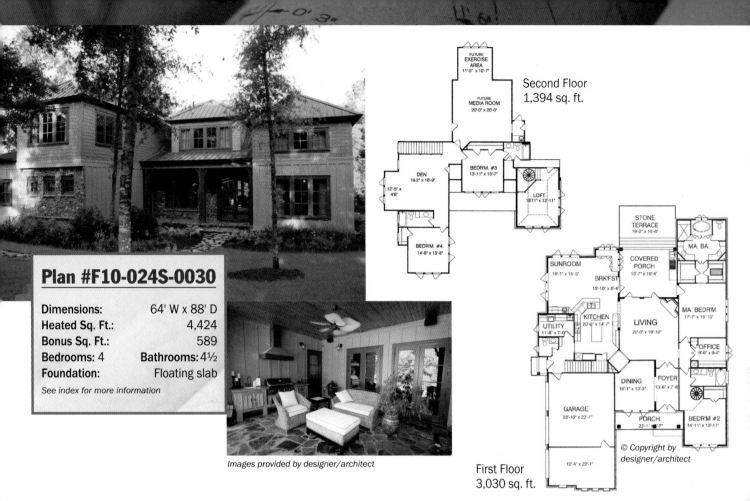

Plan #F10-024S-0030

Dimensions:	64' W x 88' D
Heated Sq. Ft.:	4,424
Bonus Sq. Ft.:	589
Bedrooms: 4	Bathrooms: 4½
Foundation:	Floating slab

See index for more information

Images provided by designer/architect

Second Floor
1,394 sq. ft.

First Floor
3,030 sq. ft.

© Copyright by
designer/architect

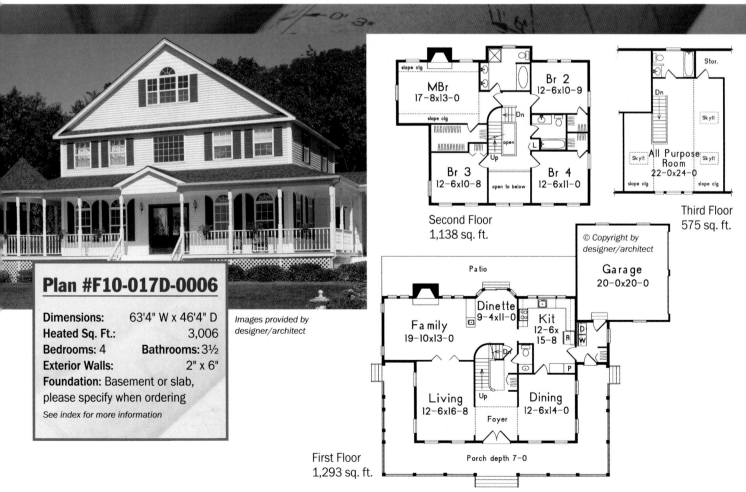

Plan #F10-017D-0006

Dimensions:	63'4" W x 46'4" D
Heated Sq. Ft.:	3,006
Bedrooms: 4	Bathrooms: 3½
Exterior Walls:	2" x 6"
Foundation: Basement or slab, please specify when ordering	

See index for more information

Images provided by designer/architect

Second Floor
1,138 sq. ft.

Third Floor
575 sq. ft.

© Copyright by
designer/architect

First Floor
1,293 sq. ft.

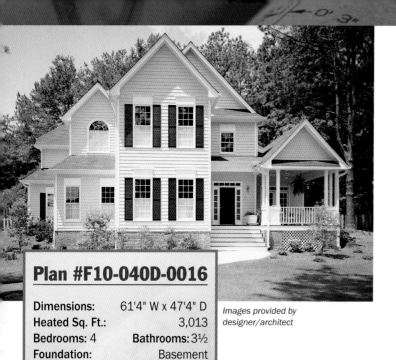

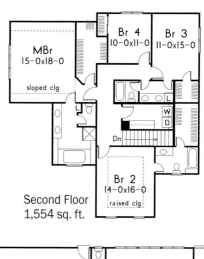

Second Floor
1,554 sq. ft.

MBr
15-0x18-0
sloped clg

Br 4
10-0x11-0

Br 3
11-0x15-0

Dn

Br 2
14-0x16-0
raised clg

Plan #F10-040D-0016

Dimensions:	61'4" W x 47'4" D
Heated Sq. Ft.:	3,013
Bedrooms: 4	**Bathrooms:** 3½
Foundation:	Basement

See index for more information

Images provided by designer/architect

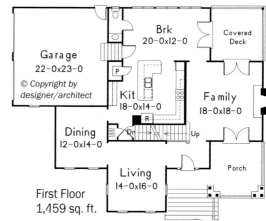

Garage
22-0x23-0

Brk
20-0x12-0

Covered
Deck

© Copyright by
designer/architect

Kit
18-0x14-0

Family
18-0x18-0

Dining
12-0x14-0

Up

Living
14-0x16-0

Porch

First Floor
1,459 sq. ft.

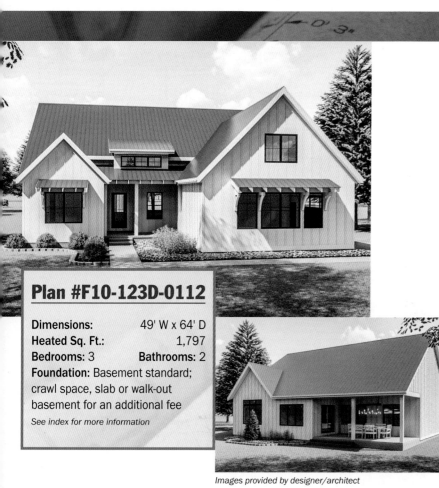

Plan #F10-123D-0112

Dimensions:	49' W x 64' D
Heated Sq. Ft.:	1,797
Bedrooms: 3	**Bathrooms:** 2

Foundation: Basement standard; crawl space, slab or walk-out basement for an additional fee

See index for more information

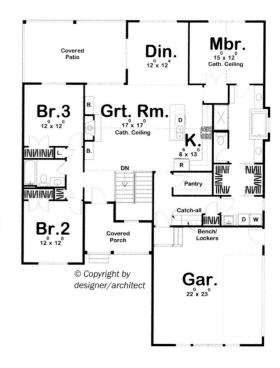

Images provided by designer/architect

Covered
Patio

Din.
12 x 12⁰⁴

Mbr.
15 x 12
Cath. Ceiling

Br.3
12 x 12

Grt. Rm.
17 x 17
Cath. Ceiling

K.
8 x 13

DN

Pantry

Catch-all

Br.2
12 x 12

Covered
Porch

Bench/
Lockers

D W

© Copyright by
designer/architect

Gar.
22 x 23⁰

Plan #F10-128D-0097

Dimensions:	39'8" W x 67'10" D
Heated Sq. Ft.:	2,479
Bonus Sq. Ft.:	552
Bedrooms: 3	**Bathrooms:** 3½

Foundation: Basement or crawl space, please specify when ordering

See index for more information

Second Floor
819 sq. ft.

FUTURE REC. ROOM 23'-4" X 18'-0"

STORAGE

STORAGE

WALK IN CLOSET

LINEN

BEDROOM 2 13'-6" x 16'-0"

BEDROOM 3 12'-2" x 16'-0"

BATH

WALK IN CLOSET

STOR.

LINEN

BATH 2 14'-2" x 10'-2"

STORAGE

ROOF AREA

SCREENED PORCH 17'-8" x 9'-2"

TWO - GARAGE 21'-0" x 22'-8"

© Copyright by designer/architect

GREAT ROOM 17'-2" x 18'-0"

UTILITY 9'-6" x 6'-2"

STORAGE 7'-0" x 6'-0"

LINEN

BREAKFAST 13'-6" x 9'-6"

WARDROBE

MASTER BATH

KITCHEN 17'-0" x 10'-0"

PANTRY

DINING ROOM 14'-4" x 11'-10"

FOYER 6'-6" x 11'-10"

MASTER BEDROOM 17'-0" x 14'-0"

COVERED PORCH 37'-8" x 8'-2"

First Floor
1,660 sq. ft.

Images provided by designer/architect

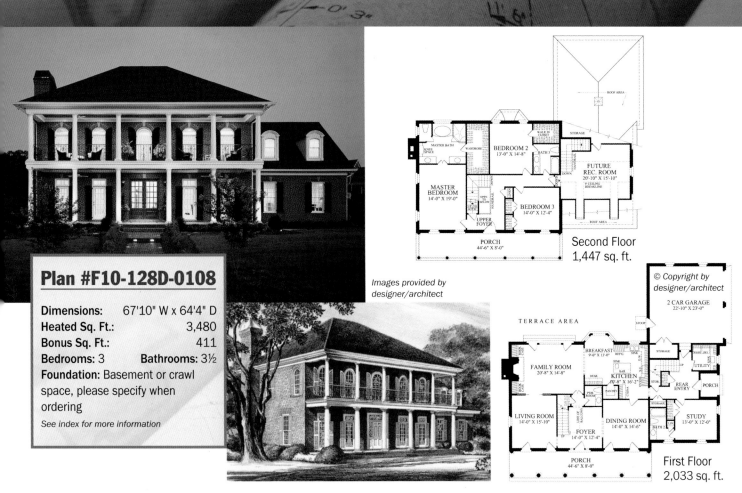

Plan #F10-128D-0108

Dimensions:	67'10" W x 64'4" D
Heated Sq. Ft.:	3,480
Bonus Sq. Ft.:	411
Bedrooms: 3	**Bathrooms:** 3½

Foundation: Basement or crawl space, please specify when ordering

See index for more information

Images provided by designer/architect

MASTER BATH

KNEE SPACE

WARDROBE

BEDROOM 2 13'-0" X 14'-8"

WALK IN CLOSET

BATH 3

STORAGE

FUTURE REC. ROOM 20'-10" X 15'-10"

MASTER BEDROOM 14'-0" X 19'-0"

OPEN TO BELOW

HANDRAIL

BEDROOM 3 14'-0" X 12'-4"

UPPER FOYER

ROOF AREA

PORCH 44'-6" X 8'-0"

Second Floor
1,447 sq. ft.

© Copyright by designer/architect

2 CAR GARAGE 22'-10" X 23'-0"

TERRACE AREA

BREAKFAST 9'-0" X 13'-0"

STORAGE

WASH. DRY.

UTILITY

FAMILY ROOM 20'-8" X 14'-8"

KITCHEN 17'-8" X 16'-2"

BAR

DESK

CHINA

PANTRY

REAR ENTRY

PORCH

PDR. ROOM

STOR.

LIVING ROOM 14'-0" X 15'-10"

DINING ROOM 14'-0" X 14'-6"

STUDY 13'-0" X 12'-0"

BATH 2

FOYER 14'-0" X 12'-4"

PORCH 44'-6" X 8'-0"

First Floor
2,033 sq. ft.

Plan #F10-055D-0215

Dimensions:	47'4" W x 58'8" D
Heated Sq. Ft.:	2,470
Bonus Sq. Ft.:	389
Bedrooms: 4	**Bathrooms:** 2½

Foundation: Slab or crawl space standard; basement or daylight basement for an additional fee

See index for more information

Images provided by designer/architect

Features

- This home combines country charm and architectural details from the Craftsman era to create a naturally rustic style unlike any other
- The functional layout keeps the kitchen orderly and organized
- An extended counter in the kitchen has dining space for four people to gather around and enjoy a meal
- Elevated to new heights, the master suite enjoys a specially designed beamed ceiling
- A media center is designed next to the fireplace in the cozy great room
- The bonus room above the garage has an additional 389 square feet of living area
- 2-car front entry garage

Second Floor
875 sq. ft.

First Floor
1,595 sq. ft.

© Copyright by
designer/architect

Plan #F10-051D-1009

Dimensions:	55' W x 66'8" D
Heated Sq. Ft.:	4,388
Bedrooms: 6	Bathrooms: 4½
Exterior Walls:	2" x 6"

Foundation: Walk-out basement standard; crawl space or slab for an additional fee

See index for more information

Images provided by designer/architect

Features

- A two-story ceiling in the entry opens to an open floor plan where the kitchen overlooks the dining and great rooms to create a stunning living space
- A den with French double doors is to the left of the entry, while a flex room that would be perfect as a man cave can be accessed off the storage space in the garage
- Three bedrooms, including a master suite with a sitting room are all located on the second floor
- The finished lower level adds two more bedrooms, a full bath, and a spacious family room with a wet bar
- 3-car front entry garage

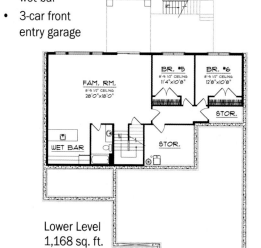

Lower Level
1,168 sq. ft.

First Floor
1,517 sq. ft.

© Copyright by designer/architect

Second Floor
1,703 sq. ft.

Plan #F10-101D-0113

Dimensions:	89' W x 77'9" D
Heated Sq. Ft.:	3,082
Bonus Sq. Ft.:	2,250
Bedrooms: 2	Bathrooms: 2½
Exterior Walls:	2" x 6"

Foundation: Basement, daylight basement or walk-out basement, please specify when ordering

See index for more information

Images provided by designer/architect

Features

- This one-story beauty has an inviting enclosed courtyard entrance
- Once inside, the great room draws you in with its openness and views of the backyard
- The kitchen has a huge island facing into the sunny dining area
- The private master bedroom enjoys a posh bath with a huge walk-in closet
- An office can be found behind the kitchen
- The optional lower level has an additional 2,250 square feet of living area and includes a rec room with a wet bar, an exercise room, two additional bedrooms, two full baths and one half bath
- 3-car front entry garage

© Copyright by designer/architect

First Floor
3,082 sq. ft.

Optional Lower Level
2,250 sq. ft.

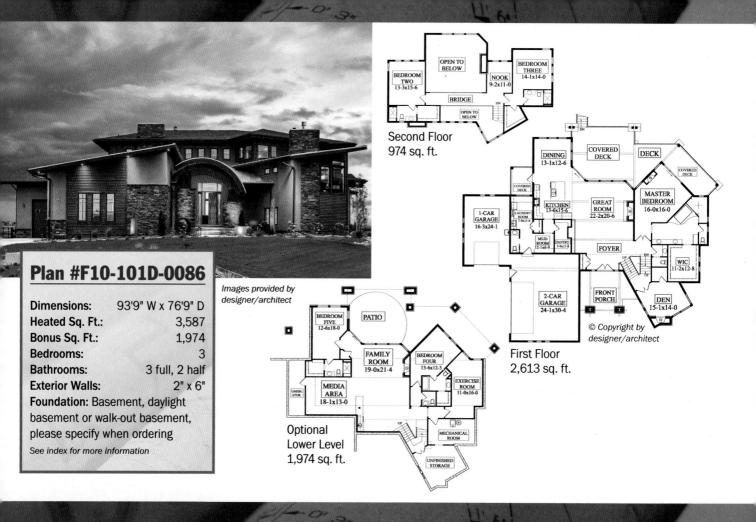

Second Floor
974 sq. ft.

BEDROOM TWO
13-3x15-6

OPEN TO BELOW

NOOK
9-2x11-0

BEDROOM THREE
14-1x14-0

BRIDGE

OPEN TO BELOW

DN

Plan #F10-101D-0086

Images provided by designer/architect

Dimensions:	93'9" W x 76'9" D
Heated Sq. Ft.:	3,587
Bonus Sq. Ft.:	1,974
Bedrooms:	3
Bathrooms:	3 full, 2 half
Exterior Walls:	2" x 6"

Foundation: Basement, daylight basement or walk-out basement, please specify when ordering

See index for more information

DINING
13-1x12-6

COVERED DECK

DECK

COVERED DECK

COVERED DECK

1-CAR GARAGE
16-3x24-1

LAUNDRY ROOM
7-9x11-6

KITCHEN
13-6x15-6

GREAT ROOM
22-2x20-6

MASTER BEDROOM
16-0x16-0

MUD ROOM
12-1x6-9

PANTRY
5-9x11-3

UP

FOYER

WIC
11-2x12-8

2-CAR GARAGE
24-1x30-4

FRONT PORCH

DEN
15-1x14-0

First Floor
2,613 sq. ft.

© Copyright by designer/architect

BEDROOM FIVE
12-6x18-0

PATIO

FAMILY ROOM
19-0x21-4

BEDROOM FOUR
13-6x12-3

EXERCISE ROOM
11-0x16-0

UNFIN. STOR.

MEDIA AREA
18-1x13-0

UP

MECHANICAL ROOM

UNFINISHED STORAGE

Optional
Lower Level
1,974 sq. ft.

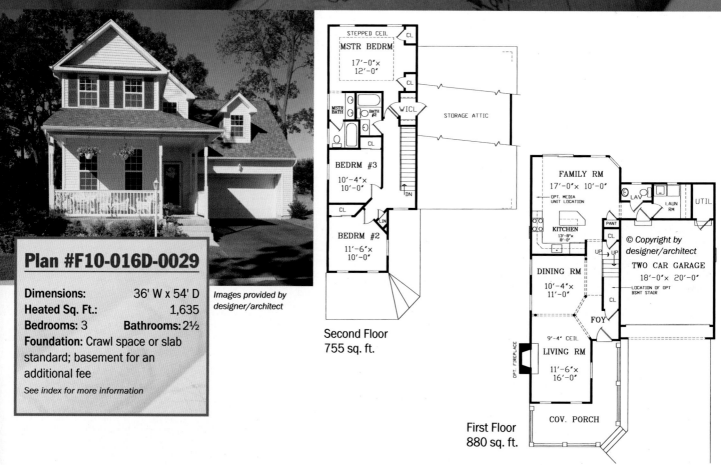

STEPPED CEIL.

CL

MSTR BEDRM
17'-0" x 12'-0"

CL

MSTR BATH

BATH #2

WICL

STORAGE ATTIC

CL

BEDRM #3
10'-4" x 10'-0"

DN

CL

BEDRM #2
11'-6" x 10'-0"

Second Floor
755 sq. ft.

Plan #F10-016D-0029

Images provided by designer/architect

Dimensions:	36' W x 54' D
Heated Sq. Ft.:	1,635
Bedrooms: 3	Bathrooms: 2½

Foundation: Crawl space or slab standard; basement for an additional fee

See index for more information

FAMILY RM
17'-0" x 10'-0"

LAV

LAUN RM

UTIL

OPT. MEDIA UNIT LOCATION

KITCHEN
13'-8" x 8'-0"

PANT

CL

© Copyright by designer/architect

DINING RM
10'-4" x 11'-0"

UP

UP

TWO CAR GARAGE
18'-0" x 20'-0"

LOCATION OF OPT BSMT STAIR

CL

FOY

OPT. FIREPLACE

9'-4" CEIL.

LIVING RM
11'-6" x 16'-0"

COV. PORCH

First Floor
880 sq. ft.

Second Floor
1,472 sq. ft.

Master Suite
15-8 x 18-6
pan vault

Br 2
12-0 x 11-4

Br 4
12-8 x 13-0

Br 3
11-0 x 13-0

open to foyer

Plan #F10-038D-0086

Dimensions:	78' W x 60' D
Heated Sq. Ft.:	3,526
Bedrooms: 4	Bathrooms: 3½
Exterior Walls:	2" x 6"
Foundation:	Walk-out basement

See index for more information

Images provided by designer/architect

Brkfst
15-8 x 10-0

Deck

Kitchen
15-8 x 14-10

Family Rm
17-0 x 22-0

Study
12-8 x 13-1

pantry

Ldry

Dining Rm
11-0 x 17-0

Foyer

Living Rm
13-0 x 19-7

Garage
31-8 x 23-8

© *Copyright by designer/architect*

First Floor
2,054 sq. ft.

Plan #F10-011D-0006

Dimensions:	70' W x 51' D
	(Width with basement is 74')
Heated Sq. Ft.:	1,873
Bedrooms: 3	Bathrooms: 2
Exterior Walls:	2" x 6"
Foundation:	Crawl space or slab standard; basement for an additional fee

See index for more information

Images provided by designer/architect

MASTER
16/2 X 14/0
(9' CLG.)

VAULTED
GREAT RM.
17/6 X 20/6

DINING
10/6 X 13/0
(9' CLG.)

SHOP / 3RD CAR
12/6 X 19/6

DEN
11/0 X 10/0
(9' CLG.)

BR. 2
11/0 X 12/6
(9' CLG.)

BR. 3
11/2 X 12/0
(9' CLG.)

GARAGE
21/0 X 22/6

© *Copyright by designer/architect*

Plan #F10-032D-1123

Dimensions:	44' W x 46'6" D
Heated Sq. Ft.:	2,496
Bonus Sq. Ft.:	1,126
Bedrooms: 4	**Bathrooms:** 2½
Exterior Walls:	2" x 6"

Foundation: Basement standard; crawl space, floating slab or monolithic slab for an additional fee

See index for more information

Images provided by designer/architect

Features

- Undeniable curb appeal as soon as you lay your eyes on this two-story modern home
- The first floor features an open layout with a kitchen featuring an island and walk-in pantry
- An attractive and convenient mud room enjoys a built-in bench seat under a trio of windows
- The two-story living room promises to maintain an open feel thanks to all of the windows spanning two stories high
- The optional lower level has an additional 1,126 square feet of living area
- 2-car front entry garage

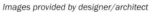

Second Floor
1,370 sq. ft.

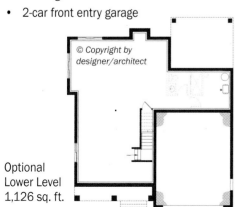

© Copyright by designer/architect

Optional
Lower Level
1,126 sq. ft.

First Floor
1,126 sq. ft.

call 1-800-373-2646   houseplansandmore.com

Plan #F10-011S-0018

Dimensions:	77' W x 65' D
Heated Sq. Ft.:	4,600
Bedrooms: 4	Bathrooms: 3½
Exterior Walls:	2" x 6"
Foundation:	Daylight basement

See index for more information

Features

- A unique glass floor leads to the staircase and allows one to look down to the lower level below
- Plant shelves adorn this house in numerous places
- The differently designed kitchen has most of its emphasis on a gracious center island
- The master bedroom flows into an open bath with a spa style tub and a double-bowl vanity
- 3-car front entry tandem garage, or use the extra space as a workshop

Images provided by designer/architect

First Floor
2,624 sq. ft.

© Copyright by
designer/architect

Lower Level
1,976 sq. ft.

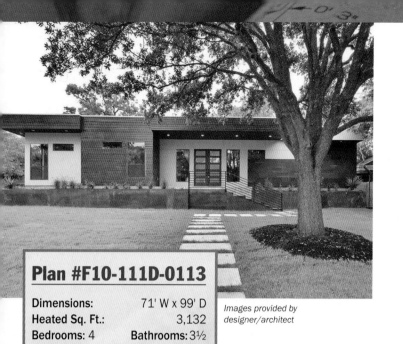

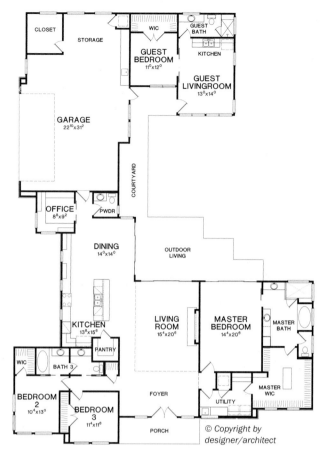

Plan #F10-111D-0113

Dimensions:	71' W x 99' D
Heated Sq. Ft.:	3,132
Bedrooms: 4	**Bathrooms:** 3½

Foundation: Slab standard; crawl space for an additional fee

See index for more information

Images provided by designer/architect

© Copyright by designer/architect

CLOSET
STORAGE
WIC
GUEST BATH
KITCHEN
GUEST BEDROOM 11'⁰x12'⁰
GUEST LIVINGROOM 13'⁰x14'⁰
GARAGE 22'¹⁰x31'²
COURTYARD
OFFICE 8'⁸x9'²
PWDR
DINING 14'⁰x14'⁰
OUTDOOR LIVING
KITCHEN 13'⁸x15'⁸
PANTRY
LIVING ROOM 15'⁴x20'⁶
MASTER BEDROOM 14'⁴x20'⁶
MASTER BATH
WIC
BATH 3
MASTER WIC
BEDROOM 2 10'⁴x13'⁰
BEDROOM 3 11'⁴x11'⁸
FOYER
UTILITY
PORCH

Plan #F10-080D-0014

Dimensions:	49'6" W x 42' D
Heated Sq. Ft.:	1,923
Bedrooms: 2	**Bathrooms:** 2
Exterior Walls:	2" x 6"
Foundation:	Crawl space

See index for more information

Images provided by designer/architect

Second Floor
754 sq. ft.

© Copyright by designer/architect

SUNDECK
SLOPED CEILING
MASTER BDRM 13'8" x 15'4" 10' HIGH CLG
MSTR BATH
SHELVES
FRENCH DRS
PLANT LEDGE OPEN TO MSTR
WASHER DRYER and TOP SPACE
OPEN TO FOYER BELOW
OPEN TO BELOW
EXPOSED FLOOR BEAMS
GLASS RAILING
LIBRARY 8'7 x 10'4 VAULTED CEILING
OPEN TO BELOW
GLASS RAILING
COVERED STAIRCASE
MULTI PURPOSE 13'2" x 11'4"
CLOSET ORGANIZER SPACE
PLANT LEDGE

First Floor
1,169 sq. ft.

SCREENED PORCH 12' x 8'
FRENCH DRS
SITTING ROOM 11'10" x 15'4"
SHELVES
BATH
PANTRY
SILL
KITCHEN 10'6" x 11'6"
REF
SUNDECK 18' x 12'
COVERED DECK
VAULTED CEILINGS
GAS FP
OPEN UNDER STAIRCASE
EXPOSED BEAMS ABOVE
GUEST RM 10'10" x 11'4"
FOYER
LIVING / DINING 12'6" x 25'
COVERED PORCH
PLANTERS

Plan #F10-013S-0013

Dimensions: 62'7" W x 81'3" D
Heated Sq. Ft.: 4,689
Bonus Sq. Ft.: 425
Bedrooms: 5   Bathrooms: 4½
Exterior Walls: 2" x 6"
Foundation: Walk-out basement standard; crawl space or slab for an additional fee

See index for more information

Images provided by designer/architect

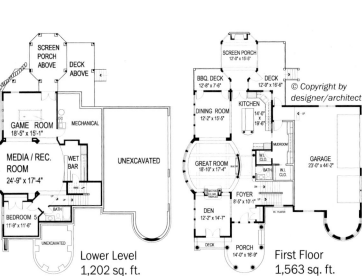

Second Floor
1,924 sq. ft.

Lower Level
1,202 sq. ft.

First Floor
1,563 sq. ft.

© Copyright by designer/architect

Plan #F10-027D-0005

Dimensions: 48' W x 34' D
Heated Sq. Ft.: 2,135
Bedrooms: 4   Bathrooms: 2½
Foundation: Basement standard; slab for an additional fee

See index for more information

Images provided by designer/architect

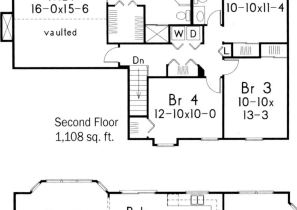

Second Floor
1,108 sq. ft.

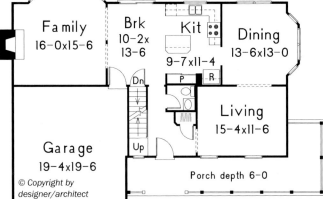

First Floor
1,027 sq. ft.

© Copyright by designer/architect

Plan #F10-011S-0210

Dimensions:	32'6" W x 99' D
Heated Sq. Ft.:	3,504
Bedrooms: 4	**Bathrooms:** 4½
Exterior Walls:	2" x 6"

Foundation: Crawl space or slab standard; basement for an additional fee

See index for more information

Images provided by designer/architect

Features

- This narrow lot home has all the amenities a homeowner could want, including a dog wash and storage in the garage
- Located near the foyer is a private dining area, perfect when entertaining
- The kitchen comes complete with a large center island, a pantry, a bench and a cozy built-in nook
- The sunny great room has a built-in media wall
- An ultra-private master bedroom enjoys a wardrobe style closet and a spacious bath with a free-standing tub and a walk-in shower
- The second floor has an additional master suite with a walk-in closet and luxury bath plus a sunny loft, great for a office or game room
- 2-car tandem style front entry garage

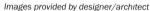

First Floor
1,777 sq. ft.

Second Floor
1,727 sq. ft.

© Copyright by designer/architect

houseplansandmore.com

Plan #F10-071S-0030

Dimensions:	85' W x 61' D
Heated Sq. Ft.:	4,336
Bonus Sq. Ft.:	384
Bedrooms: 4	Bathrooms: 3½
Exterior Walls:	2" x 6"
Foundation:	Crawl space

See index for more information

Images provided by designer/architect

Features

- A beautiful den features a tray ceiling, a bay window, and a fireplace creating a cozy and charming feel that's perfect for a home office

- The formal dining and living rooms have covered porch access and connect, which is perfect for upscale entertaining

- A comfortable guest bedroom on the second floor has its own private bath and a walk-in closet

- A casual family room is found off the kitchen and is sure to be the favorite day-to-day gathering spot

- The bonus room on the second floor has an additional 384 square feet of living area

- 3-car front entry garage

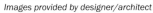

Second Floor
2,096 sq. ft.

First Floor
2,240 sq. ft.

© Copyright by
designer/architect

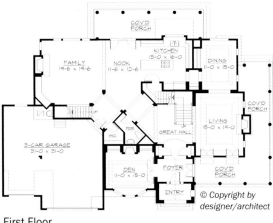

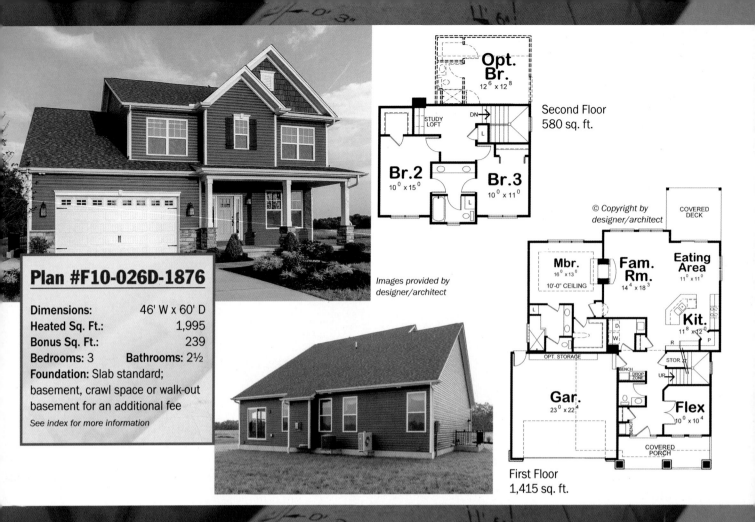

Second Floor
580 sq. ft.

**Opt.
Br.**
12⁶ x 12⁸

STUDY
LOFT

DN

L

Br.2
10⁰ x 15⁰

Br.3
10⁰ x 11⁰

L

*Images provided by
designer/architect*

© Copyright by
designer/architect

COVERED
DECK

Mbr.
16⁰ x 13⁰
10'-0" CEILING

**Fam.
Rm.**
14⁴ x 18³

**Eating
Area**
11⁰ x 11⁰

Kit.
11⁸ x 12⁰

L

D

W

R

P

OPT. STORAGE

BENCH

DROP
ZONE

STOR.

UP

Gar.
23⁰ x 22⁴

Flex
10⁰ x 10⁴

BENCH

COVERED
PORCH

First Floor
1,415 sq. ft.

Plan #F10-026D-1876

Dimensions:	46' W x 60' D
Heated Sq. Ft.:	1,995
Bonus Sq. Ft.:	239
Bedrooms: 3	Bathrooms: 2½

Foundation: Slab standard;
basement, crawl space or walk-out
basement for an additional fee

See index for more information

VAULTED
MASTER
16⁸ X 13⁸

NICHE

SEAT

MEDIA
EQUIP

9' CLG.

9' CLG.

DINING
12⁰ X 12⁰

9' CLG.

GUEST
10⁰ X 10⁰

BUFFET

GREAT RM.
20⁰ X 16²

9' CLG.

KIT.
9⁰ X 13²

9' CLG.

BENCH

STDY
9⁰ X 7⁰

9' CLG.

BR. 2
10⁴ X 11²

LINEN

PANTRY

RECYCLE

9' CLG.

GARAGE
23⁰ X 21⁰

© Copyright by
designer/architect

Plan #F10-011D-0311

Dimensions:	64' W x 54' D
Heated Sq. Ft.:	1,988
Bedrooms: 3	Bathrooms: 3
Exterior Walls:	2" x 6"

Foundation: Crawl space or slab
standard; basement for an
additional fee

See index for more information

*Images provided by
designer/architect*

PORCH 2
8' DEEP

KITCHEN/DINING
14' X 13'

GREAT ROOM
20' X 17'

LAUNDRY

BATH

BATH

LINEN

BEDROOM 1
14' X 12'

FOYER 6' WIDE

BEDROOM 2
14' X 12'

© Copyright by designer/architect

PORCH 1

Plan #F10-028D-0064

Dimensions:	38' W x 52' D
Heated Sq. Ft.:	1,292
Bedrooms: 2	Bathrooms: 2
Exterior Walls:	2" x 6"

Foundation: Monolithic slab standard; floating slab, crawl space, basement or walk-out basement for an additional fee

See index for more information

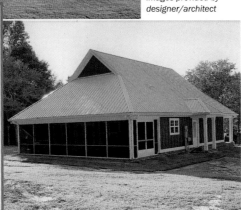

Plan #F10-111D-0101

Dimensions:	49' W x 55' D
Heated Sq. Ft.:	2,662
Bedrooms: 4	Bathrooms: 2½

Foundation: Slab standard; crawl space for an additional fee

See index for more information

Images provided by designer/architect

BEDROOM 4
12⁴ x 12⁰

STORAGE/ OPT. BA. 3

ENVIRO.

GAMEROOM
14⁶ x 14⁶

BEDROOM 2
11¹ x 11⁸

BA. 2

BEDROOM 3
11⁰ x 12⁸

W.I.C.

Second Floor
968 sq. ft.

COV. PATIO

BRKFST.
9⁸ x 10⁸

KITCHEN
13⁸ x 17⁵

MASTER BEDROOM
15² x 14⁴

FAMILY ROOM
17⁷ x 18⁴

HALL

M. BATH

UTILITY

W.I.C.

DINING/ OPT. STUDY
11⁸ x 11⁸

ENTRY

PWDR

GARAGE
20⁸ x 19⁸

PORCH

First Floor
1,694 sq. ft.

© Copyright by designer/architect

Plan #F10-013S-0015

Dimensions:	77' W x 58' D
Heated Sq. Ft.:	5,085
Bedrooms: 5	**Bathrooms:** 4½
Exterior Walls:	2" x 6"
Foundation:	Walk-out basement

See index for more information

Images provided by designer/architect

Features

- The charming exterior is graced with a covered porch and unique windows
- The kitchen is a chef's delight with an abundance of counterspace for food prep and entertaining
- The expansive great room boasts multiple windows and a fireplace
- The master bedroom features an enormous bathroom with a walk-in shower and garden tub
- 3-car front entry tandem garage

Second Floor
1,814 sq. ft.

Lower Level
1,288 sq. ft.

First Floor
1,983 sq. ft.

© Copyright by designer/architect

8'-0" X 8'-4"
2,40 X 2,50

8'-0" X 8'-4"
2,40 X 2,50

23'-0" X 10'-4"
6,90 X 3,10

Plan #F10-032D-0709

Dimensions:	24' W x 20' D
Heated Sq. Ft.:	480
Bedrooms: 2	**Bathrooms:** 1
Exterior Walls:	2" x 6"

Foundation: Screw pile standard; crawl space, floating slab or monolithic slab for an additional fee

See index for more information

Second Floor
517 sq. ft.

BEDROOM 2
12-0 X 11-8
SLOPED
CEILING

MEZZANINE

BEDROOM 3
9-10 X 11-8
SLOPED
CEILING

BATHROOM
SLOPED CEILING

TERRACE

LIVING ROOM
20-0 X 14-0
CATHEDRAL
CEILING

KITCHEN
14-0 X 20-0

MASTER
BEDROOM
13-8 X 12-8

WALK-IN

BATH
ROOM

MUD
ROOM

FOYER

COVERED
PORCH

First Floor
1,108 sq. ft.

Plan #F10-032D-0368

Dimensions:	36' W x 36' D
Heated Sq. Ft.:	1,625
Bedrooms: 3	**Bathrooms:** 2
Exterior Walls:	2" x 6"

Foundation: Basement standard; crawl space, floating slab or monolithic slab for an additional fee

See index for more information

Plan #F10-011D-0335

Images provided by designer/architect

Dimensions: 78' W x 62'6" D
Heated Sq. Ft.:   2,557
Bedrooms: 3   Bathrooms: 2½
Exterior Walls: 2" x 6"
Foundation: Crawl space or slab standard; basement for an additional fee

See index for more information

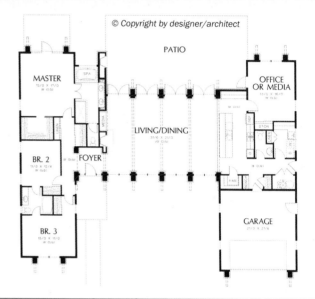

© Copyright by designer/architect

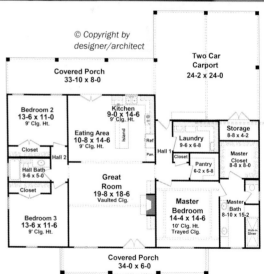

© Copyright by designer/architect

Images provided by designer/architect

Plan #F10-077D-0293

Dimensions: 58' W x 58'6" D
Heated Sq. Ft.:   1,800
Bedrooms: 3   Bathrooms: 2
Foundation: Crawl space or slab, please specify when ordering

See index for more information

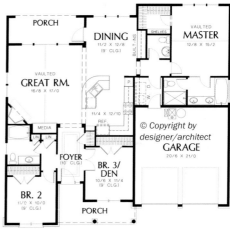

Plan #F10-011D-0007

Dimensions: 50' W x 48' D
Heated Sq. Ft.: 1,580
Bedrooms: 3 **Bathrooms:** 2½
Exterior Walls: 2" x 6"
Foundation: Crawl space or slab standard; basement for an additional fee

See index for more information

Images provided by designer/architect

Plan #F10-084D-0016

Dimensions: 56' W x 45'8" D
Heated Sq. Ft.: 1,492
Bedrooms: 3 **Bathrooms:** 2
Foundation: Slab standard; crawl space or basement for an additional fee

See index for more information

Images provided by designer/architect

Images provided by designer/architect

Plan #F10-016D-0062

Dimensions:	48' W x 43'4" D
Heated Sq. Ft.:	1,380
Bonus Sq. Ft.:	385
Bedrooms: 3	Bathrooms: 2

Foundation: Slab or crawl space standard; walk-out basement or basement for an additional fee

See index for more information

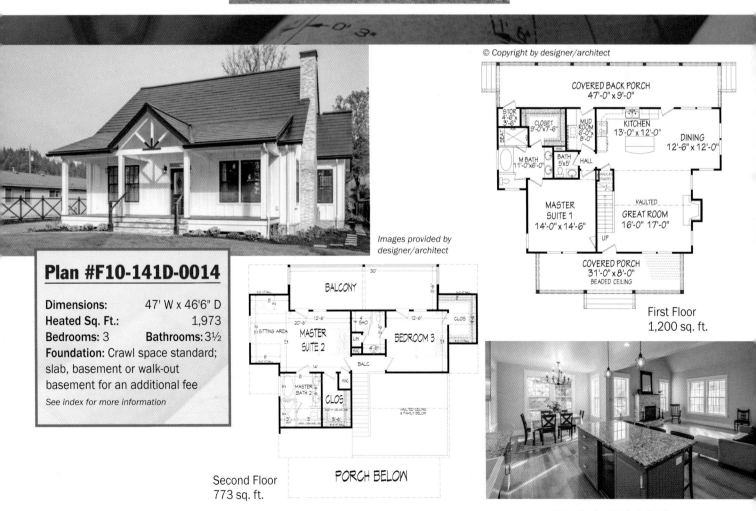

Images provided by designer/architect

First Floor
1,200 sq. ft.

Plan #F10-141D-0014

Dimensions:	47' W x 46'6" D
Heated Sq. Ft.:	1,973
Bedrooms: 3	Bathrooms: 3½

Foundation: Crawl space standard; slab, basement or walk-out basement for an additional fee

See index for more information

Second Floor
773 sq. ft.

Plan #F10-076D-0255

Dimensions: 68'4" W x 63'7" D
Heated Sq. Ft.: 2,435
Bonus Sq. Ft.: 472
Bedrooms: 4   **Bathrooms:** 2½
Foundation: Basement, crawl space or slab, please specify when ordering

See index for more information

Images provided by designer/architect

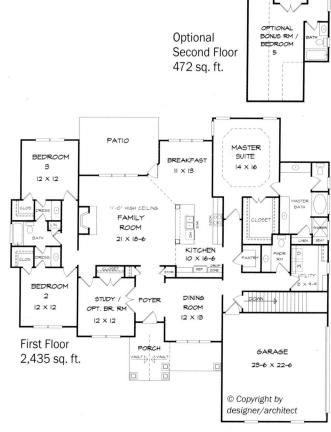

Optional Second Floor 472 sq. ft.

OPTIONAL BONUS RM / BEDROOM 5

BEDROOM 3 12 X 12

PATIO

BREAKFAST 11 X 13

MASTER SUITE 14 X 16

11'-0" HIGH CEILING FAMILY ROOM 21 X 18-6

KITCHEN 10 X 16-6

MASTER BATH

CLOSET

PANTRY

UTILITY 8 X 9-9

BEDROOM 2 12 X 12

STUDY / OPT. BR. RM 12 X 12

FOYER

DINING ROOM 12 X 13

GARAGE 23-6 X 22-6

PORCH

First Floor 2,435 sq. ft.

© Copyright by designer/architect

Plan #F10-169D-0002

Dimensions: 41' W x 60'4" D
Heated Sq. Ft.: 1,762
Bedrooms: 3   **Bathrooms:** 2
Foundation: Basement standard; crawl space or slab for an additional fee

See index for more information

Images provided by designer/architect

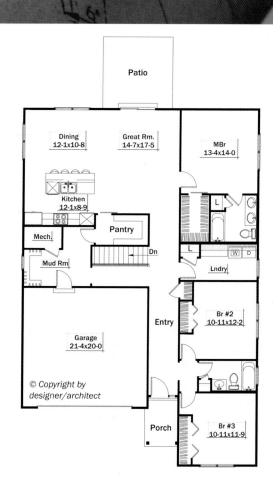

Patio

Dining 12-1x10-8

Great Rm. 14-7x17-5

MBr 13-4x14-0

Kitchen 12-1x8-9

Mech.

Pantry

Dn

Mud Rm

Lndry

Garage 21-4x20-0

Entry

Br #2 10-11x12-2

© Copyright by designer/architect

Porch

Br #3 10-11x11-9

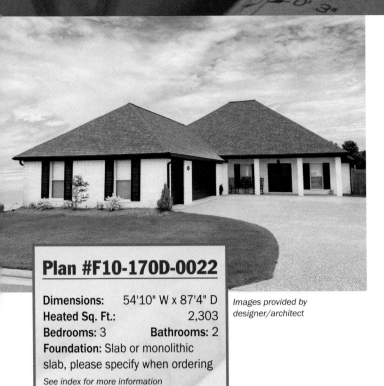

Plan #F10-170D-0022

Dimensions: 54'10" W x 87'4" D
Heated Sq. Ft.: 2,303
Bedrooms: 3   **Bathrooms:** 2
Foundation: Slab or monolithic slab, please specify when ordering

See index for more information

Images provided by designer/architect

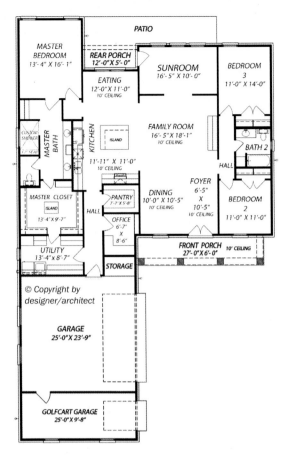

© Copyright by designer/architect

PATIO

MASTER BEDROOM 13'-4" X 16'-1"

REAR PORCH 12'-0" X 5'-0"

SUNROOM 16'-5" X 10'-0"

BEDROOM 3 11'-0" X 14'-0"

EATING 12'-0" X 11'-0" 10' CEILING

CUSTOM SHOWER 5'X5' SEAT

MASTER BATH

KITCHEN 11'-11" X 11'-0" 10' CEILING

FAMILY ROOM 16'-5" X 18'-1" 10' CEILING

ISLAND

BATH 2

HALL

MASTER CLOSET 13'-4" X 9'-7"   ISLAND

PANTRY 7'-7" X 5'-8"

DINING 10'-0" X 10'-5" 10' CEILING

FOYER 6'-5" X 10'-5" 10' CEILING

BEDROOM 2 11'-0" X 11'-0"

HALL

OFFICE 6'-7" X 8'-6"

UTILITY 13'-4" X 8'-7"

STORAGE

FRONT PORCH 27'-0" X 6'-0"   10' CEILING

GARAGE 25'-0" X 23'-9"

GOLFCART GARAGE 25'-0" X 9'-8"

Plan #F10-011D-0683

Dimensions: 17' W x 41' D
Heated Sq. Ft.: 944
Bedrooms: 1   **Bathrooms:** 1
Exterior Walls: 2" x 6"
Foundation: Crawl space or slab standard; basement for an additional fee

See index for more information

Images provided by designer/architect

© Copyright by designer/architect

T.W.H

REF

8/0 X 9/0 (9' CLG)

SHLVS

PAN

STOR

LIV/DIN 11/6 X 20/0 (9' CLG.)

UP

PORCH

First Floor 489 sq. ft.

BR. 2 11/6 X 10/0 (8' CLG.)

W/D

LIN

DN.

BR. 1 11/6 X 10/0 (8' CLG.)

SEAT

Second Floor 455 sq. ft.

Plan #F10-032D-1145

Dimensions:	41' W x 46' D
Heated Sq. Ft.:	2,814
Bedrooms: 3	Bathrooms: 2½
Exterior Walls:	2" x 6"

Foundation: Basement standard; crawl space, monolithic slab or floating slab for an additional fee

See index for more information

Features

- This stunning Modern Farmhouse style home has a terrific layout that has tons of great amenities in a smaller footprint
- The living room is completely open to the dining room with the kitchen island just behind the dining table
- The first floor master suite enjoys a walk-in closet and private bath with both a freestanding tub and a walk-in shower
- A private home office is near the master suite
- A large walk-in pantry keeps the kitchen organized
- The lower level features an open family room, a large laundry room, two bedrooms and a bath
- 1-car front entry garage

Images provided by designer/architect

© Copyright by designer/architect

First Floor
1,407 sq. ft.

Lower Level
1,407 sq. ft.

houseplansandmore.com

Plan #F10-011D-0347

Dimensions:	113'4" W x 62'8" D
Heated Sq. Ft.:	2,910
Bedrooms: 3	**Bathrooms:** 3
Exterior Walls:	2" x 6"

Foundation: Crawl space or slab standard; basement for an additional fee

See index for more information

Features

- The foyer has 11' ceilings with wood columns into the vaulted great room straight ahead
- The vaulted great room has gorgeous exposed beams, and a fireplace with built-in bookcases
- An open floor plan combines the great room, kitchen, and dining room into one big "family triangle," with no walls to cramp the space
- The kitchen has an island with a double sink, 10' ceilings, and plenty of counterspace
- 3-car side entry garage

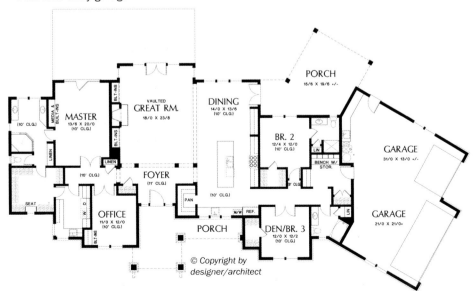

Images provided by designer/architect

Plan #F10-155D-0134

Dimensions: 70'6" W x 56'2" D
Heated Sq. Ft.: 2,031
Bonus Sq. Ft.: 406
Bedrooms: 3   **Bathrooms:** 2½
Foundation: Crawl space or slab standard; basement or daylight basement for an additional fee

See index for more information

Optional
Second Floor
406 sq. ft.

First Floor
2,031 sq. ft.

Plan #F10-169D-0001

Dimensions: 50' W x 30' D
Heated Sq. Ft.: 1,400
Bedrooms: 3   **Bathrooms:** 2
Foundation: Crawl space standard; slab for an additional fee

See index for more information

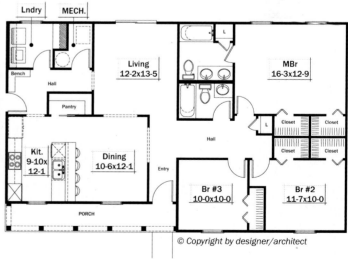

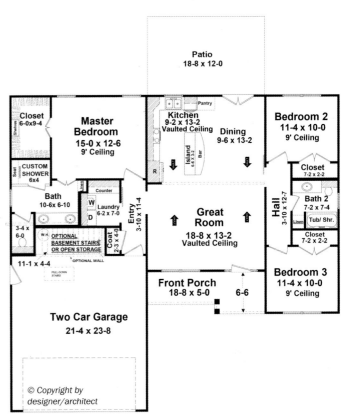

Patio
18-8 x 12-0

Closet
6-0x9-4

Master Bedroom
15-0 x 12-6
9' Ceiling

Kitchen
9-2 x 13-2
Vaulted Ceiling

Pantry

Dining
9-6 x 13-2

Bedroom 2
11-4 x 10-0
9' Ceiling

Island
6-8 x 3-2

Bar

Closet
7-2 x 2-2

CUSTOM SHOWER
6x4

Seat

Bath
10-6 6-10

Counter

W
D

Laundry
6-2 x 7-0

Entry
3-10 x 11-4

Great Room
18-8 x 13-2
Vaulted Ceiling

Hall
3-10 x 12-7

Bath 2
7-2 x 7-4

Tub/ Shr.

Linen

3-4 x
6-0

W.H.

OPTIONAL BASEMENT STAIRS OR OPEN STORAGE

Coat
2-3 x 4-0

Closet
7-2 x 2-2

11-1 x 4-4

OPTIONAL WALL

PULL-DOWN STAIRS

Front Porch
18-8 x 5-0

6-6

Bedroom 3
11-4 x 10-0
9' Ceiling

Two Car Garage
21-4 x 23-8

© Copyright by designer/architect

Plan #F10-077D-0295

Dimensions: 52'8" W x 60'10" D
Heated Sq. Ft.: 1,416
Bedrooms: 3   **Bathrooms:** 2
Foundation: Crawl space, slab, basement or walk-out basement, please specify when ordering
See index for more information

Images provided by designer/architect

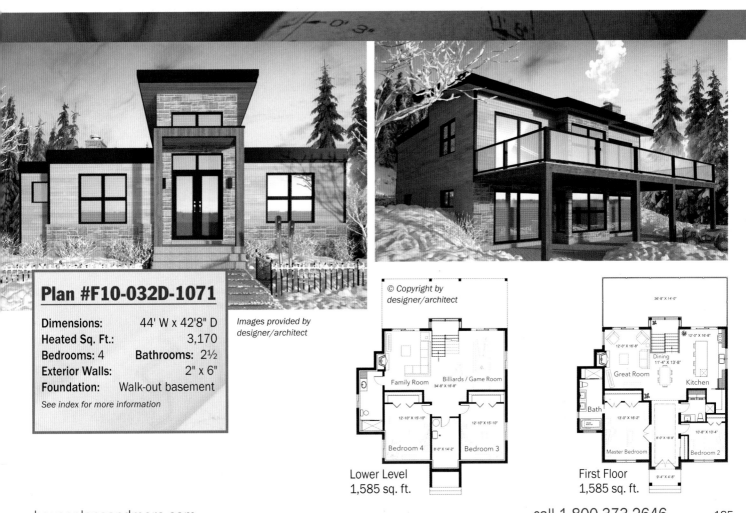

Images provided by designer/architect

Plan #F10-032D-1071

Dimensions: 44' W x 42'8" D
Heated Sq. Ft.: 3,170
Bedrooms: 4   **Bathrooms:** 2½
Exterior Walls: 2" x 6"
Foundation: Walk-out basement
See index for more information

© Copyright by designer/architect

Family Room

Billiards / Game Room
34-8 x 16-8

Bedroom 4
12-10 x 15-10

Bedroom 3
12-10 x 15-10

8-0 x 14-2

Lower Level
1,585 sq. ft.

36-8 X 14-0

Dining
11-4 X 13-8

12-0 X 16-8

Great Room

Kitchen

Bath

Master Bedroom
13-0 X 16-2

8-0 X 18-8

Bedroom 2
10-8 X 14-0

9-4 X 4-8

First Floor
1,585 sq. ft.

Plan #F10-011D-0037

Dimensions:	40' W x 40' D
Heated Sq. Ft.:	2,262
Bedrooms: 3	**Bathrooms:** 2½
Exterior Walls:	2" x 6"
Foundation:	Walk-out basement

See index for more information

Images provided by designer/architect

Features

- The formal dining room is cheerful and sunny with two walls of windows and a decorative ceiling
- A wonderful great room has a two-story ceiling as well as access to an enchanting deck
- The open great room flows effortlessly into the kitchen with a handy cooktop island boasting ample counterspace
- All of the bedrooms are located on the second floor for privacy
- 3-car drive under front entry garage

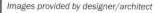

Second Floor
960 sq. ft.

BR. 2
12/0 X 10/0
(9' CLG.)

BR. 3
12/0 X 10/8
(9' CLG.)

LOFT
14/2 X 7/0
(9' CLG.)

GREAT RM
BELOW

VAULTED
MASTER
14/0 X 16/0

First Floor
1,302 sq. ft.

DINING
11/0 X 16/0
(9' CLG.)

NOOK
9/0 X 10/8 +/-
(9' CLG.)

REF

PAN

MEDIA
CENTER

GREAT RM.
15/6 X 16/0

2 STORY

DEN
12/2 X 12/0
(9' CLG.)

BUILT-IN

DECK

PLANTER

© Copyright by
designer/architect

Plan #F10-126D-0903

Dimensions:	52'10" W x 44' D
Heated Sq. Ft.:	2,145
Bedrooms: 4	**Bathrooms:** 2½
Exterior Walls:	2" x 6"
Foundation:	Basement

See index for more information

Images provided by designer/architect

Features

- This home has a stylish Prairie feel and a clean, open interior floor plan
- The first floor combines the kitchen, dining and living areas into one space
- There is also another dining space that is separated from the kitchen by pocket doors
- The master bath is truly luxurious with its amazing tub enhanced with a window above adding natural light
- The first floor half bath includes the washer and dryer
- 2-car front entry garage

© Copyright by designer/architect

First Floor
1,028 sq. ft.

Second Floor
1,117 sq. ft.

Plan #F10-076D-0280

Dimensions: 61'8" W x 78'4" D
Heated Sq. Ft.: 2,585
Bonus Sq. Ft.: 492
Bedrooms: 4   **Bathrooms:** 3½
Foundation: Crawl space or slab, please specify when ordering

See index for more information

Features

- The family room boasts a fireplace and an 11'-6" ceiling
- A center island in the kitchen includes an eating bar providing ample prep space and casual dining space
- The private master suite enjoys a remote location away from the other bedrooms
- The optional bonus room has an additional 492 square feet of living area
- 2-car side entry garage

First Floor
2,230 sq. ft.

© Copyright by designer/architect

Second Floor
355 sq. ft.

Images provided by designer/architect

Plan #F10-019S-0007

Dimensions: 103'6" W x 88'5" D
Heated Sq. Ft.: 3,886
Bedrooms: 4   **Bathrooms:** 3½
Foundation: Slab standard; crawl space or basement for an additional fee

See index for more information

Images provided by designer/architect

© Copyright by designer/architect

Plan #F10-011D-0674

Dimensions: 40' W x 60'6" D
Heated Sq. Ft.: 1,552
Bedrooms: 3   **Bathrooms:** 2
Exterior Walls: 2" x 6"
Foundation: Crawl space or slab standard; basement for an additional fee

See index for more information

Images provided by designer/architect

© Copyright by designer/architect

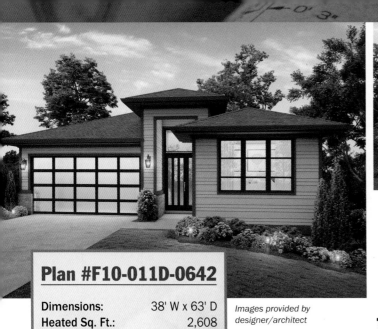

Plan #F10-011D-0642

Dimensions:	38' W x 63' D
Heated Sq. Ft.:	2,608
Bedrooms: 4	Bathrooms: 3
Exterior Walls:	2" x 6"
Foundation:	Walk-out basement

See index for more information

Images provided by designer/architect

Lower Level
1,085 sq. ft.

First Floor
1,523 sq. ft.

© Copyright by designer/architect

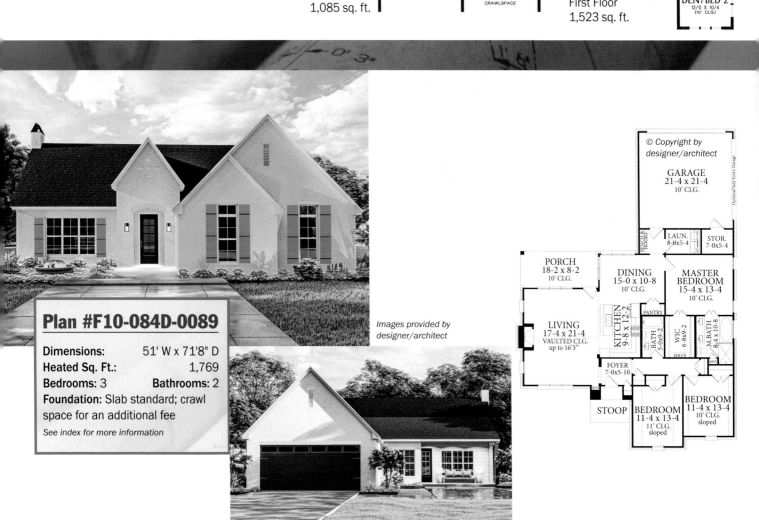

Plan #F10-084D-0089

Dimensions:	51' W x 71'8" D
Heated Sq. Ft.:	1,769
Bedrooms: 3	Bathrooms: 2
Foundation:	Slab standard; crawl space for an additional fee

See index for more information

Images provided by designer/architect

© Copyright by designer/architect

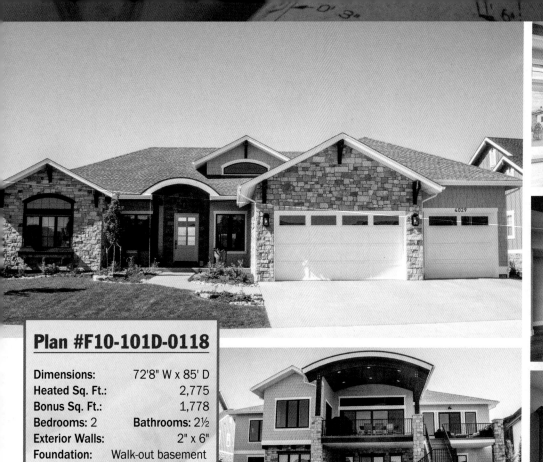

Plan #F10-101D-0118

Dimensions:	72'8" W x 85' D
Heated Sq. Ft.:	2,775
Bonus Sq. Ft.:	1,778
Bedrooms: 2	Bathrooms: 2½
Exterior Walls:	2" x 6"
Foundation:	Walk-out basement

See index for more information

Features

- Lovely arches with stone and rustic accents create a beautiful front facade
- The entry leads to a beautiful family room with sliding glass doors leading to a covered deck
- The kitchen has a large island facing the great room
- The master bedroom has deck access, two walk-in closets, and a posh bath with a freestanding tub
- The optional lower level has an additional 1,778 square feet of living area including a rec room, media area, wet bar, two bedrooms, two full baths, and a half bath
- 3-car front entry garage

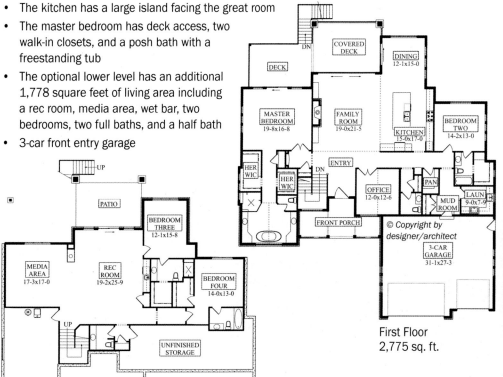

First Floor
2,775 sq. ft.

Optional
Lower Level
1,778 sq. ft.

© Copyright by designer/architect

Images provided by designer/architect

Plan #F10-047D-0083

Dimensions:	51' W x 74'4" D
Heated Sq. Ft.:	2,293
Bonus Sq. Ft.:	509
Bedrooms: 3	Bathrooms: 2
Foundation:	Slab

See index for more information

Images provided by designer/architect

Features

- The family and dining rooms feature 12' ceilings and a barrier-free open floor plan creating a more spacious feel
- The cozy nook area brings in an abundance of warm natural light and features a U-shaped sitting arrangement built into a box-bay window
- The master bedroom, with a unique ceiling, enjoys private access onto the covered patio and includes a bath with double walk-in closets, a separate tub and shower, and a double-bowl vanity
- Upon entering the home is a den with a double-door entry that could easily be converted to a home office
- The optional second floor has an additional 509 square feet of living area with room for a bedroom and bath
- 2-car side entry garage

Optional Second Floor 509 sq. ft.

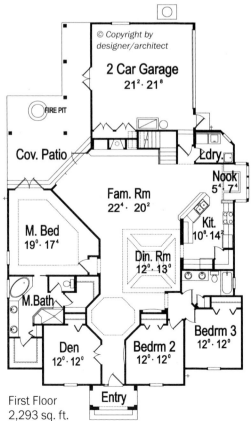

First Floor 2,293 sq. ft.

Plan #F10-026D-2113

Dimensions: 38' W x 54' D
Heated Sq. Ft.: 1,390
Bedrooms: 2 **Bathrooms:** 2
Foundation: Basement standard; slab, crawl space or walk-out basement for an additional fee

See index for more information

Images provided by designer/architect

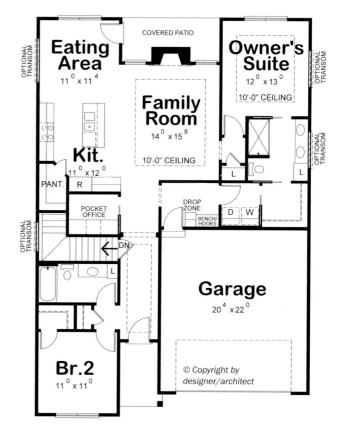

COVERED PATIO

Eating Area
11⁰ x 11⁴

Owner's Suite
12⁰ x 13⁰
10'-0" CEILING

Family Room
14⁰ x 15⁸
10'-0" CEILING

Kit.
11⁰ x 12⁰

OPTIONAL TRANSOM

PANT.

R

POCKET OFFICE

DROP ZONE
BENCH/ HOOKS

D W

DN

L

Garage
20⁴ x 22⁰

Br.2
11⁰ x 11⁰

© Copyright by designer/architect

Plan #F10-077D-0142

Dimensions: 70' W x 56' D
Heated Sq. Ft.: 2,067
Bonus Sq. Ft.: 379
Bedrooms: 3 **Bathrooms:** 2½
Foundation: Slab or crawl space, please specify when ordering; for basement version, see Plan #077D-0164 at houseplansandmore.com

See index for more information

Images provided by designer/architect

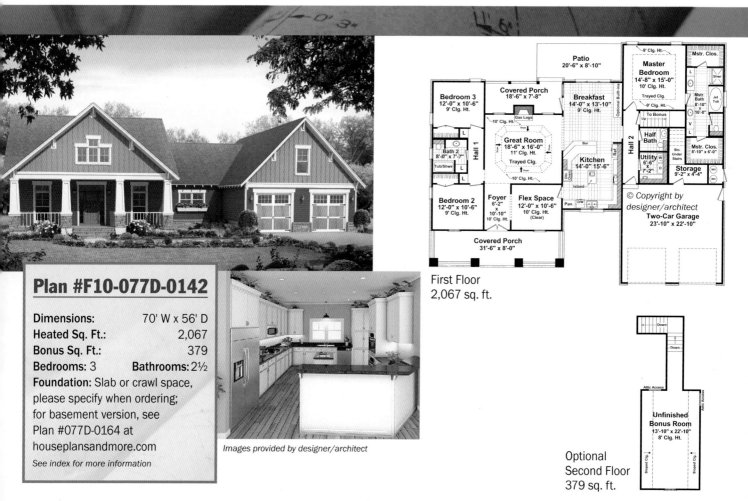

Patio 20'-6" x 8'-10"

Covered Porch 18'-6" x 7'-8"

Bedroom 3 12'-0" x 10'-6" 9' Clg. Ht.

Bath 2 8'-0" x 7'-7"
Tub/Shwr

Hall 1

Great Room 18'-6" x 16'-0" 11' Clg. Ht. Trayed Clg.
Gas Logs

Breakfast 14'-0" x 13'-10" 9' Clg. Ht.

Optional Built-Ins

Master Bedroom 14'-8" x 15'-0" 10' Clg. Ht. Trayed Clg.

9' Clg. Ht.

To Bonus
Up

Mstr. Clos.

Mstr. Bath 8'-10" x 16'-0"

Shwr

Jet Tub

Kitchen 14'-0" 15'-6"
Bar
Island
Ref.

Hall 2

Half Bath

Sto. Under Stairs

Mstr. Clos. 8'-10" x 6'-0"

Bedroom 2 12'-0" x 10'-6" 9' Clg. Ht.

Foyer 6'-2" x 10'-10" 10' Clg. Ht.

Flex Space 12'-0" x 10'-6" 10' Clg. Ht. (Clear)

Pan.

D/W

Utility 6'-6" x 7'-2"

W D

Storage 9'-2" x 4'-4"

© Copyright by designer/architect

Two-Car Garage 23'-10" x 22'-10"

Covered Porch 31'-6" x 8'-0"

First Floor 2,067 sq. ft.

Down

Down

Attic Access

Attic Access

Unfinished Bonus Room 13'-10" x 22'-10" 8' Clg. Ht.

Sloped Clg.

Sloped Clg.

Optional Second Floor 379 sq. ft.

Plan #F10-028D-0100

Dimensions: 46' W x 42'6" D
Heated Sq. Ft.: 1,311
Bedrooms: 3 **Bathrooms:** 2
Exterior Walls: 2" x 6"
Foundation: Floating slab standard; monolithic slab, crawl space, basement or walk-out basement for an additional fee

See index for more information

Images provided by designer/architect

8' WIDE DECK

BEDROOM 3
12-0 X 11-6

KITCHEN/DINING
17-8 X 12-6

LAUNDRY
14-0 X 6-8

CLO

BEDROOM 2
12-0 X 11-6

GREAT ROOM
17-8 X 16-0

MASTER BEDROOM
14-0 X 12-6

COVERED PORCH

© Copyright by designer/architect

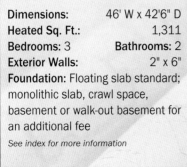

Plan #F10-011D-0676

Dimensions: 40' W x 55'6" D
Heated Sq. Ft.: 1,196
Bedrooms: 3 **Bathrooms:** 2
Exterior Walls: 2" x 6"
Foundation: Crawl space or slab standard; basement for an additional fee

See index for more information

Images provided by designer/architect

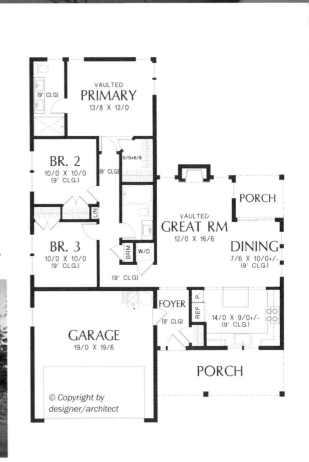

VAULTED PRIMARY
13/8 X 12/0
(9' CLG)

BR. 2
10/0 X 10/0
(9' CLG.)

BR. 3
10/0 X 10/0
(9' CLG.)

PORCH

VAULTED GREAT RM
12/0 X 16/6

DINING
7/6 X 10/0+/-
(9' CLG.)

GARAGE
19/0 X 19/6

FOYER
(9' CLG)

14/0 X 9/0+/-
(9' CLG.)

PORCH

© Copyright by designer/architect

what home buyers want
WIDE OPEN SPACES

When having a party, do you ever feel cut off from your guests as you scurry between rooms? You're trying to take care of kitchen tasks, while maintaining a connection with your guests, but it's a struggle to do so in a floor plan so disconnected. Or, perhaps there are times when work in the kitchen is begging your attention, but so are the children playing in the family room. Too many homeowners can relate with the desire to be in more than one place at one time within their home. Thankfully, today's dream homes offer the luxury of an open floor plan allowing homeowners to feel as though they are in more than one place at a time!

Open floor plans are the answer to this common problem in the past, and luckily open layouts are the future in home design. Open floor plans combine all gathering spaces into one large space. The kitchen, dining area, and great room form one large place where cooking, eating, relaxing, and other tasks can be done together. With as many distractions as there are today, both inside and outside our homes that keep us from being together with family and friends, the open floor plan at least has found a way to bring people together.

feeling lonely?
Are there ways to open up your kitchen to your great room in your home? Could columns replace walls? These changes can be customized in a new home, too.

an open mind is a good place to start

Today's floor plans are often designed with little or no divisions between rooms. But, what if you fall in love with a floor plan that isn't quite as open as you'd like for it to be? There are some creative ways to open it up.

spread out

Even homes with modest square footage can be transformed into airy, open spaces. Wherever possible, eliminate doorways, widen passages, and remove boundaries. Ultimately, you're turning your home into a "universal" home design which means, it suits all people of all ages and accommodates all physical abilities. This is a smart move for resale values and allows all those who enter your home to feel welcome and able to move about freely. Allowing traffic to flow easily from one "room" to another is important in making a home feel more spacious.

lighten up

Natural light can make any space inviting and warm. Use large windows and long views to connect with the outdoors and make an open room appear even larger. If window walls are not appropriate, consider skylights and strategically placed mirrors to make the most of some natural light and space.

family functionality with personality

Open floor plans that combine kitchens, dining, and living rooms are imperative for busy families. When open, these spaces transition easily into one another, allowing family members to take on various tasks without being entirely separated, or tripping over one another. A great addition to open kitchens is the snack bar/preparation island. Kids can keep busy and close, while still allowing mom and dad enough room to visit and get meals underway.

There are simple steps homeowners can take to open up their homes

Page 198, top: Spacious vaulted living area, REAL LOG HOMES®, realloghomes.com, James Ray Spahn, photographer; bottom: ClosetMaid® game room with smart storage ideas, closetmaid.com; Page 199, top: Open floor plan with rustic ceiling, Plan #055D-0932; Open kitchen and eating bar, Plan #F10-111S-0005 on page 222; Page 200, top, right: Plan #F10-011D-0266 on page 431, Bob Greenspan, photographer; bottom: Plan #F10-055D-0748 on page 109; See more photos and purchase plans at houseplansandmore.com.

use it or lose it

It's important to make the most of the space you have, using every corner and nook. The formal dining room is becoming a space of the past in small or moderate sized homes where square footage is a high commodity. If you find a floor plan that includes a formal dining room in addition to a more casual dining space, open up the walls and turn it into a media room, home office, playroom or other space that better suits your families' needs. Most often windows, deck access, fireplaces, and bay windows can be incorporated into these new open spaces making them feel seamless with other areas.

open up and get together

Like the dining room and kitchen, opening the great room presents numerous benefits to families. This once formally enclosed space sometimes referred to as a den in the past, can now be a spacious area perfect for daily family activities, or ideal for keeping guests comfortable when entertaining.

By building a home with an open floor plan, or customizing a plan to create a more open feel, there is no longer any reason to limit your spaces or banish particular tasks to designated rooms. Your home's floor plan should offer a seamless space where guests and hosts, and parents and children, can all interact and enjoy an area that is completely multi-purpose.

nowhere to hide

Not only does your home appear twice as large as it normally would, an open floor plan is a great way to get the entire family into one space, sharing cooking, hobbies and relaxation together.

200

Plan #F10-128D-0065

Dimensions:	50' W x 82'6" D
Heated Sq. Ft.:	2,441
Bonus Sq. Ft.:	479
Bedrooms: 3	Bathrooms: 3½
Foundation:	Crawl space

See index for more information

Features

- There's plenty of outdoor living space offered within this home including a large covered front porch that graces the entire width of the front facade, a rear terrace/deck area, and also a screen porch

- The balcony/lounge area is flanked by two bedrooms, each with their own walk-in closet and full bath

- A private first floor master suite has two walk-in closets and a bath with all the amenities, including a corner whirlpool tub

- Perfect for the family member trying to transition into their own home, there is a future apartment above the garage with a kitchenette, living room, a bedroom and a bath that has an additional 479 square feet of living area

- 2-car rear entry garage

Second Floor
737 sq. ft.

First Floor
1,704 sq. ft.

© Copyright by designer/architect

Images provided by designer/architect

Plan #F10-080D-0012

Dimensions:	36' W x 46'6" D
Heated Sq. Ft.:	1,370
Bedrooms: 3	**Bathrooms:** 2
Exterior Walls:	2" x 6"

Foundation: Basement or crawl space, please specify when ordering

See index for more information

Images provided by designer/architect

Features

- An enormous sundeck surrounds this home providing space for relaxing and dining outdoors
- The second floor vaulted master bedroom has a private balcony and unique interior windows
- The great room is open and bright with a partial two-story ceiling topped with skylights

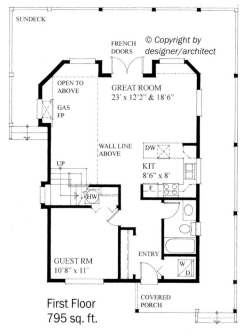

First Floor
795 sq. ft.

SUNDECK

FRENCH DOORS

© Copyright by designer/architect

OPEN TO ABOVE

GREAT ROOM
23' x 12'2" & 18'6"

GAS FP

WALL LINE ABOVE

DW

KIT
8'6" x 8'

UP

HW

F

GUEST RM
10'8" x 11'

ENTRY

W D

COVERED PORCH

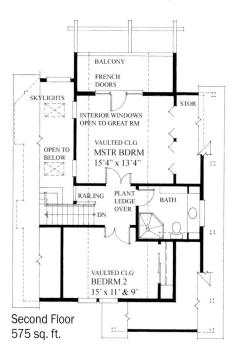

Second Floor
575 sq. ft.

BALCONY

FRENCH DOORS

SKYLIGHTS

STOR

INTERIOR WINDOWS OPEN TO GREAT RM

OPEN TO BELOW

VAULTED CLG
MSTR BDRM
15'4" x 13'4"

RAILING

PLANT LEDGE OVER

BATH

DN

VAULTED CLG
BEDRM 2
15' x 11' & 9'

Plan #F10-013S-0009

Dimensions:	62' W x 66' D
Heated Sq. Ft.:	3,799
Bonus Sq. Ft.:	1,634
Bedrooms: 4	Bathrooms: 3½
Exterior Walls:	2" x 6"
Foundation:	Walk-out basement

See index for more information

Images provided by designer/architect

Features

- The perfect home for entertaining including a lovely island in the kitchen for gathering
- Today's busy family will enjoy the loft with a built-in desk that overlooks the great room below
- The vaulted master bedroom includes a spacious bath with a corner shower that leaves plenty of room for getting ready
- The optional lower level has an additional 1,634 square feet of living area and features a recreation room, a home theater, a wet bar, a bedroom, a full bath, and an exercise room
- 3-car side entry garage

Second Floor
1,848 sq. ft.

Optional
Lower Level
1,634 sq. ft.

© Copyright by
designer/architect

First Floor
1,951 sq. ft.

Plan #F10-055S-0036

Dimensions:	89' W x 104' D
Heated Sq. Ft.:	4,121
Bonus Sq. Ft.:	1,826
Bedrooms: 3	Bathrooms: 3

Foundation: Slab or crawl space standard; basement or daylight basement for an additional fee
See index for more information

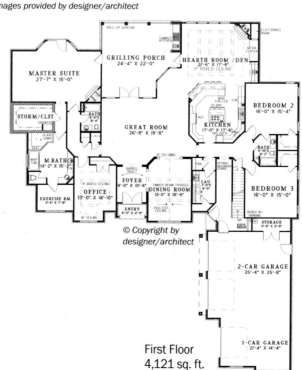

Images provided by designer/architect

Features

- An 11' boxed ceiling, a media center, a wet bar, and a cozy corner fireplace make the hearth room/den the center of activity

- The master suite is full of amenities including a corner fireplace, a luxury bath, an exercise room, and a unique reinforced storm closet for shelter

- An immense home theater/game room and bonus room on the second floor provide an additional 1,826 square feet of living space for entertaining and fun for the whole family

- 3-car side entry garage

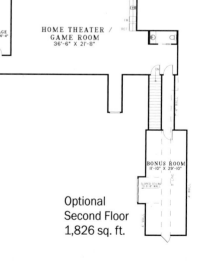

Optional
Second Floor
1,826 sq. ft.

First Floor
4,121 sq. ft.

© Copyright by designer/architect

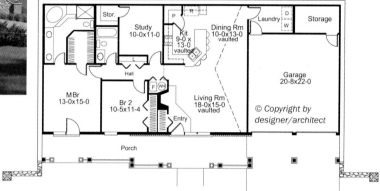

Plan #F10-007D-0161

Dimensions:	70' W x 36' D
Heated Sq. Ft.:	1,480
Bedrooms: 2	Bathrooms: 2
Exterior Walls:	2" x 6"
Foundation:	Slab

See index for more information

Images provided by designer/architect

© Copyright by designer/architect

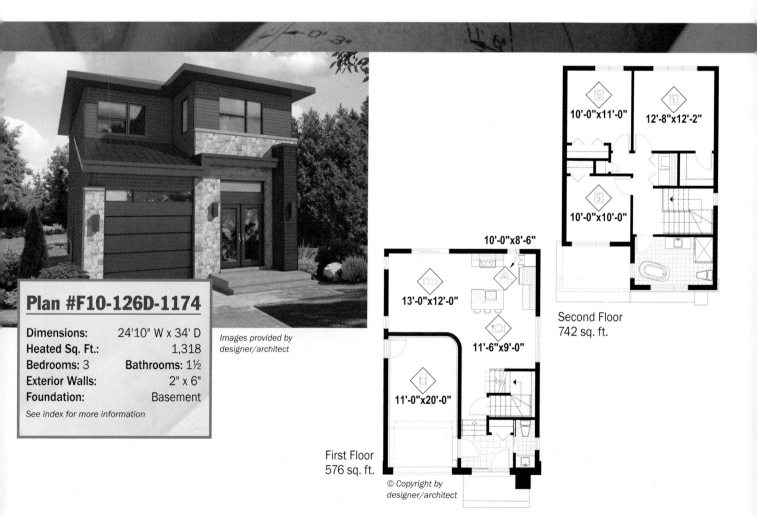

Plan #F10-126D-1174

Dimensions:	24'10" W x 34' D
Heated Sq. Ft.:	1,318
Bedrooms: 3	Bathrooms: 1½
Exterior Walls:	2" x 6"
Foundation:	Basement

See index for more information

Images provided by designer/architect

Second Floor
742 sq. ft.

First Floor
576 sq. ft.

© Copyright by designer/architect

Plan #F10-056D-0137

Dimensions: 62'10" W x 68'5" D
Heated Sq. Ft.: 2,342
Bonus Sq. Ft.: 1,054
Bedrooms: 3 **Bathrooms:** 2
Foundation: Basement standard; crawl space or slab for an additional fee

See index for more information

Images provided by designer/architect

First Floor
2,342 sq. ft.

© Copyright by designer/architect

Optional Lower Level
1,054 sq. ft.

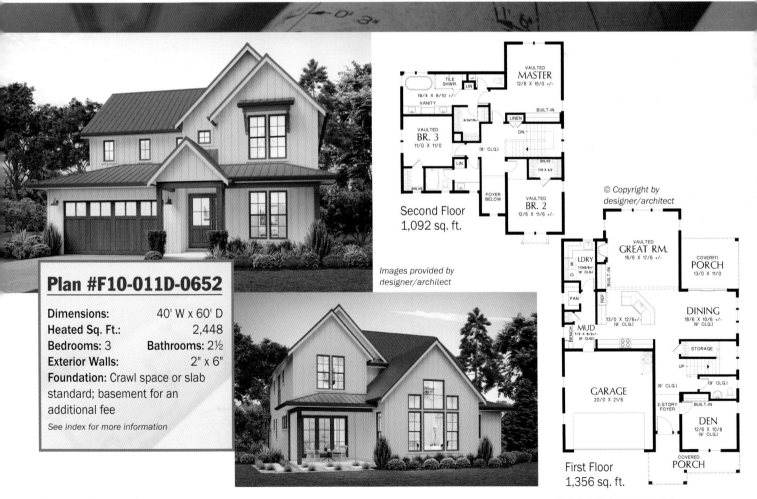

Plan #F10-011D-0652

Dimensions: 40' W x 60' D
Heated Sq. Ft.: 2,448
Bedrooms: 3 **Bathrooms:** 2½
Exterior Walls: 2" x 6"
Foundation: Crawl space or slab standard; basement for an additional fee

See index for more information

Images provided by designer/architect

Second Floor
1,092 sq. ft.

© Copyright by designer/architect

First Floor
1,356 sq. ft.

Plan #F10-167D-0010

Dimensions: 70'11" W x 84'10" D
Heated Sq. Ft.: 3,409
Bedrooms: 4   **Bathrooms:** 4½
Exterior Walls: 2" x 6"
Foundation: Crawl space standard; slab for an additional fee

See index for more information

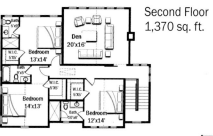

Second Floor
1,370 sq. ft.

Images provided by designer/architect

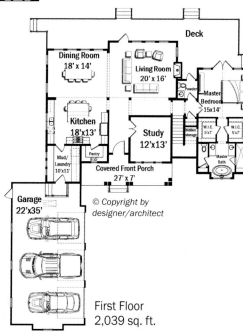

© Copyright by designer/architect

First Floor
2,039 sq. ft.

Plan #F10-172D-0041

Dimensions: 53' W x 47'6" D
Heated Sq. Ft.: 2,313
Bonus Sq. Ft.: 1,615
Bedrooms: 4   **Bathrooms:** 2½
Exterior Walls: 2" x 6"
Foundation: Basement standard; crawl space, monolithic slab, stem wall slab, daylight basement or walk-out basement for an additional fee

See index for more information

Second Floor
1,187 sq. ft.

Images provided by designer/architect

Optional Lower Level
1,615 sq. ft.

First Floor
1,126 sq. ft.

© Copyright by designer/architect

Plan #F10-157D-0006

Dimensions:	89'11" W x 75' D
Heated Sq. Ft.:	2,883
Bonus Sq. Ft.:	397
Bedrooms: 3	Bathrooms: 2½

Foundation: Crawl space standard; slab or basement for an additional fee

See index for more information

Images provided by designer/architect

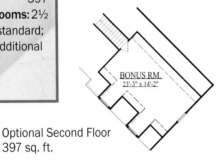

BONUS RM.
23'-3" x 14'-2"

Optional Second Floor
397 sq. ft.

Porch 23'-11" x 12'-8"
Brkf. 12'-0" x 8'-10"
Master Bdrm 14'-6" x 18'-7"
Living 21'-11" x 18'-7"
Bdrm#2 10'-10" x 13'-10"
Kitchen 13'-6" x 18'-7"
Bdrm#3 13'-0" x 12'-1"
Closet 8'-10" x 16'-1"
Study 11'-10" x 13'-3"
Entry 8'-11" x 16'-1"
Dining 11'-11" x 13'-3"
Laundry 10'-5" x 10'-1"
Porch 45'-11" x 9'-3"
Garage 23'-3" x 23'-1"

First Floor
2,883 sq. ft.

© Copyright by designer/architect

Plan #F10-139D-0038

Dimensions:	56'11" W x 59'9" D
Heated Sq. Ft.:	2,368
Bonus Sq. Ft.:	491
Bedrooms: 3	Bathrooms: 2½
Exterior Walls:	2" x 6"

Foundation: Crawl space standard; slab, basement, daylight basement or walk-out basement for an additional fee

See index for more information

Images provided by designer/architect

OPT. BONUS 22'-0" x 20'-11"
ATTIC ACCESS
STORAGE 8'-0" x 17'-0"

Optional Second Floor 491 sq. ft.

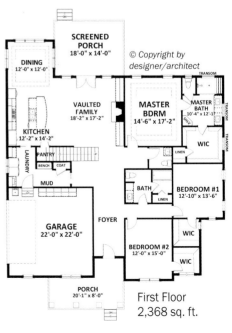

© Copyright by designer/architect

SCREENED PORCH 18'-0" x 14'-0"
DINING 12'-0" x 12'-0"
VAULTED FAMILY 18'-2" x 17'-2"
MASTER BDRM 14'-6" x 17'-2"
MASTER BATH 10'-4" x 12'-1"
WIC
KITCHEN 12'-2" x 14'-2"
LAUNDRY
PANTRY
BENCH COAT
MUD
LINEN
BATH
LINEN
BEDROOM #1 12'-10" x 13'-6"
GARAGE 22'-0" x 22'-0"
FOYER
WIC
BEDROOM #2 12'-0" x 15'-0"
WIC
PORCH 20'-1" x 8'-0"

First Floor
2,368 sq. ft.

SCREENED PORCH 16'-0" x 13'-11"

DECK 10'-1" x 10'-1"

14' CEILING

HERS

SITTING

BEDROOM SUITE #3 13'-0" x 11'-0"

MASTER SUITE 21'-4" x 15'-6"

HIS

14' CEILING

CASUAL DINING 11'-0" x 12'-5"

MASTER BATH 9'-4" x 13'-8"

FAMILY ROOM 16'-0" x 21'-0"

KITCHEN 11'-0" x 13'-3"

UP TO BONUS

LAUNDRY 8'-0" x 6'-5"

KNEE SPACE

COATS

COFFEE CORNER 11'-0" x 8'-0"

STAIRS TO BASEMENT (OPTIONAL)

BEDROOM SUITE #2 13'-0" x 11'-0"

12' CEILING

FLEX ROOM 11'-0" x 13'-0"

10' CEILING

10' TRAY CEILING

PORCH 15'-4" x 5'-7"

LINE OF BONUS ROOM ABOVE 13'-4" x 33'-0"

3 CAR GARAGE 21'-4" x 34'-2"

7'

2 CAR GARAGE OPTION

Plan #F10-013D-0168

Dimensions:	63' W x 62'8" D
Heated Sq. Ft.:	2,000
Bonus Sq. Ft.:	503
Bedrooms: 3	Bathrooms: 3½

Foundation: Slab standard; crawl space or basement for an additional fee

See index for more information

Images provided by designer/architect

Plan #F10-155D-0048

Images provided by designer/architect

Dimensions:	56'2" W x 57' D
Heated Sq. Ft.:	2,071
Bonus Sq. Ft.:	435
Bedrooms: 4	Bathrooms: 2

Foundation: Slab or crawl space, please specify when ordering

See index for more information

DN

ATTIC STRG

9' CEILING

BONUS ROOM 13'-8" x 21'-0"

9' CEILING

Optional Second Floor 435 sq. ft.

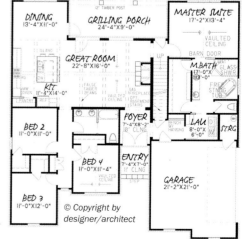

DINING 13'-4" x 11'-0"

12' TIMBER POST

GRILLING PORCH 24'-4" x 9'-0"

MASTER SUITE 17'-2" x 13'-4"

VAULTED CEILING

GREAT ROOM 22'-8" x 16'-0"

BARN DOOR

M.BATH 17'-0" x 9'-0"

KIT 11'-4" x 14'-0"

FALSE RAISED BEAMS

VAULTED CEILING

GAS FIREPLACE

FOYER 7'-4" x 8'-2" 10' CLNG

LAU 8'-0" x 6'-0"

STRG

BED 2 11'-0" x 11'-0"

BED 4 11'-0" x 11'-4"

ENTRY 7'-4" x 7'-0" 11' CLNG

GARAGE 21'-2" x 21'-0"

BED 3 11'-0" x 12'-0"

VAULTED CEILING

First Floor 2,071 sq. ft.

© Copyright by designer/architect

First Floor
1,264 sq. ft.

Second Floor
1,000 sq. ft.

Plan #F10-088D-0594

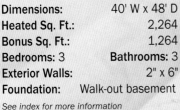

Dimensions:	40' W x 48' D
Heated Sq. Ft.:	2,264
Bonus Sq. Ft.:	1,264
Bedrooms: 3	Bathrooms: 3
Exterior Walls:	2" x 6"
Foundation:	Walk-out basement

See index for more information

Images provided by designer/architect

Front View

Optional Lower Level
1,264 sq. ft.

Plan #F10-007D-0135

Dimensions:	57' W x 36'4" D
Heated Sq. Ft.:	801
Bedrooms: 2	Bathrooms: 1
Foundation:	Slab

See index for more information

Images provided by designer/architect

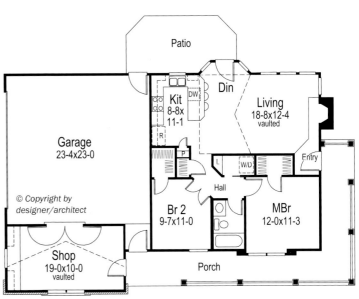

© Copyright by designer/architect

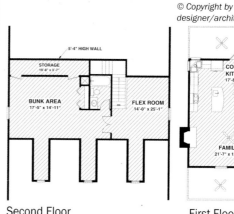

Second Floor
911 sq. ft.

First Floor
1,059 sq. ft.

Images provided by designer/architect

© Copyright by designer/architect

Plan #F10-013D-0253

Dimensions:	40'3" W x 42'4" D
Heated Sq. Ft.:	2,943
Bedrooms: 3	Bathrooms: 3

Foundation: Basement standard; crawl space or slab for an additional fee

See index for more information

Lower Level
973 sq. ft.

First Floor
2,535 sq. ft.

© Copyright by designer/architect

Images provided by designer/architect

Plan #F10-076D-0290

Dimensions:	52'5" W x 68' D
Heated Sq. Ft.:	2,535
Bonus Sq. Ft.:	821
Bedrooms: 3	Bathrooms: 2½
Foundation:	Basement

See index for more information

Optional Lower Level
821 sq. ft.

Second Floor
885 sq. ft.

First Floor
1,117 sq. ft.

*Images provided by
designer/architect*

© Copyright by
designer/architect

Plan #F10-011D-0440

Dimensions:	40' W x 45' D
Heated Sq. Ft.:	2,002
Bedrooms: 3	Bathrooms: 2½
Exterior Walls:	2" x 6"

Foundation: Crawl space or slab
standard; basement for an
additional fee

See index for more information

First Floor
2,213 sq. ft.

Optional
Second Floor
442 sq. ft.

*Images provided by
designer/architect*

© Copyright by
designer/architect

Plan #F10-011D-0650

Dimensions:	60' W x 53' D
Heated Sq. Ft.:	2,213
Bonus Sq. Ft.:	442
Bedrooms: 3	Bathrooms: 2
Exterior Walls:	2" x 6"

Foundation: Crawl space or slab
standard; basement for an
additional fee

See index for more information

Optional
In-Law Cottage
514 sq. ft.

First Floor
1,671 sq. ft.

© Copyright by designer/architect

Plan #F10-013D-0204

Dimensions:	42' W x 55' D
Heated Sq. Ft.:	1,671
Bonus Sq. Ft.:	514
Bedrooms: 4	Bathrooms: 2
Exterior Walls:	2" x 6"

Foundation: Slab standard; crawl space or basement for an additional fee

See index for more information

Images provided by designer/architect

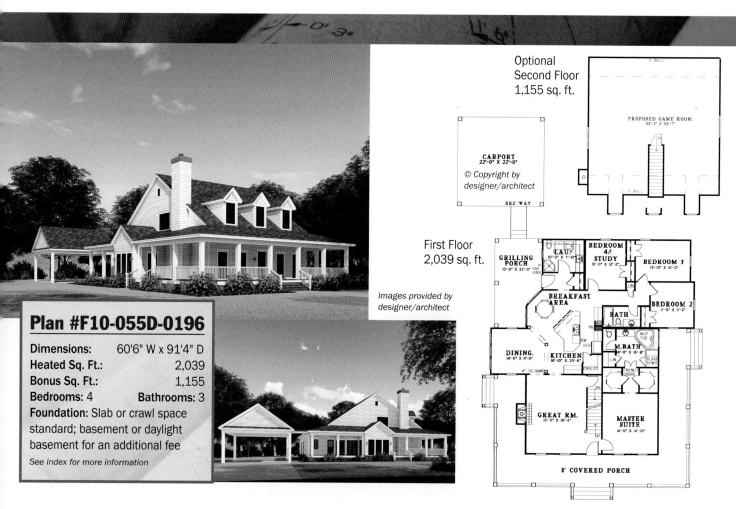

Optional
Second Floor
1,155 sq. ft.

PROPOSED GAME ROOM.
33'-2" X 33'-7"

CARPORT
22'-0" X 22'-0"

© Copyright by
designer/architect

First Floor
2,039 sq. ft.

*Images provided by
designer/architect*

Plan #F10-055D-0196

Dimensions:	60'6" W x 91'4" D
Heated Sq. Ft.:	2,039
Bonus Sq. Ft.:	1,155
Bedrooms: 4	Bathrooms: 3

Foundation: Slab or crawl space standard; basement or daylight basement for an additional fee

See index for more information

Plan #F10-011D-0069

Dimensions: 40' W x 52'6" D
Heated Sq. Ft.: 1,999
Bedrooms: 3   **Bathrooms:** 2½
Exterior Walls: 2" x 6"
Foundation: Daylight basement

See index for more information

Lower Level
769 sq. ft.

Images provided by designer/architect

© Copyright by designer/architect

First Floor
1,230 sq. ft.

Plan #F10-011D-0617

Dimensions: 69' W x 58' D
Heated Sq. Ft.: 2,104
Bonus Sq. Ft.: 268
Bedrooms: 3   **Bathrooms:** 2½
Exterior Walls: 2" x 6"
Foundation: Crawl space or slab standard; basement for an additional fee

See index for more information

© Copyright by designer/architect

First Floor
2,104 sq. ft.

Optional
Second Floor
268 sq. ft.

Images provided by designer/architect

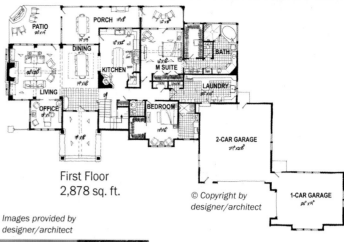

First Floor
2,878 sq. ft.

© Copyright by
designer/architect

Plan #F10-163D-0001

Dimensions:	129'1" W x 81'2" D
Heated Sq. Ft.:	3,922
Bonus Sq. Ft.:	348
Bedrooms: 4	Bathrooms: 3½
Exterior Walls:	2" x 6"
Foundation:	Slab

See index for more information

Second Floor
1,044 sq. ft.

Plan #F10-032D-1124

Dimensions:	66' W x 50' D
Heated Sq. Ft.:	2,117
Bonus Sq. Ft.:	360
Bedrooms: 3	Bathrooms: 2
Exterior Walls:	2" x 6"

Foundation: Crawl space standard;
floating slab, monolithic slab,
basement or walk-out basement for
an additional fee

See index for more information

Optional
Second Floor
360 sq. ft.

First Floor
2,117 sq. ft.

© Copyright by
designer/architect

Plan #F10-051D-0850

Dimensions:	38' W x 52' D
Heated Sq. Ft.:	1,334
Bedrooms: 2	Bathrooms: 2
Exterior Walls:	2" x 6"

Foundation: Basement standard; slab or crawl space for an additional fee

See index for more information

Images provided by designer/architect

DECK

DIN. RM. GRT. RM.
10'-1 1/8" STEP CEILING
24'4"x14'4"

MBR.
10'-1 1/8" STEP CEILING
12'4"x15'0"

KIT.
9'-1 1/8" CEILING
12'4"x9'0"

PAN.

LIN.
LIN.

DN.

BR. #2
9'-1 1/8" CEILING
12'0"x11'8"

E.
10'-1 1/8"
STEP
CEILING

2 CAR GARAGE
19'4"x21'8"

© Copyright by designer/architect

Plan #F10-013D-0236

Dimensions:	71'2" W x 64'6" D
Heated Sq. Ft.:	2,183
Bonus Sq. Ft.:	1,670
Bedrooms: 3	Bathrooms: 3½

Foundation: Crawl space or pier standard; slab or basement for an additional fee

See index for more information

Images provided by designer/architect

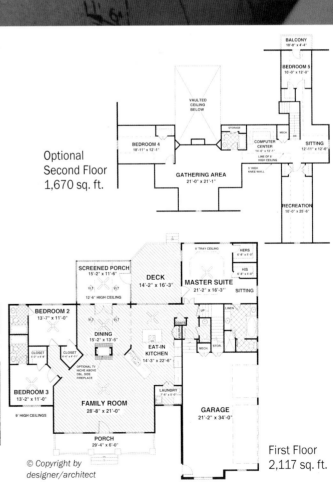

Optional Second Floor 1,670 sq. ft.

BALCONY
10'-6" x 4'-4"

BEDROOM 5
10'-0" x 12'-0"

VAULTED CEILING BELOW

STORAGE

BEDROOM 4
18'-11" x 12'-1"

COMPUTER CENTER
14'-0" x 12'-1"

MECH

DN

SITTING
12'-11" x 12'-0"

GATHERING AREA
21'-0" x 21'-1"

RECREATION
10'-0" x 25'-6"

SCREENED PORCH
15'-2" x 11'-6"

DECK
14'-2" x 16'-3"

HERS

HIS

MASTER SUITE
21'-2" x 16'-3"

SITTING

BEDROOM 2
13'-7" x 11'-0"

DINING
15'-2" x 13'-5"

EAT-IN KITCHEN
14'-3" x 22'-6"

BEDROOM 3
13'-2" x 11'-0"

FAMILY ROOM
28'-8" x 21'-0"

LAUNDRY
7'-4" x 6'-0"

GARAGE
21'-2" x 34'-0"

PORCH
29'-4" x 6'-0"

First Floor 2,117 sq. ft.

© Copyright by designer/architect

Plan #F10-011D-0526

Dimensions:	72' W x 65'6" D
Heated Sq. Ft.:	2,735
Bonus Sq. Ft.:	379
Bedrooms: 3	Bathrooms: 2½
Exterior Walls:	2" x 6"

Foundation: Crawl space or slab standard; basement for an additional fee

See index for more information

Images provided by designer/architect

Features

- The vaulted great room with fireplace and covered porch views commands full attention when you enter this home
- A quiet home office is tucked away near the foyer
- The kitchen has an efficient angled island and breakfast bar that overlooks the great room and breakfast nook
- Two secondary bedrooms find themselves located behind the kitchen and share a full bath
- The optional second floor has an additional 379 square feet of living area
- 3-car front entry garage

Optional
Second Floor
379 sq. ft.

First Floor
2,735 sq. ft.

© Copyright by designer/architect

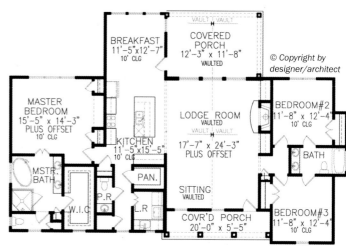

Plan #F10-056D-0104

Dimensions:	63'1" W x 41'10" D
Heated Sq. Ft.:	1,925
Bedrooms: 3	Bathrooms: 2½
Foundation:	Slab

See index for more information

Images provided by designer/architect

© Copyright by designer/architect

BREAKFAST 11'-5"x12'-7" 10' CLG

COVERED PORCH 12'-3" x 11'-8" VAULTED

MASTER BEDROOM 15'-5" x 14'-3" PLUS OFFSET 10' CLG

KITCHEN 11'-5"x15'-5" 10' CLG

LODGE ROOM VAULTED 17'-7" x 24'-3" PLUS OFFSET

BEDROOM#2 11'-8" x 12'-4" 10' CLG

BATH

MSTR. BATH

PAN.

P.R

W.I.C

L.R

SITTING VAULTED

COVR'D PORCH 20'-0" x 5'-5"

BEDROOM#3 11'-8" x 12'-4" 10' CLG

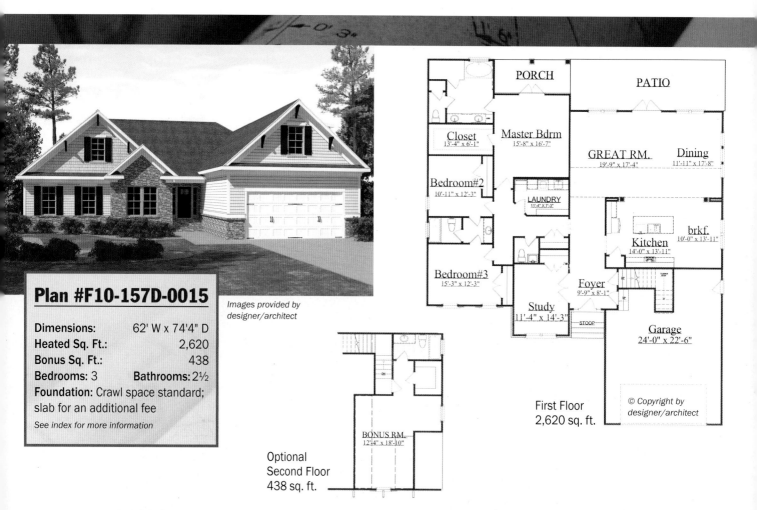

Plan #F10-157D-0015

Dimensions:	62' W x 74'4" D
Heated Sq. Ft.:	2,620
Bonus Sq. Ft.:	438
Bedrooms: 3	Bathrooms: 2½
Foundation:	Crawl space standard; slab for an additional fee

See index for more information

Images provided by designer/architect

PORCH

PATIO

Closet 13'-4" x 6'-1"

Master Bdrm 15'-8" x 16'-7"

GREAT RM. 19'-9" x 17'-4"

Dining 11'-11" x 17'-8"

Bedroom#2 10'-11" x 12'-3"

LAUNDRY 13'-4" x 7'-3"

Kitchen 14'-0" x 13'-11"

brkf. 10'-0" x 13'-11"

Bedroom#3 15'-3" x 12'-3"

Foyer 9'-9" x 8'-1"

Study 11'-4" x 14'-3"

STOOP

Garage 24'-0" x 22'-6"

First Floor 2,620 sq. ft.

© Copyright by designer/architect

BONUS RM. 12'-4" x 18'-10"

Optional Second Floor 438 sq. ft.

Plan #F10-111D-0037

Dimensions: 28'4" W x 51'8" D
Heated Sq. Ft.: 1,466
Bedrooms: 3   **Bathrooms:** 2½
Foundation: Slab standard; crawl space for an additional fee

See index for more information

Images provided by designer/architect

© Copyright by designer/architect

Second Floor
490 sq. ft.

BEDROOM 2
11² x 10⁶

BEDROOM 3
10⁰ x 10²

BATH 2

LOFT

BALCONY

ATTIC

WOOD DECK

MASTER BEDROOM
12⁸ x 11¹⁰

WIC

M. BATH

PANTRY

KITCHEN
18⁸ x 19⁰

WOOD DECK

LIVING & DINING
14⁸ x 19⁰

CARPORT

ENTRY

PWDR

STORAGE

PORCH

First Floor
976 sq. ft.

Plan #F10-076D-0259

Dimensions: 46' W x 57'2" D
Heated Sq. Ft.: 1,730
Bonus Sq. Ft.: 312
Bedrooms: 3   **Bathrooms:** 2
Foundation: Slab

See index for more information

Images provided by designer/architect

Optional Second Floor
312 sq. ft.

DOWN

BONUS ROOM
12-3 X 14-9

© Copyright by designer/architect

MASTER BATH

HER

COVERED TERRACE

BREAKFAST
11 X 12

KITCHEN

MASTER BEDROOM
15 X 14

FAMILY ROOM
18 X 20
11'-0" HIGH CLG

REF

HIM

UTIL

BEDROOM 3
12 X 12

BATH

FOYER

LIN

CLOSET

GARAGE
21-6 X 22

PORCH

BEDROOM 2
12 X 12

First Floor
1,730 sq. ft.

Plan #F10-111S-0005

Dimensions: 96'5" W x 63'11" D
Heated Sq. Ft.: 3,937
Bonus Sq. Ft.: 328
Bedrooms: 5   **Bathrooms:** 4½
Foundation: Slab standard; crawl space or basement for an additional fee

See index for more information

Features

- This Craftsman style two-story has perfect outdoor living areas like the covered porch and courtyard
- This home's exterior features stone, stucco and cedar and the interior uses stone, wood, granite and plastered arches
- Located off the open kitchen, the breakfast area is the perfect nook
- Walls of windows provide views in the great room and breakfast area
- The vaulted master bedroom offers endless luxury with a posh bath and two walk-in closets
- A bonus room and flex space make this floor plan very versatile for future needs with the bonus room having an additional 328 square feet of living area
- 3-car side entry garage

Second Floor
1,106 sq. ft.

First Floor
2,831 sq. ft.

© Copyright by designer/architect

Images provided by designer/architect

Plan #F10-032D-0887

Dimensions:	42' W x 40' D
Heated Sq. Ft.:	1,212
Bonus Sq. Ft.:	1,212
Bedrooms: 2	**Bathrooms:** 1
Exterior Walls:	2" x 6"

Foundation: Basement standard; crawl space, floating slab or monolithic slab for an additional fee

See index for more information

Images provided by designer/architect

Features

- This highly efficient home offers an open floor plan with beamed ceilings above adding a tremendous amount of architectural interest to the interior
- A fireplace acts like a partition between the bedroom hall and the main gathering spaces
- The large covered porch is a wonderful extension of the interior living spaces
- The island in the kitchen includes casual dining space and a double basin sink and dishwasher
- The optional lower level has an additional 1,212 square feet of living area

First Floor
1,212 sq. ft.

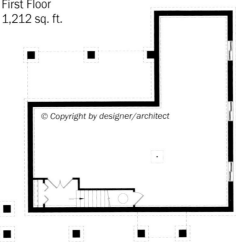

© Copyright by designer/architect

Optional Lower Level
1,212 sq. ft.

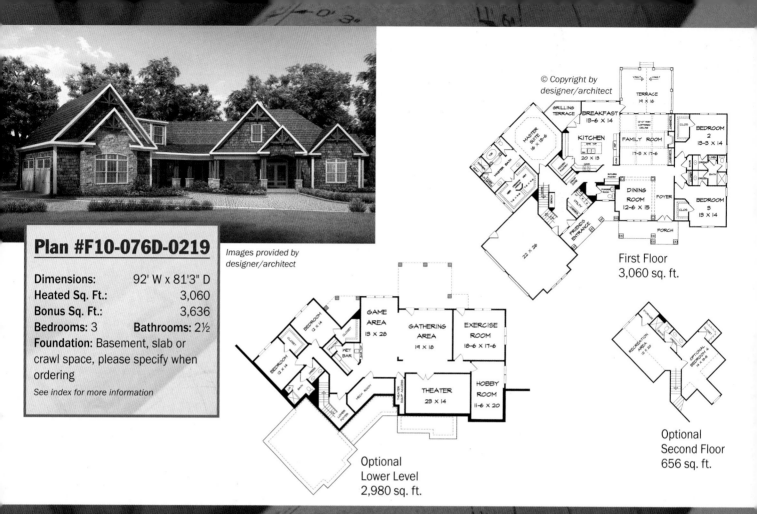

Plan #F10-076D-0219

Dimensions:	92' W x 81'3" D
Heated Sq. Ft.:	3,060
Bonus Sq. Ft.:	3,636
Bedrooms: 3	**Bathrooms:** 2½

Foundation: Basement, slab or crawl space, please specify when ordering

See index for more information

Images provided by designer/architect

First Floor
3,060 sq. ft.

© Copyright by designer/architect

Optional
Lower Level
2,980 sq. ft.

Optional
Second Floor
656 sq. ft.

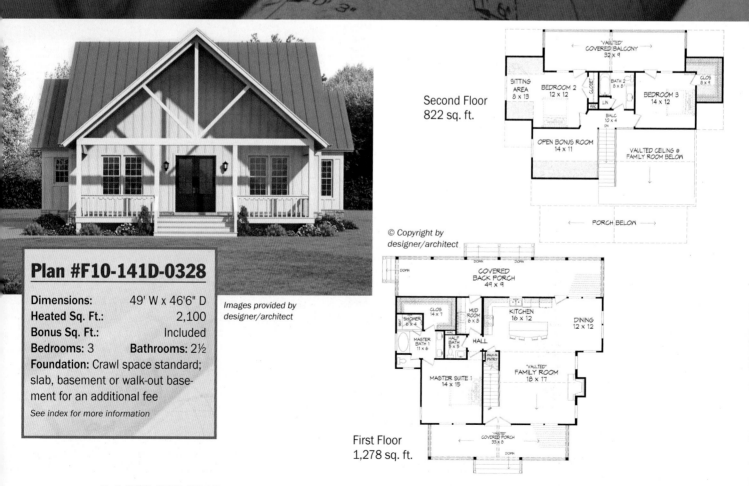

Plan #F10-141D-0328

Dimensions:	49' W x 46'6" D
Heated Sq. Ft.:	2,100
Bonus Sq. Ft.:	Included
Bedrooms: 3	**Bathrooms:** 2½

Foundation: Crawl space standard; slab, basement or walk-out basement for an additional fee

See index for more information

Images provided by designer/architect

Second Floor
822 sq. ft.

© Copyright by designer/architect

First Floor
1,278 sq. ft.

Plan #F10-144D-0001

Dimensions: 28' W x 40' D
Heated Sq. Ft.: 1,677
Bedrooms: 2   Bathrooms: 2
Exterior Walls: 2" x 6"
Foundation: Crawl space standard; slab, basement, daylight basement or walk-out basement for an additional fee

See index for more information

Images provided by designer/architect

First Floor
1,064 sq. ft.

© Copyright by designer/architect

Second Floor
613 sq. ft.

Plan #F10-159D-0010

Dimensions: 72'8" W x 65'4" D
Heated Sq. Ft.: 2,900
Bonus Sq. Ft.: 1,500
Bedrooms: 4   Bathrooms: 2½
Exterior Walls: 2" x 6"
Foundation: Walk-out basement

See index for more information

Second Floor
900 sq. ft.

Images provided by designer/architect

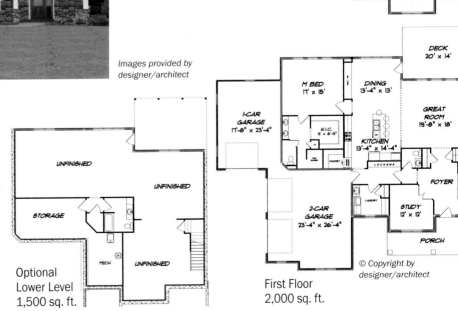

Optional Lower Level
1,500 sq. ft.

First Floor
2,000 sq. ft.

© Copyright by designer/architect

Plan #F10-011D-0586

Dimensions:	36'6" W x 56' D
Heated Sq. Ft.:	2,988
Bedrooms: 4	**Bathrooms:** 4
Exterior Walls:	2" x 6"
Foundation:	Walk-out basement

See index for more information

Images provided by designer/architect

Features

- This Industrial style modern home simplifies living with its open floor plan, which expands the size of the gathering spaces
- The outdoor covered porch enjoys a built-in grill and deck
- The second floor has a master suite, a bedroom with a private bath, a laundry room, and an exercise room
- The lower level enjoys an apartment style layout with a covered porch
- 1-car front entry garage

Second Floor
1,123 sq. ft.

© Copyright by
designer/architect

First Floor
1,175 sq. ft.

Lower Level
690 sq. ft.

houseplansandmore.com

Plan #F10-101D-0121

Dimensions:	116'6" W x 62' D
Heated Sq. Ft.:	3,380
Bonus Sq. Ft.:	2,027
Bedrooms: 2	Bathrooms: 2½
Exterior Walls:	2" x 6"

Foundation: Basement, daylight basement or walk-out basement, please specify when ordering

See index for more information

Images provided by designer/architect

Features

- This stunning Modern home has a touch of a Modern Farmhouse feel
- This unique floor plan has a separate apartment style suite that features its own living room, a separate entrance, a covered patio and a kitchen with an island
- The main home offers an open kitchen with massive island, a cozy great room with fireplace, a casual dining space, a laundry room and a master bedroom and bath in a private location
- There's also a first floor study, ideal as a home office
- The lower level has an additional 2,027 square feet of living area and features a rec room, media area, bar, an exercise room, two bedrooms and two full baths
- 3-car side entry garage

First Floor
3,380 sq. ft.

© Copyright by designer/architect

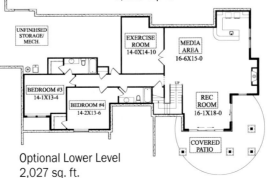

Optional Lower Level
2,027 sq. ft.

Second Floor
745 sq. ft.

First Floor
2,885 sq. ft.

© Copyright by designer/architect

Optional Lower Level
2,102 sq. ft.

Plan #F10-013D-0256

Dimensions: 57'10" W x 66'4" D
Heated Sq. Ft.: 3,630
Bonus Sq. Ft.: 2,502
Bedrooms: 4   **Bathrooms:** 4½
Foundation: Basement standard; crawl space or slab for an additional fee

See index for more information

Images provided by designer/architect

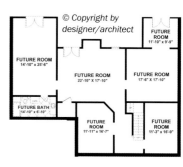

8' DEEP COVERED PORCH

© Copyright by designer/architect

Images provided by designer/architect

Plan #F10-028D-0103

Dimensions: 40' W x 46' D
Heated Sq. Ft.: 1,520
Bedrooms: 2   **Bathrooms:** 1
Exterior Walls: 2" x 6"
Foundation: Crawl space standard; floating slab, monolithic slab, basement or walk-out basement for an additional fee

See index for more information

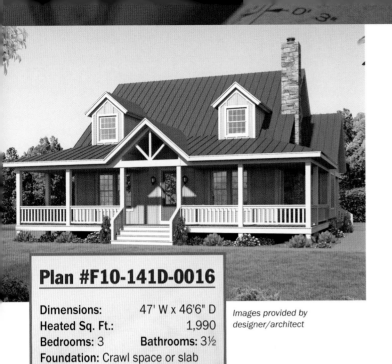

Second Floor
790 sq. ft.

First Floor
1,200 sq. ft.

Plan #F10-141D-0016

Dimensions:	47' W x 46'6" D
Heated Sq. Ft.:	1,990
Bedrooms: 3	**Bathrooms:** 3½

Foundation: Crawl space or slab standard; basement or walk-out basement for an additional fee

See index for more information

Images provided by designer/architect

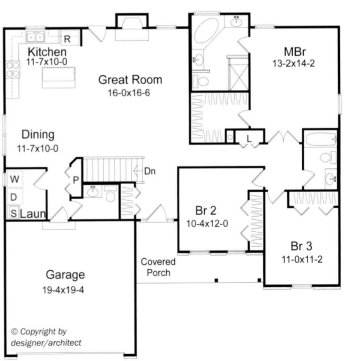

Plan #F10-058D-0171

Dimensions:	51' W x 50'4" D
Heated Sq. Ft.:	1,635
Bedrooms: 3	**Bathrooms:** 2½
Foundation:	Basement

See index for more information

Images provided by designer/architect

Plan #F10-167D-0008

Dimensions:	62'4" W x 50'7" D
Heated Sq. Ft.:	3,328
Bedrooms: 4	**Bathrooms:** 3½
Exterior Walls:	2" x 6"

Foundation: Crawl space standard;
slab for an additional fee

See index for more information

Features

- Classic American Farmhouse style with a Modern Farmhouse twist
- The first floor has a living and dining area, and an open kitchen
- Handy laundry and mud rooms offer an opportunity for great organizing
- Two doors off the living area lead to a private home office
- The vaulted owner's suite has two walk-in closets, a private bath with a huge walk-in shower and free-standing tub, and access to a deck
- 2-car detached side entry garage

Detached Garage

garage
21'x19'

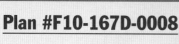

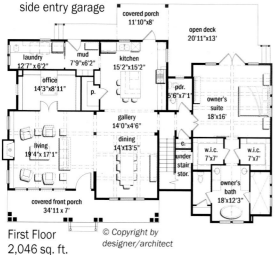

First Floor
2,046 sq. ft.

© Copyright by
designer/architect

Second Floor
1,282 sq. ft.

Images provided by designer/architect

houseplansandmore.com

Plan #F10-101D-0052

Dimensions:	129'8" W x 70'8" D
Heated Sq. Ft.:	2,611
Bonus Sq. Ft.:	2,456
Bedrooms: 2	Bathrooms: 2½
Exterior Walls:	2" x 6"
Foundation:	Walk-out basement

See index for more information

Images provided by designer/architect

Features

- Open living at its finest in this Craftsman style home with barrier free living spaces
- An angled den off the foyer creates a private home office
- The U-shaped kitchen has a large island
- There is a convenient mud room and laundry area as you enter from the garage
- The optional lower level has an additional 2,456 square feet of living area including two bedrooms
- 3-car front entry garage

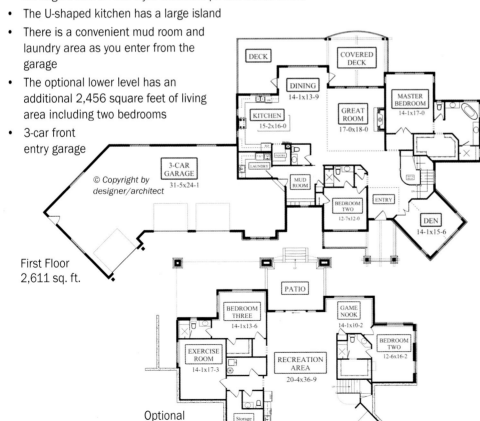

First Floor
2,611 sq. ft.

© Copyright by designer/architect

Optional
Lower Level
2,456 sq. ft.

Plan #F10-101D-0125

Dimensions:	118'3" W x 70' D
Heated Sq. Ft.:	2,970
Bonus Sq. Ft.:	2,014
Bedrooms: 2	Bathrooms: 2½
Exterior Walls:	2" x 6"
Foundation:	Walk-out basement

See index for more information

Features

- This rustic modern masterpiece offers an open concept floor plan with the utmost style and distinction
- Step into the foyer and be greeted by an open and expansive great room topped with a stunning ceiling
- The bright and stylish kitchen has a huge island, rustic beams above and plenty of cabinet space for maintaining a sleek appearance free of clutter
- The first floor master bedroom enjoys a beamed ceiling, covered deck access, a luxury bath and a huge walk-in closet
- A guest room with its own private bath can be found on the opposite side of the first floor from the master bedroom for extra privacy
- The optional lower level has an additional 2,014 square feet of living area including a wet bar with island, a rec room, a game nook, three additional bedrooms, one full bath and a half bath
- 2-car front entry garage, and a 1-car side entry garage

Images provided by designer/architect

Optional Lower Level
2,014 sq. ft.

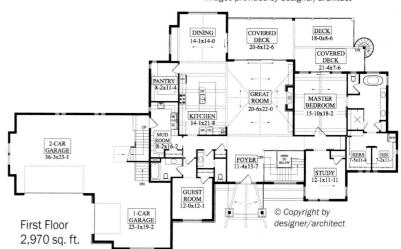

First Floor
2,970 sq. ft.

© Copyright by designer/architect

Plan #F10-028D-0099

Dimensions:	30' W x 49' D
Heated Sq. Ft.:	1,320
Bedrooms: 3	**Bathrooms:** 2
Exterior Walls:	2" x 6"

Foundation: Crawl space or monolithic slab, please specify when ordering

See index for more information

Features

- In a sensible size, this cottage can easily incorporate popular Modern Farmhouse style trends into its floor plan with a barn style door from the master bedroom into the bath

- The great room and kitchen/dining area blend together making the interior feel larger than its true size

- All three of the bedrooms are located near each other for convenience

- The laundry room is centrally located adding ease with this chore

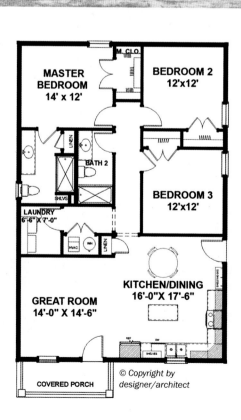

MASTER BEDROOM 14' x 12'

M. CLO.

BEDROOM 2 12'x12'

BATH 2

LAUNDRY 6'-6" X 7'-0"

BEDROOM 3 12'x12'

LINEN

HVAC

LINEN

KITCHEN/DINING 16'-0" X 17'-6"

GREAT ROOM 14'-0" X 14'-6"

COVERED PORCH

© Copyright by designer/architect

Images provided by designer/architect

Plan #F10-013S-0011

Images provided by designer/architect

Dimensions:	75' W x 60' D
Heated Sq. Ft.:	5,565
Bedrooms:	4
Bathrooms:	3 full, 2 half
Foundation:	Walk-out basement

standard; crawl space or slab for
an additional fee

See index for more information

Features

- The living and dining rooms share a warming see-through fireplace
- A built-in bench wraps around the kitchen creating additional seating and cozy spaces for entertaining as well as dining
- The lower level is spacious with a recreational room, a wet bar, a billiards area, a game area, an exercise space, a laundry room, and three additional large bedrooms, perfect for guests
- 3-car front entry garage

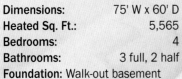

First Floor
2,884 sq. ft.

Lower Level
2,681 sq. ft.

Images provided by designer/architect

© Copyright by designer/architect

Plan #F10-011D-0640

Dimensions:	58' W x 62' D
Heated Sq. Ft.:	1,834
Bedrooms: 3	**Bathrooms:** 2
Exterior Walls:	2" x 6"

Foundation: Crawl space or slab standard; basement for an additional fee

See index for more information

© Copyright by designer/architect

Optional Second Floor 473 sq. ft.

First Floor 2,015 sq. ft.

Optional Lower Level 1,367 sq. ft.

Plan #F10-123D-0156

Dimensions:	53' W x 67' D
Heated Sq. Ft.:	2,015
Bonus Sq. Ft.:	1,840
Bedrooms: 3	**Bathrooms:** 2

Foundation: Basement standard; crawl space, slab or walk-out basement for an additional fee

See index for more information

Images provided by designer/architect

Images provided by designer/architect

Plan #F10-111D-0081

Dimensions: 54'6" W x 54'9" D
Heated Sq. Ft.: 2,137
Bonus Sq. Ft.: 247
Bedrooms: 3   **Bathrooms:** 2
Foundation: Slab standard; crawl space for an additional fee
See index for more information

Optional
Detached Garage
Second Floor
247 sq. ft.

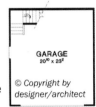

GARAGE
20¹⁰ x 23²

Detached Garage
First Floor

© Copyright by
designer/architect

© Copyright by
designer/architect

Images provided by designer/architect

First Floor
2,021 sq. ft.

Plan #F10-077D-0131

Dimensions: 69' W x 63'10" D
Heated Sq. Ft.: 2,021
Bonus Sq. Ft.: 354
Bedrooms: 3   **Bathrooms:** 2½
Foundation: Basement; for slab or crawl space versions, see Plan #077D-0128 at houseplansandmore.com
See index for more information

Unfinished
Bonus
Room
14-0 x 23-6
(Clear)
8-0 Clg. Ht.

Optional
Second Floor
354 sq. ft.

Plan #F10-024S-0025

Dimensions:	72' W x 78' D
Heated Sq. Ft.:	4,099
Bedrooms: 4	Bathrooms: 3½
Foundation:	Basement

See index for more information

Images provided by designer/architect

Features

- The large kitchen with center cooktop island overlooks the cozy casual family room with a corner fireplace
- An amazing private master bath boasts a peninsula whirlpool tub with a built-in flat screen television that has a walk-through shower behind it
- The second floor media room is the perfect spot for watching your favorite film in a quiet place
- 3-car drive under side entry garage

First Floor
3,163 sq. ft.

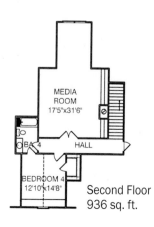

Second Floor
936 sq. ft.

houseplansandmore.com

Plan #F10-032D-0963

Dimensions:	34' W x 38' D
Heated Sq. Ft.:	1,178
Bonus Sq. Ft.:	1,178
Bedrooms: 1	**Bathrooms:** 1
Exterior Walls:	2" x 6"

Foundation: Basement standard; crawl space, floating slab or monolithic slab for an additional fee

See index for more information

Images provided by designer/architect

Features

- This small Modern Farmhouse inspired home takes simplicity and style to a new level
- Step into the entry from the covered front porch and discover an oversized walk-in closet
- The open-concept floor plan has the kitchen and dining area blended perfectly
- The kitchen has a large walk-in pantry with a barn style door for a farmhouse feel
- The bedroom enjoys close proximity to the pampering bath that features a shower as well as a free-standing tub in one corner
- The optional lower level has an additional 1,178 square feet of living area

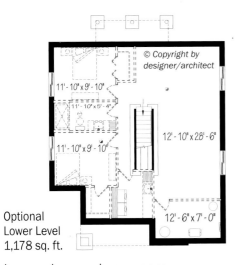

© Copyright by designer/architect

11' - 10" x 9' - 0"
11' - 10" x 5' - 4"
11' - 10" x 9' - 10"
12' - 10" x 28' - 6"
12' - 6" x 7' - 0"

Optional Lower Level
1,178 sq. ft.

11' - 0" x 12' - 0"
DINING

LIVING
11' - 0" x 16' - 0"

KITCHEN
10' - 8" x 12' - 0"

BATH

BEDROOM
13' - 10" x 12' - 0"

OFFICE
13' - 2" x 8' - 2"

First Floor
1,178 sq. ft.

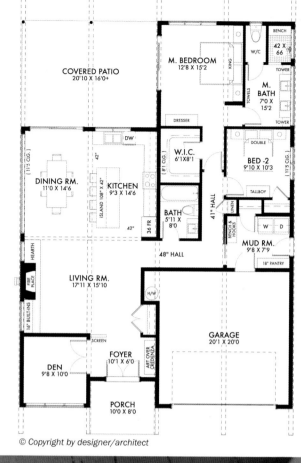

Images provided by designer/architect

© Copyright by designer/architect

Plan #F10-180D-0043

Dimensions:	42' W x 58' D
Heated Sq. Ft.:	1,627
Bedrooms: 2	Bathrooms: 2
Exterior Walls:	2" x 6"

Foundation: Crawl space or slab, please specify when ordering

See index for more information

Images provided by designer/architect

First Floor
1,583 sq. ft.

© Copyright by designer/architect

Optional Lower Level
1,583 sq. ft.

Plan #F10-032D-1122

Dimensions:	63'8" W x 38'4" D
Heated Sq. Ft.:	1,583
Bonus Sq. Ft.:	1,583
Bedrooms: 3	Bathrooms: 1
Exterior Walls:	2" x 6"
Foundation:	Basement

See index for more information

Plan #F10-077D-0088

Dimensions:	30' W x 36' D
Heated Sq. Ft.:	800
Bedrooms: 2	Bathrooms: 1
Foundation:	Slab

See index for more information

Images provided by designer/architect

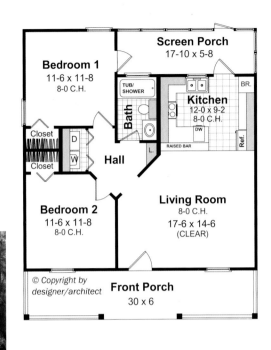

Bedroom 1
11-6 x 11-8
8-0 C.H.

Screen Porch
17-10 x 5-8

TUB/SHOWER

Bath

BR.

Kitchen
12-0 x 9-2
8-0 C.H.

DW

Ref.

Closet

D

W

RAISED BAR

Closet

L.

Hall

Bedroom 2
11-6 x 11-8
8-0 C.H.

Living Room
8-0 C.H.
17-6 x 14-6
(CLEAR)

© Copyright by designer/architect

Front Porch
30 x 6

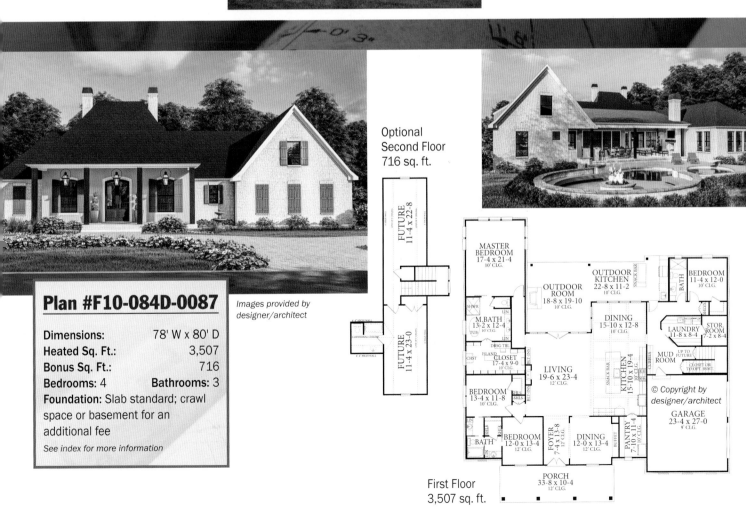

Plan #F10-084D-0087

Images provided by designer/architect

Dimensions:	78' W x 80' D
Heated Sq. Ft.:	3,507
Bonus Sq. Ft.:	716
Bedrooms: 4	Bathrooms: 3
Foundation:	Slab standard; crawl space or basement for an additional fee

See index for more information

Optional
Second Floor
716 sq. ft.

FUTURE
11-4 x 22-8

FUTURE
11-4 x 23-0

MASTER BEDROOM
17-4 x 21-4
10' CLG.

OUTDOOR ROOM
18-8 x 19-10
10' CLG.

OUTDOOR KITCHEN
22-8 x 11-2
10' CLG.

SNACK BAR

BATH

BEDROOM
11-4 x 12-0
10' CLG.

M.BATH
13-2 x 12-4
10' CLG.

SHWR

TUB

LIN

LIN

DINING
15-10 x 12-8
10' CLG.

LAUNDRY
11-8 x 8-4

STOR. ROOM
7-2 x 8-4

DRSG TBL

CHST

ISLAND

CLOSET
17-4 x 9-0
10' CLG.

KITCHEN
15-10 x 19-4

SNACK BAR

LIVING
19-6 x 23-4
12' CLG.

MUD ROOM

UP TO FUTURE

CLOSET OR OPT. BSMT.

BEDROOM
13-4 x 11-8
10' CLG.

© Copyright by designer/architect

GARAGE
23-4 x 27-0
9' CLG.

BATH

LIN

BEDROOM
12-0 x 13-4
12' CLG.

FOYER
7-4 x 13-8
12' CLG.

DINING
12-0 x 13-4
12' CLG.

PANTRY
7-10 x 11-4
10' CLG.

BUFFET

PORCH
33-8 x 10-4
12' CLG.

First Floor
3,507 sq. ft.

Plan #F10-032D-0919

Dimensions:	32'8" W 36' D
Heated Sq. Ft.:	2,021
Bedrooms: 3	**Bathrooms:** 1½
Exterior Walls:	2" x 6"

Foundation: Basement standard; crawl space, monolithic slab or floating slab for an additional fee

See index for more information

Images provided by designer/architect

Features

- Stylish European home offers tremendous curb appeal and a feeling of luxury in a popular size
- An open first floor plan has the main gathering spaces combining in an L-shape as you enter the great room on the left from the foyer
- The dining area is sunny and bright thanks to a bay window, and a series of sliding glass doors on another wall leading outdoors
- All of the bedrooms are located on the second floor for privacy

15'-8" X 13'-4"
4,70 X 4,00

15'-8" X 11'-0"
4,70 X 3,30

13'-0" X 19'-0"
3,90 X 5,70

10'-8" X 8'-0"
3,20 X 2,40

© Copyright by designer/architect

First Floor
1,133 sq. ft.

15'-8" X 11'-0"
4,70 X 3,30

14'-0" X 9'-0"
4,20 X 2,70

13'-10" X 14'-0"
4,15 X 4,20

Second Floor
888 sq. ft.

Plan #F10-032D-1151

Dimensions:	45' W x 38' D
Heated Sq. Ft.:	2,113
Bonus Sq. Ft.:	1,056
Bedrooms: 3	Bathrooms: 2½
Exterior Walls:	2" x 6"

Foundation: Basement standard;
crawl space for an additional fee

See index for more information

Images provided by designer/architect

Features

- The open living room features a beautiful modern fireplace creating dramatic ambiance
- The kitchen has an island and walk-in pantry
- Sliding glass doors make the dining room cheerful
- The optional lower level has an additional 1,056 square feet of living area
- 1-car side entry garage

Optional Lower Level
1,056 sq. ft.

© Copyright by designer/architect

Second Floor
1,057 sq. ft.

First Floor
1,056 sq. ft.

Plan #F10-076D-0304

Dimensions:	89' W x 76'4" D
Heated Sq. Ft.:	2,162
Bonus Sq. Ft.:	412
Bedrooms: 3	Bathrooms: 2½
Foundation:	Slab

See index for more information

Images provided by designer/architect

Optional
Second Floor
412 sq. ft.

BONUS ROOM
15-6 X 22-6
DOWN

COVERED TERRACE
18-3 X 14

MASTER SUITE
13-6 X 16

M. BATH
11 X 16-6

SHOWER
TUB

LINEN

CLOSET
4-8 X 10-9

KITCHEN
11-6 X 16-6

ISLAND
5 X 6-9

SINK
DW
COOK
REF

FAMILY ROOM
18-3 X 16-6

BEDROOM 3
13 X 12

CLOSET

DRESS

BATH

LINEN

CLOSET

DRESS

PANTRY
7-6 X 4-6
SHELVING

UTILITY
11 X 7-6

FOLDING
HANGING
FOLDING
HANGING
BENCH

UP

PNTR RM 1

COAT

DINING ROOM
14-6 X 13

FOYER
7-3 X 13

BEDROOM 2
13 X 12

PORCH

2 CAR GARAGE
26 X 22-6

10-0 X 8-0
10-0 X 8-0
10-0 X 8-0

© Copyright by designer/architect

First Floor
2,162 sq. ft.

Plan #F10-028D-0120

Dimensions:	56' W x 52' D
Heated Sq. Ft.:	2,096
Bedrooms: 4	Bathrooms: 2
Exterior Walls:	2" x 6"

Foundation: Floating slab standard; monolithic slab, crawl space, basement or walk-out basement for an additional fee

See index for more information

Images provided by designer/architect

Laundry
7-5 X 12-0

Suite 1
15-0 X 16-0

clo
6-0 X 12-0

bath
9-0 X 12-0

clo
6-0 X 14-0

Suite 2
16-5 X 14-0

Porch 2
7-6 ft deep

Kitchen/Dining
19-7 X 15-0

COUNTER HIGH SNACK BAR

Great Room
19-7 X 19-6

Bedroom 4
14-0 X 12-0

bath
10-0 X 5-6

Bedroom 3
14-0 X 12-0

© Copyright by designer/architect

Porch 1
10-0 ft deep

Plan #F10-011D-0660

Dimensions: 52' W x 53' D
Heated Sq. Ft.: 1,704
Bedrooms: 3 **Bathrooms:** 2½
Exterior Walls: 2" x 6"
Foundation: Crawl space or slab
standard; basement for an
additional fee

See index for more information

Images provided by designer/architect

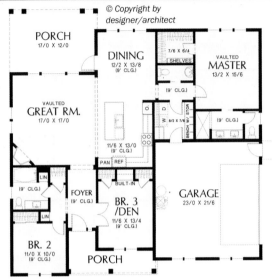

Plan #F10-121D-0046

Dimensions: 60' W x 61' D
Heated Sq. Ft.: 1,983
Bedrooms: 3 **Bathrooms:** 2½
Foundation: Basement standard;
crawl space or slab for an
additional fee

See index for more information

Images provided by designer/architect

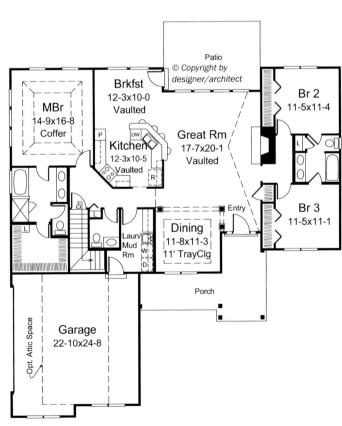

Plan #F10-076D-0239

Dimensions:	91'5" W x 79'5" D
Heated Sq. Ft.:	2,772
Bonus Sq. Ft.:	433
Bedrooms: 4	**Bathrooms:** 2½

Foundation: Slab or crawl space, please specify when ordering

See index for more information

Images provided by designer/architect

Features

- Friendly Craftsman architecture takes center stage on the exterior of this stylish 1-story home
- The vaulted beamed family room is open and inviting with the kitchen island able to be a part of the family room activity
- The kitchen also enjoys a sizable walk-in pantry for keeping the highly visible kitchen free of clutter and excess appliances
- The master suite enjoys its remote location and provides the homeowners with a dressing room style closet space and a private bath
- The bonus room on the second floor has an additional 433 square feet of living area
- 2-car front entry garage

Optional Second Floor
433 sq. ft.

© Copyright by designer/architect

First Floor
2,772 sq. ft.

Plan #F10-170D-0019

Dimensions: 87'2" W x 60'4" D
Heated Sq. Ft.: 2,648
Bedrooms: 4   **Bathrooms:** 2½
Foundation: Slab or monolithic slab, please specify when ordering

See index for more information

Images provided by designer/architect

Features

- This one-story has a tremendous amount of open space ideal for those who like an airy atmosphere
- There is a formal dining room as well as a casual eating area off the kitchen
- A large kitchen island overlooks the family room and its centered fireplace
- A small office is right around the corner from the kitchen in a secluded hallway
- The master bedroom enjoys its privacy, a large bath with both a shower and a spa style tub, and a large walk-in closet
- 3-car side entry garage

Plan #F10-084D-0090

Dimensions: 73'6" W x 61' D
Heated Sq. Ft.: 2,221
Bonus Sq. Ft.: 403
Bedrooms: 4 **Bathrooms:** 2
Foundation: Slab standard; crawl space or basement for an additional fee

See index for more information

Images provided by designer/architect

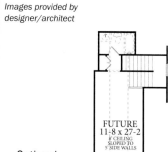

Optional
Second Floor
403 sq. ft.

FUTURE
11-8 x 27-2
8' CEILING
SLOPED TO
5' SIDE WALLS

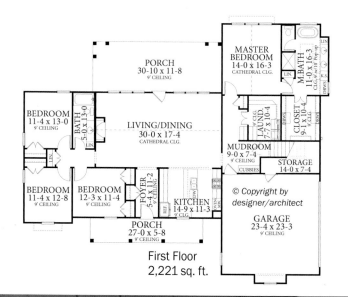

First Floor
2,221 sq. ft.

PORCH
30-10 x 11-8
9' CEILING

MASTER
BEDROOM
14-0 x 16-3
CATHEDRAL CLG.

M.BATH
11-0 x 16-3

BEDROOM
11-4 x 13-0
9' CEILING

BATH
5-0 x 13-0

LIVING/DINING
30-0 x 17-4
CATHEDRAL CLG.

CLOSET
9-1 x 10-4

LAUND.
7-7 x 10-4

BEDROOM
11-4 x 12-8
9' CEILING

BEDROOM
12-3 x 11-4
9' CEILING

FOYER
5-4 x 11-2
9' CEILING

KITCHEN
14-9 x 11-3
9' CLG.

MUDROOM
9-0 x 7-4
9' CEILING

STORAGE
14-0 x 7-4

PORCH
27-0 x 5-8
9' CEILING

GARAGE
23-4 x 23-3
9' CEILING

© Copyright by designer/architect

Plan #F10-141D-0223

Dimensions: 52'10" W x 67'2" D
Heated Sq. Ft.: 2,095
Bedrooms: 3 **Bathrooms:** 2½
Exterior Walls: 2" x 6"
Foundation: Slab or crawl space standard; basement or walk-out basement for an additional fee

See index for more information

Images provided by designer/architect

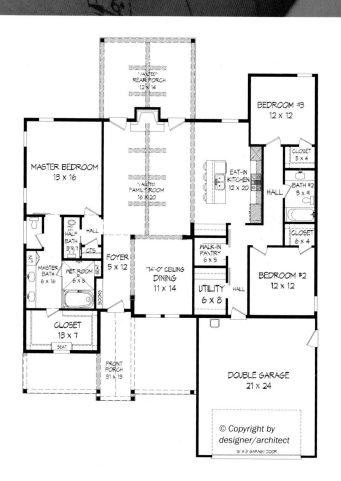

VAULTED
REAR PORCH
12 x 14

MASTER BEDROOM
13 x 16

VAULTED
FAMILY ROOM
16 x 20

EAT-IN
KITCHEN
12 x 20

BEDROOM #3
12 x 12

CLOSET
5 x 4

BATH #2
5 x 9

HALL

HALF
BATH

MASTER
BATH
6 x 16

WET ROOM
6 x 8

FOYER
5 x 12

WALK-IN
PANTRY
6 x 5

CLOSET
6 x 4

BEDROOM #2
12 x 12

14'-0" CEILING
DINING
11 x 14

UTILITY
6 x 8

HALL

CLOSET
13 x 7

FRONT
PORCH
31 x 13

DOUBLE GARAGE
21 x 24

© Copyright by designer/architect

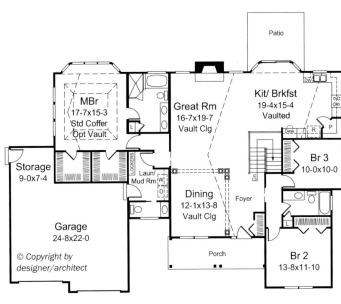

Plan #F10-121D-0020

Dimensions:	70'8" W x 47' D
Heated Sq. Ft.:	2,037
Bedrooms: 3	Bathrooms: 2½

Foundation: Basement standard; crawl space or slab for an additional fee

See index for more information

Images provided by designer/architect

© Copyright by designer/architect

Plan #F10-026D-2072

Dimensions:	45' W x 62' D
Heated Sq. Ft.:	1,619
Bedrooms: 3	Bathrooms: 2
Exterior Walls:	2" x 6"

Foundation: Slab standard; crawl space, basement or walk-out basement for an additional fee

See index for more information

Images provided by designer/architect

© Copyright by designer/architect

Plan #F10-051D-0852

Dimensions:	40' W x 56' D
Heated Sq. Ft.:	1,432
Bedrooms: 2	Bathrooms: 2
Exterior Walls:	2" x 6"

Foundation: Basement standard; crawl space or slab for an additional fee

See index for more information

Features

- This modern style home has an up-to-date look that's simple and less cluttered
- A 10' step ceiling greets you as you enter the home for added spaciousness
- An open concept floor plan combines the kitchen, dining and great rooms for a comfortable and more open living space
- The kitchen enjoys an open feel thanks to its island overlooking the great room
- The master suite is tucked behind the garage and includes a private bath with dual sinks, an oversized walk-in shower, and a walk-in closet
- 2-car front entry garage

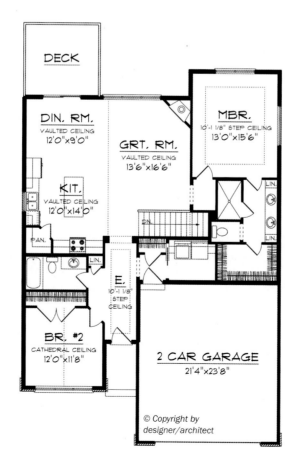

DECK

DIN. RM.
VAULTED CEILING
12'0"x9'0"

GRT. RM.
VAULTED CEILING
13'6"x16'6"

MBR.
10'-1 1/8" STEP CEILING
13'0"x15'6"

KIT.
VAULTED CEILING
12'0"x14'0"

PAN.

LIN.

E.
10'-1 1/8"
STEP
CEILING

DN.

LIN.

LIN.

BR. #2
CATHEDRAL CEILING
12'0"x11'8"

2 CAR GARAGE
21'4"x23'8"

© Copyright by
designer/architect

Images provided by designer/architect

Plan #F10-028D-0116

Dimensions:	28' W x 48' D
Heated Sq. Ft.:	1,120
Bedrooms: 2	**Bathrooms:** 2
Exterior Walls:	2" x 6"

Foundation: Floating slab standard; monolithic slab, crawl space, basement or walk-out basement for an additional fee

See index for more information

Images provided by designer/architect

Features

- Spacious and open this home's interior feels much larger than its true size thanks to the absence of walls between spaces

- The kitchen features a sizable island with seating for up to four people

- Two symmetrical bedrooms and baths comprise the rear of the home and offer equal amenities

- The laundry room has a handy sink and outdoor access

- The great room/dining area extend off the kitchen and provide a quality open living concept

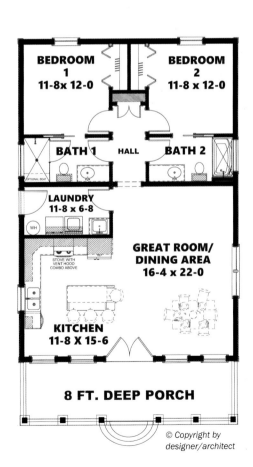

BEDROOM 1
11-8x 12-0

BEDROOM 2
11-8 x 12-0

BATH 1 HALL BATH 2

LAUNDRY
11-8 x 6-8

WH

STOVE WITH
VENT HOOD
COMBO ABOVE

GREAT ROOM/
DINING AREA
16-4 x 22-0

KITCHEN
11-8 X 15-6

8 FT. DEEP PORCH

© Copyright by
designer/architect

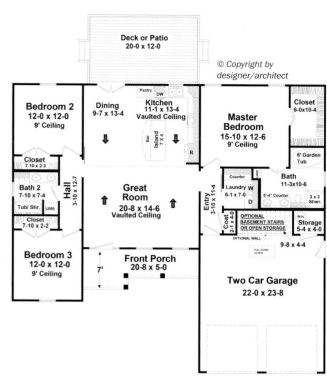

© Copyright by designer/architect

Deck or Patio 20-0 x 12-0

Bedroom 2 12-0 x 12-0 9' Ceiling

Closet 7-10 x 2-3

Bath 2 7-10 x 7-4

Closet 7-10 x 2-2

Bedroom 3 12-0 x 12-0 9' Ceiling

Dining 9-7 x 13-4

Pantry DW

Kitchen 11-1 x 13-4 Vaulted Ceiling

Bar Island 7 x 4

Hall 3-10 x 12-7

Great Room 20-8 x 14-6 Vaulted Ceiling

Master Bedroom 15-10 x 12-6 9' Ceiling

Closet 6-0x10-4

6' Garden Tub

Counter

Laundry W D 6-1 x 7-0

Bath 11-3x10-6

5'-4" Counter

3 x 3 Shwr.

Entry 3-10 x 11-4

Coat 2-1 x 4-0

OPTIONAL BASEMENT STAIRS OR OPEN STORAGE

OPTIONAL WALL

W.H. **Storage** 5-4 x 4-0

9-8 x 4-4

PULL DOWN STAIRS

Front Porch 20-8 x 5-0

7'

Two Car Garage 22-0 x 23-8

Plan #F10-077D-0294

Dimensions: 56' W x 62'4" D
Heated Sq. Ft.: 1,600
Bedrooms: 3   Bathrooms: 2
Foundation: Crawl space, slab, basement or daylight basement, please specify when ordering

See index for more information

Images provided by designer/architect

Plan #F10-123D-0171

Dimensions: 37' W x 49' D
Heated Sq. Ft.: 1,030
Bonus Sq. Ft.: 815
Bedrooms: 1   Bathrooms: 1½
Foundation: Basement standard; crawl space, slab or walk-out basement for an additional fee

See index for more information

Images provided by designer/architect

Br.2 11 x 11

UP

Fam. 13 x 19

Storage

Br.3 11 x 11

Lin

Optional
Lower Level
815 sq. ft.

D

Pantry

K. 15 x 14 10'-0" Ceiling

Lin.

Mbr. 12 x 13 10'-0" Ceiling

Din. 15 x 8 10'-0" Ceiling

Coffee Bar

R

W D

DN

Mud Room

Liv. 14 x 13 10'-0" Ceiling

Bench/ Lockers

Covered Porch

Gar. 19 x 22

© Copyright by designer/architect

First Floor
1,030 sq. ft.

Breezeway

© Copyright by designer/architect

DOUBLE GARAGE
20 x 22

COVERED/PATIO
BREEZEWAY
11 x 20

UTILITY
7 x 6

CLOSET
4 x 12

MASTER BEDROOM
12 x 16

HALL

STO
3 x 4

STUDY
7 x 6

KITCHEN
14 x 14

SHR
3 x 5

BATH
8 x 10

PAN

STO

DINING
10 x 12

FAMILY ROOM
13 x 18

PORCH
9 x 11

BEDROOM 3
13 x 17

LIN
STO
3 x 3

BATH #2
9 x 9

CLO
5 x 5

HALL

MECH
5 x 6

HVAC

CLO
5 x 5

BEDROOM 2
13 x 17

PORCH
BELOW

Garage
Attached Via
Breezeway

First Floor
1,210 sq. ft.

Second Floor
769 sq. ft.

Plan #F10-141D-0018

Dimensions:	23'9" W x 57' D
Heated Sq. Ft.:	1,979
Bedrooms: 3	**Bathrooms:** 2

Foundation: Slab standard; crawl space, basement or walk-out basement for an additional fee

See index for more information

Images provided by designer/architect

COVERED PATIO
30'-2" X 11'-9"

BEDROOM 2
13'-8" X 11'-1"

MASTER BDRM
14'-0" X 17'-5"

NOOK
10'-4" X 9'-9"

GREAT ROOM
20'-2" X 19'-3"

BEDROOM 3
15'-8" X 10'-6"

TLT
5'-8" X 6'-1"

MASTER BATH
8'-10" X 12'-9"

KITCHEN
13'-5" X 13'-9"

SHR
5'-8" X 6'-2"

GALLERY
11'-11" X 3'-9"

MSTR CLOSET
6'-11" X 10'-5"

LNDRY/FAM ENTRY
9'-6" X 9'-0"

OFFICE
9'-4" X 7'-3"

ENTRY
5'-6" X 11'-5"

FORMAL
11'-7" X 14'-5"

BEDROOM 4 / STUDY
13'-8" X 12'-4"

© Copyright by designer/architect

COVERED PORCH
11'-3" X 5'-0"

GARAGE
21'-0" X 29'-1"

Plan #F10-166D-0004

Dimensions:	63'10" W x 71'5" D
Heated Sq. Ft.:	2,512
Bedrooms: 4	**Bathrooms:** 3
Exterior Walls:	2" x 6"
Foundation:	Slab

See index for more information

Images provided by designer/architect

Plan #F10-011D-0662

Dimensions:	76' W x 62' D
Heated Sq. Ft.:	2,460
Bedrooms: 3	Bathrooms: 2½
Exterior Walls:	2" x 6"

Foundation: Crawl space or slab standard; basement for an additional fee

See index for more information

Images provided by designer/architect

Features

- Stunning curb appeal can be noted upon seeing this stylish one-story home
- The covered front porch welcomes you into the interior where you will find a formal dining room right off the foyer
- The vaulted great room enjoys direct access to the amazing vaulted outdoor living area with a fireplace, an outdoor kitchen and a sunny patio
- The bayed breakfast nook right off the kitchen will enjoy views of the outdoors
- The private master suite has a posh bath and a spacious walk-in closet with direct laundry room access
- Two additional bedrooms and a bath complete this home
- 2-car side entry garage

© Copyright by designer/architect

Plan #F10-032D-0885

Dimensions:	60' W x 43'6" D
Heated Sq. Ft.:	2,808
Bedrooms: 3	**Bathrooms:** 3
Exterior Walls:	2" x 6"

Foundation: Basement standard; crawl space, floating slab or monolithic slab for an additional fee

See index for more information

Features

- This stylish Contemporary would make an excellent home for a sloping lot, or as a vacation home thanks to its simple, uncluttered layout
- Enter the home at the lower level and discover small apartment style living with a kitchenette, a bedroom, a bath on one side, and another living space and bedroom on the other side
- The first floor above has a large kitchen, spacious open dining room, and a great room that merge to form the main gathering space
- 1-car front entry drive under garage

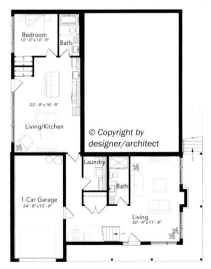

Lower Level
1,272 sq. ft.

First Floor
1,536 sq. ft.

Plan #F10-011D-0687

Dimensions:	74' W x 55' D
Heated Sq. Ft.:	1,975
Bedrooms: 4	Bathrooms: 2
Exterior Walls:	2" x 6"

Foundation: Crawl space or slab standard; basement for an additional fee

See index for more information

Images provided by designer/architect

© Copyright by designer/architect

Plan #F10-077D-0138

Images provided by designer/architect

Dimensions:	61' W x 47'4" D
Heated Sq. Ft.:	1,509
Bedrooms: 3	Bathrooms: 2

Foundation: Slab, crawl space or basement, please specify when ordering

See index for more information

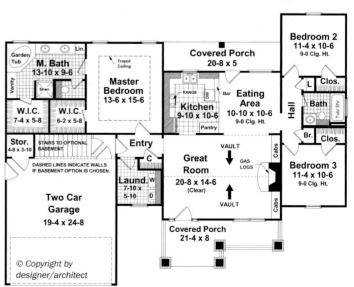

© Copyright by designer/architect

Plan #F10-008D-0134

Dimensions: 28' W x 32' D
Heated Sq. Ft.: 1,275
Bedrooms: 4 **Bathrooms:** 2
Foundation: Basement standard; crawl space or slab for an additional fee

See index for more information

Images provided by designer/architect

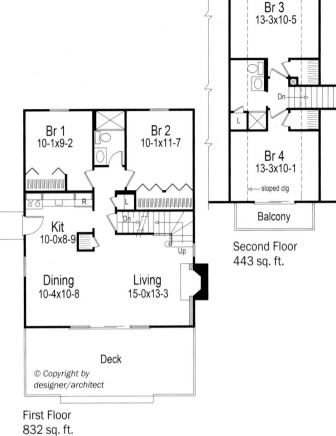

Br 3
13-3x10-5

Br 4
13-3x10-1
← sloped clg

Balcony

Second Floor
443 sq. ft.

Br 1
10-1x9-2

Br 2
10-1x11-7

Kit
10-0x8-9

Dining
10-4x10-8

Living
15-0x13-3

Up

Deck

© Copyright by designer/architect

First Floor
832 sq. ft.

Plan #F10-167D-0006

Dimensions: 68'11" W x 69'10" D
Heated Sq. Ft.: 2,939
Bedrooms: 4 **Bathrooms:** 3½
Exterior Walls: 2" x 6"
Foundation: Slab standard; crawl space for an additional fee

See index for more information

Images provided by designer/architect

M. BEDROOM
16'-7"x15'-0"

DINING
12'-6"x13'-6"

MEDIA
15'-8"x14'-0"

W.I.C.

M.BATH

BATH

LIVING
20'-5"x18'-10"

BEDROOM
12'-0"x12'-0"

KITCHEN
12'-6"x18'-10"

BATH

W.I.C.

LAUNDRY

PDR

BEDROOM
12'-0"x12'-0"

GARAGE
21'-5"x32'-6"

OFFICE
12'-6"x12'-0"

FOYER
7'-4"x17'-3"

BEDROOM
12'-6"x12'-0"

© Copyright by designer/architect

call 1-800-373-2646

Plan #F10-011S-0066

Dimensions:	80'6" W x 78' D
Heated Sq. Ft.:	4,270
Bedrooms:	4
Bathrooms:	3 full, 2 half
Exterior Walls:	2" x 6"
Foundation:	Daylight basement

See index for more information

Images provided by designer/architect

Features

- Three levels of stunning rustic Craftsmanship create a home perfect for a sloping lot, near a lake, or mountains
- Enjoy the outdoors with the exquisite porch that features a cozy fireplace
- The master bedroom has many amenities including a spa tub in the private bath and large walk-in closet
- A sizable island makes the kitchen very functional, while offering extra casual dining space near the breakfast nook
- There is also a walk-in pantry near the kitchen and an activity center, perfect for a computer, homework, or hobby time
- 2-car drive under front entry garage

Second Floor
1,543 sq. ft.

Lower Level
342 sq. ft.

First Floor
2,385 sq. ft.

© Copyright by designer/architect

Plan #F10-011D-0272

Dimensions:	40' W x 57' D
Heated Sq. Ft.:	1,899
Bedrooms: 2	Bathrooms: 2½
Exterior Walls:	2" x 6"

Foundation: Crawl space or slab standard; basement for an additional fee

See index for more information

Features

- Playful colors and sleek angles join forces and create a one-of-a-kind Contemporary home that's ready to stand out from the crowd, whether it's built in an urban or suburban setting

- Step inside and find an office ready for high function with a U-shaped built-in desk maximizing every last inch of square footage

- The living/dining space is all in one and has a built-in seat that spans the depth of the room offering a place to relax, or pull up a table and add extra dining space

- The kitchen has a sizable island that faces into the living/dining space unifying it with the surrounding spaces

- The second floor has a vaulted guest room with its own bath

- The master bedroom is also vaulted, has a sun-filled bath with an oversized shower, and a walk-in closet that can handle a plentiful wardrobe

- 2-car front entry garage

Second Floor
721 sq. ft.

First Floor
1,178 sq. ft.

© Copyright by designer/architect

Images provided by designer/architect

Plan #F10-101D-0044

Dimensions:	101'6" W x 82'8" D
Heated Sq. Ft.:	3,897
Bonus Sq. Ft.:	1,678
Bedrooms: 4	Bathrooms: 3½
Exterior Walls:	2" x 6"
Foundation:	Walk-out basement

See index for more information

Features

- No detail has been overlooked in this Craftsman inspired luxury home
- The first floor offers a central gathering spot with the great room that has direct access to the open kitchen that features a huge island with food preparation space, as well as, casual dining
- The covered deck wraps the rear of the home and includes a spot off the master bedroom with a pergola above and an outdoor fireplace
- The optional lower level has an additional 1,678 square feet of living area and is comprised of a game area, a TV room, an exercise room, a wet bar, and guest space with a bath
- The garage includes a toy storage space that could be designated for children's toys, or adult toys like an ATV or sports equipment
- 2-car front entry garage, and a 1-car side entry garage

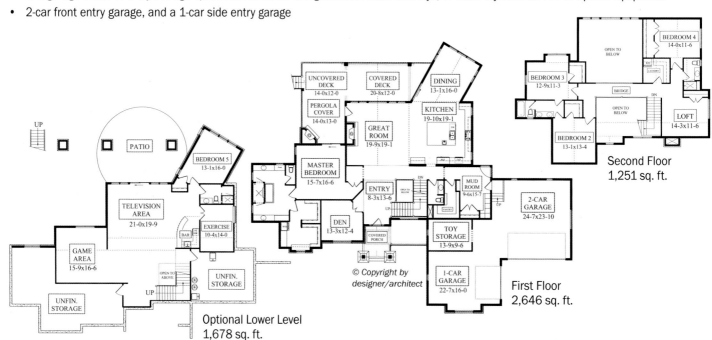

© Copyright by designer/architect

Optional Lower Level
1,678 sq. ft.

First Floor
2,646 sq. ft.

Second Floor
1,251 sq. ft.

Plan #F10-011D-0342

Dimensions:	63' W x 61'6" D
Heated Sq. Ft.:	2,368
Bedrooms: 3	**Bathrooms:** 2½
Exterior Walls:	2" x 6"

Foundation: Crawl space or slab standard; basement for an additional fee

See index for more information

Images provided by designer/architect

Features

- This Craftsman home's curb appeal will make it a standout in any neighborhood with its tasteful combination of stone, siding and gables
- The family chef will love the island kitchen, with its walk-in pantry and spacious snack bar
- The nearby laundry room is bright and cheerful, with plenty of counter space for folding clothes
- The secluded office could serve as a guest room, or a place for hobbies
- The well-appointed master suite features a vaulted ceiling, and a nice window arrangement with transoms overlooking the backyard
- A sit-down shower anchors the posh master bath, which also includes a private toilet, dual sinks and a walk-in closet
- 3-car front entry garage

First Floor
2,368 sq. ft.

© Copyright by designer/architect

Basement Stair Location

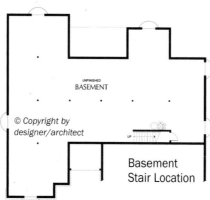

Plan #F10-055S-0127

Dimensions: 83'8" W x 88' D
Heated Sq. Ft.:   3,766
Bonus Sq. Ft.:   947
Bedrooms: 3   Bathrooms: 3½
Foundation: Slab or crawl space standard; basement or daylight basement for an additional fee

See index for more information

Features

- The enormous outdoor living/grilling porch features a corner stone fireplace and a convenient outdoor kitchen with a grill
- The beautiful beamed great room enjoys views of the backyard and covered porch
- The luxurious kitchen boasts two islands, one for the preparation of meals, and the other with seating space for casual dining
- Bedroom #4/optional game room has an additional 947 square feet of living area
- 3-car side entry garage

First Floor
3,766 sq. ft.

Optional
Second Floor
947 sq. ft.

Images provided by designer/architect

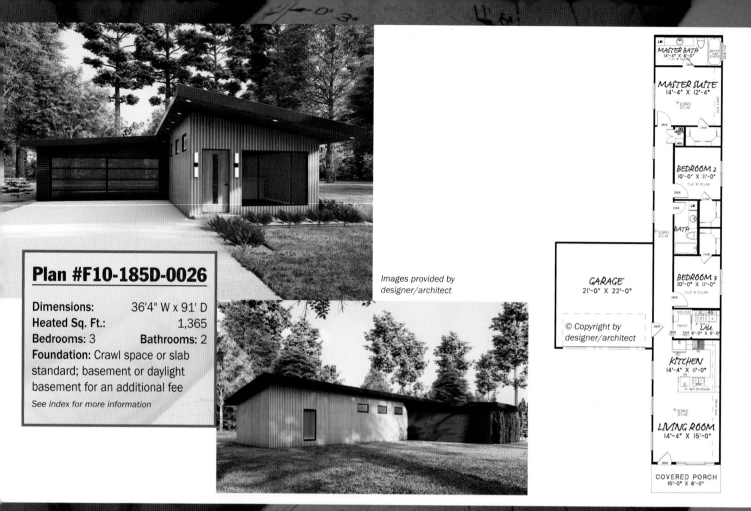

Plan #F10-185D-0026

Dimensions:	36'4" W x 91' D
Heated Sq. Ft.:	1,365
Bedrooms: 3	**Bathrooms:** 2

Foundation: Crawl space or slab standard; basement or daylight basement for an additional fee

See index for more information

Images provided by designer/architect

MASTER BATH
14'-4" X 8'-0"

MASTER SUITE
14'-4" X 12'-4"

BEDROOM 2
10'-0" X 11'-0"

BATH

GARAGE
21'-0" X 22'-0"

BEDROOM 3
10'-0" X 11'-0"

PANTRY   LAU.
6'-0" X 8'-0"

KITCHEN
14'-4" X 11'-0"

LIVING ROOM
14'-4" X 15'-0"

COVERED PORCH
15'-0" X 6'-0"

Plan #F10-026D-2134

Dimensions:	38' W x 55' D
Heated Sq. Ft.:	1,387
Bedrooms: 2	**Bathrooms:** 2

Foundation: Basement standard; crawl space, slab or walk-out basement for an additional fee

See index for more information

Images provided by designer/architect

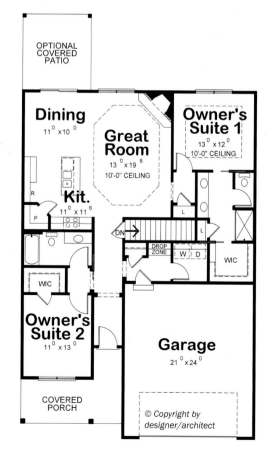

OPTIONAL COVERED PATIO

Dining
11'0" x 10'0"

Great Room
13'0" x 19'8"
10'-0" CEILING

Owner's Suite 1
13'0" x 12'0"
10'-0" CEILING

Kit.
11'0" x 11'6"

DN

DROP ZONE

W D

WIC

WIC

Owner's Suite 2
11'0" x 13'0"

Garage
21'0" x 24'0"

COVERED PORCH

Images provided by designer/architect

© Copyright by designer/architect

Plan #F10-055D-1077

Dimensions: 40'4" W x 60'2" D
Heated Sq. Ft.: 1,516
Bedrooms: 3   Bathrooms: 2
Foundation: Crawl space or slab standard; basement or daylight basement for an additional fee

See index for more information

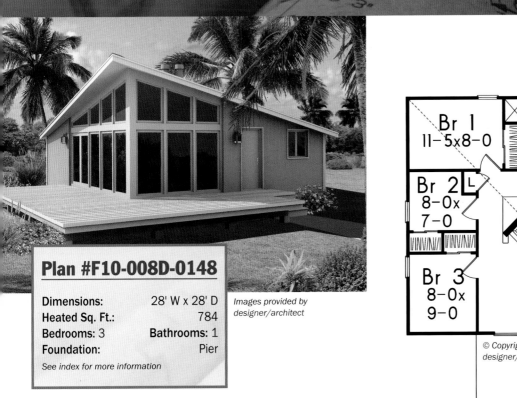

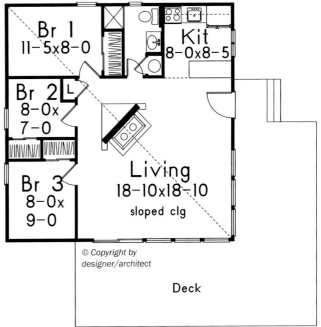

Images provided by designer/architect

© Copyright by designer/architect

Plan #F10-008D-0148

Dimensions: 28' W x 28' D
Heated Sq. Ft.: 784
Bedrooms: 3   Bathrooms: 1
Foundation: Pier

See index for more information

Plan #F10-161D-0028

Dimensions:	75' W x 119' D
Heated Sq. Ft.:	4,021
Bedrooms: 4	Bathrooms: 4½
Exterior Walls:	2" x 6"
Foundation:	Crawl space

See index for more information

Features

- This stunning modern masterpiece enjoys the luxury of two master suites on opposite ends of the house from one another creating total privacy
- The den is surrounded in windows for added light and outdoor views
- The kitchen, dining area and great room flow together offering a wonderfully large and inviting space
- There are plenty of outdoor living spaces including a terrace courtyard in the front and a covered outdoor space in the back including a spa space
- The bonus room is included in the second floor square footage
- 4-car side entry garage

Second Floor
926 sq. ft.

First Floor
3,095 sq. ft.

Images provided by designer/architect

houseplansandmore.com

Plan #F10-026D-1872

Dimensions:	58'4" W x 54' D
Heated Sq. Ft.:	2,495
Bonus Sq. Ft.:	402
Bedrooms: 4	**Bathrooms:** 3½

Foundation: Slab standard; crawl space, basement or walk-out basement for an additional fee

See index for more information

Images provided by designer/architect

Features

- The den offers flexibility creating space for a home office, a nursery, in-law suite, or dining
- The two-story great room has an open feel
- The island kitchen has dining space
- The first floor master suite enjoys a luxury bath, a walk-in closet, and a convenient washer and dryer
- The second floor has three bedrooms with walk-in closets, and easy access to the laundry room
- The bonus area on the second floor has an additional 402 square feet of living area
- 3-car side entry garage

Second Floor
831 sq. ft.

First Floor
1,664 sq. ft.

© Copyright by designer/architect

Plan #F10-065D-0372

Dimensions: 69'10" W x 64'10" D
Heated Sq. Ft.: 2,479
Bedrooms: 3 Bathrooms: 2½
Foundation: Basement standard;
crawl space for an additional fee

See index for more information

Images provided by designer/architect

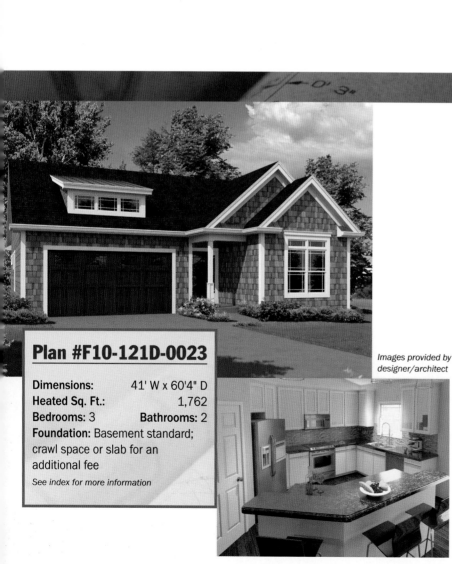

Plan #F10-121D-0023

Dimensions: 41' W x 60'4" D
Heated Sq. Ft.: 1,762
Bedrooms: 3 Bathrooms: 2
Foundation: Basement standard;
crawl space or slab for an
additional fee

See index for more information

Images provided by designer/architect

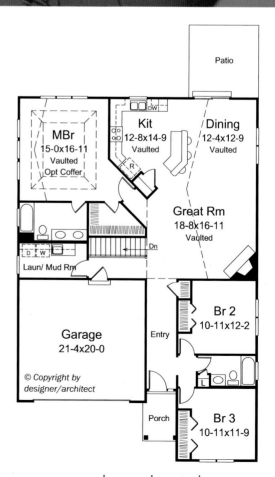

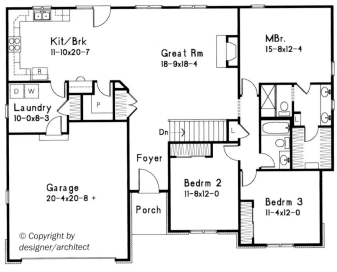

Plan #F10-058D-0249

Dimensions:	56'4" W x 42'4" D
Heated Sq. Ft.:	1,699
Bedrooms: 3	**Bathrooms:** 2
Foundation:	Basement

See index for more information

Images provided by designer/architect

© Copyright by designer/architect

Plan #F10-051D-0736

Dimensions:	40' W x 70'8" D
Heated Sq. Ft.:	1,662
Bedrooms: 2	**Bathrooms:** 2
Exterior Walls:	2" x 6"

Foundation: Basement standard; crawl space or slab for an additional fee

See index for more information

Images provided by designer/architect

© Copyright by designer/architect

Plan #F10-011S-0184

Dimensions:	123'11" W x 78'8" D
Heated Sq. Ft.:	5,266
Bedrooms:	5
Bathrooms:	3 full, 2 half
Exterior Walls:	2" x 6
Foundation:	Daylight basement

See index for more information

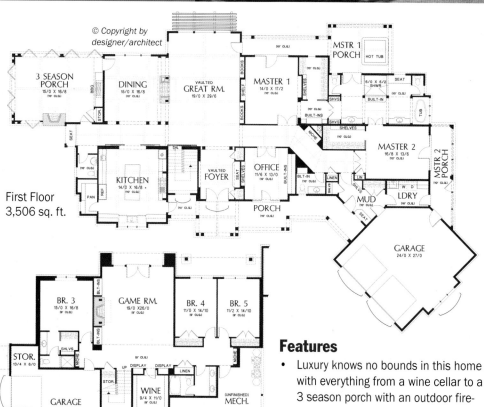

First Floor
3,506 sq. ft.

Lower Level
1,760 sq. ft.

Features

- Luxury knows no bounds in this home with everything from a wine cellar to a 3 season porch with an outdoor fireplace
- The first floor has a home office, mud and laundry rooms, two master suites, and a see-through fireplace shared by the dining and great rooms
- 2-car front entry garage, and a 1-car drive under side entry garage

Images provided by designer/architect

Plan #F10-032D-1104

Dimensions:	32' W x 30' D
Heated Sq. Ft.:	1,920
Bedrooms: 3	**Bathrooms:** 2
Exterior Walls:	2" x 6"

Foundation: Basement standard; crawl space for an additional fee

See index for more information

Features

- This stylish Modern Farmhouse inspired home has an open floor plan making it appear larger than its true size
- The kitchen features a large island with dining space and an oversized corner walk-in pantry with a window
- The master bedroom has a walk-in closet and enjoys the close proximity of the luxury bath
- The lower level enjoys a spacious laundry room with walk-in closet, an open family room, two additional bedrooms and a full bath

Images provided by designer/architect

© Copyright by designer/architect

First Floor
960 sq. ft.

Lower Level
960 sq. ft.

Images provided by designer/architect

Plan #F10-028D-0122

Dimensions:	56' W x 52' D
Heated Sq. Ft.:	2,352
Bedrooms: 3	Bathrooms: 2
Exterior Walls:	2" x 6"

Foundation: Floating slab standard; monolithic slab, crawl space, basement or walk-out basement for an additional fee

See index for more information

BEDROOM 1
16-8x13-0

COVERED PORCH 2

CLO

CUSTOM SHOWER

BATH

LAUNDRY

HVAC

KITCHEN
19-7 x 15-0

REF
PANTRY PANTRY

COUNTER-HIGH SNACK BAR

BEDROOM 3
14-0 x 12-0

BATH 2

GREAT ROOM
22-5 X 19-6

FIREPLACE

DINING AREA
19-7 x 19-6

BEDROOM 2
14-0 x 12-0

© Copyright by designer/architect   **COVERED PORCH 1**

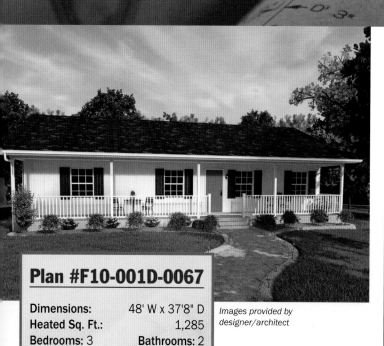

Plan #F10-001D-0067

Dimensions:	48' W x 37'8" D
Heated Sq. Ft.:	1,285
Bedrooms: 3	Bathrooms: 2

Foundation: Crawl space standard; basement or slab for an additional fee

See index for more information

Images provided by designer/architect

Storage

D W
W R

MBr
12-0x14-5

Furn

Kit
9-10x
10-11

Dining
10-3x
10-11

L   P

Br 2
15-6x10-8

Br 3
10-1x10-8

Living
18-10x14-2

Porch depth 6-0

© Copyright by designer/architect

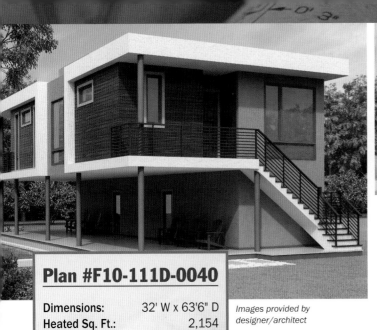

© Copyright by designer/architect

Plan #F10-111D-0040

Dimensions: 32' W x 63'6" D
Heated Sq. Ft.: 2,154
Bedrooms: 4   **Bathrooms:** 3
Foundation: Slab standard; crawl space for an additional fee

See index for more information

Images provided by designer/architect

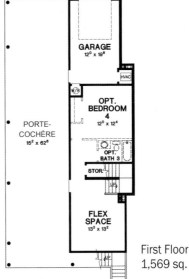

Lower Level
585 sq. ft.

First Floor
1,569 sq. ft.

Plan #F10-026D-2092

Dimensions: 45' W x 59'8" D
Heated Sq. Ft.: 2,448
Bedrooms: 4   **Bathrooms:** 3½
Foundation: Basement standard; crawl space or slab for an additional fee

See index for more information

Images provided by designer/architect

Second Floor
1,336 sq. ft.

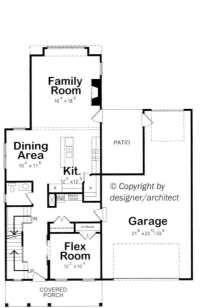

© Copyright by designer/architect

First Floor
1,112 sq. ft.

Plan #F10-071S-0001

Dimensions:	96' W x 145' D
Heated Sq. Ft.:	7,900
Bedrooms:	4
Bathrooms:	5 full, 2 half
Exterior Walls:	2" x 6"
Foundation:	Crawl space

See index for more information

Images provided by designer/architect

Features

- The grand, open kitchen has ample counter space and a center island
- A circular music room sits just off the living room providing entertainment and relaxation
- An impressive rotunda staircase leads you to the immense second floor that features all of the bedrooms, a theater, a kitchenette, and a game room with double-door access to a lovely deck
- 3-car side entry garage, 1-car side entry garage

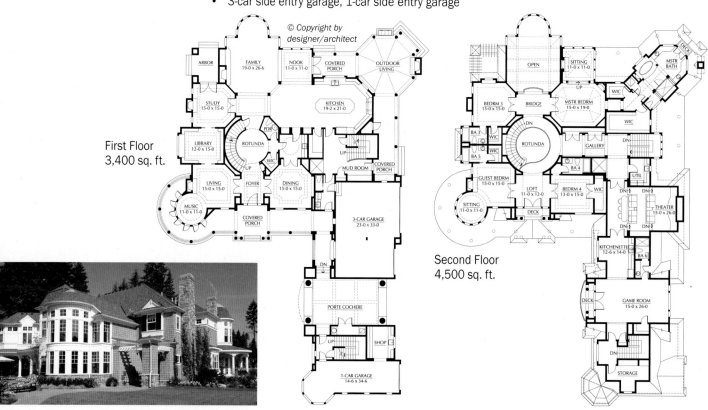

First Floor
3,400 sq. ft.

© Copyright by designer/architect

Second Floor
4,500 sq. ft.

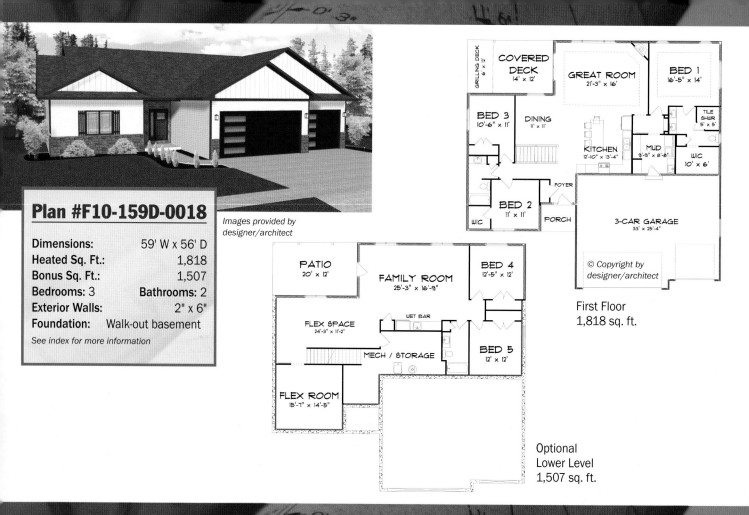

Plan #F10-159D-0018

Dimensions:	59' W x 56' D
Heated Sq. Ft.:	1,818
Bonus Sq. Ft.:	1,507
Bedrooms: 3	Bathrooms: 2
Exterior Walls:	2" x 6"
Foundation:	Walk-out basement

See index for more information

Images provided by designer/architect

© Copyright by designer/architect

First Floor
1,818 sq. ft.

Optional Lower Level
1,507 sq. ft.

Plan #F10-167D-0004

Dimensions:	42'4" W x 53' D
Heated Sq. Ft.:	2,589
Bonus Sq. Ft.:	465
Bedrooms: 4	Bathrooms: 3
Exterior Walls:	2" x 6"
Foundation:	Crawl space standard; slab for an additional fee

See index for more information

Optional Second Floor
465 sq. ft.

Detached Garage

Second Floor
754 sq. ft.

First Floor
1,835 sq. ft.

© Copyright by designer/architect

Images provided by designer/architect

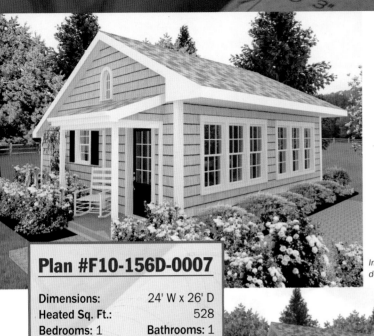

Bedroom
9'-6" × 10'-5"

Living area
11'-1" × 10'-9"

CLO.
2' x 8'-3"

Bath
5'-7" x 10'-7"

Kitchen
17'-5" × 10'-7"

PORCH
8'-1" X 3'-9"

© Copyright by
designer/architect

Plan #F10-156D-0007

Dimensions: 24' W x 26' D
Heated Sq. Ft.: 528
Bedrooms: 1   **Bathrooms:** 1
Foundation: Slab standard; crawl
space for an additional fee

See index for more information

*Images provided by
designer/architect*

Plan #F10-121D-0006

Dimensions: 68'4" W x 56' D
Heated Sq. Ft.: 2,241
Bedrooms: 4   **Bathrooms:** 2½
Exterior Walls: 2" x 6"
Foundation: Basement standard;
crawl space or slab for an
additional fee

See index for more information

*Images provided by
designer/architect*

Patio

Kitchen
15-4x18-4
11' Clg

MBr
15-1x17-4
Coffer Clg

Dining
12-2x16-4
11' Clg

Table

Brkfst Area

Br 3
13-8x11-0

Br 4/ Study
12-0x10-0

Dn

Laun/
Mud Rm
D W

Great Rm
20-1x16-11
11' Clg

Entry

Br 2
13-8x11-6

Garage
23-4x25-4

Porch

© Copyright by
designer/architect

Plan #F10-139D-0047

Dimensions:	73' W x 81'3" D
Heated Sq. Ft.:	4,086
Bedrooms: 4	**Bathrooms:** 4
Exterior Walls:	2" x 6"

Foundation: Walk-out basement standard; crawl space, slab, basement or daylight basement for an additional fee

See index for more information

Images provided by designer/architect

Features

- The floor plan of this home includes both casual and formal dining options, perfect for entertaining of all kinds
- A private office is located near the front entry and offers a sliding door for added privacy if needed
- The kitchen is filled with storage including an island with cabinets, a walk-in pantry and a nearby wet bar with cabinets above
- 3-car side entry garage

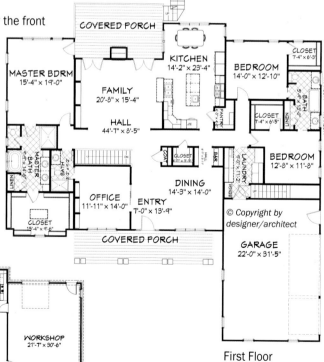

First Floor
2,720 sq. ft.

Lower Level
1,366 sq. ft.

© Copyright by designer/architect

Plan #F10-101D-0080

Dimensions:	79' W x 97'9" D
Heated Sq. Ft.:	2,682
Bonus Sq. Ft.:	1,940
Bedrooms: 2	Bathrooms: 2½
Exterior Walls:	2" x 6"

Foundation: Basement, daylight basement or walk-out basement, please specify when ordering

See index for more information

Features

- This home typifies the best in design with unique architectural features
- A family can enjoy the outdoors with the rear deck complete with a fireplace
- Private den with deck access is a secluded retreat
- The optional lower level has an additional 1,940 square feet of living area including three additional bedrooms, two baths, a laundry room, and rec room
- 3-car side entry garage

Images provided by designer/architect

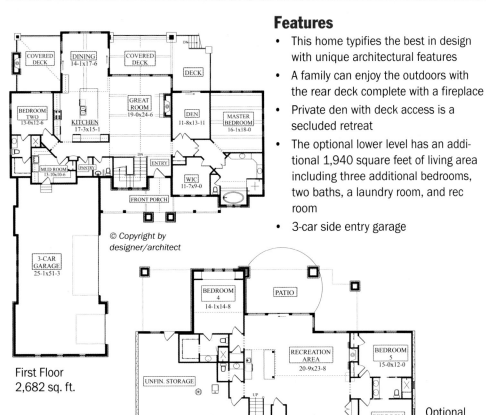

© Copyright by designer/architect

First Floor
2,682 sq. ft.

Optional
Lower Level
1,940 sq. ft.

Plan #F10-024D-0797

Dimensions:	48' W x 111' D
Heated Sq. Ft.:	2,780
Heated Sq. Ft.:	897
Bedrooms: 3	Bathrooms: 3
Foundation:	Floating slab

See index for more information

Images provided by designer/architect

Features

- The covered rear porch is a delight in every season with a corner fireplace for added warmth
- The living and dining rooms combine offering one large gathering space that is both beautiful and functional
- In addition to the utility room is a handy mud room with plenty of extra storage space
- The optional second floor has an additional 897 square feet of living area
- 2-car rear entry garage

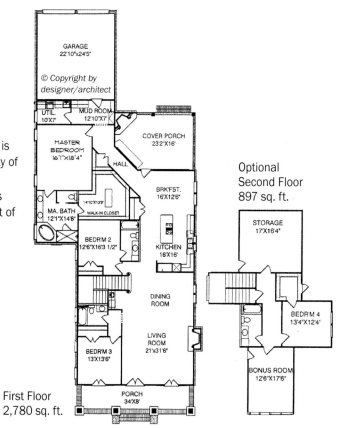

First Floor
2,780 sq. ft.

Optional
Second Floor
897 sq. ft.

houseplansandmore.com

Plan #F10-101D-0077

Dimensions:	68' W x 77' D
Heated Sq. Ft.:	2,422
Heated Sq. Ft.:	1,491
Bedrooms: 2	Bathrooms: 2½
Exterior Walls:	2" x 6"

Foundation: Basement or daylight basement, please specify when ordering

See index for more information

Images provided by designer/architect

Features

- Rustic ranch living has been achieved with this beautiful home
- The kitchen enjoys a massive island that overlooks the great room and dining area
- The master bedroom is tucked away nicely and includes a huge walk-in shower, and an oversized walk-in closet
- The spacious mud room/ laundry will keep everyone organized
- The optional lower level has an additional 1,491 square feet of living area and includes two additional bedrooms, a family room with wet bar, and an exercise room
- 2-car side entry garage, and a 1-car front entry garage

© Copyright by designer/architect

First Floor
2,422 sq. ft.

Optional
Lower Level
1,491 sq. ft.

bonus rooms & basements
finding flexibility within your home

You found it – the perfect dream home! It has the exact number of bedrooms and bathrooms. The open floor plan is great. The kitchen is spacious, the mud room ideal, and the storage is awesome. You even have a bonus room. Now, what to do with that space? Here lies the beauty of this space – you can do whatever you like! From newlyweds to families of five, the bonus room holds numerous possibilities for every homeowner to customize their design as they see fit. Many one-story homes today are designed with bonus or flex spaces that give families that wiggle room when additional space is needed. Let your imagination run wild! There are so many opportunities to make this your area for fun, fitness, work or relaxation; you name it.

think big
Maximize your home's fun quotient by finishing your flex or bonus space for a big time fun spot everyone will love! Better yet, your basement may be below ground, but there's nothing sub-par about these ideas!

Unless noted, copyright by designer/architect; Page 282, top, left: Plan #101D-0197; above: Plan #101D-0199; Page 283, top: Plan #F10-011S-0018 on page 167; Bonus room playroom, istockphoto.com; Plan #F10-055D-0748 on page 109; Plan #101S-0019; See more photos or to purchase plans, please visit houseplansandmore.com.

here's some favorites

play room

Every mom wishes she had a place where she could put those extra toys, keeping them from clashing with her living room décor, or ending up under her feet while she tries to fix dinner. So why not put that bonus room to good use as a designated play room? Organizational systems of cubbies, baskets, and shelves will keep an unruly collection of toys organized, while providing enough space to enjoy playing with them. Bean bag chairs and play rugs in bright colors keep the room fun and functional. You could even break the room down into stations – an art area with chalkboard paint walls for your budding Van Gogh, a reading corner with special pillows and lighting, or a block table for the young architect. Keep this room child-friendly and fun and your kids will flock there, all while keeping the mess out of the rest of the house.

the home theater

To turn your bonus room into your own personal theater experience, you need surprisingly few items. A quality television, proper media players, and surround sound are the best setup. Now that your theater is functional it's time to personalize your movie watching experience. Are you going to put in oversized reclining chairs and couches, or movie theater seats? Will you put in dimming ambient lights? How about a popcorn machine? After all, the primary reason you have a home theater is to enjoy cinema entertainment in unsurpassed comfort. Some homeowners with serious theater systems choose to have professional input and installation. Whether home designed or professionally outfitted, the home theater is a bonus room design enjoyed by all.

the family gathering spot

Often called a recreation or game room, this family gathering spot is the place where family can get together and relax. Filled with games, movies, and perhaps a snack area or wet bar, this bonus room use is great for families that need an informal space to hang out in that doesn't necessarily need to be kept perfect like the highly visible great room. Keep this space cozy and inviting for making family memories.

the home gym

We all know someone who has purchased home workout equipment only to realize that the plan was not thought out. Bulky equipment is a pain to set up and take down everyday, so it often goes unused. If the equipment is left out, those machines always manage to take up awkward amounts of space. Even small free weights often find themselves in the way, causing stubbed toes and storage woes. Turning your bonus room into a home gym, or exercise room creates a designated space for all that equipment, plus it allows options of customized flooring or built-in sound systems. It will definitely make exercising less of a chore since you won't have to leave the house!

the home office

If you choose to work from home, there is no more valuable a space than a bonus room that's been turned into a home office. Remember that your home office is a reflection of you and the work you produce. Make it a priority to keep the space efficient and eye-appealing with necessary storage, noise buffers, and organizational systems. Keeping this room working for you makes working from home a pleasant affair and ensures the bonus room is never a wasted space.

double your square footage ╋ customize your basement into something special

many of today's one-story homes like the ones featured in this book are designed with an optional lower level. Offering flexibility if additional square footage is needed or desired, finishing a lower level can instantly increase a home's square footage providing added bedrooms, gathering space, or whatever you need to make your home more functional and work for you. Gone are the days of a home's basement being only used as a place for old boxes. The basements, or lower levels of today are nothing in comparison. Basement storage is being transformed into finished family spaces. The most popular options are best broken into specialized areas. From gaming to movie theaters, much like a bonus or flex room, your basement can be designed to your unique desires.

need ideas?

game on

What you do with your dedicated game room depends on the game to be played. Families may choose to have a special table for game play, with shelves installed to organize their extensive board game collections. Poker, or Texas Hold'em are popular and if you love to play, then a personalized table, chips, and cards would be great additions to this space. Pool tables, air hockey, shuffleboard, and even full-scale arcade games are also available for purchase, allowing fans to recreate their favorite gaming experiences – without worrying about their high scores being challenged!

make the most of the media

As family lifestyles become more hectic, the free time they spend together is often wanted at home. The availability of flat screen smart televisions, surround sound (often wireless), and multiple video, audio, gaming systems and apps allow any media experience to be enjoyed at full capacity without ever leaving home. Specialized lighting can add the appropriate ambiance when movie watching or having gaming tournaments with just a click of the remote.

lounging around

For some families, extra space is best outfitted with the amenities needed to relax. Cozy furniture, warm lighting, blankets and bookshelves create a desirable place to retreat to while enjoying one another's company.

Many families choose to mix and match the different suggestions, creating zones of activity within the basement. Additionally, refreshment centers are becoming more popular in finished basements, adding to the level of comfort. These can be uniquely designed, ranging from full-scale kitchens to specialized wet bars. Wine cellars and humidors are also popular in many households. Keep in mind that with refreshments usually come bathrooms. Full baths, saunas, hot tubs, and even guest rooms are prevalent in basements when resources allow.

When it comes to decorating and creating a specific atmosphere, it may be best to consider a theme. This works particularly well for dedicated rooms. If you are choosing to outfit your basement for multiple uses, stick to something that will be enjoyed by everyone without overshadowing any particular area. Your basement is one more opportunity to show how creative you are – so, don't hold back!

Attempt to use as much of the space as you can. Vertical shelves are great for visible, neat storage, while also giving you further places to display pictures and other treasures while also promoting a feeling of spaciousness with their height.

hot tip

Make your finished basement feel like an extension of your main level. Use the same finishes and remove the doors that separate each floor and now you have twice the house with twice the personality and comfort!

hit the floor

Flooring is important, and the basement will likely be exposed to heavy traffic flow. Durability and comfort are both vital in addition to stain resistance and sound proofing. Cork flooring is growing in popularity for these reasons. Another popular choice is luxury vinyl laminate, or ceramic tile. Both of these options can look exactly like stone or wood flooring, but are entirely waterproof, perfect for damper environments like basements and areas where there will be plenty of entertaining and the chance for frequent spills.

let there be light

Recessed lighting eliminates overhead and wasting floor space, but can be expensive. Sconces are another idea to prevent wasting precious entertainment space, but try to include as much natural light as possible to avoid the feeling of being underground. Today, many areas have code requirements for egress windows in basements, these windows are larger than their traditional counterparts and allow much more natural light to filter into the space. They alleviate the feeling of a dark, damp basement instantly, and they also allow any bedroom designed into a basement space to be considered a true bedroom when you plan to resell your home. Per code, a bedroom must have a proper escape method if there's a fire, and an egress window is large enough for just that.

make it multi-task

Some homeowners like the idea of multiple uses but really desire the peace of reading a book without overhearing the poker game going on across the room. Don't give up the hope of having both a flexible and functional recreation room. Curtain rails and bi-fold doors/walls can be installed, sectioning off areas in use or opening up the room to its greatest space potential, perfect for privacy or parties.

As you ponder finishing your basement with a festive and fun game room, or a tranquil spa and meditation area, keep in mind the space allowed as well as your budget, time constrictions and future needs. Measure the area and plan for traffic flow and adequate seating. It will be beneficial to pick a large space and plot the exact layout you desire. Homeowners are often surprised to find that a simple ping-pong table can take up a third of a room's floor space when unfolded. It is essential to have a defined plan for what amenities you definitely need to include in your new basement, in addition to where they will be located. Then, discuss your desires with your contractor. They can re-evaluate your design, ensuring the availability of your preferences. Although tempting, avoid purchasing items until your contractor has agreed to a layout. If you already own specific items, inform your contractor of their existence so those components are not ruled out when adjustments are made. With a little creativity, your former damp, dark basement will become the family's favorite gathering place, or the much-needed comfortable guest or living quarters you've always wanted.

Second Floor
1,481 sq. ft.

First Floor
1,025 sq. ft.

Plan #F10-026D-2007

Dimensions:	40' W x 48' D
Heated Sq. Ft.:	2,506
Bedrooms: 5	Bathrooms: 3½
Exterior Walls:	2" x 6"

Foundation: Basement standard; crawl space or slab for an additional fee

See index for more information

Images provided by designer/architect

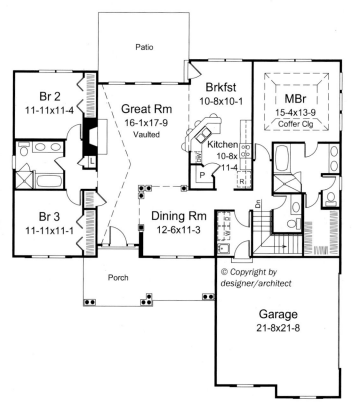

Plan #F10-121D-0040

Dimensions:	58' W x 58' D
Heated Sq. Ft.:	1,863
Bedrooms: 3	Bathrooms: 2½

Foundation: Basement standard; crawl space or slab for an additional fee

See index for more information

Images provided by designer/architect

Plan #F10-167D-0002

Dimensions:	74' W x 49'5" D
Heated Sq. Ft.:	2,063
Bedrooms: 3	Bathrooms: 2½
Exterior Walls:	2" x 6"

Foundation: Slab standard; crawl space for an additional fee

See index for more information

Images provided by designer/architect

© Copyright by designer/architect

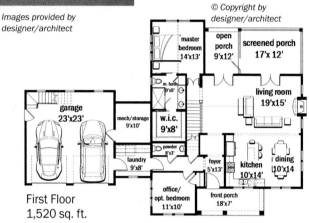

First Floor
1,520 sq. ft.

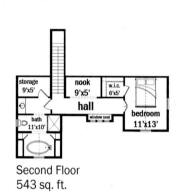

Second Floor
543 sq. ft.

Plan #F10-141D-0315

Dimensions:	25' W x 40' D
Heated Sq. Ft.:	750
Bedrooms: 1	Bathrooms: 1
Exterior Walls:	2" x 6"
Foundation:	Pier

See index for more information

Images provided by designer/architect

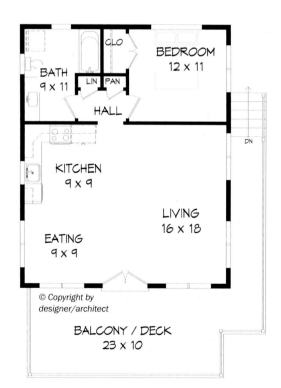

© Copyright by designer/architect

Plan #F10-026D-1913

Dimensions: 34' W x 60'4" D
Heated Sq. Ft.: 3,322
Bedrooms: 6   **Bathrooms:** 3½
Exterior Walls: 2" x 6"
Foundation: Basement standard; walk-out basement for an additional fee

See index for more information

Images provided by designer/architect

Features

- This eye-catching modern home is very unique and eclectic
- The two-story living room has an open atmosphere and brings the outdoors with its large windows
- The lower level includes a family room, two bedrooms, and a bath making it a private living space all to itself, and there's also space for mechanical equipment, storage and cold storage
- Tucked away by the garage is an office and a half bath with a private entrance
- The laundry room is centrally located on the second floor for convenience to the bedrooms
- 3-car rear entry garage

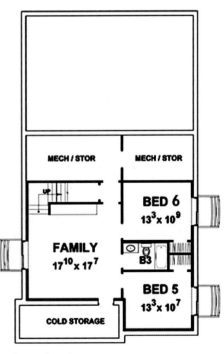

Lower Level
806 sq. ft.

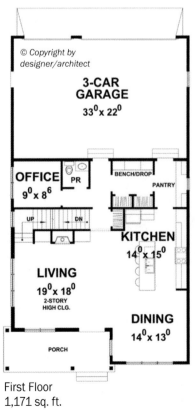
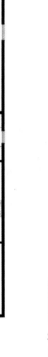

First Floor
1,171 sq. ft.

Second Floor
1,345 sq. ft.

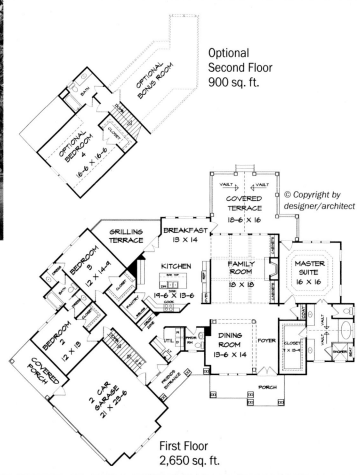

Optional
Second Floor
900 sq. ft.

OPTIONAL
BONUS ROOM

BATH

OPTIONAL
BEDROOM
4
16-6 X 16-6

CLOSET

© Copyright by
designer/architect

VAULT VAULT

COVERED
TERRACE
18-6 X 16

GRILLING
TERRACE

BREAKFAST
13 X 14

BEDROOM
3
12 X 14-9

KITCHEN
19-6 X 13-6

FAMILY
ROOM
18 X 18

MASTER
SUITE
16 X 16

PANTRY

BEDROOM
2
12 X 13

UTIL

DINING
ROOM
13-6 X 14

FOYER

CLOSET

VAULT

SHOWER SEAT

COVERED
PORCH

2 CAR
GARAGE
21 X 23-6

POWDER
RM

FRIENDS
ENTRANCE

PORCH

First Floor
2,650 sq. ft.

Plan #F10-076D-0210

Images provided by designer/architect

Dimensions: 91'9" W x 76'4" D
Heated Sq. Ft.:   2,650
Bonus Sq. Ft.:   900
Bedrooms: 3   **Bathrooms:** 2½
Foundation: Basement, crawl space or slab, please specify when ordering

See index for more information

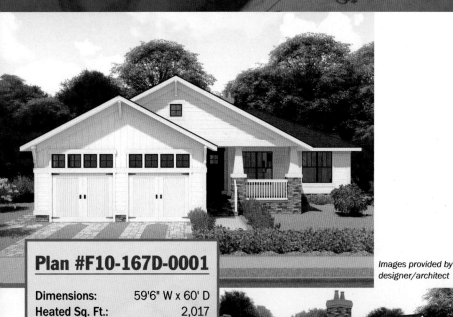

OWNER'S
SUITE
14'11"X13'7"

DINING
11'10"X10'3"

SCREENED
PORCH

GREAT ROOM
16'8" X 18'3"

BED 3
12'4" X 11'0"

O'S BATH

KITCHEN

BATH

WIC

WIC

WIC

UTIL.

BATH

WIC

BED 2
12'4"X11'0"

GARAGE
24'5" X 22'0"

FOYER

STUDY
11'1"X11'7"

FRONT PORCH

© Copyright by
designer/architect

Images provided by designer/architect

Plan #F10-167D-0001

Dimensions: 59'6" W x 60' D
Heated Sq. Ft.:   2,017
Bedrooms: 3   **Bathrooms:** 3
Exterior Walls: 2" x 6"
Foundation: Crawl space standard; slab for an additional fee

See index for more information

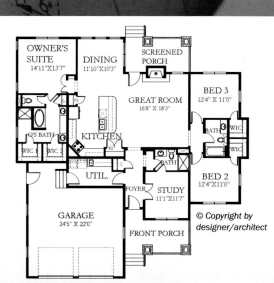

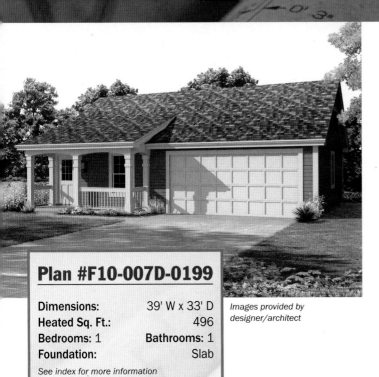

Plan #F10-007D-0199

Dimensions:	39' W x 33' D
Heated Sq. Ft.:	496
Bedrooms: 1	Bathrooms: 1
Foundation:	Slab

See index for more information

Images provided by designer/architect

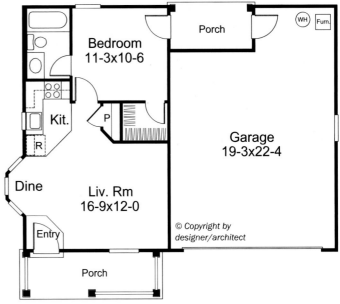

© Copyright by designer/architect

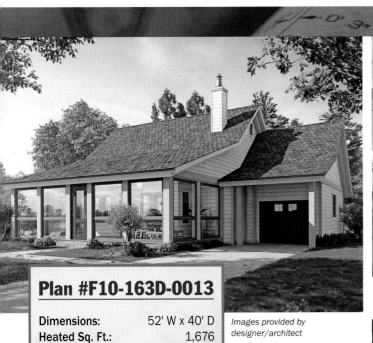

Plan #F10-163D-0013

Dimensions:	52' W x 40' D
Heated Sq. Ft.:	1,676
Bedrooms: 3	Bathrooms: 3
Exterior Walls:	2" x 6"

Foundation: Crawl space or slab, please specify when ordering

See index for more information

Images provided by designer/architect

Second Floor
257 sq. ft.

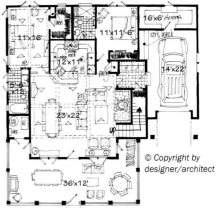

© Copyright by designer/architect

First Floor
1,419 sq. ft.

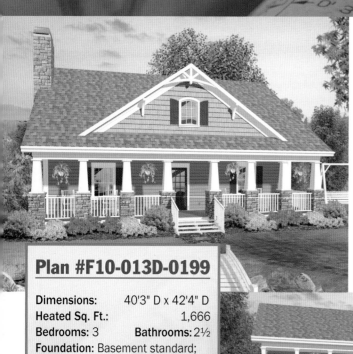

Second Floor
607 sq. ft.

First Floor
1,059 sq. ft.

© Copyright by
designer/architect

Images provided by
designer/architect

Plan #F10-013D-0199

Dimensions: 40'3" D x 42'4" D
Heated Sq. Ft.: 1,666
Bedrooms: 3   Bathrooms: 2½
Foundation: Basement standard;
crawl space or slab for an
additional fee

See index for more information

Lower Level

Plan #F10-121D-0047

Dimensions: 60' W x 70' D
Heated Sq. Ft.: 1,983
Bonus Sq. Ft.: 404
Bedrooms: 3   Bathrooms: 2
Foundation: Basement standard;
crawl space or slab for an
additional fee

See index for more information

Images provided by
designer/architect

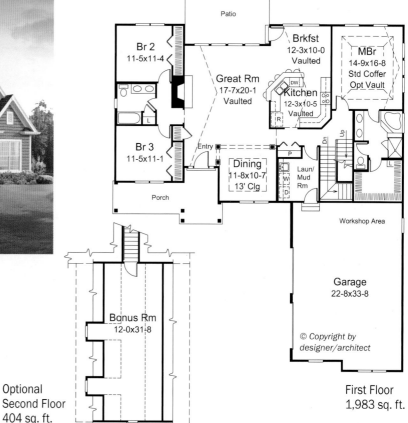

Optional
Second Floor
404 sq. ft.

First Floor
1,983 sq. ft.

© Copyright by
designer/architect

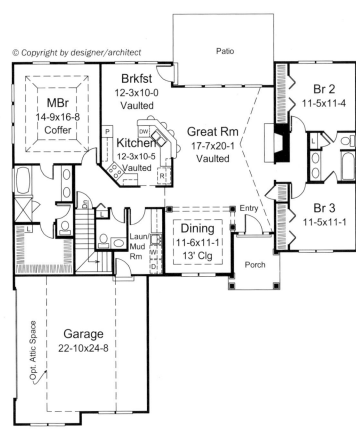

Patio

Brkfst
12-3x10-0
Vaulted

MBr
14-9x16-8
Coffer

Kitchen
12-3x10-5
Vaulted

Great Rm
17-7x20-1
Vaulted

Br 2
11-5x11-4

Br 3
11-5x11-1

Entry

Laun/
Mud
Rm

Dining
11-6x11-1
13' Clg

Porch

Opt. Attic Space

Garage
22-10x24-8

Images provided by designer/architect

Plan #F10-121D-0015

Dimensions:	60' W x 61' D
Heated Sq. Ft.:	1,983
Bonus Sq. Ft.:	273
Bedrooms: 3	Bathrooms: 2½

Foundation: Basement standard; crawl space or slab for an additional fee

See index for more information

COVERED PORCH
12' x 10'

CLOS.
5' x 6'

M. BATH
10'6" x 16'

M. BEDROOM
(VAULTED)
14'6" x 16'

KIT.
12' x 11'

DINING ROOM
11' x 16'

BED #2
12' x 12'

CLOS.
5' x 6'

BATH

STOR.
11' x 8'

UTIL.
6'6" x 8'

ENTRY

COAT

GREAT ROOM
23' x 16'

HALL

LIN

MEDIA
8' x 9'

ATTIC ACCESS

2 CAR GARAGE
22' x 22'

COVERED PORCH
23' x 4'

BED #3
12' x 12'

Images provided by designer/architect

Plan #F10-077D-0052

Dimensions:	65' W x 50'10" D
Heated Sq. Ft.:	1,802
Bedrooms: 3	Bathrooms: 2

Foundation: Slab, crawl space or basement or daylight basement, please specify when ordering

See index for more information

Optional
Second Floor
591 sq. ft.

Plan #F10-091D-0506

Images provided by designer/architect

Dimensions:	82' W x 71' D
Heated Sq. Ft.:	2,241
Bonus Sq. Ft.:	591
Bedrooms: 3	Bathrooms: 2½
Exterior Walls:	2" x 6"

Foundation: Basement standard; slab, crawl space, daylight basement or walk-out basement for an additional fee

See index for more information

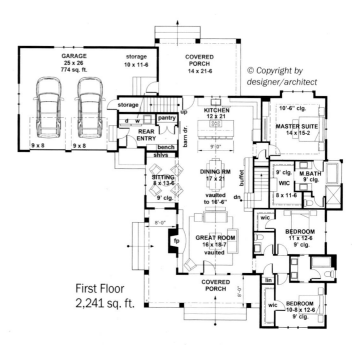

© Copyright by designer/architect

First Floor
2,241 sq. ft.

Plan #F10-143D-0005

Images provided by designer/architect

Dimensions:	50'4" W x 27'6" D
Heated Sq. Ft.:	1,381
Bedrooms: 3	Bathrooms: 2
Exterior Walls:	2" x 6"

Foundation: Basement, crawl space or slab, please specify when ordering

See index for more information

© Copyright by designer/architect

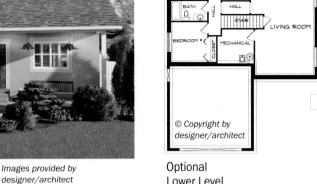

**Optional
Lower Level
1,069 sq. ft.**

**First Floor
1,069 sq. ft.**

© Copyright by
designer/architect

Plan #F10-172D-0023

*Images provided by
designer/architect*

Dimensions:	39'6" W x 49' D
Heated Sq. Ft.:	1,069
Bonus Sq. Ft.:	1,069
Bedrooms: 2	**Bathrooms:** 2

Foundation: Basement standard;
crawl space, monolithic slab, stem
wall slab, daylight basement or
walk-out basement for an
additional fee

See index for more information

**Second Floor
2,054 sq. ft.**

© Copyright by designer/architect

Plan #F10-088D-0608

*Images provided by
designer/architect*

Dimensions:	74'6" W x 57' D
Heated Sq. Ft.:	4,234
Bonus Sq. Ft.:	1,594
Bedrooms: 4	**Bathrooms:** 3½
Exterior Walls:	2" x 6"

Foundation: Partial basement/
crawl space

See index for more information

**Optional
Lower Level
1,594 sq. ft.**

**First Floor
2,180 sq. ft.**

Plan #F10-155D-0171

Dimensions:	53'8" W x 41'4" D
Heated Sq. Ft.:	1,131
Bedrooms: 3	**Bathrooms:** 2
Foundation: Crawl space or slab, please specify when ordering	

See index for more information

Images provided by designer/architect

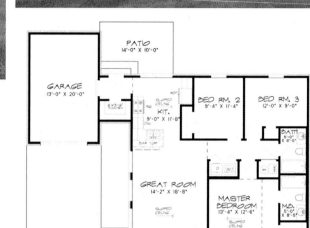

PATIO
14'-0" X 10'-0"

GARAGE
13'-0" X 20'-0"

KIT.
9'-0" X 11'-8"

BED RM. 2
9'-4" X 11'-4"

BED RM. 3
12'-0" X 9'-0"

GREAT ROOM
14'-2" X 18'-8"

MASTER BEDROOM
13'-4" X 12'-6"

SLOPED CEILING

SLOPED CEILING

Plan #F10-181D-0002

Dimensions:	60' W x 50' D
Heated Sq. Ft.:	1,578
Bonus Sq. Ft.:	1,158
Bedrooms: 3	**Bathrooms:** 2½
Exterior Walls:	2" x 6"
Foundation: Slab standard; crawl space or basement for an additional fee	

Please see the index for more information

Images provided by designer/architect

Second Floor
1,158 sq. ft.

MASTER BEDROOM
20'x11'7"

PERGOLA OVER DECK
16'11"x12'

MASTER BATHROOM
6'6"x7'8"

LIVING /DINING
25'x16'

BEDROOM
12'9"x10'2"

WARDROBE
12'10"x7'8"

LAUNDRY
6'9"x6'3"

BATHROOM
9'2"x9'2"

KITCHEN
16'2"x10'5"

FOYER
5'6"x10'5"

BEDROOM
12'9"x10'1"

GARAGE
20'x20'2"

FRONT PORCH
8'4"x8'0"

First Floor
1,578 sq. ft.

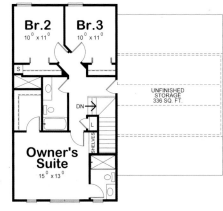

Second Floor
752 sq. ft.

Br.2
10⁰ x 11⁰

Br.3
10⁰ x 11⁰

UNFINISHED STORAGE 336 SQ. FT.

Owner's Suite
15⁰ x 13⁰

Plan #F10-026D-2079

Images provided by designer/architect

Dimensions: 42' W x 42' D
Heated Sq. Ft.: 1,600
Bonus Sq. Ft.: 336
Bedrooms: 3   **Bathrooms:** 2½
Foundation: Basement standard; crawl space, slab or walk-out basement for an additional fee

See index for more information

Kit.
10⁰ x 12⁶

Dining Area
10⁴ x 10⁰

DROP ZONE

STORAGE

POCKET OFFICE

Garage
20⁸ x 24⁰

Family Room
16⁸ x 17⁰

© Copyright by designer/architect

First Floor
848 sq. ft.

COVERED PORCH

Plan #F10-032D-1143

Images provided by designer/architect

Dimensions: 37' W x 38' D
Heated Sq. Ft.: 1,891
Bonus Sq. Ft.: 880
Bedrooms: 3   **Bathrooms:** 2½
Exterior Walls: 2" x 6"
Foundation: Basement standard; crawl space, monolithic slab or floating slab for an additional fee

See index for more information

Second Floor
1,011 sq. ft.

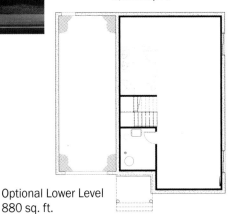

First Floor
880 sq. ft.

© Copyright by designer/architect

Optional Lower Level
880 sq. ft.

Second Floor
947 sq. ft.

Plan #F10-111D-0095

Dimensions: 46' W x 50'8" D
Heated Sq. Ft.: 2,458
Bedrooms: 3 **Bathrooms:** 3
Foundation: Slab standard; crawl
space for an additional fee

See index for more information

Images provided by designer/architect

© Copyright by designer/architect

First Floor
1,511 sq. ft.

Plan #F10-141D-0021

Dimensions: 33'4" W x 46' D
Heated Sq. Ft.: 1,267
Bedrooms: 2 **Bathrooms:** 2
Foundation: Pier standard; slab,
crawl space, basement or walk-out
basement for an additional fee

See index for more information

Images provided by designer/architect

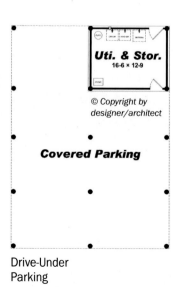

© Copyright by designer/architect

Drive-Under Parking

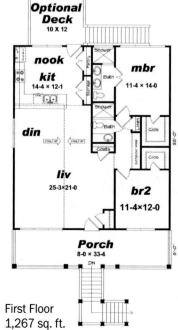

First Floor
1,267 sq. ft.

Images provided by
designer/architect

© Copyright by
designer/architect

Plan #F10-013D-0257

Dimensions: 40'3" W x 42'4" D
Heated Sq. Ft.: 1,059
Bedrooms: 2   **Bathrooms:** 1½
Foundation: Basement standard;
crawl space or slab for an
additional fee

See index for more information

Plan #F10-077D-0297

Dimensions: 37'2" W x 36' D
Heated Sq. Ft.: 904
Bedrooms: 1   **Bathrooms:** 1½
Foundation: Basement or daylight
basement, please specify when
ordering; for crawl space or slab
versions of this plan, see Plan
#077D-0296 at
houseplansandmore.com

See index for more information

Images provided by
designer/architect

© Copyright by
designer/architect

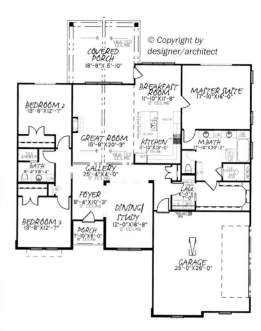

Images provided by designer/architect

Plan #F10-155D-0179

Dimensions: 60'8" W x 73'10" D
Heated Sq. Ft.: 2,382
Bedrooms: 3 **Bathrooms:** 2
Foundation: Crawl space or slab standard; basement or daylight basement for an additional fee

See index for more information

First Floor
1,787 sq. ft.

Images provided by designer/architect

Plan #F10-007D-0085

Dimensions: 59'8" W x 40' D
Heated Sq. Ft.: 1,787
Bonus Sq. Ft.: 415
Bedrooms: 3 **Bathrooms:** 2
Foundation: Walk-out basement

See index for more information

Optional
Lower Level
415 sq. ft.

Plan #F10-028D-0106

Dimensions: 68' W x 84' D
Heated Sq. Ft.: 2,525
Bedrooms: 3 **Bathrooms:** 2½
Exterior Walls: 2" x 6"
Foundation: Basement standard; floating slab, monolithic slab, crawl space or walk-out basement for an additional fee

See index for more information

Images provided by designer/architect

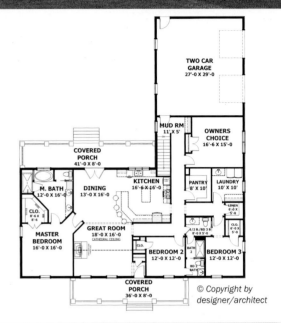

© Copyright by designer/architect

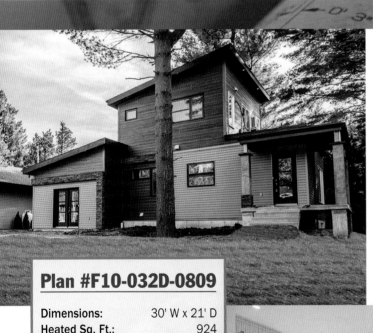

Plan #F10-032D-0809

Dimensions: 30' W x 21' D
Heated Sq. Ft.: 924
Bedrooms: 2 **Bathrooms:** 2
Exterior Walls: 2" x 6"
Foundation: Floating slab standard; crawl space or monolithic slab for an additional fee

See index for more information

Images provided by designer/architect

Second Floor
294 sq. ft.

© Copyright by designer/architect

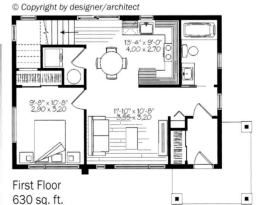

First Floor
630 sq. ft.

Plan #F10-101D-0047

Dimensions:	99' W x 81' D
Heated Sq. Ft.:	2,478
Bonus Sq. Ft.:	1,795
Bedrooms: 2	Bathrooms: 2½
Exterior Walls:	2" x 6"
Foundation:	Walk-out basement

See index for more information

Images provided by designer/architect

Features

- The architectural style of this home has interesting features and great curb appeal

- Directly off the foyer is a study that is private and could easily be converted to a home office

- Open living at its finest with the combination of the great room, kitchen and dining area for a relaxed casual atmosphere

- The master bedroom features double walk-in closets, and a bath with a separate tub and shower and a double bowl vanity

- The optional lower level has an additional 1,795 square feet of living area and features a craft area, a sitting area, a family room, two additional bedrooms and a bath

- 5-car front entry tandem garage, and a 2-car side entry garage

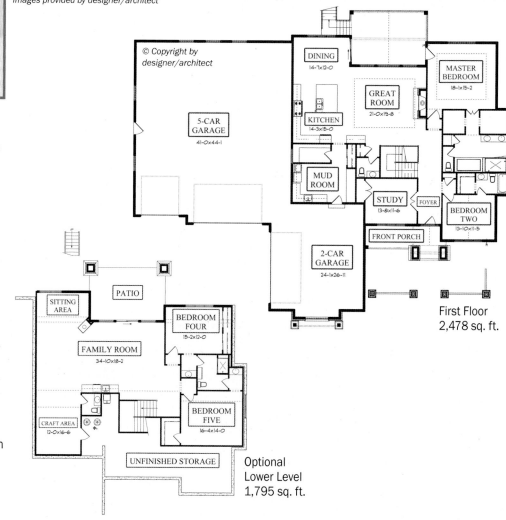

© Copyright by designer/architect

First Floor
2,478 sq. ft.

Optional
Lower Level
1,795 sq. ft.

Plan #F10-123D-0056

Dimensions:	55' W x 55' D
Heated Sq. Ft.:	1,701
Bedrooms: 3	Bathrooms: 2

Foundation: Basement standard; crawl space, slab or walk-out basement for an additional fee

See index for more information

Images provided by designer/architect

Features

- This attractive home draws inspiration from Modern Farmhouse style and has an open floor plan
- The great room has a 10' ceiling and enjoy views through a large window wall
- The kitchen is completely open and has an island angled to take in great room views plus a large walk-in pantry for keeping everything neat and organized
- The mud room provides a place to drop daily necessities when entering the home
- 3-car front entry garage

Plan #F10-013S-0010

Dimensions:	97' W x 78'9" D
Heated Sq. Ft.:	6,342
Bedrooms: 5	Bathrooms: 4½
Exterior Walls:	2" x 6"

Foundation: Walk-out basement standard; crawl space or slab for an additional fee

See index for more information

Images provided by designer/architect

Features

- The elegant pergola covered entry welcomes guests and leads them to a spacious covered porch
- Once inside, this lovely home expands to include an open great room/hearth room, which shares a double-sided fireplace
- The kitchen includes a pantry, in addition to a passage way and serving area into the formal dining room
- The screen porch with fireplace will make for cozy family gatherings all year round
- 4-car side entry garage

Second Floor
2,757 sq. ft.

© Copyright by designer/architect

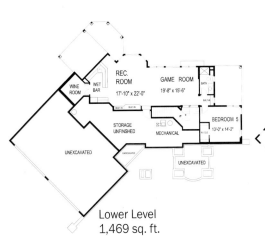

Lower Level
1,469 sq. ft.

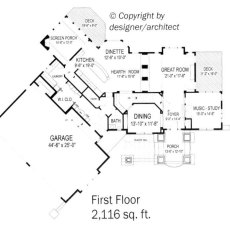

First Floor
2,116 sq. ft.

© Copyright by designer/architect

Plan #F10-077D-0042

Images provided by designer/architect

Dimensions: 64' W x 45'10" D
Basement depth is 49'10"
Heated Sq. Ft.: 1,752
Bedrooms: 3   **Bathrooms:** 2
Foundation: Basement, slab or crawl space, please specify when ordering

See index for more information

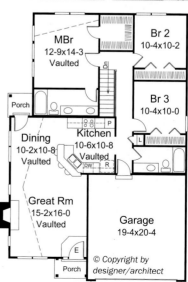

Plan #F10-121D-0010

Images provided by designer/architect

Dimensions: 37'6" W x 52' D
Heated Sq. Ft.: 1,281
Bedrooms: 3   **Bathrooms:** 2
Foundation: Basement standard; crawl space or slab for an additional fee

See index for more information

© Copyright by designer/architect

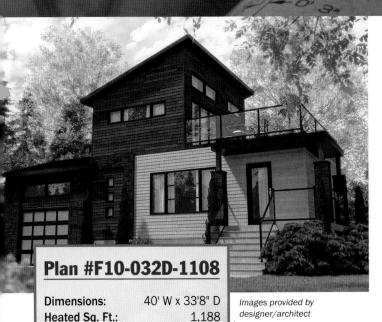

Plan #F10-032D-1108

Dimensions:	40' W x 33'8" D
Heated Sq. Ft.:	1,188
Bonus Sq. Ft.:	843
Bedrooms: 2	Bathrooms: 2
Exterior Walls:	2" x 6"

Foundation: Basement standard; crawl space, monolithic slab or floating slab for an additional fee

See index for more information

Images provided by designer/architect

© Copyright by designer/architect

Second Floor
345 sq. ft.

Optional Lower Level
843 sq. ft.

First Floor
843 sq. ft.

Plan #F10-007D-0060

Dimensions:	38'8" W x 48'4" D
Heated Sq. Ft.:	1,268
Bedrooms: 3	Bathrooms: 2

Foundation: Basement standard; crawl space or slab for an additional fee

See index for more information

Images provided by designer/architect

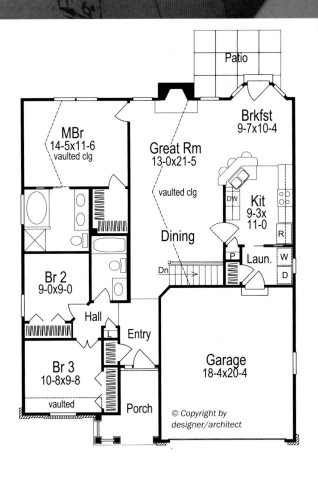

© Copyright by designer/architect

Plan #F10-007D-0136

Dimensions:	71'8" W x 38' D
Heated Sq. Ft.:	1,532
Bonus Sq. Ft.:	740
Bedrooms: 3	**Bathrooms:** 2
Foundation:	Walk-out basement

See index for more information

Features

- Multiple gables and stonework deliver a warm and inviting exterior to this wonderful home
- The vaulted great room has a stylish fireplace and spectacular views accomplished with a two-story atrium window wall
- A rear covered deck is easily accessed from the charming breakfast room, or the garage
- The optional lower level has an additional 740 square feet of living area
- 2-car front entry garage

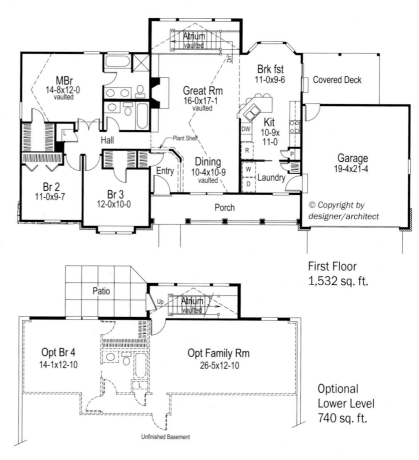

First Floor
1,532 sq. ft.

© Copyright by designer/architect

Optional
Lower Level
740 sq. ft.

Plan #F10-007D-0010

Dimensions:	83' W x 42'4" D
Heated Sq. Ft.:	1,845
Bonus Sq. Ft.:	889
Bedrooms: 3	**Bathrooms:** 2

Foundation: Walk-out basement standard; crawl space or slab for an additional fee

See index for more information

Features

- Vaulted dining and great rooms are immersed in sunlight from an atrium window wall
- The bayed breakfast room opens onto the covered porch
- The kitchen has a wrap-around casual counter with seating for four and a large corner pantry
- The optional lower level has an additional 889 square feet of living area
- 3-car front entry garage

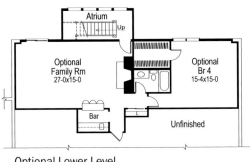

Optional Lower Level
889 sq. ft.

First Floor
1,845 sq. ft.

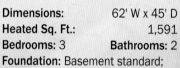

Plan #F10-007D-0140

Dimensions:	62' W x 45' D
Heated Sq. Ft.:	1,591
Bedrooms: 3	Bathrooms: 2

Foundation: Basement standard; crawl space or slab for an additional fee

See index for more information

© Copyright by designer/architect

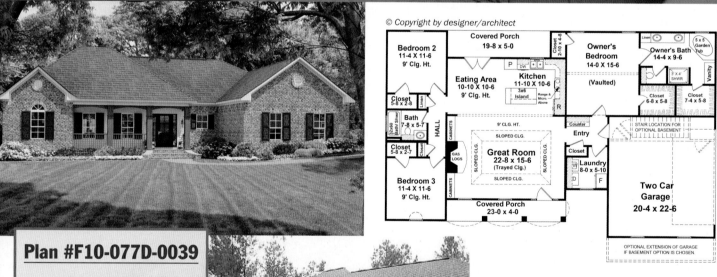

Plan #F10-077D-0039

Dimensions:	64' W x 39' D
Heated Sq. Ft.:	1,654
Bedrooms: 3	Bathrooms: 2

Foundation: Slab, crawl space, basement or daylight basement, please specify when ordering

See index for more information

Optional Second Floor
809 sq. ft.

FUTURE BONUS
12-4 x 20-4

FUTURE DESK/STUDY

WIC
5-2 x 8-0

FUTURE BONUS
13-4 x 16-4

GARAGE
23-4 x 21-4

PATIO

© Copyright by designer/architect

LAUN.
15-0 x 9-2

PORCH
15-2 x 9-8

M.BATH
12-4 x 13-2

W.I.C.
12-4 x 6-8

STORAGE
8-0 x 3-2

PANTRY
6-4 x 6-8

BEDROOM
13-4 x 12-4

KITCHEN
19-8 x 9-6

LIVING
19-8 x 20-5
VAULTED

MASTER BEDROOM
13-4 x 20-4
VAULTED

BATH

DINING/FOYER
18-10 x 11-2

BEDROOM
13-4 x 12-4

PORCH
19-2 x 7-4

First Floor
2,366 sq. ft.

Plan #F10-084D-0092

Dimensions:	58' W x 80'2" D
Heated Sq. Ft.:	2,366
Bonus Sq. Ft.:	809
Bedrooms: 3	**Bathrooms:** 2

Foundation: Slab standard; basement or crawl space for an additional fee

See index for more information

Images provided by designer/architect

Images provided by designer/architect

Plan #F10-155D-0065

Dimensions:	72'6" W x 64'8" D
Heated Sq. Ft.:	1,897
Heated Sq. Ft.:	373
Bedrooms: 4	**Bathrooms:** 2

Foundation: Crawl space or slab standard; basement or daylight basement for an additional fee

See index for more information

Optional Second Floor
373 sq. ft.

ATTIC STORAGE

½ BATH

BONUS ROOM
11'-8"X21'-8"

MASTER SUITE
13'-0"X15'-0"

BEDROOM 4
11'-0"X10'-10"

GRILLING PORCH

DINING
12'-0"X9'-5"

STORAGE
11'-8"X3'-8"

BATH

GREAT ROOM
18'-8"X15'-10"

M. BATH
13'-0"X10'-0"

GARAGE
11'-8"X21'-4"

BEDROOM 3
11'-0"X12'-0"

FOYER
7'-4"X6'-2"

LAUNDRY
9'-4"X8'-4"

BEDROOM/OFFICE
11'-4"X12'-0"

4' ENTRY

GARAGE
22'-4"X21'-8"

© Copyright by designer/architect

First Floor
1,897 sq. ft.

Images provided by designer/architect

Plan #F10-058D-0020

Dimensions:	46' W x 42'6" D
Heated Sq. Ft.:	1,428
Bedrooms: 3	**Bathrooms:** 2
Foundation:	Basement

See index for more information

Features

- This home is entirely surrounded by a wrap-around porch making it perfect for a lot with great views in every direction

- The large family room with fireplace opens to a cheerful dining area and charming kitchen with a handy breakfast bar for casual dining

- The first floor master bedroom offers a large and comfortable private bath, a sizable walk-in closet, and nearby laundry facilities

- A spacious loft/bedroom #3 overlooks the wonderful family room

- An additional bedroom and bath complement the second floor and includes a walk-in closet

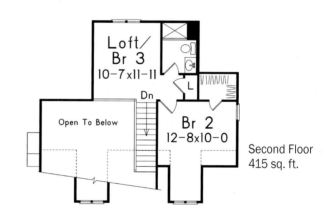

Second Floor
415 sq. ft.

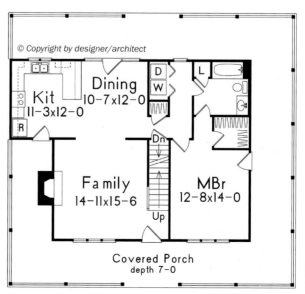

© Copyright by designer/architect

First Floor
1,013 sq. ft.

Images provided by designer/architect

Plan #F10-007D-0055

Dimensions: 67' W x 51'4" D
Heated Sq. Ft.: 2,029
Bedrooms: 3   **Bathrooms:** 2
Foundation: Basement standard; crawl space or slab for an additional fee

See index for more information

Features

- Stonework, gables, roof dormer and double porches create a country flavor
- The kitchen enjoys extravagant cabinetry and counterspace in a bay, island snack bar, built-in pantry and cheery dining area with multiple tall windows
- An angled stair descends from the large entry with wood columns and is open to a vaulted great room with corner fireplace
- A lovely master bedroom boasts two walk-in closets, a private bath with double-door entry and a secluded porch
- 2-car side entry garage

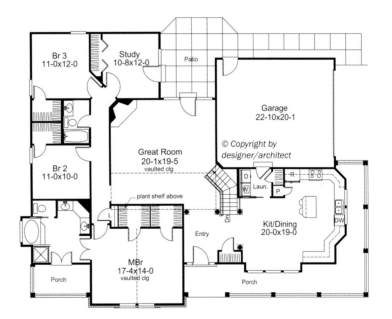

Optional
Second Floor
812 sq. ft.

Plan #F10-055D-0162

Dimensions:	84' W x 55'6" D
Heated Sq. Ft.:	1,921
Bonus Sq. Ft.:	812
Bedrooms: 3	Bathrooms: 2

Foundation: Crawl space or slab standard; basement or daylight basement for an additional fee

See index for more information

First Floor
1,921 sq. ft.

© Copyright by designer/architect

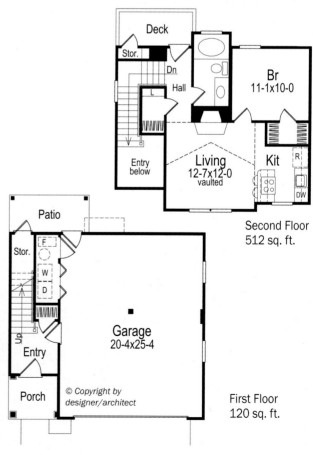

Second Floor
512 sq. ft.

Plan #F10-007D-0040

Dimensions:	28' W x 26' D
Heated Sq. Ft.:	632
Bedrooms: 1	Bathrooms: 1
Foundation:	Slab

See index for more information

© Copyright by designer/architect

First Floor
120 sq. ft.

Plan #F10-007D-0114

Dimensions: 32' W x 39'4" D
Heated Sq. Ft.: 1,671
Bedrooms: 3   **Bathrooms:** 2½
Foundation: Basement standard; crawl space or slab for an additional fee

See index for more information

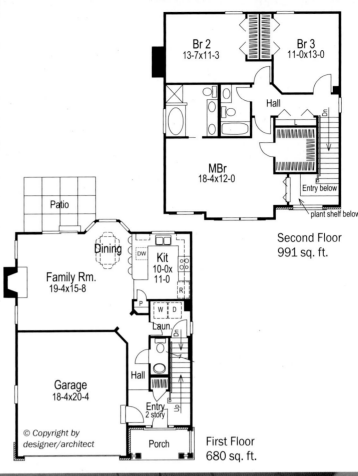

Second Floor
991 sq. ft.

First Floor
680 sq. ft.

© Copyright by designer/architect

Plan #F10-155D-0162

Dimensions: 73'4" W x 82' D
Heated Sq. Ft.: 2,294
Bonus Sq. Ft.: 444
Bedrooms: 4   **Bathrooms:** 2½
Foundation: Crawl space or slab standard; basement or daylight basement for an additional fee

See index for more information

Images provided by designer/architect

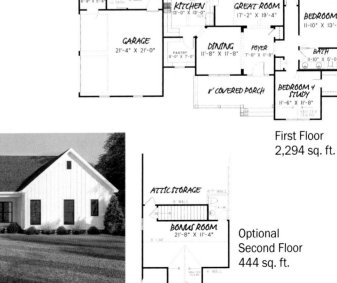

© Copyright by designer/architect

First Floor
2,294 sq. ft.

Optional Second Floor
444 sq. ft.

Plan #F10-101D-0228

Dimensions:	105'6" W x 72'3" D
Heated Sq. Ft.:	2,730
Bedrooms: 4	**Bathrooms:** 3½
Exterior Walls:	2" x 6"
Foundation:	Daylight basement

See index for more information

Images provided by designer/architect

Features

- Stunning rustic Modern style prevails in this stylish new home design with a spacious split bedroom floor plan
- The master suite enjoys a private location with a see-through fireplace it shares with a covered deck, a posh bath with a free-standing tub, and a huge walk-in closet with laundry room access
- The kitchen is filled with cabinets, a center island, and a walk-in pantry around the corner
- 3-car front entry garage

© Copyright by designer/architect

Plan #F10-011D-0770

Dimensions:	62' W x 94' D
Heated Sq. Ft.:	2,588
Bedrooms: 3	**Bathrooms: 3½**
Exterior Walls:	2" x 6"

Foundation: Crawl space or slab standard; basement for an additional fee

See index for more information

Images provided by designer/architect

Features

- This home typifies the best in country design with unique barn style architectural features
- A family can enjoy the outdoors with the wrap-around porch and screened porch
- A private office makes working from home a breeze
- The entertainment space offers plenty of room for a pool table and includes a cozy fireplace
- 6-car side entry garage

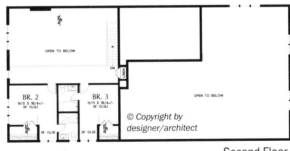

© Copyright by designer/architect

Second Floor
776 sq. ft.

First Floor
1,812 sq. ft.

Plan #F10-005D-0001

Dimensions:	72' W x 34'4" D
Heated Sq. Ft.:	1,400
Bedrooms: 3	**Bathrooms:** 2

Foundation: Basement standard; crawl space or slab for an additional fee

See index for more information

Features

- Triple roof dormers and an inviting covered front porch add great curb appeal
- The vaulted living room creates a spacious feel
- A raised snack bar creates a smooth transition from the kitchen to the dining room
- A split bedroom design offers privacy
- The oversized two-car garage has additional storage
- 2-car front entry garage

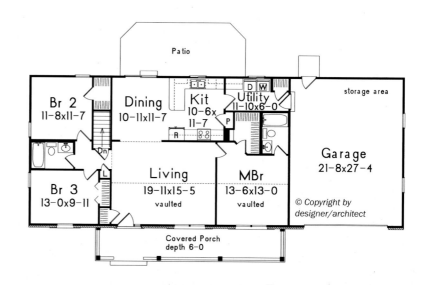

Patio

Br 2
11-8x11-7

Dining
10-11x11-7

Kit
10-6x
11-7

Utility
11-10x6-0

storage area

Living
19-11x15-5
vaulted

MBr
13-6x13-0
vaulted

Garage
21-8x27-4

Br 3
13-0x9-11

Covered Porch
depth 6-0

© Copyright by designer/architect

Plan #F10-007D-0077

Dimensions:	76'8" W x 47'4" D
Heated Sq. Ft.:	1,978
Bonus Sq. Ft.:	1,295
Bedrooms: 4	**Bathrooms:** 2½
Foundation:	Walk-out basement

See index for more information

Features

- A home with a classic exterior that's always in style
- The spacious great room boasts a vaulted ceiling, a dining area, an atrium window wall with an elegant staircase and feature windows
- The kitchen has an angled snack bar with seating for four people
- The optional lower level has an additional 1,295 square feet of living area that consists of a family room, two bedrooms, two baths, and a study
- 3-car side entry garage

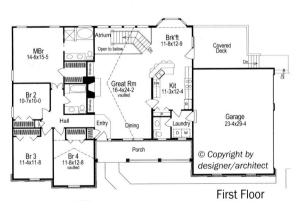

First Floor
1,978 sq. ft.

© Copyright by designer/architect

Optional
Lower Level
1,295 sq. ft.

Images provided by designer/architect

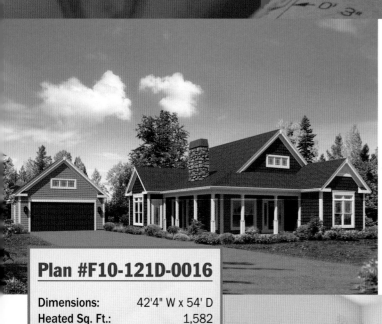

Detached Garage
23-4x23-4

© Copyright by
designer/architect

Plan #F10-121D-0016

Dimensions: 42'4" W x 54' D
Heated Sq. Ft.: 1,582
Bedrooms: 3 **Bathrooms:** 2
Foundation: Basement standard; crawl space or slab for an additional fee

See index for more information

© Copyright by
designer/architect

Plan #F10-001D-0013

Dimensions: 60'10" W x 51'2" D
Heated Sq. Ft.: 1,882
Bedrooms: 3 **Bathrooms:** 2
Foundation: Basement standard; crawl space or slab for an additional fee

See index for more information

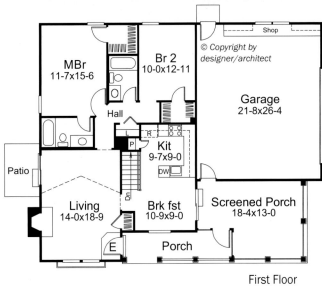

Plan #F10-007D-0128

Dimensions:	52' W x 40'8" D
Heated Sq. Ft.:	1,072
Bonus Sq. Ft.:	345
Bedrooms: 2	**Bathrooms:** 2
Foundation:	Walk-out basement

See index for more information

First Floor
1,072 sq. ft.

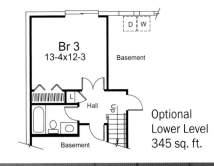

Optional
Lower Level
345 sq. ft.

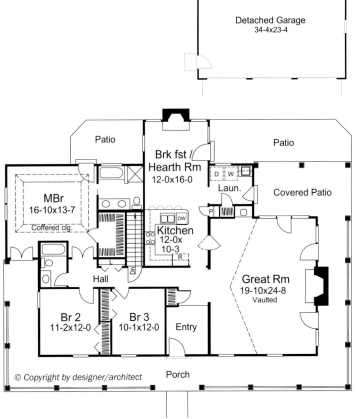

Plan #F10-007D-0124

Dimensions:	65' W x 51' D
Heated Sq. Ft.:	1,944
Bedrooms: 3	**Bathrooms:** 2
Foundation:	Basement standard; crawl space or slab for an additional fee

See index for more information

Plan #F10-088D-0141

Dimensions:	65' W x 56'6" D
Heated Sq. Ft.:	3,304
Bedrooms: 2	**Bathrooms:** 3
Exterior Walls:	ICF
Foundation:	Walk-out basement

See index for more information

Features

- A wrap-around deck and a covered porch add tons of outdoor living space
- Double doors lead into the den/office
- The master suite has access to an open deck, two walk-in closets and a private bath
- The lower level has a wet bar, a family room, a sitting room, a bedroom, and covered porch access
- 2-car front entry garage

Images provided by designer/architect

© Copyright by designer/architect

Lower Level
1,652 sq. ft.

First Floor
1,652 sq. ft.

houseplansandmore.com

Images provided by designer/architect

Plan #F10-051D-0246

Dimensions:	71' W x 62' D
Heated Sq. Ft.:	3,099
Bedrooms: 4	**Bathrooms:** 2½
Exterior Walls:	2" x 6"

Foundation: Basement standard; crawl space or slab for an additional fee

See index for more information

First Floor
2,143 sq. ft.

© Copyright by
designer/architect

Second Floor
956 sq. ft.

Features

- A see-through fireplace warms the formal living room and the casual family room equally, and is a beautiful focal point in both spaces
- The gourmet kitchen features an abundance of counterspace, a stovetop island and a walk-in pantry
- The breakfast nook/sun room has access to a screen porch through sliding glass doors
- 3-car front entry garage

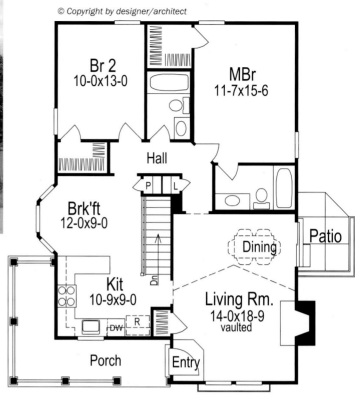

Plan #F10-007D-0105

Dimensions: 35' W x 40'8" D
Heated Sq. Ft.: 1,084
Bedrooms: 2 **Bathrooms:** 2
Foundation: Basement standard; crawl space or slab for an additional fee

See index for more information

Images provided by designer/architect

Br 2
10-0x13-0

MBr
11-7x15-6

Hall

Brk'ft
12-0x9-0

Patio

Kit
10-9x9-0

Dining

Living Rm.
14-0x18-9
vaulted

Porch

Entry

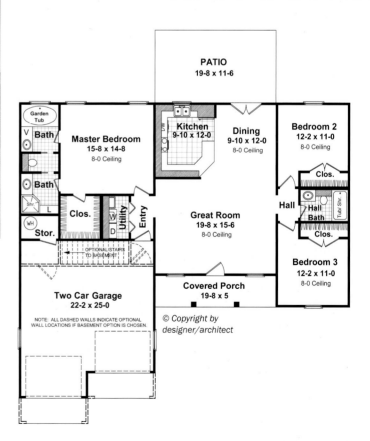

PATIO
19-8 x 11-6

Garden Tub

Bath

Master Bedroom
15-8 x 14-8
8-0 Ceiling

Kitchen
9-10 x 12-0

Dining
9-10 x 12-0
8-0 Ceiling

Bedroom 2
12-2 x 11-0
8-0 Ceiling

Bath

Clos.

Hall

Clos.

Hall Bath

Utility

Entry

Great Room
19-8 x 15-6
8-0 Ceiling

Stor.

OPTIONAL STAIRS TO BASEMENT

Bedroom 3
12-2 x 11-0
8-0 Ceiling

Two Car Garage
22-2 x 25-0

Covered Porch
19-8 x 5

NOTE: ALL DASHED WALLS INDICATE OPTIONAL WALL LOCATIONS IF BASEMENT OPTION IS CHOSEN.

Plan #F10-077D-0019

Dimensions: 54' W x 47' D
Heated Sq. Ft.: 1,400
Bedrooms: 3 **Bathrooms:** 2
Foundation: Slab, crawl space, basement, or walk-out basement please specify when ordering

See index for more information

Images provided by designer/architect

Plan #F10-032D-0808

Dimensions:	32' W x 24' D
Heated Sq. Ft.:	900
Bedrooms: 2	Bathrooms: 1½
Exterior Walls:	2" x 6"

Foundation: Basement standard; crawl space, floating slab or monolithic slab for an additional fee

See index for more information

Second Floor
420 sq. ft.

First Floor
480 sq. ft.

Plan #F10-121D-0025

Dimensions:	50' W x 34'6" D
Heated Sq. Ft.:	1,368
Bedrooms: 3	Bathrooms: 2

Foundation: Basement standard; crawl space or slab for an additional fee

See index for more information

Images provided by designer/architect

Plan #F10-055D-0193

Dimensions: 63'10" W x 72'2" D
Heated Sq. Ft.: 2,129
Bedrooms: 3 **Bathrooms:** 2½
Foundation: Slab or crawl space
standard; basement or daylight
basement for an additional fee

See index for more information

*Images provided by
designer/architect*

© Copyright by
designer/architect

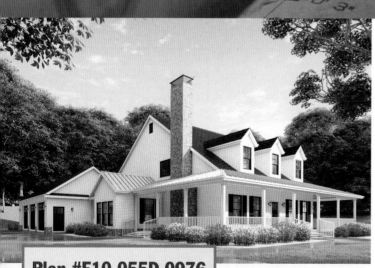

Plan #F10-055D-0976

Dimensions: 62'6" W x 93'10" D
Heated Sq. Ft.: 2,180
Bonus Sq. Ft.: 1,214
Bedrooms: 4 **Bathrooms:** 3
Foundation: Crawl space or slab
standard; basement or daylight
basement for an additional fee

See index for more information

*Images provided by
designer/architect*

© Copyright by
designer/architect

PROPOSED GAME ROOM
33'-2" X 35'-7"

Optional Second Floor
1,214 sq. ft.

First Floor
2,180 sq. ft.

houseplansandmore.com

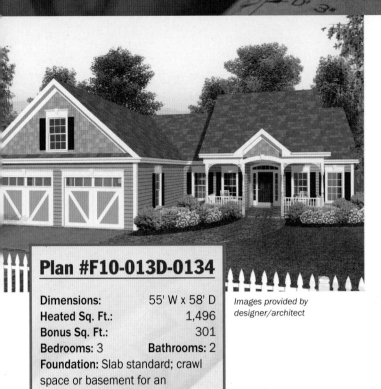

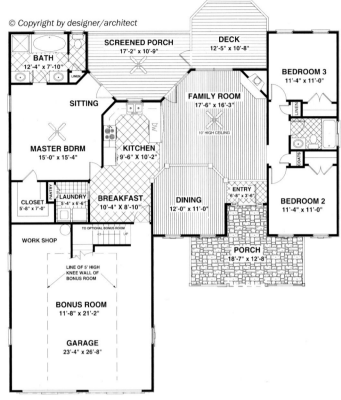

© Copyright by designer/architect

BATH 12'-4" x 7'-10"

SCREENED PORCH 17'-2" x 10'-9"

DECK 12'-5" x 10'-8"

BEDROOM 3 11'-4" x 11'-0"

SITTING

FAMILY ROOM 17'-6" x 16'-3"

10' HIGH CEILING

MASTER BDRM 15'-0" x 15'-4"

KITCHEN 9'-6" X 10'-2"

CLOSET 5'-8" x 7'-0"

LAUNDRY 5'-4" x 6'-6"

BREAKFAST 10'-4" X 8'-10"

DINING 12'-0" x 11'-0"

ENTRY 6'-8" x 3'-6"

BEDROOM 2 11'-4" x 11'-0"

WORK SHOP

LINE OF 5' HIGH KNEE WALL OF BONUS ROOM

TO OPTIONAL BONUS ROOM

UP

PORCH 18'-7" x 12'-8"

BONUS ROOM 11'-8" x 21'-2"

GARAGE 23'-4" x 26'-8"

Plan #F10-013D-0134

Dimensions:	55' W x 58' D
Heated Sq. Ft.:	1,496
Bonus Sq. Ft.:	301
Bedrooms: 3	**Bathrooms:** 2

Foundation: Slab standard; crawl space or basement for an additional fee

See index for more information

Images provided by designer/architect

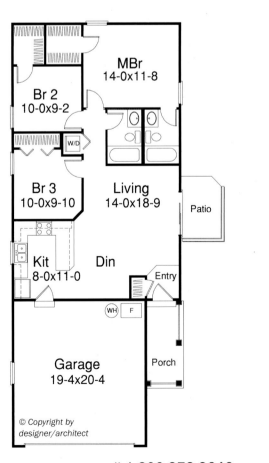

MBr 14-0x11-8

Br 2 10-0x9-2

W/D

Br 3 10-0x9-10

Living 14-0x18-9

Patio

Kit 8-0x11-0

Din

Entry

WH   F

Garage 19-4x20-4

Porch

© Copyright by designer/architect

Plan #F10-007D-0108

Dimensions:	25' W x 60' D
Heated Sq. Ft.:	983
Bedrooms: 3	**Bathrooms:** 2

Foundation: Crawl space standard; slab for an additional fee

See index for more information

Images provided by designer/architect

Plan #F10-011D-0757

Dimensions:	87' W x 76' D
Heated Sq. Ft.:	2,456
Bedrooms: 3	Bathrooms: 2½
Exterior Walls:	2" x 6"

Foundation: Crawl space or slab standard; basement for an additional fee

See index for more information

Images provided by designer/architect

Features

- A popular sprawling country farmhouse is sure to delight all those who lay eyes on this home
- An open floor plan has the great room with fireplace flowing effortlessly into the kitchen and dining area
- The master bedroom enjoys a private location with a luxurious bath and walk-in closet
- Two secondary bedrooms are located on the opposite side of the home and share a full bath
- 3-car side entry garage

BR. 3
12/0 X 14/8
(9' CLG.)

PATIO
(93 SQ. FT.)

VAULTED
DINING
12/0 X 14/10

REAR PORCH
(194 SQ. FT.)

VAULTED
MBR
14/0 X 17/0

PANTRY
5/2 X 8/8

GREAT RM.
20/0 X 19/0 +/-
(15' CLG.)

11/6 X 16/2+/-
(15' CLG.)

FOYER
(9' CLG.)

9/8X8/10+/-
(9' CLG.)

BR. 2
12/0 X 11/10 +/-
(9' CLG.)

BROOM

FRONT PORCH
(255 SQ. FT.)

VAULTED
OFFICE
14/0 X 11/6

MUD

© Copyright by
designer/architect

GARAGE
23/0 X 21/0 +

19/0 X 12/0

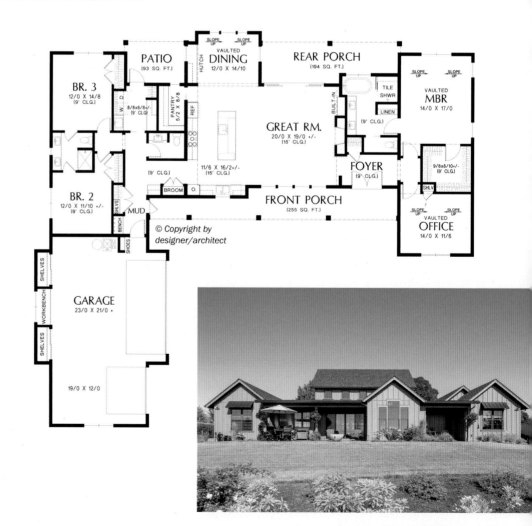

Plan #F10-011D-0738

Dimensions:	59' W x 59'6" D
Heated Sq. Ft.:	2,117
Bedrooms: 3	**Bathrooms:** 2½
Exterior Walls:	2" x 6"

Foundation: Crawl space or slab standard; basement for an additional fee

See index for more information

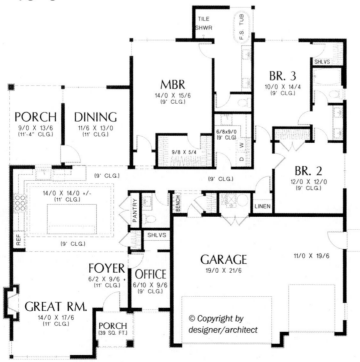

Features

- With its sleek style, this modern home feels uncomplicated and inviting
- The dining area and great room all remain open to the kitchen creating an overwhelming sense of spaciousness
- A quiet home office is tucked near foyer
- The central master bedroom offers the homeowners a peaceful bath and a walk-in closet
- 3-car front entry garage

Images provided by designer/architect

Floor Plan

PORCH 9/0 X 13/6 (11'-4" CLG.)

DINING 11/6 X 13/0 (11' CLG.)

MBR 14/0 X 15/6 (9' CLG.)

BR. 3 10/0 X 14/4 (9' CLG.)

TILE SHWR • F.S. TUB • SHLVS

6/8 X 9/0 (9' CLG.)

9/8 X 5/4

14/0 X 14/0 +/- (11' CLG.)

(9' CLG.)

(9' CLG.)

D W

BR. 2 12/0 X 12/0 (9' CLG.)

REF

PANTRY • BENCH • LINEN

SHLVS

GARAGE 19/0 X 21/6

11/0 X 19/6

FOYER 6/2 X 9/6 + (11' CLG.)

OFFICE 6/10 X 9/6 (9' CLG.)

GREAT RM. 14/0 X 17/6 (11' CLG.)

PORCH (39 SQ. FT.)

© Copyright by designer/architect

Plan #F10-032D-1212

Dimensions:	32' W x 30' D
Heated Sq. Ft.:	1,940
Bedrooms: 2	Bathrooms: 2
Exterior Walls:	2" x 6"
Foundation:	Walk-out basement

See index for more information

Images provided by designer/architect

Features

- This friendly home has the perfect layout for waterfront or hillside views
- The vaulted first floor has a centered fireplace as the focal point
- The kitchen has a large island that overlooks the dining and living areas
- The lower level features a cozy family room, a bedroom and a full bath
- A covered terrace, screened porch and large lower level patio offer plenty of great options for relaxing outdoors
- 1-car drive under rear entry garage

© Copyright by designer/architect

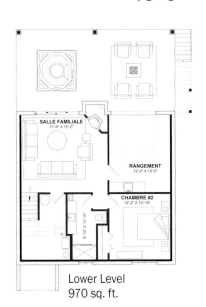

Lower Level
970 sq. ft.

First Floor
970 sq. ft.

Plan #F10-007D-0162

Dimensions:	47'8" W x 47'4" D
Heated Sq. Ft.:	1,519
Bedrooms: 4	**Bathrooms:** 2

Foundation: Crawl space standard; basement or slab for an additional fee

See index for more information

Images provided by designer/architect

Patio

Br 2
12-0x12-0

Br 3
10-4x12-0

Living Rm
13-1x18-5
vaulted

Dining
10-3x12-8
vaulted

Hall

Plant Shelf
Above

Kit
10-0x
13-0
vaulted

DW

Entry

W
D

Laundry

R

P

Study/Br 4
10-0x9-0

MBr
15-0x14-0

Porch

Garage
19-4x20-4

Sitting

© Copyright by
designer/architect

Plan #F10-007D-0117

Dimensions:	76'8" W x 57'6" D
Heated Sq. Ft.:	2,695
Bedrooms: 3	**Bathrooms:** 2½

Foundation: Basement standard; crawl space or slab for an additional fee

See index for more information

Images provided by designer/architect

Patio

Brk'ft
14-10x11-1

MBr
18-8x17-0

Br 2
14-0x14-0

Great Room
18-6x23-0

Kit
15-2x11-4

DW

vaulted

Hall

L

Hall

Br 3
14-0x14-8

Entry

Dining
13-2x15-0
tray clg.

Laun

W
D

© Copyright by
designer/architect

Garage
21-4x20-10

Porch

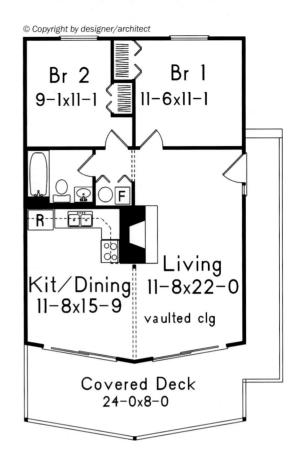

© Copyright by designer/architect

Br 2
9-1x11-1

Br 1
11-6x11-1

R

F

Living
11-8x22-0
vaulted clg

Kit/Dining
11-8x15-9

Covered Deck
24-0x8-0

Plan #F10-008D-0153

Dimensions: 24' W x 42' D
Heated Sq. Ft.: 792
Bedrooms: 2   **Bathrooms:** 1
Foundation: Crawl space standard;
slab for an additional fee

See index for more information

Images provided by designer/architect

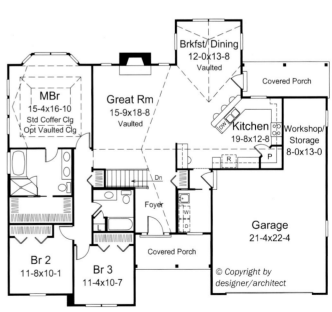

Brkfst/ Dining
12-0x13-8
Vaulted

Covered Porch

MBr
15-4x16-10
Std Coffer Clg
Opt Vaulted Clg

Great Rm
15-9x18-8
Vaulted

Kitchen
19-8x12-8

Workshop/ Storage
8-0x13-0

R   **P**

Dn

Foyer

Garage
21-4x22-4

Br 2
11-8x10-1

Br 3
11-4x10-7

Covered Porch

© Copyright by designer/architect

Plan #F10-121D-0036

Dimensions: 60'4" W x 52' D
Heated Sq. Ft.: 1,820
Bedrooms: 3   **Bathrooms:** 2
Foundation: Basement standard;
crawl space or slab for an
additional fee

See index for more information

Images provided by designer/architect

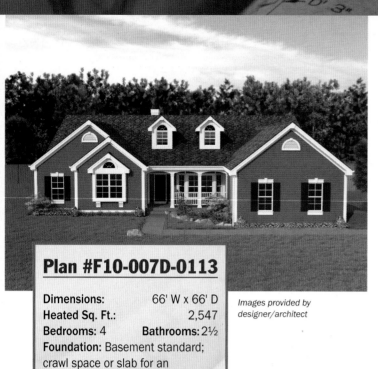

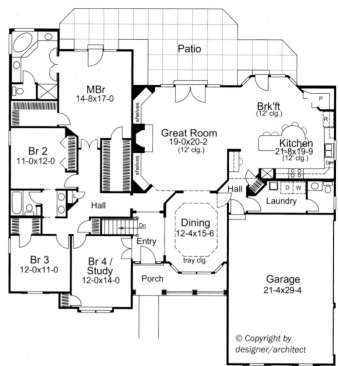

Images provided by designer/architect

Plan #F10-007D-0113

Dimensions: 66' W x 66' D
Heated Sq. Ft.: 2,547
Bedrooms: 4   **Bathrooms:** 2½
Foundation: Basement standard; crawl space or slab for an additional fee

See index for more information

© Copyright by designer/architect

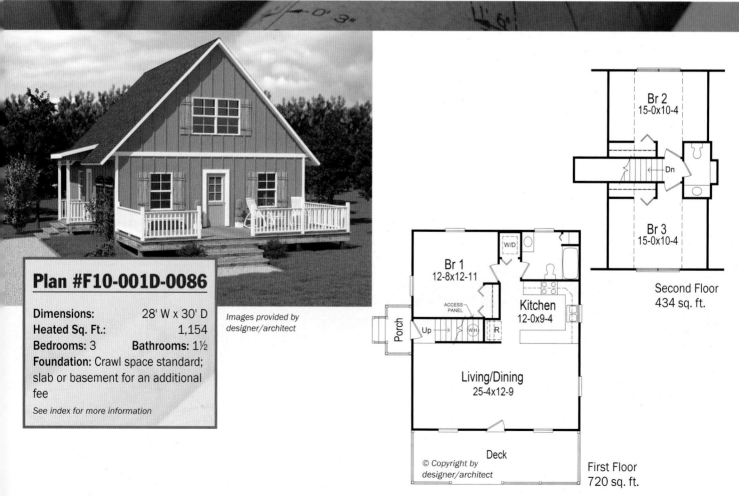

Images provided by designer/architect

Second Floor
434 sq. ft.

First Floor
720 sq. ft.

© Copyright by designer/architect

Plan #F10-001D-0086

Dimensions: 28' W x 30' D
Heated Sq. Ft.: 1,154
Bedrooms: 3   **Bathrooms:** 1½
Foundation: Crawl space standard; slab or basement for an additional fee

See index for more information

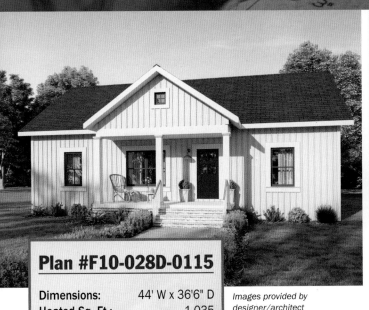

Plan #F10-028D-0115

Dimensions:	44' W x 36'6" D
Heated Sq. Ft.:	1,035
Bedrooms: 3	Bathrooms: 2
Exterior Walls:	2" x 6"

Foundation: Floating slab standard; monolithic slab, crawl space, basement or walk-out basement for an additional fee

See index for more information

Images provided by designer/architect

© Copyright by designer/architect

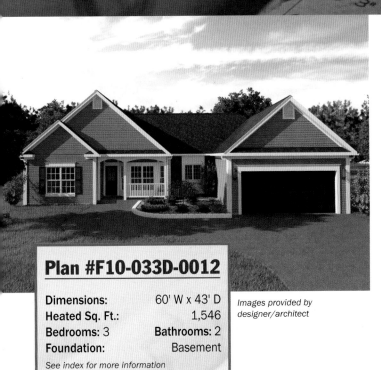

Plan #F10-033D-0012

Dimensions:	60' W x 43' D
Heated Sq. Ft.:	1,546
Bedrooms: 3	Bathrooms: 2
Foundation:	Basement

See index for more information

Images provided by designer/architect

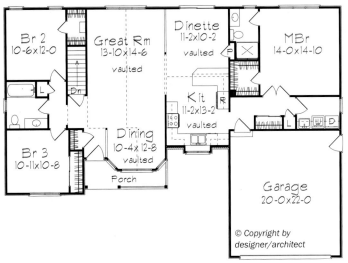

© Copyright by designer/architect

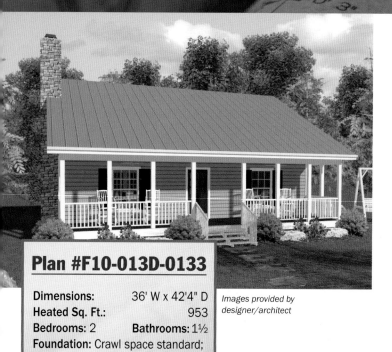

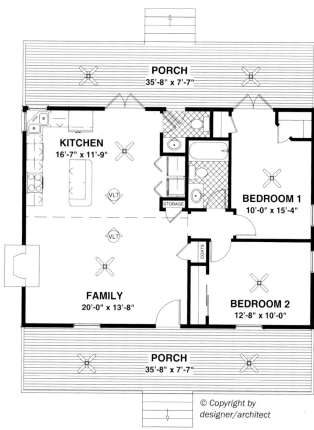

Plan #F10-013D-0133

Dimensions:	36' W x 42'4" D
Heated Sq. Ft.:	953
Bedrooms: 2	Bathrooms: 1½

Foundation: Crawl space standard; basement or slab for an additional fee

See index for more information

Images provided by designer/architect

PORCH
35'-8" x 7'-7"

KITCHEN
16'-7" x 11'-9"

VLT

VLT

STORAGE

BEDROOM 1
10'-0" x 15'-4"

COATS

FAMILY
20'-0" x 13'-8"

BEDROOM 2
12'-8" x 10'-0"

PORCH
35'-8" x 7'-7"

Plan #F10-001D-0041

Dimensions:	40' W x 25' D
Heated Sq. Ft.:	1,000
Bedrooms: 3	Bathrooms: 1

Foundation: Crawl space standard; basement or slab for an additional fee

See index for more information

Images provided by designer/architect

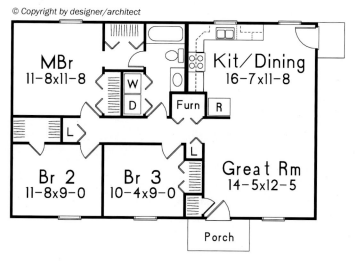

MBr
11-8x11-8

W
D

Furn

Kit/Dining
16-7x11-8

R

L

L

Br 2
11-8x9-0

Br 3
10-4x9-0

Great Rm
14-5x12-5

Porch

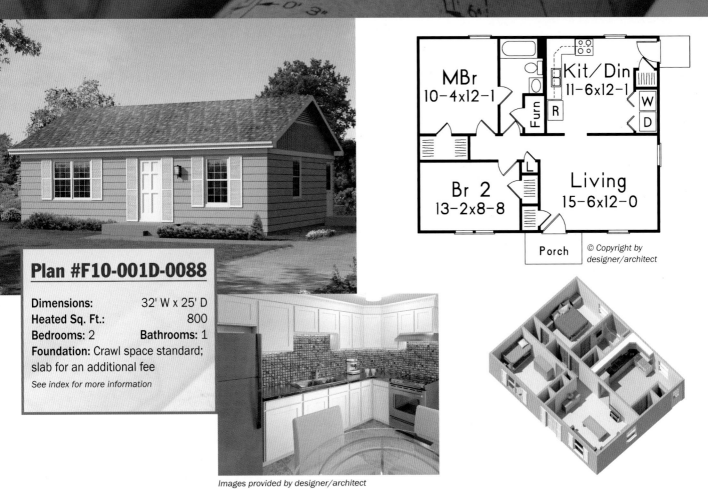

Plan #F10-001D-0088

Dimensions: 32' W x 25' D
Heated Sq. Ft.: 800
Bedrooms: 2   **Bathrooms:** 1
Foundation: Crawl space standard; slab for an additional fee

See index for more information

Images provided by designer/architect

Plan #F10-065D-0062

Images provided by designer/architect

Dimensions: 50' W x 55'8" D
Heated Sq. Ft.: 1,390
Bedrooms: 3   **Bathrooms:** 2
Foundation: Walk-out basement standard; crawl space or slab for an additional fee

See index for more information

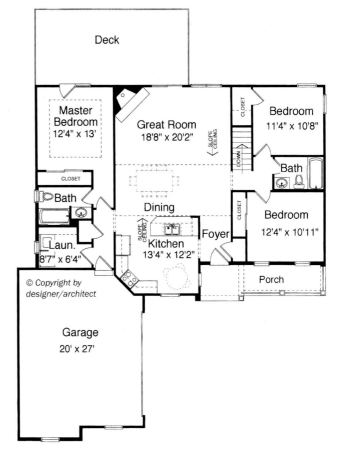

Plan #F10-051D-0757

Dimensions: 55' W x 51'8" D
Heated Sq. Ft.: 1,501
Bedrooms: 3 **Bathrooms:** 2
Exterior Walls: 2" x 6"
Foundation: Basement standard; crawl space or slab for an additional fee

See index for more information

CVRD. PORCH
16'0"x10'4"

GRT. RM.
VAULTED CEILING
17'8"x14'6"

MBR.
10'-1 1/8" STEP CEILING
14'0"x12'0"

BR. #3
9'-1 1/8" CEILING
10'0"x11'0"

DIN.
VAULTED CEILING
14'0"x11'6"

KIT.
VAULTED CEILING
10'6"x12'4"

E.
VAULTED CEILING

BR. #2
9'-1 1/8" CEILING
11'0"x11'0"

3 CAR GARAGE
29'4"x21'8"

© Copyright by designer/architect

Images provided by designer/architect

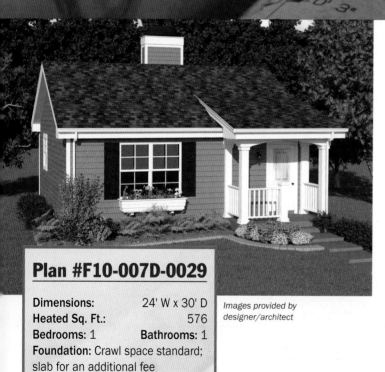

Plan #F10-007D-0029

Dimensions: 24' W x 30' D
Heated Sq. Ft.: 576
Bedrooms: 1 **Bathrooms:** 1
Foundation: Crawl space standard; slab for an additional fee

See index for more information

Images provided by designer/architect

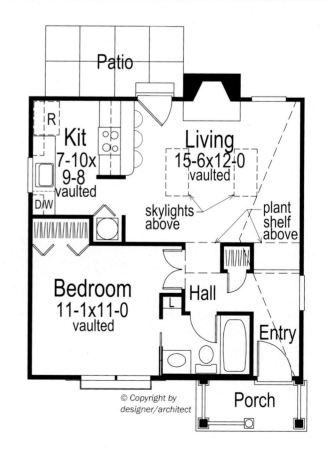

Patio

R

Kit
7-10x 9-8
vaulted

DW

Living
15-6x12-0
vaulted

skylights above

plant shelf above

Bedroom
11-1x11-0
vaulted

Hall

Entry

Porch

© Copyright by designer/architect

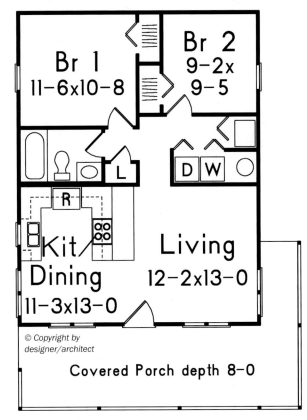

Br 1
11-6x10-8

Br 2
9-2x
9-5

L

D W

R

Kit/
Dining
11-3x13-0

Living
12-2x13-0

© Copyright by
designer/architect

Covered Porch depth 8-0

Plan #F10-001D-0085

Dimensions: 28' W x 38' D
Heated Sq. Ft.:   720
Bedrooms: 2   Bathrooms: 1
Foundation: Crawl space standard;
slab for an additional fee

See index for more information

*Images provided by
designer/architect*

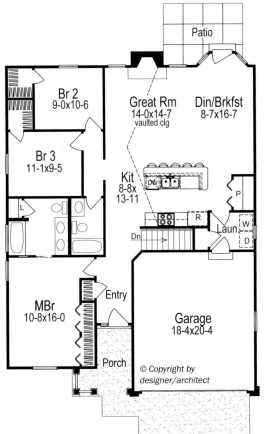

Patio

Br 2
9-0x10-6

Great Rm
14-0x14-7
vaulted clg

Din/Brkfst
8-7x16-7

Br 3
11-1x9-5

L

Kit
8-8x
13-11

P

Dn

R

Laun

W
D

MBr
10-8x16-0

Entry

Garage
18-4x20-4

Porch

© Copyright by
designer/architect

Plan #F10-007D-5060

Dimensions: 38' W x 48'4" D
Heated Sq. Ft.:   1,344
Bedrooms: 3   Bathrooms: 2
Foundation: Basement standard;
crawl space or slab for an addition-
al fee

See index for more information

*Images provided by
designer/architect*

Alternate
Slab or
Crawl Space
Layout

Plan #F10-001D-0024

Dimensions: 68' W x 38' D
Heated Sq. Ft.: 1,360
Bedrooms: 3   **Bathrooms:** 2
Foundation: Basement standard;
crawl space or slab for an additional fee

See index for more information

Images provided by designer/architect

© Copyright by designer/architect

Plan #F10-007D-0043

Dimensions: 40' W x 22' D
Heated Sq. Ft.: 647
Bedrooms: 1   **Bathrooms:** 1
Foundation: Crawl space standard;
slab for an additional fee

See index for more information

Images provided by designer/architect

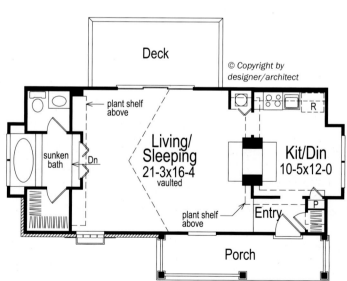

© Copyright by designer/architect

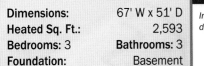

Plan #F10-007D-0252

Dimensions: 67' W x 51' D
Heated Sq. Ft.: 2,593
Bedrooms: 3   Bathrooms: 3
Foundation: Basement

See index for more information

Images provided by designer/architect

Second Floor
614 sq. ft.

Sloped Clg
Std Loft Area
32-2x18-0
Balcony to Great Rm Below

Opt Br 4
13-10x10-7

Opt Office
15-7x18-0

Sloped Clg

Sloped Clg   Sloped Clg

Open to Great Rm Below

Garage
34-4x23-4

© Copyright by designer/architect

First Floor
1,979 sq. ft.

Patio   Brkfst/ Hearth 12-0x16-8   Patio

MBr 15-5x16-8 Std Vault Clg Opt Coffer Clg

Up

W D

Laundry   Grilling Porch

Kitchen 12-0x9-7
DW
R

Great Rm 19-10x24-8 Vault Clg

Dn

Br 2 11-2x12-0   Br 3 10-1x12-0   Foyer

Porch

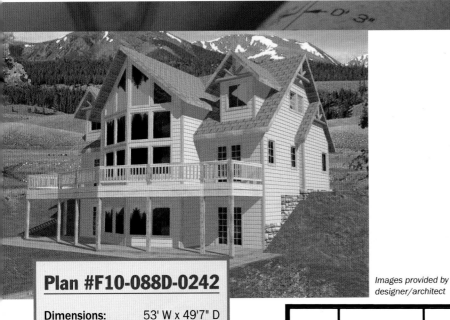

Plan #F10-088D-0242

Dimensions: 53' W x 49'7" D
Heated Sq. Ft.: 2,281
Bonus Sq. Ft.: 1,436
Bedrooms: 3   Bathrooms: 2½
Exterior Walls: 2" x 6"
Foundation: Walk-out basement

See index for more information

Images provided by designer/architect

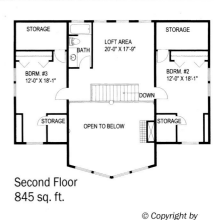

Second Floor
845 sq. ft.

STORAGE   STORAGE
BATH
LOFT AREA 20'-0" X 17'-9"
BDRM. #3 12'-0" X 18'-1"   BDRM. #2 12'-0" X 18'-1"
DOWN
STORAGE   OPEN TO BELOW   STORAGE

© Copyright by designer/architect

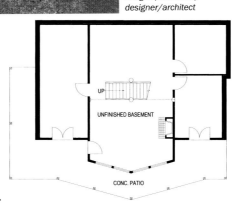

Optional Lower Level
1,436 sq. ft.

UP
UNFINISHED BASEMENT
CONC. PATIO

First Floor
1,436 sq. ft.

COVERED ENTRY PORCH

KITCHEN 12'X13'6"
UTILITY 6'8"X10
6'X5'
FOYER 6'-10" X 14'-0"   WIC   13'8"X10'8
WIC

DINING RM. 12'-0" X 12'-5"
UP
GREAT RM. 20'-0" X 17'-0"
DOWN
MASTER SUITE 12'-0" X 15'-10"

DECK AREA   DECK AREA

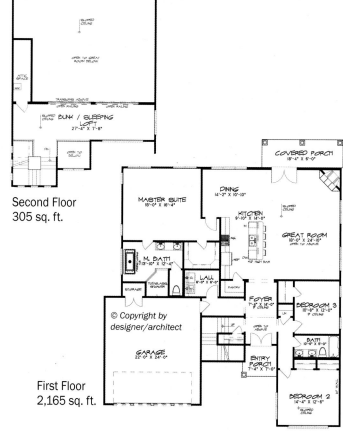

Plan #F10-155D-0023

Dimensions:	55'2" W x 64'8" D
Heated Sq. Ft.:	2,470
Bedrooms: 3	**Bathrooms:** 2

Foundation: Slab or crawl space, please specify when ordering

See index for more information

Images provided by designer/architect

Second Floor
305 sq. ft.

First Floor
2,165 sq. ft.

© Copyright by designer/architect

Plan #F10-076D-0249

Dimensions:	71' W x 70'6" D
Heated Sq. Ft.:	2,488
Bonus Sq. Ft.:	330
Bedrooms: 3	**Bathrooms:** 2½

Foundation: Basement, crawl space or slab, please specify when ordering

See index for more information

Images provided by designer/architect

Optional
Second Floor
330 sq. ft.

First Floor
2,488 sq. ft.

© Copyright by designer/architect

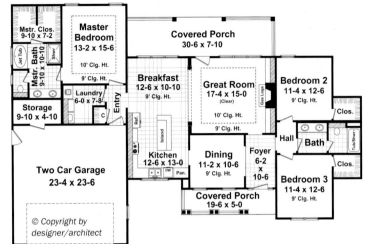

Plan #F10-077D-0165

Dimensions: 72'4" W x 48' D
Heated Sq. Ft.: 1,800
Bedrooms: 3   **Bathrooms:** 2
Foundation: Slab or crawl space,
please specify when ordering; for
basement version, see
Plan #077D-0256 at
houseplansandmore.com

See index for more information

Images provided by designer/architect

Mstr. Clos. 9-10 x 7-2

Master Bedroom 13-2 x 15-6 — 10' Clg. Ht.

Covered Porch 30-6 x 7-10

Jet Tub

Mstr. Bath 9-10 x 10-10

Shwr

Breakfast 12-6 x 10-10 — 9' Clg. Ht.

Great Room 17-4 x 15-0 (Clear) — 10' Clg. Ht. — 9' Clg. Ht.

Gas Logs

Bedroom 2 11-4 x 12-6 — 9' Clg. Ht.

Clos.

Laundry 6-0 x 7-8

Entry

Storage 9-10 x 4-10

Reff.

C

Island

Hall

Bath

Tub/Shwr

Clos.

Two Car Garage 23-4 x 23-6

Kitchen 12-6 x 13-0

DW   Pan.

Dining 11-2 x 10-6 — 9' Clg. Ht.

Foyer 6-2 x 10-6

Bedroom 3 11-4 x 12-6 — 9' Clg. Ht.

Covered Porch 19-6 x 5-0

© Copyright by designer/architect

Plan #F10-126D-1175

Dimensions: 28' W x 26' D
Heated Sq. Ft.: 910
Bedrooms: 2   **Bathrooms:** 1½
Exterior Walls: 2" x 6"
Foundation: Slab

See index for more information

Images provided by designer/architect

9'-2"x11'-0"
2,79x3,35

13'-0"x13'-8"
3,96x4,17

11'-0"x12'-8"
3,35x3,86

Second Floor
494 sq. ft.

© Copyright by designer/architect

11'-0''x12'-6''
3,35x3,81

11'-6''x24'-6''
3,51x7,47

11'-0''x12'-0''
3,35x3,66

First Floor
416 sq. ft.

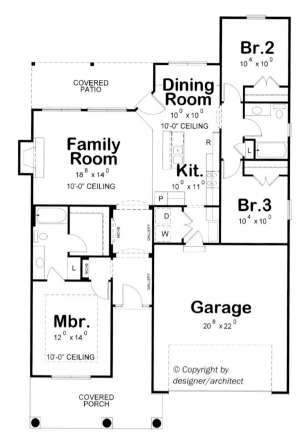

Plan #F10-026D-1997

Dimensions: 40' W x 62' D
Heated Sq. Ft.: 1,356
Bedrooms: 3   **Bathrooms:** 2
Foundation: Slab standard; crawl space, basement or walk-out basement for an additional fee

See index for more information

Images provided by designer/architect

© Copyright by designer/architect

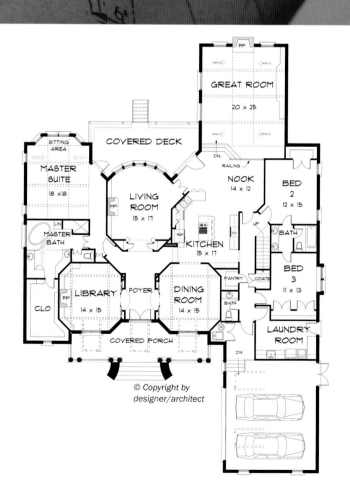

Plan #F10-164D-0044

Images provided by designer/architect

Dimensions: 69' W x 98' D
Heated Sq. Ft.: 3,287
Bedrooms: 3   **Bathrooms:** 2½
Foundation: Slab

See index for more information

© Copyright by designer/architect

First Floor
1,493 sq. ft.

Plan #F10-172D-0031

Dimensions:	63' W x 43' D
Heated Sq. Ft.:	1,493
Bonus Sq. Ft.:	1,470
Bedrooms: 3	Bathrooms: 2
Exterior Walls:	2" x 6"

Foundation: Basement standard; crawl space, monolithic slab, stem wall slab, daylight basement or walk-out basement for an additional fee

See index for more information

Images provided by designer/architect

Optional Lower Level
1,470 sq. ft.

Images provided by designer/architect

Plan #F10-156D-0011

Dimensions:	28' W x 32' D
Heated Sq. Ft.:	710
Bedrooms: 1	Bathrooms: 1

Foundation: Slab standard; crawl space for an additional fee

See index for more information

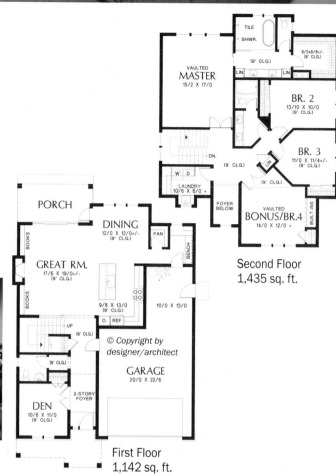

Plan #F10-011D-0681

Dimensions:	38' W x 55' D
Heated Sq. Ft.:	2,577
Bonus Sq. Ft.:	Included
Bedrooms: 4	Bathrooms: 2½
Exterior Walls:	2" x 6"

Foundation: Crawl space or slab standard; basement for an additional fee

See index for more information

Images provided by designer/architect

Second Floor
1,435 sq. ft.

First Floor
1,142 sq. ft.

© Copyright by designer/architect

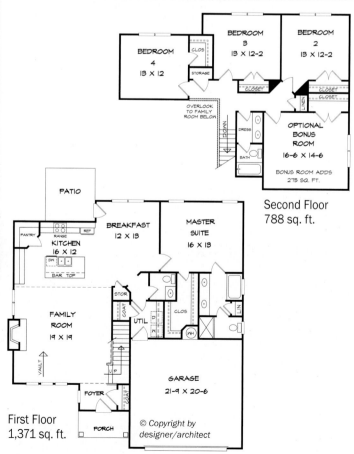

Plan #F10-076D-0287

Dimensions:	46' W x 47' D
Heated Sq. Ft.:	2,159
Bonus Sq. Ft.:	275
Bedrooms: 4	Bathrooms: 2½
Foundation:	Slab

See index for more information

Images provided by designer/architect

Second Floor
788 sq. ft.

First Floor
1,371 sq. ft.

© Copyright by designer/architect

Plan #F10-032D-1023

Dimensions:	52' W x 56' D
Heated Sq. Ft.:	1,556
Bonus Sq. Ft.:	409
Bedrooms: 2	Bathrooms: 1½
Exterior Walls:	2" x 6"

Foundation: Basement standard; crawl space or floating slab for an additional fee

See index for more information

Images provided by designer/architect

First Floor
1,556 sq. ft.

© Copyright by designer/architect

BONUS ROOM
12-0 X 22-0

Optional
Second Floor
409 sq. ft.

Plan #F10-077D-0291

Dimensions:	57' W x 74' D
Heated Sq. Ft.:	2,149
Bonus Sq. Ft.:	429
Bedrooms: 3	Bathrooms: 2½

Foundation: Slab, crawl space, basement or walk-out basement, please specify when ordering

See index for more information

Images provided by designer/architect

Bonus Room
13-0 x 22-6
8' Clg. Ht.

Bonus Bath
7-2 x 8-10

Optional
Second Floor
429 sq. ft.

© Copyright by designer/architect

First Floor
2,149 sq. ft.

Plan #F10-011D-0692

Dimensions: 29' W x 54'6" D
Heated Sq. Ft.: 1,855
Bedrooms: 4   **Bathrooms:** 3
Exterior Walls: 2" x 6"
Foundation: Crawl space or slab standard; basement for an additional fee

See index for more information

Images provided by designer/architect

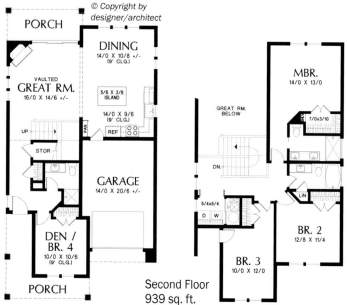

© Copyright by designer/architect

First Floor
916 sq. ft.

Second Floor
939 sq. ft.

PORCH

DINING
14/0 X 10/8 +/-
(9' CLG.)

VAULTED
GREAT RM.
16/0 X 14/6 +/-

5/6 X 3/6
ISLAND

14/0 X 9/6
(9' CLG.)

UP

REF

STOR

GARAGE
14/0 X 20/6 +/-

DEN /
BR. 4
10/0 X 10/6
(9' CLG.)

PORCH

MBR.
14/0 X 13/0

7/0x3/10

GREAT RM.
BELOW

DN.

5/4x5/4

D   W

LIN

BR. 2
12/8 X 11/4

BR. 3
10/0 X 12/0

Plan #F10-121D-0037

Dimensions: 56'8" W x 57'4" D
Heated Sq. Ft.: 2,240
Bedrooms: 3   **Bathrooms:** 2½
Foundation: Basement standard; crawl space or slab for an additional fee

See index for more information

Images provided by designer/architect

Second Floor
630 sq. ft.

Great Rm Below

Br 3
13-4x11-6

Dn

Foyer
Below

Plant Shelf

Loft
10-3x13-11

Br 2
13-7x10-3

First Floor
1,610 sq. ft.

Patio

MBr
13-4x17-3

Std Coffer Clg
Opt Vaulted Clg

Great Rm
18-1x18-2
Vaulted

Brkfst
13-4x13-2

DW

Kitchen
13-4x11-2

P

R

Dn

Foyer

Up

Dining
12-3x13-8

Mud Rm

Laun

W D

Porch

Garage
21-2x25-4

© Copyright by designer/architect

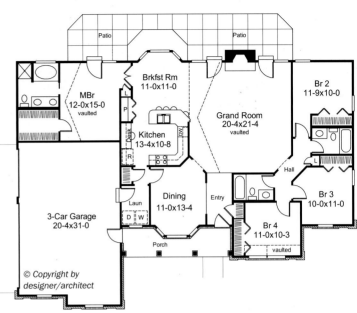

Plan #F10-007D-0146

Dimensions:	68' W x 49'8" D
Heated Sq. Ft.:	1,929
Bedrooms: 4	**Bathrooms:** 3

Foundation: Crawl space standard; basement or slab for an additional fee

See index for more information

Images provided by designer/architect

© Copyright by designer/architect

Plan #F10-052D-0157

Dimensions:	40'4" W x 42' D
Heated Sq. Ft.:	2,067
Bonus Sq. Ft.:	356
Bedrooms: 4	**Bathrooms:** 2½
Foundation:	Basement

See index for more information

Images provided by designer/architect

Second Floor
860 sq. ft.

Lower Level
88 sq. ft.

First Floor
1,119 sq. ft.

© Copyright by designer/architect

Plan #F10-076D-0265

Dimensions:	27'6" W x 47'9" D
Heated Sq. Ft.:	1,276
Bedrooms: 3	Bathrooms: 2½
Foundation:	Slab

See index for more information

Images provided by designer/architect

© Copyright by designer/architect

First Floor
874 sq. ft.

Second Floor
402 sq. ft.

Plan #F10-007D-0164

Dimensions:	53' W x 55' D
Heated Sq. Ft.:	1,741
Bedrooms: 4	Bathrooms: 2
Foundation:	Crawl space standard; slab or basement for an additional fee

See index for more information

Images provided by designer/architect

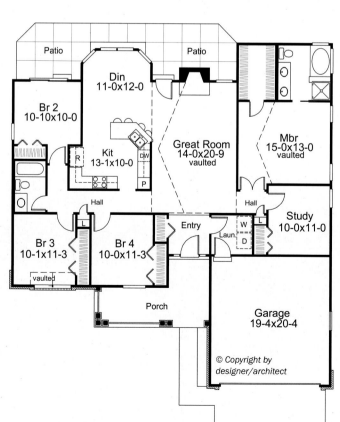

© Copyright by designer/architect

PORCH
8'-0" DEEP

LAUNDRY
7-3 X 6-6

BEDROOM 2
14-0 X 10-0

BATH
7-0 X 10-0

KITCHEN
12-0 X 11-6

GREAT ROOM
20-0 X 14-0

BEDROOM 1
13-0 X 10-0

© Copyright by designer/architect

PORCH
8'-0" DEEP

Plan #F10-028D-0109

Dimensions: 33' W x 40' D
Heated Sq. Ft.: 890
Bedrooms: 2   **Bathrooms:** 1
Exterior Walls: 2" x 6"
Foundation: Floating slab standard; monolithic slab, crawl space, basement or walk-out basement for an additional fee

See index for more information

BATH

BREAKFAST ROOM
12'-4" X 9'-6"

PORCH

KNEE SPACE

GUEST ROOM/
BEDROOM 4
12'-8" X 11'-6"

MASTER SUITE
TRAY CEILING
13'-4" X 15'-8"

WHP TUB

GREAT ROOM
12' CEILING
15'-0" X 18'-4"

M.BATH
8'-10" X 2'-0"

KITCHEN
12'-8" X 13'-6"

LAU.
12'-8" X 5'-10"

REF

PAN

BATH

LIN

8" BOX COL.

FOYER
12' CEILING
7'-4" X 7'-10"

LIN

DINING ROOM
10' BOX CEILING
12'-2" X 13'-4"

BEDROOM 3
11'-0" X 10'-4"

BEDROOM 2
11'-2" X 11'-6"

GARAGE
20'-10" X 25'-0"

PORCH
7'-0" X 5'-6"

VAULTED CEILING

© Copyright by designer/architect

Plan #F10-055D-0205

Dimensions: 64'2" W x 49' D
Heated Sq. Ft.: 1,989
Bedrooms: 4   **Bathrooms:** 3
Foundation: Slab or crawl space standard; basement or daylight basement for an additional fee

See index for more information

Plan #F10-157D-0001

Dimensions: 69'9" W x 56' D
Heated Sq. Ft.: 2,182
Bonus Sq. Ft.: 327
Bedrooms: 3 **Bathrooms:** 2½
Foundation: Crawl space standard; slab for an additional fee

See index for more information

Images provided by designer/architect

© Copyright by designer/architect

Optional Second Floor
327 sq. ft.

BONUS RM.
13'-0" X 23'-4"

First Floor
2,182 sq. ft.

Bedroom#3 12'-8" x 11'-8"
Porch 19'-0" x 6'-4"
Brkf. 12'-11" x 10'-7"
Master Bdrm 14'-0" x 15'-1"
Great rm. 19'-2" x 16'-8"
Laundry 9'-9" x 6'-3"
Closet 9'-0" x 12'-7"
Kitchen 13'-1" x 12'-2"
UP
Bedroom#2 12'-8" x 11'-8"
Entry 5'-11" x 11'-8"
Dining 12'-8" x 11'-8"
Pantry 12'-11" x 5'-2"
Garage 23'-4" x 23'-4"
Porch

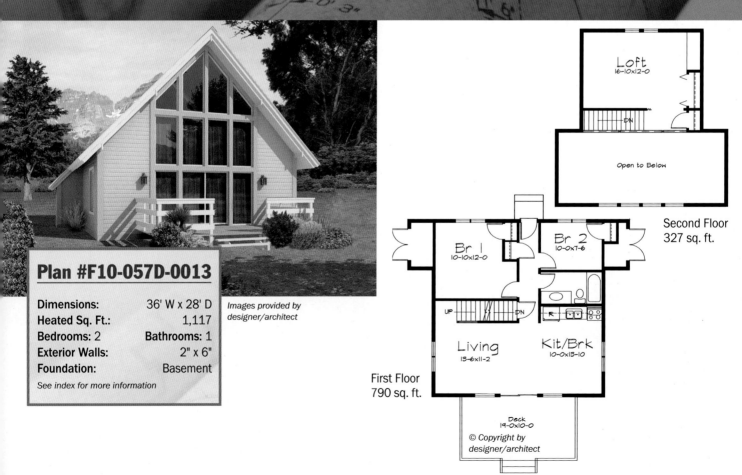

Plan #F10-057D-0013

Dimensions: 36' W x 28' D
Heated Sq. Ft.: 1,117
Bedrooms: 2 **Bathrooms:** 1
Exterior Walls: 2" x 6"
Foundation: Basement

See index for more information

Images provided by designer/architect

Loft 16-10x12-0

Open to Below

Second Floor
327 sq. ft.

Br 1 10-10x12-0
Br 2 10-0x7-6
UP
DN
Living 13-6x11-2
Kit/Brk 10-0x13-10

First Floor
790 sq. ft.

Deck 19-0x10-0

© Copyright by designer/architect

Plan #F10-091D-0520

Dimensions:	64' W x 52' D
Heated Sq. Ft.:	2,751
Bedrooms: 4	Bathrooms: 3½
Exterior Walls:	2" x 6"

Foundation: Crawl space standard; slab, basement or walk-out basement for an additional fee

See index for more information

Images provided by designer/architect

Second Floor
796 sq. ft.

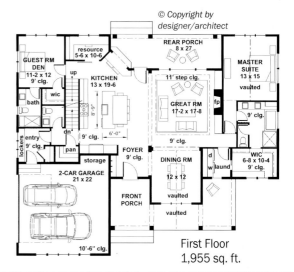

© Copyright by designer/architect

First Floor
1,955 sq. ft.

Images provided by designer/architect

© Copyright by designer/architect

Plan #F10-144D-0024

Dimensions:	32' W x 32' D
Heated Sq. Ft.:	1,024
Bedrooms: 1	Bathrooms: 1½
Exterior Walls:	2" x 6"

Foundation: Crawl space or slab standard; basement or walk-out basement for an additional fee

See index for more information

Plan #F10-161D-0016

Dimensions:	76' W x 120' D
Heated Sq. Ft.:	3,275
Bedrooms: 4	Bathrooms: 3½
Exterior Walls:	2" x 6"
Foundation:	Crawl space

See index for more information

Features

- With its sleek style, this modern home feels uncomplicated and inviting
- The kitchen, dining area and great room all remain open to one another creating an overwhelming sense of spaciousness
- Stair-stepped rooms and walls of windows at the rear of this home create amazing views from every angle
- A centrally located great room takes center stage and does not disappoint, with its built-in niches and cabinetry there is plenty of space to display art as well as store family treasures
- Located off the garage is a laundry room that is perfect for organizing your family; it features not only a large bench with hooks above, but cubbies and an L-shaped counter for folding and sorting clothes
- The master suite has dramatic floor to ceiling corner windows and a luxurious bath complete with shower, tub, large walk-in close and double bowl vanity
- The second floor features a den/studio for the artist in the family as well as a guest room/TV room and a convenient full bath
- 3-car side entry garage

Images provided by designer/architect

© Copyright by designer/architect

First Floor
2,729 sq. ft.

Second Floor
546 sq. ft.

Plan #F10-164D-0036

Dimensions:	110'7" W x 86'4" D
Heated Sq. Ft.:	5,303
Bedrooms: 5	**Bathrooms:** 4½
Foundation:	Slab

See index for more information

Images provided by designer/architect

Features

- Stunning European style two-story is adorned with Tudor accents and beautiful stonework creating tons of curb appeal
- The circular staircase in the foyer is an impressive feature that is sure to "wow" guests upon entering
- Beautiful circular window walls grace the master bedroom, dining nook, and the two-story great room
- A peaceful guest bedroom can be found tucked away near the garage and has its own walk-in closet and private bath
- The second floor game room/theater is sure to be a favorite gathering spot
- 2-car front entry garage, and a 1-car rear entry garage

Second Floor
1,771 sq. ft.

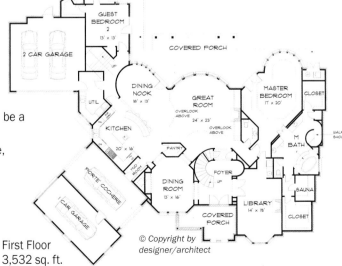

First Floor
3,532 sq. ft.

© Copyright by
designer/architect

Plan #F10-011S-0112

Dimensions:	124'4" W x 84'3" D
Heated Sq. Ft.:	5,155
Bonus Sq. Ft.:	553
Bedrooms: 4	Bathrooms: 3½
Exterior Walls:	2" x 6"
Foundation:	Walk-out basement

See index for more information

Images provided by designer/architect

Features

- This breathtaking home incorporates the best elements of classic, lodge-inspired rustic Northwest living on the exterior with an open, floor plan on the interior
- The outdoor kitchen connects to the breakfast nook offering a great way to conveniently dine in the great outdoors without any hassle
- The large great room features a high vaulted ceiling and generous built-ins
- The two-island kitchen features an adjoining nook, built-in wine cooler, and a built-in desk, emphasizing this home's great function
- The bonus area has an additional 553 square feet of living area
- Two 2-car front entry garages

© Copyright by designer/architect

First Floor
2,966 sq. ft.

Lower Level
2,189 sq. ft.

houseplansandmore.com

Plan #F10-032D-0880

Dimensions:	40' W x 44' D
Heated Sq. Ft.:	1,944
Bedrooms: 4	Bathrooms: 2
Exterior Walls:	2" x 6"

Foundation: Floating slab standard; basement, crawl space or monolithic slab for an additional fee

See index for more information

Features

- This modern farmhouse inspired home offers an open floor plan that maintains an airy feel throughout the interior
- The kitchen is entirely open to the two-story great room that feature a soaring fireplace
- There is a bedroom located on the first floor for convenience and it has outdoor access onto a covered patio
- The second floor has three additional bedrooms including one with its own private outdoor balcony
- 1-car front entry garage

Second Floor
831 sq. ft.

© Copyright by
designer/architect

First Floor
1,113 sq. ft.

Images provided by designer/architect

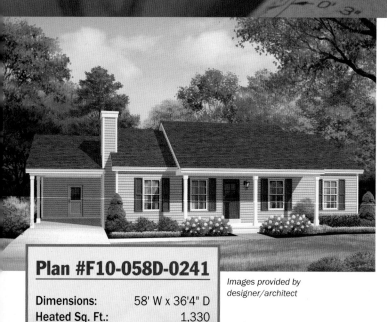

Plan #F10-058D-0241

Dimensions:	58' W x 36'4" D
Heated Sq. Ft.:	1,330
Bedrooms: 3	Bathrooms: 2
Foundation:	Basement

See index for more information

Images provided by designer/architect

© Copyright by designer/architect

Storage

Carport
13-8x21-4

Dn

Kit/Brk
22-1x12-1

Island

R

Pantry

MBr
10-4x12-8

Lin.

Family
22-1x13-4

Bedrm 2
10-4x10-6

Bedrm 3
10-4x10-6

Porch
24-8x6-4

Plan #F10-143D-0007

Dimensions:	49'2" W x 47' D
Heated Sq. Ft.:	1,380
Bedrooms: 3	Bathrooms: 2
Exterior Walls:	2" x 6"

Foundation: Basement, crawl space or slab, please specify when ordering

See index for more information

Images provided by designer/architect

BEDROOM #2
13'-0" X 13'-0"

DINING ROOM
10'-0" X 11'-0"

KITCHEN
11'-0" X 11'-0"

MASTER BEDROOM
15'-0" X 15'-0"

BATH

LIVING ROOM
16'-0" X 15'-0"

PANTRY

W.I.C.

BEDROOM #3
13'-0" X 13'-0"

UTILITY

MASTER BATH

COVERED PORCH
16'-0" X 4'-0"

GARAGE
20'-0" X 20'-0"

© Copyright by designer/architect

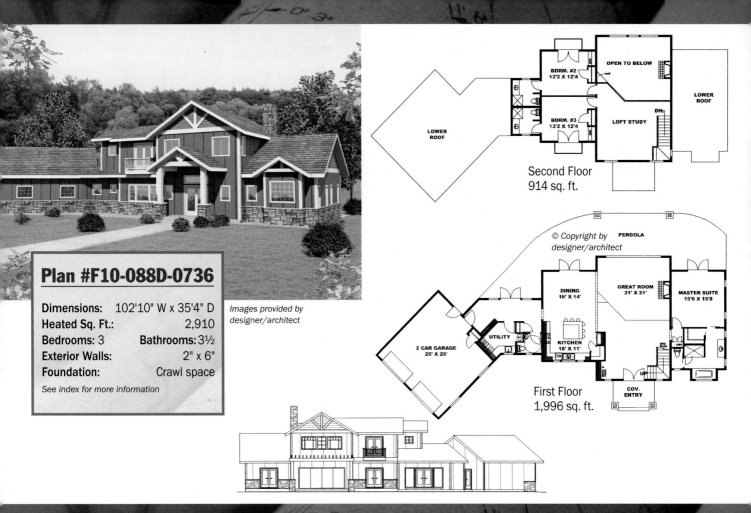

Plan #F10-088D-0736

Dimensions:	102'10" W x 35'4" D
Heated Sq. Ft.:	2,910
Bedrooms: 3	Bathrooms: 3½
Exterior Walls:	2" x 6"
Foundation:	Crawl space

See index for more information

Images provided by designer/architect

Second Floor
914 sq. ft.

BDRM. #2
13'2 X 12'4

OPEN TO BELOW

LOWER ROOF

BDRM. #3
13'2 X 12'4

LOFT STUDY

DN

LOWER ROOF

© Copyright by designer/architect

PERGOLA

DINING
16' X 14'

GREAT ROOM
21' X 21'

MASTER SUITE
15'6 X 15'8

2 CAR GARAGE
25' X 25'

UTILITY

KITCHEN
18' X 11'

UP

COV. ENTRY

First Floor
1,996 sq. ft.

Plan #F10-007D-0104

Dimensions:	31'4" W x 38' D
Heated Sq. Ft.:	1,207
Bedrooms: 2	Bathrooms: 1
Foundation:	Walk-out basement

See index for more information

Images provided by designer/architect

Garage Below

Br 2
12-0x11-0

Atrium

Dn

Living Rm.
16-0x18-2

Hall

Dining

MBr
12-0x13-3
(9' clg.)

Kitchen
9-0x9-0

Entry

R

Porch

First Floor
969 sq. ft.

© Copyright by designer/architect

Up

Atrium above

Garage
11-8x21-0

Family Rm.
15-1x18-8

D
W

F

HW

Laundry/stor.

Lower Level
238 sq. ft.

Plan #F10-172D-0051

Dimensions:	41'6" W x 64' D
Heated Sq. Ft.:	1,635
Bonus Sq. Ft.:	2,204
Bedrooms: 3	**Bathrooms:** 2
Exterior Walls:	2" x 6"

Foundation: Basement standard; crawl space, monolithic slab, stem wall slab, daylight basement or walk-out basement for an additional fee

See index for more information

Images provided by designer/architect

Features

- This one-story has great curb appeal and plenty of room for expansion
- The family room is open to the kitchen
- A home office is right off the entry for convenience
- The kitchen features a small dining area nearby and a large walk-in pantry
- The optional lower level has an additional 2,204 square feet of living area and includes an apartment that can be accessed directly from the outdoors
- 2-car front entry garage

© Copyright by designer/architect
2 CAR GARAGE
22' 1" x 22' 8"
Main Floor
1,635 Sq Ft.

First Floor
1,635 sq. ft.

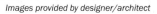

Optional Lower Level
2,204 sq. ft.

Plan #F10-056S-0021

Dimensions: 64'4" W x 67'10" D
Heated Sq. Ft.: 3,314
Bonus Sq. Ft.: 1,956
Bedrooms: 5 **Bathrooms:** 4
Foundation: Basement standard; crawl space or slab for an additional fee

See index for more information

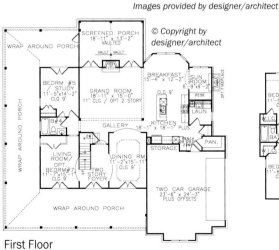

Images provided by designer/architect

Features

- Luxury Modern Farmhouse is perfectly designed for a sloping lot
- Bedroom #5/study is a private space perfect for guests
- An open first floor plan includes formal spaces as well as casual areas
- The optional lower level has an additional 1,956 square feet of living area
- 2-car side entry garage

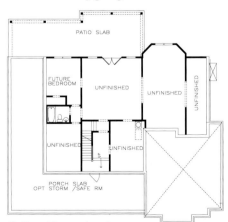

Optional Lower Level
1,956 sq. ft.

First Floor
1,672 sq. ft.

Second Floor
1,642 sq. ft.

© Copyright by designer/architect

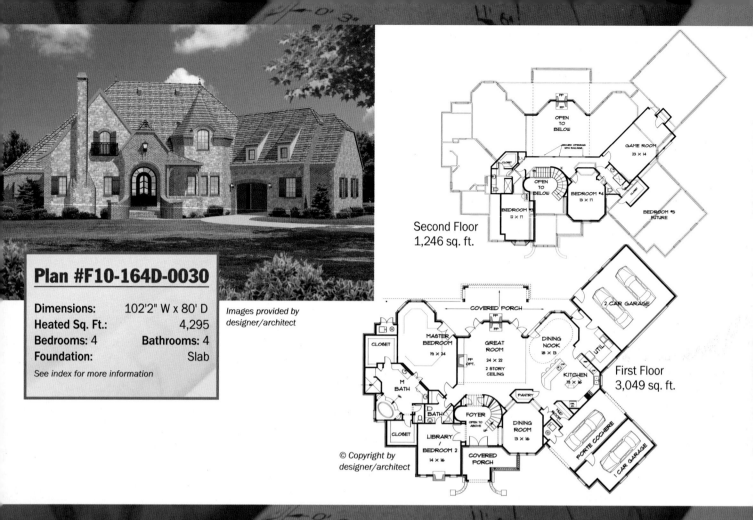

Second Floor
1,246 sq. ft.

First Floor
3,049 sq. ft.

© Copyright by
designer/architect

Plan #F10-164D-0030

Dimensions:	102'2" W x 80' D
Heated Sq. Ft.:	4,295
Bedrooms: 4	Bathrooms: 4
Foundation:	Slab

See index for more information

Images provided by designer/architect

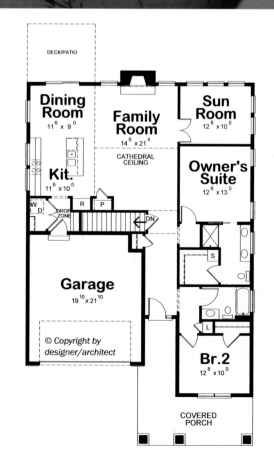

© Copyright by
designer/architect

Plan #F10-026D-2117

Dimensions:	40' W x 62' D
Heated Sq. Ft.:	1,511
Bedrooms: 2	Bathrooms: 2
Exterior Walls:	2" x 6"

Foundation: Basement standard;
crawl space, slab or walk-out
basement for an additional fee

See index for more information

Images provided by designer/architect

Plan #F10-084D-0063

Dimensions: 62'11" W x 77'1" D
Heated Sq. Ft.: 2,280
Bonus Sq. Ft.: 1,166
Bedrooms: 3 **Bathrooms:** 2½
Foundation: Basement, slab or crawl space, please specify when ordering

See index for more information

Images provided by designer/architect

First Floor
2,280 sq. ft.

Optional Second Floor
1,166 sq. ft.

Plan #F10-051D-0849

Dimensions: 39' W x 48' D
Heated Sq. Ft.: 1,170
Bedrooms: 3 **Bathrooms:** 1
Exterior Walls: 2" x 6"
Foundation: Basement standard; crawl space or slab for an additional fee

See index for more information

Images provided by designer/architect

Plan #F10-111D-0039

Dimensions:	40' W x 47'4" D
Heated Sq. Ft.:	1,846
Bedrooms: 3	Bathrooms: 2½
Foundation:	Slab

See index for more information

Features

- Striking Craftsman symmetry promises to add major curb appeal to any neighborhood
- The wrap-around covered porch is perfect for extending your living to the outdoors
- The kitchen is designed for function and includes a center island and an eating bar
- The living and dining areas surround the kitchen and maximize the first floor square footage to the fullest
- The second floor features two bedrooms, and an open loft space, ideal as an office or computer area

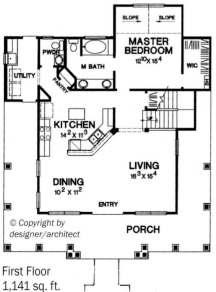

First Floor
1,141 sq. ft.

Second Floor
705 sq. ft.

Images provided by designer/architect

Plan #F10-155D-0111

Dimensions:	106' W x 110' D
Heated Sq. Ft.:	4,575
Bedrooms: 4	**Bathrooms:** 4½

Foundation: Daylight basement standard; slab or basement for an additional fee

See index for more information

Images provided by designer/architect

Features

- This one-story luxury home has a Craftsman style exterior that's both rustic and refined
- The kitchen enjoys two islands with one designated for casual dining
- The beautiful beamed ceiling and fireplace add a cozy feel to the great room
- The enormous laundry/hobby room will be a great place to keep everything organized
- A fun game room can be found on the lower level along with bedroom 4, a full bath, and an unfinished basement area
- 3-car front entry garage

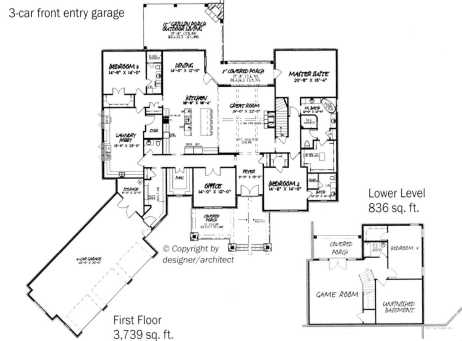

© Copyright by designer/architect

First Floor
3,739 sq. ft.

Lower Level
836 sq. ft.

Plan #F10-026D-1871

Dimensions: 59'4" W x 64'4" D
Heated Sq. Ft.: 1,945
Bedrooms: 3   Bathrooms: 2½
Foundation: Basement standard;
crawl space, slab or walk-out
basement for an additional fee

See index for more information

Images provided by designer/architect

© Copyright by designer/architect

Plan #F10-013D-0229

Dimensions: 53'8" W x 60'1" D
Heated Sq. Ft.: 1,800
Bonus Sq. Ft.: 3,124
Bedrooms: 3   Bathrooms: 2
Foundation: Basement standard;
crawl space or slab for an
additional fee

See index for more information

Images provided by designer/architect

© Copyright by designer/architect

Optional Second Floor 1,224 sq. ft.

Optional Lower Level 1,900 sq. ft.

First Floor 1,800 sq. ft.

Plan #F10-051D-0847

Dimensions:	40' W x 46' D
Heated Sq. Ft.:	1,047
Bedrooms: 2	Bathrooms: 1
Exterior Walls:	2" x 6"

Foundation: Basement standard; slab or crawl space for an additional fee

See index for more information

Images provided by designer/architect

DECK

MBR.
9'-1 1/8" CEILING
15'8"x13'0"

KIT.
VAULTED CEILING
9'0"x9'6"

DIN. RM.
VAULTED CEILING
8'6"x9'6"

BR. #2
9'-1 1/8" CEILING
11'8"x10'6"

GRT. RM.
VAULTED CEILING
17'6"x14'6"

E.
CATHEDRAL
CEILING

2 CAR GARAGE
20'4"x20'8"

Plan #F10-007D-0110

Dimensions:	37'4" W x 46'8" D
Heated Sq. Ft.:	1,169
Bedrooms: 3	Bathrooms: 2
Foundation:	Basement

See index for more information

Images provided by designer/architect

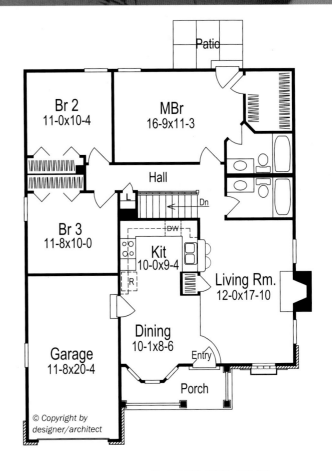

Patio

Br 2
11-0x10-4

MBr
16-9x11-3

Hall

Br 3
11-8x10-0

Dn

DW

Kit
10-0x9-4

Living Rm.
12-0x17-10

R

Garage
11-8x20-4

Dining
10-1x8-6

Entry

Porch

looking inside today's best
smart homes

Since the beginning of time, interest in making life easier has always brought curiosity to inventors as well as architects. Even as far back as the Victorian era homebuilders included "dumbwaiters" in homes. Similar to an elevator but on a smaller scale that often used pulleys, a dumbwaiter was an easy method to help homeowners move things from one floor to another. So, it comes as no surprise that homeowners are still constantly searching for ways to make life easier. Whether the gadget or appliance is small such as the crockpot in the 60s and 70s, or the Keurig® of today, we are always yearning for the latest technology to tackle life's everyday hassles with better ease.

Today's gadgets and smart home features are more seamless than ever. Most are now powered by an app that can be downloaded onto your tablet or smart phone allowing your home to be managed even while you're away. Often these added conveniences are time-saving, but they also provide better safety and health benefits. If you're interested in incorporating smart features into your new home, there are many innovative options available to homeowners and the market is continuing to grow.

Page 370, left: Google Home Smart Assistant 2, store.google.com, photo from gadgetflow.com; right: Iris Hub, irisbylowes.com, photo from techive.com; Page 371, clockwise from top right: Ecobee4 is more than a thermostat, shop.ecobee.com; GE Z-Wave Wireless Smart Lighting Control Appliance Module works with Amazon Alexa, amazon.com; Quirky + GE Aros Smart Window Air Conditioner, amazon.com; The Smart Bridge and Lutron App for Caséta Wireless are the perfect foundations for creating a connected home system, casetawireless.com; Nest Learning Thermostat, store.nest.com.

command attention

From automated lock systems to apps that manage the temperature on your thermostat, tech companies have responded to the homeowner's need for a central command hub. A hub device is designed to allow you to control all of the various apps managing functions throughout your home in one master application. Some of the top hubs on the market today include: Google Echo, Samsung SmartThings *(smartthings.com)*, Iris Smart Hub® *(lowes. com)*, Staples Connect™ *(staples.com)*, and Wink *(homedepot.com)*. If you're a homeowner that's also a tech junkie, then seamlessly managing all of your apps and home functions in one central hub really cuts down on the app clutter and confusion.

Other wireless options include Wi-Fi plug modules. GE's appliance module plugs into the wall, then plug any small appliance into the module and it instantly goes wireless and can be managed from your smart phone. There are also in-wall outlets that make the outlets themselves app-adjustable. Don't ever fear again that you left the curling iron on, and you won't be home for hours. Yes, there's now an app for that!

home basics 101

Digital thermostats, such as the ones from Nest®, sync with an app on your smart phone and even learn your habits. Then, they program themselves to turn up the temperature, or turn it down based on your routine. The Ecobee4 has a responsive display, a remote sensor and tons of smart integrations, including a built-in Amazon Alexa speaker, making it unmatched on the market.

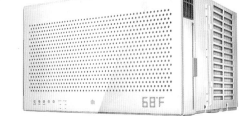

Or, install Quirky + GE Aros Smart Air Conditioner that responds to commands from your smart phone and also uses GPS to turn itself on and off depending on where you are, resulting in money and energy savings.

Ceiling fans have also gone high tech. The Vizia RF +® Fan Speed Control *(leviton.com)* can adjust a fan to any speed, turn it off, set it to start at a certain time, and can also coordinate with light dimmers all while using Wi-Fi.

Control the amount of light throughout your home and the intensity with app controlled light dimmers. Some great options on the market include: Lutron Caseta® Wireless In-Wall Dimmer, left *(homedepot.com)*, Aspire RF with Z-Wave® Dimmer *(staples.com)*, and Leviton DZMX Z-Wave Dimmer *(leviton.com)*. If you're interested in other smart lighting options, then the Philips Hue Wireless Dimming Kit is a simple and affordable way to get started.

Tech is even moving outdoors and getting in on the smart stuff with the Skydrop™ sprinkler system that reviews the local weather forecasts to determine watering needs and adjusts its settings accordingly. It includes both automatic and manual modes, and now works with Nest®.

interior decor

Windows, Blinds & Shades

Control the amount of light that enters your home even remotely with shades from Bali or Serena. Or, automate your shades so that as the sun shifts in the sky, the shades adjust for better efficiency and privacy.

Flooring

From cutting edge carpets to floor textiles, some new flooring options are able to track your every move and even show you the way. Lauzon Pure Genius® Smart Floor breaks down airborne contaminants. Activated by light, Pure Genius® flooring works on its own and acts as if having 3 trees inside your home. Natural or artificial light activates the titanium dioxide in Pure Genius®, setting the air-purifying agent in motion. The flooring is triggered by movement, whether from movement through a room, or a fan. The active nanoparticles in Pure Genius® decompose toxic contaminants in the air (formaldehyde and other pollutants) and convert them into harmless water and carbon dioxide molecules. Toto's Hydrotect Tile has a special coating that's antimicrobial and repels oil and dirt. So, cleaning the floor just got a whole lot faster and easier. A house coated in HydroTect purifies the same amount of air as a forest the size of four tennis courts, or decomposes the same amount of pollution produced by 30 cars driving a little over 18 miles a day.

Home Accessories

You spend more time in bed than anywhere else in your home. So why not invest in a smart bed? Sensors in the Sleep Number Mattress using their SleepIQ® Technology *(sleepnumber.com)* communicate with a corresponding app that calculates your breathing, heart rate, and frequency of movement. Then, outfit your smart bed with the Outlast® Temperature Regulating Sheets System that absorbs and releases excess body heat and moisture, so no need to steal, or kick the blankets off all night long anymore.

engage your senses

Today's homeowners are interested in living cleaner lifestyles free of chemicals and allergens trapped within their home. Becoming less popular are unnatural chemical laden room freshening sprays and deodorizers and taking their place are aromatherapy diffusers. These diffusers can be adjusted to run for any period of time and they use natural essential oils to eliminate odors, relieve stress, or discourage germs.

A method for monitoring home air quality is placing smoke and carbon monoxide detectors around your home. Now, these devices send your phone alerts and communicate with other units. Some distinguish between smoke and carbon dioxide and even tell you where the problem lies in a human voice. If you're concerned with water leaks and mold, then a Wally Sensor *(wallyhome.com)* can send you alerts about leaks and mold. a WallyHome Multi-Sensor detects and alerts you of water leaks, temperature and humidity changes, and when doors and windows open.

If you love having live plants and flowers around your home, but hate not knowing how to keep them thriving, then the Click and Grow Smartpot *(clickandgrow.com)* was created just for you. It dispenses the correct amount of water and nutrients for up to a month making it also great for those who travel frequently. Or, use a Parrot® Flower Power *(global.parrot.com)* and place the sensor into the soil and it will tell you exactly how to tend to the plant via your smart phone.

Page 372, top: Skydrop™ Smart Watering Sprinkler Controller has 8 built-in zones using the most advanced technology that accesses local weather data, calculates water, and adjusts watering schedules helping you spend less money, skydrop.com; Lauzon Pure Genius® flooring, lauzon.com; Page 373, top: i10 with FlexFit 3 and Sleep IQ®, sleepnumber.com; top, middle: Your WallyHome Sensor connects your home and keeps you informed through text message, email, push notifications or phone calls, wallyhome.com; right: The Click and Grow Smartpot enables you to grow fresh herbs, fruits and flowers with zero effort, clickandgrow.com.

Let yourself wake up in a more peaceful state thanks to the Yantouch Diamond+ Speaker and Alarm *(yantouch.com)*. This unique device washes the wall in soft light in millions of colors and wakes you up with sunrise hues all while playing accompanying music. Or, if drifting off to sleep tends to be more of a problem for you, then use a Drift™ Light by Saffron *(drift-light.com)*, which functions as a normal bulb until you flip the switch twice, then it softly fades in 37 minutes, which is the average time of a sunset. The bulb's warm light also induces melatonin production, which naturally controls your body's sleep and wake cycles.

Even your bathroom can be outfitted with amazing smart features such as the Sunstruck® Bathtub with Bask® *(us.kohler.com)*. This tub acts as a Bluetooth speaker when empty, but when it's filled the music waves ripple through the water and creates a hydrotherapy spa. It will even play your music library, or select one of their programmed mixes for total relaxation. Shower controls can also be set and regulated so the water is the optimal temperature or, sing along with your favorite playlist right inside your shower with Kohler's Moxie™ showerhead with removable speaker by Harman Kardon.

Page 374 top: Yantouch Diamond+ world's first Music+Light LED Lifestyle Bluetooth Speaker, yantouch.com/diamond; bottom: Kohler's Sunstruck® Oval Freestanding bathtub with Bask® heated surface, us.kohler.com; Moxie™ showerhead with built-in Harman Kardon speaker, us.kohler.com; Page 375, top, left and right: Crock-Pot® 6-Quart Smart Slow Cooker with WeMo® App, Item #SCCPWM600-V2, crock-pot.com; middle, right: Samsung French Door Refrigerator with Family Hub™, samsung.com; Bottom: Dacor Discovery™ iQ Wall Oven is controllable from an app, Item# DYO230, dacor.com; middle, left: 782 Taylor TemPerfect™ Floating Thermometers, taylor-enviro.com.

no excuse for the perfect meal

Kitchen gadgets and appliances have come a long way and almost make it impossible to ruin a meal. For instance, there's no longer a need to hang by the oven or stove when cooking thanks to a kitchen thermometer that will ping you via an app when the meat you're cooking in the oven reaches the correct temperature. So, you can finally enjoy spending time with family and friends on the patio before dinner is served thanks to this handy device.

Or, upgrade your crockpot to the Crock-Pot® 6-Quart. Smart Slow Cooker with WeMo® (crock-pot.com). It monitors and adjusts the time and temperature remotely and will send you a notification to your smart phone when the set time has finished.

Taylor's TEMPerfect™ Floating Rings indicate a liquid's ideal temperature for poaching, simmering or boiling. Or, try their butter dish that changes color when the butter reaches room temperature.

innovative home appliances

Refrigerators

Sub-Zero's® IT-36CIID Refrigerator and Freezer (subzero-wolf.com) uses NASA technology and includes an air purifier that rids the inside of mold and bacteria every 20 minutes. Another popular option great for busy families is the Samsung® Smart Hub Refrigerator that has a large touchscreen that lets you leave notes, view other family members' schedules, order groceries, play music, and even watch TV. It also has three cameras on the inside that can take a picture and email it to you every time you close the door. Now you can stop guessing if you need milk when grocery shopping.

Ovens

Dacor's Discovery™ iQ Wall Oven (dacor.com) not only screams fun since it's available in a variety of colors, but it can be controlled via Wi-Fi and features an LCD screen where you can access recipes.

Stoves

The Alno Kitchen Display, left (alno-usa.com) allows the chef of the family to look up recipes on-line, watch cooking shows, or even take a video call, while sautéing tonight's dinner.

Washers & Dryers

The Whirlpool® Smart Front-Load Washer and Dryer sends alerts making you aware of peak energy-using hours and connects to your Amazon account so you can order laundry supplies easily.

other top-notch smart home electronics

Televisions

The Roku™ TV comes with fully integrated streaming and works with gaming consoles and other devices to provide hundreds of channels and platforms like Netflix™.

Sound Systems

BeoLab18 speaker towers, left (bang-olufsen.com) operate on a frequency that's not affected by other wireless networks. So, gone are the days of having a song stop right in the middle, or showing other signs of interference with static. You will be able to enjoy crystal clear uninterrupted sound.

Monitoring Systems

Fido feeling lonely? Then, Petcube (petcube.com) may be the answer. Place the cube where your pet stays when you aren't home and it streams video to your tablet or smart phone. Or, monitor your pet with PetChatz HD®, left (petchatz.com), or Petzi Treat Cam® (petzi.com), which is similar to the Petcube, but instead of a laser that plays with your pet, it dispenses treats.

If outdoor security is your interest, then SkyBell's® video doorbell quality is terrific, and integrations with Alexa, Nest®, and If This Then That (IFTTT) help it stand out in an increasingly competitive market. It also includes free online video storage and a resolution of 1080p, which are also major pluses.

Page 376 top: Alno kitchen displays allow you to look up recipes online while cooking, alno-usa.com; middle: Bang Olufsen's BeoLab 18 delivers exceptional wireless sound, and placement flexibility, bang-olufsen.com; bottom: PetChatz HD® Pet Camera Two-Way Audio/Video System dispenses treats and provides motion/noise sensing, petchatz.com.

Voice Activated Assistance

Amazon's Echo and Alexa retrieve on-line information, play music, set reminders and more all by using voice commands. Jibo *(myjibo.com)* recognizes faces, learns your tastes, gives you reminders and communicates with you using sound effects and graphics.

Robots

Robot vacuums are one of the most popular gadgets that make cleaning less of a chore. These machines are only getting better with some that now even mop.

And, don't protect these fancy gadgets and electronics the old-fashioned way with a standard surge protector, use the Wink Pivot Surge Protector, which of course is Wi-Fi enabled.

With homeowners constantly being bombarded by alerts, messages, notifications, texts and emails, it's easy to see why gadgets and devices that reduce the amount of clutter electronically are the latest rage in home design. Incorporating these smart products into your new home will take it into the future and generally make life easier from the minute you move in. Stop wasting time and let these savvy tech items run your household like a champ; giving you more time to relax and enjoy life.

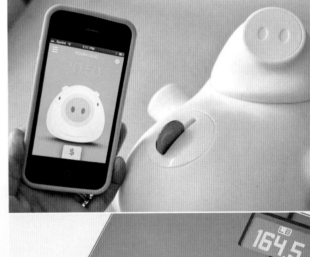

quirky finds

- Porkfolio *(wink.com)* is a piggy bank that tracks your savings and deposits, and helps you set goals. And, you can actually drop in coins and its snout lights up!

- Nokia's Body+ Health Mate Body Composition Wi-Fi Scale (health. nokia.com) monitors your weight, BMI, body fat percentage and heart rate.

- GlowCap® *(nanthealth.com/vitality)* is a pill bottle lid that reminds you to take your medicine by lighting up. It shares information with your doctor and submits prescription refills.

- Petnet iO Smartfeeder schedules pet feeding times, manages portions, and sends notifications right to your phone.

Page 377 clockwise from top: Amazon Echo uses Alexa to play music, make calls, send messages, and get information instantly, amazon. com; Porkfolio Piggy bank uses the Wink app to monitor the amount of change you've put into its belly and track your savings goals, wink. com; Nokia's Body+ Health Mate Body Composition Wi-Fi Scale centralizes your health information to help you achieve your health goals, health.nokia.com; Vitality Glowcap® syncs with an app and reminds you to take your medicine by lighting up the cap, nanthealth.com/vitality; The Petnet iO SmartFeeder is an automatic pet feeder that dispenses food on a schedule, petnet.io.

Plan #F10-106S-0070

Dimensions:	90'5" W x 78' D
Heated Sq. Ft.:	7,100
Bedrooms: 6	**Bathrooms:** 7½
Exterior Walls:	Concrete block
Foundation:	Monolithic slab

See index for more information

Images provided by designer/architect

Features

- A popular summer kitchen can be found on the covered patio overlooking the space designated for a pool as well as plenty of additional covered patio space for entertaining
- A gorgeous staircase in a circular turret ascends to the second floor creating quite a dramatic statement upon entering the grand foyer
- A unique V.I.P. suite is the perfect place for guests featuring a lavish bath, a walk-in closet, and direct access to the pool and patio
- 3-car front entry garage

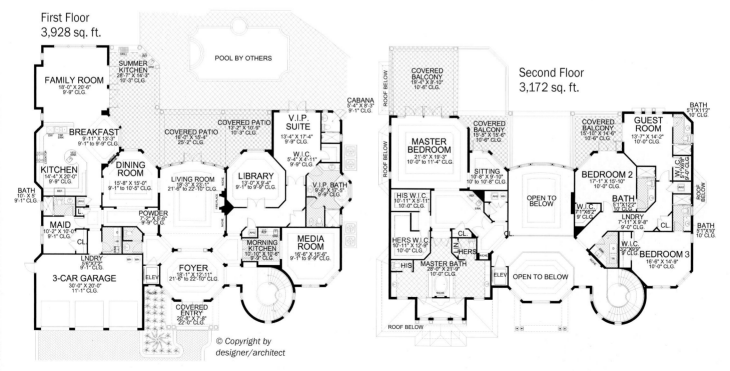

First Floor
3,928 sq. ft.

Second Floor
3,172 sq. ft.

© Copyright by designer/architect

Plan #F10-091D-0523

Dimensions:	69' W x 57'6" D
Heated Sq. Ft.:	2,514
Bonus Sq. Ft.:	390
Bedrooms: 4	Bathrooms: 3½
Exterior Walls:	2" x 6"

Foundation: Crawl space standard; slab, basement, daylight basement or walk-out basement for an additional fee

See index for more information

Images provided by designer/architect

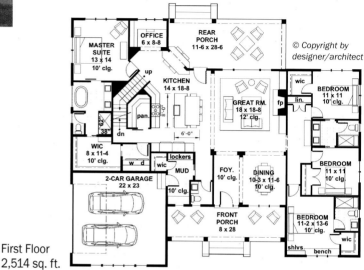

© Copyright by designer/architect

Optional Second Floor
390 sq. ft.

First Floor
2,514 sq. ft.

Plan #F10-143D-0006

Dimensions:	50' W x 28' D
Heated Sq. Ft.:	1,400
Bedrooms: 3	Bathrooms: 2
Exterior Walls:	2" x 6"

Foundation: Basement, crawl space or slab, please specify when ordering

See index for more information

Images provided by designer/architect

© Copyright by designer/architect

Plan #F10-084D-0085

Dimensions:	85' W x 64' D
Heated Sq. Ft.:	2,252
Bonus Sq. Ft.:	1,341
Bedrooms: 3	**Bathrooms:** 2
Foundation: Slab standard; crawl space or basement for an additional fee	

See index for more information

Images provided by designer/architect

© Copyright by designer/architect

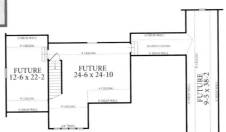

Optional Second Floor
1,341 sq. ft.

First Floor
2,252 sq. ft.

Plan #F10-088D-0731

Dimensions:	75' W x 92'4" D
Heated Sq. Ft.:	3,643
Bedrooms: 2	**Bathrooms:** 5
Exterior Walls:	2" x 8"
Foundation:	Crawl space

See index for more information

Images provided by designer/architect

Front Elevation

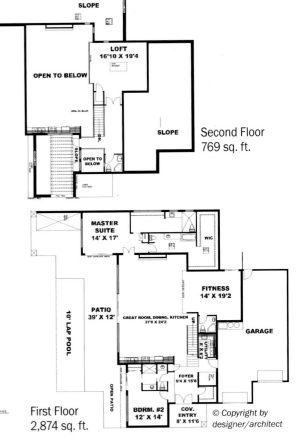

Second Floor
769 sq. ft.

First Floor
2,874 sq. ft.

© Copyright by designer/architect

Plan #F10-147D-0012

Dimensions:	80' W x 32'4" D
Heated Sq. Ft.:	1,500
Bedrooms: 3	**Bathrooms:** 2

Foundation: Crawl space standard; slab for an additional fee

See index for more information

Images provided by designer/architect

© Copyright by designer/architect

Plan #F10-141D-0036

Dimensions:	72'4" W x 74'8" D
Heated Sq. Ft.:	3,500
Bedrooms: 4	**Bathrooms:** 3½

Foundation: Slab standard; crawl space, basement or walk-out basement for an additional fee

Pricing subject to change

Images provided by designer/architect

© Copyright by designer/architect

First Floor
2,400 sq. ft.

Second Floor
1,100 sq. ft.

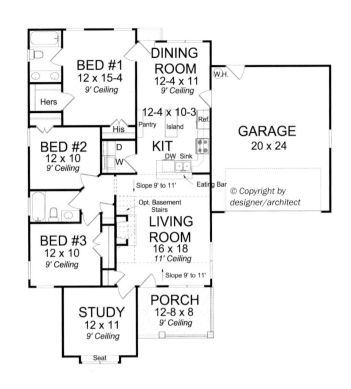

BED #1
12 x 15-4
9' Ceiling

Hers

DINING ROOM
12-4 x 11
9' Ceiling

W.H.

12-4 x 10-3

Pantry

Island

Ref.

GARAGE
20 x 24

© Copyright by designer/architect

BED #2
12 x 10
9' Ceiling

His

D

W

KIT

DW

Sink

Slope 9' to 11'

Eating Bar

Opt. Basement Stairs

LIVING ROOM
16 x 18
11' Ceiling

BED #3
12 x 10
9' Ceiling

Slope 9' to 11'

STUDY
12 x 11
9' Ceiling

PORCH
12-8 x 8
9' Ceiling

Seat

Plan #F10-130D-0395

Images provided by designer/architect

Dimensions: 51' W x 54'4" D
Heated Sq. Ft.: 1,420
Bedrooms: 3   **Bathrooms:** 2
Foundation: Slab standard; crawl space or basement for an additional fee

See index for more information

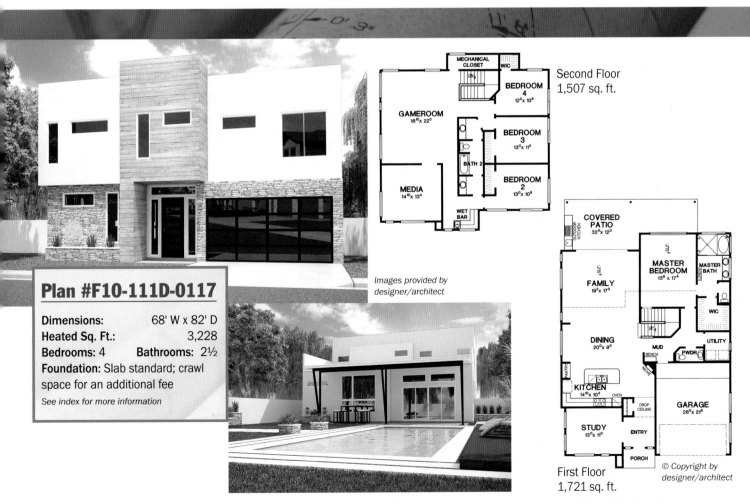

MECHANICAL CLOSET

WIC

GAMEROOM
18¹⁰ x 22⁰

BEDROOM 4
12⁰ x 10⁸

Second Floor
1,507 sq. ft.

BATH 2

BEDROOM 3
13⁰ x 11⁰

MEDIA
14¹⁰ x 13⁴

BEDROOM 2
13⁰ x 10⁸

WET BAR

Images provided by designer/architect

COVERED PATIO
32¹¹ x 12⁰

OUTDOOR KITCHEN

MASTER BEDROOM
13⁸ x 17⁴

MASTER BATH

FAMILY
19² x 17⁰

WIC

DINING
20⁰ x 9⁰

MUD

PWDR

UTILITY

KITCHEN
14¹⁰ x 10⁴

OVEN

DROP CEILING

GARAGE
28⁸ x 21⁸

STUDY
13⁵ x 11⁰

ENTRY

PORCH

First Floor
1,721 sq. ft.

© Copyright by designer/architect

Plan #F10-111D-0117

Dimensions: 68' W x 82' D
Heated Sq. Ft.: 3,228
Bedrooms: 4   **Bathrooms:** 2½
Foundation: Slab standard; crawl space for an additional fee

See index for more information

Second Floor
888 sq. ft.

Plan #F10-026D-1901

Images provided by
designer/architect

Dimensions:	57'6" W x 51' D
Heated Sq. Ft.:	1,973
Bonus Sq. Ft.:	1,436
Bedrooms: 3	Bathrooms: 3
Exterior Walls:	2" x 6"

Foundation: Basement standard;
walk-out basement for an
additional fee

See index for more information

Optional
Lower Level
863 sq. ft.

© Copyright by
designer/architect

First Floor
1,085 sq. ft.

Plan #F10-065D-0315

Images provided by
designer/architect

Dimensions:	60' W x 49'6" D
Heated Sq. Ft.:	1,597
Bedrooms: 3	Bathrooms: 2

Foundation: Basement standard;
crawl space or slab for an
additional fee

See index for more information

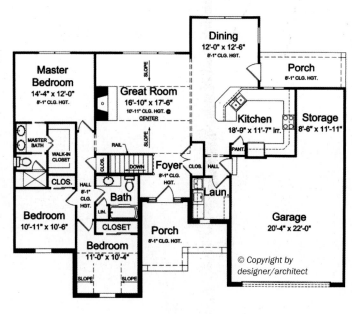

© Copyright by
designer/architect

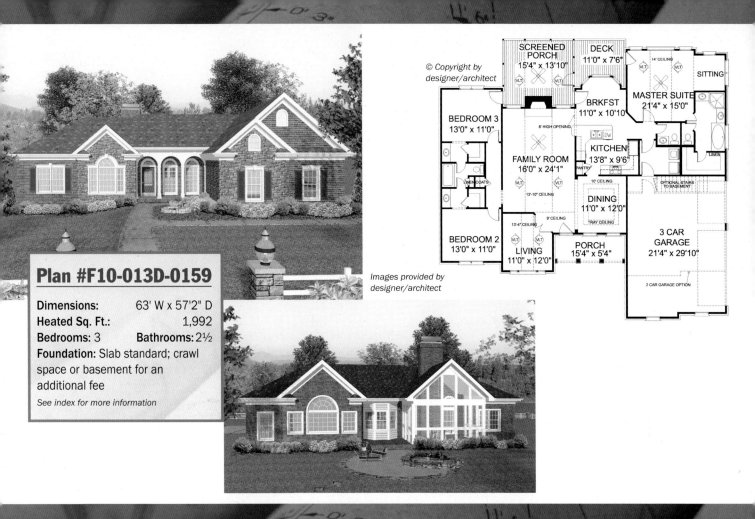

© Copyright by designer/architect

SCREENED PORCH 15'4" x 13'10"

DECK 11'0" x 7'6"

14' CEILING

SITTING

MASTER SUITE 21'4" x 15'0"

BEDROOM 3 13'0" x 11'0"

BRKFST 11'0" x 10'10

8' HIGH OPENING

KITCHEN 13'8" x 9'6"

LINEN

FAMILY ROOM 16'0" x 24'1"

PANTRY

10' CEILING

13'-10" CEILING

OPTIONAL STAIRS TO BASEMENT

DINING 11'0" x 12'0"

TRAY CEILING

9' CEILING

BEDROOM 2 13'0" x 11'0"

13'-4" CEILING

LIVING 11'0" x 12'0"

PORCH 15'4" x 5'4"

3 CAR GARAGE 21'4" x 29'10"

2 CAR GARAGE OPTION

Images provided by designer/architect

Plan #F10-013D-0159

Dimensions: 63' W x 57'2" D
Heated Sq. Ft.: 1,992
Bedrooms: 3 **Bathrooms:** 2½
Foundation: Slab standard; crawl space or basement for an additional fee

See index for more information

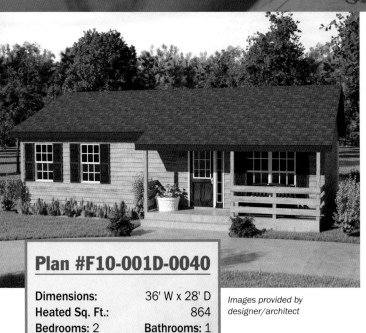

Plan #F10-001D-0040

Dimensions: 36' W x 28' D
Heated Sq. Ft.: 864
Bedrooms: 2 **Bathrooms:** 1
Foundation: Crawl space standard; basement or slab for an additional fee

See index for more information

Images provided by designer/architect

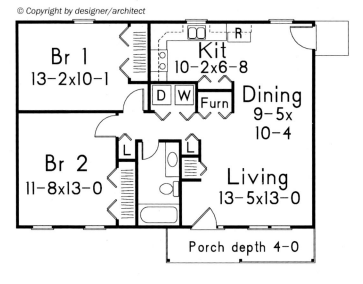

© Copyright by designer/architect

Br 1 13-2x10-1

Kit 10-2x6-8

R

Dining 9-5x 10-4

D W Furn

Br 2 11-8x13-0

L L

Living 13-5x13-0

Porch depth 4-0

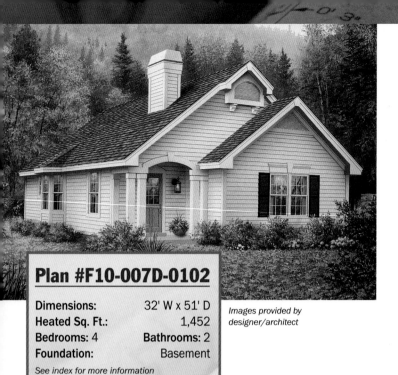

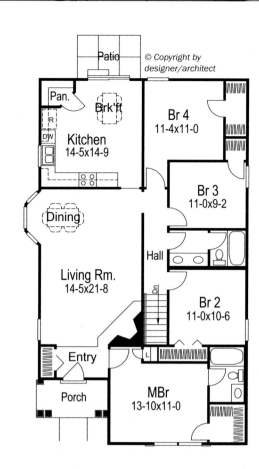

Images provided by
designer/architect

Plan #F10-007D-0102

Dimensions: 32' W x 51' D
Heated Sq. Ft.: 1,452
Bedrooms: 4 **Bathrooms:** 2
Foundation: Basement

See index for more information

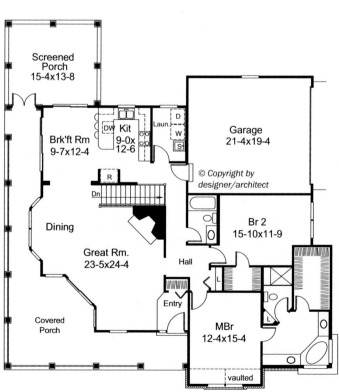

Images provided by
designer/architect

Plan #F10-007D-0172

Dimensions: 56'4" W x 61'4" D
Heated Sq. Ft.: 1,646
Bedrooms: 2 **Bathrooms:** 2
Foundation: Basement standard;
crawl space or slab for an
additional fee

See index for more information

Plan #F10-147D-0001

Dimensions: 40'8" W x 49'4" D
Heated Sq. Ft.: 1,472
Bedrooms: 3   **Bathrooms:** 2
Foundation: Basement, standard;
crawl space or slab for an
additional fee

See index for more information

*Images provided by
designer/architect*

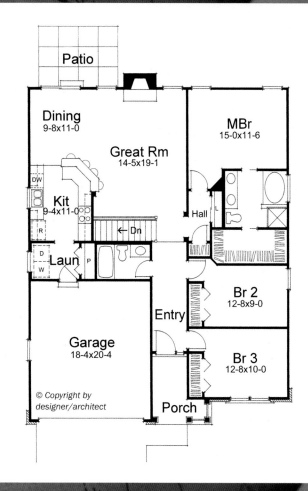

Plan #F10-008D-0133

Dimensions: 26' W x 24' D
Heated Sq. Ft.: 624
Bedrooms: 2   **Bathrooms:** 1
Foundation: Pier

See index for more information

*Images provided by
designer/architect*

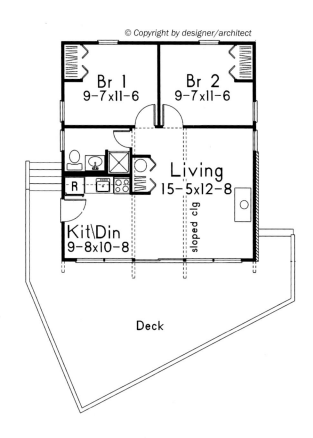

© Copyright by designer/architect

Images provided by designer/architect

Plan #F10-013D-0027

Dimensions: 71'2" W x 58'1" D
Heated Sq. Ft.: 2,184
Bonus Sq. Ft.: 379
Bedrooms: 3   Bathrooms: 3
Foundation: Slab standard; crawl space or basement for an additional fee

See index for more information

Images provided by designer/architect

Plan #F10-123D-0060

Dimensions: 52' W x 38' D
Heated Sq. Ft.: 1,185
Bedrooms: 3   Bathrooms: 2
Foundation: Basement standard; crawl space, slab or walk-out basement for an additional fee

See index for more information

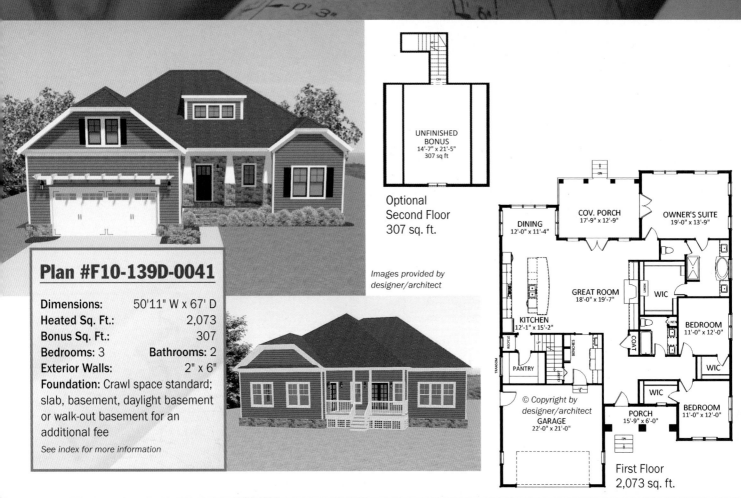

Plan #F10-139D-0041

Dimensions: 50'11" W x 67' D
Heated Sq. Ft.: 2,073
Bonus Sq. Ft.: 307
Bedrooms: 3   **Bathrooms:** 2
Exterior Walls: 2" x 6"
Foundation: Crawl space standard; slab, basement, daylight basement or walk-out basement for an additional fee

See index for more information

UNFINISHED BONUS
14'-7" x 21'-5"
307 sq ft

Optional
Second Floor
307 sq. ft.

Images provided by designer/architect

COV. PORCH
17'-9" x 12'-9"

DINING
12'-0" x 11'-4"

OWNER'S SUITE
19'-0" x 13'-9"

GREAT ROOM
18'-0" x 19'-7"

WIC

KITCHEN
12'-1" x 15'-2"

BEDROOM
11'-0" x 12'-0"

WIC

PANTRY

WIC

© Copyright by designer/architect

GARAGE
22'-0" x 21'-0"

PORCH
15'-9" x 6'-0"

BEDROOM
11'-0" x 12'-0"

First Floor
2,073 sq. ft.

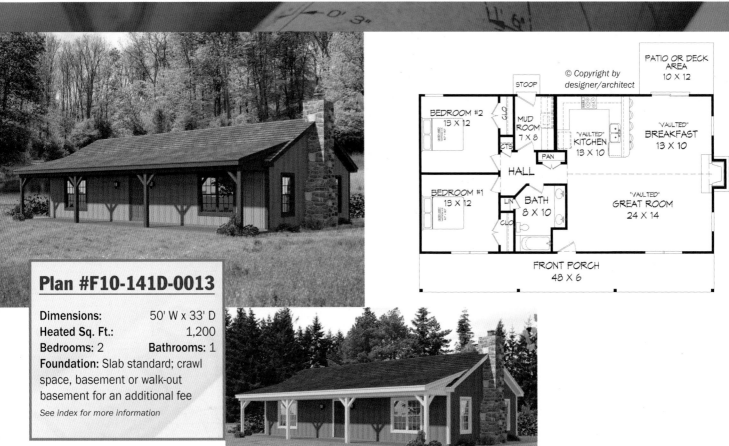

Plan #F10-141D-0013

Dimensions: 50' W x 33' D
Heated Sq. Ft.: 1,200
Bedrooms: 2   **Bathrooms:** 1
Foundation: Slab standard; crawl space, basement or walk-out basement for an additional fee

See index for more information

© Copyright by designer/architect

PATIO OR DECK AREA
10 X 12

BEDROOM #2
13 X 12

MUD ROOM
7 X 8

STOOP

"VAULTED" KITCHEN
13 X 10

"VAULTED" BREAKFAST
13 X 10

HALL

BEDROOM #1
13 X 12

PAN

BATH
8 X 10

"VAULTED" GREAT ROOM
24 X 14

FRONT PORCH
48 X 6

Images provided by designer/architect

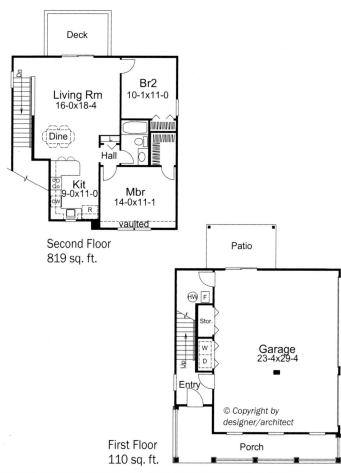

Deck

Living Rm
16-0x18-4

Br2
10-1x11-0

Dine

Hall

Kit
9-0x11-0

Mbr
14-0x11-1

vaulted

Second Floor
819 sq. ft.

Patio

HW F

Stor.

W
D

Garage
23-4x29-4

Entry

© Copyright by
designer/architect

First Floor
110 sq. ft.

Porch

Plan #F10-007D-0070

*Images provided by
designer/architect*

Dimensions:	31' W x 35' D
Heated Sq. Ft.:	929
Bedrooms: 2	Bathrooms: 1
Foundation:	Slab

See index for more information

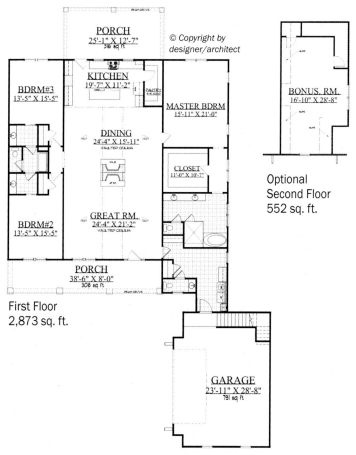

© Copyright by
designer/architect

PORCH
25'-1" X 12'-7"
316 sq ft

KITCHEN
19'-7" X 11'-2"

BDRM#3
13'-5" X 15'-5"

PANTRY

MASTER BDRM
15'-11" X 21'-0"

DINING
24'-4" X 15'-11"
VAULTED CEILING

CLOSET
11'-0" X 10'-7"

BDRM#2
13'-5" X 15'-5"

GREAT RM.
24'-4" X 21'-2"
VAULTED CEILING

PORCH
38'-6" X 8'-0"
308 sq ft

First Floor
2,873 sq. ft.

BONUS. RM.
16'-10" X 28'-8"

Optional
Second Floor
552 sq. ft.

GARAGE
23'-11" X 28'-8"
791 sq ft

Plan #F10-157D-0023

*Images provided by
designer/architect*

Dimensions:	65'11" W x 107' D
Heated Sq. Ft.:	2,873
Bonus Sq. Ft.:	552
Bedrooms: 3	Bathrooms: 2½
Foundation:	Crawl space standard; slab for an additional fee

See index for more information

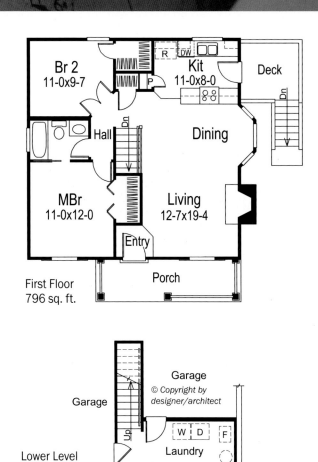

Plan #F10-007D-0042

Dimensions: 30' W x 33' D
Heated Sq. Ft.: 914
Bedrooms: 2 **Bathrooms:** 1
Foundation: Basement

See index for more information

Images provided by designer/architect

Br 2
11-0x9-7

Kit
11-0x8-0

Deck

Hall

Dining

MBr
11-0x12-0

Living
12-7x19-4

Entry

First Floor
796 sq. ft.

Porch

Garage

Garage

© Copyright by designer/architect

Laundry

Lower Level
118 sq. ft.

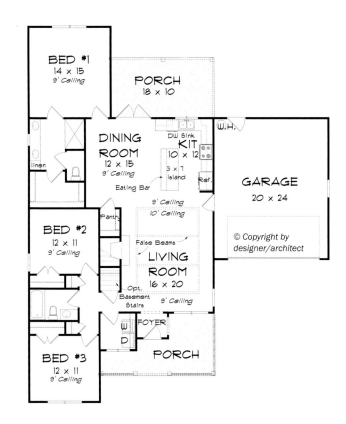

Plan #F10-130D-0391

Dimensions: 52'8" W x 44' D
Heated Sq. Ft.: 1,558
Bedrooms: 3 **Bathrooms:** 2
Foundation: Slab standard; crawl space or basement for an additional fee

See index for more information

Images provided by designer/architect

BED #1
14 x 15
9' Ceiling

PORCH
18 x 10

DINING ROOM
12 x 15
9' Ceiling

KIT
10 x 12

GARAGE
20 x 24

BED #2
12 x 11
9' Ceiling

LIVING ROOM
16 x 20
9' Ceiling

© Copyright by designer/architect

BED #3
12 x 11
9' Ceiling

FOYER

PORCH

Plan #F10-024D-0795

Dimensions:	71' W x 95' D
Heated Sq. Ft.:	3,076
Bedrooms: 4	**Bathrooms:** 3
Foundation:	Floating slab

See index for more information

Images provided by designer/architect

Features

- This unique home features all of the living areas near each other for ease with family activities and easy, comfortable gathering
- The cheerful breakfast room enjoys views of the enormous covered rear porch featuring a corner outdoor fireplace for year-round enjoyment
- The elegant master bedroom has its own sitting area with views of the rear covered porch and also a private pampering spa style bath with a walk-in closet
- 2-car rear entry garage, and a 1-car rear entry carport

Plan #F10-161D-0002

Dimensions:	81'9" W x 95'6" D
Heated Sq. Ft.:	3,959
Bedrooms: 3	Bathrooms: 4½
Exterior Walls:	2" x 6"
Foundation:	Crawl space

See index for more information

Images provided by designer/architect

© Copyright by designer/architect

First Floor
2,907 sq. ft.

Second Floor
1,052 sq. ft.

Features

- This home defines rustic Craftsman style to a tee with its mix of stone, rustic beams and shingle cedar siding
- The massive great room is vaulted and has a towering fireplace
- Although large and open, the kitchen has a cozy feel with its dark wood ceilings above
- The spacious dining room offers the ability to entertain in comfort and style
- The den would make a nice secluded office
- The bonus room on the second floor is included in the square footage
- 3-car side entry garage

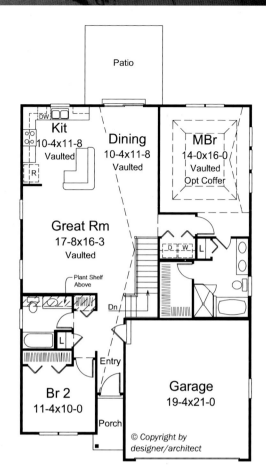

Plan #F10-121D-0028

Dimensions:	36' W x 54' D
Heated Sq. Ft.:	1,433
Bedrooms: 2	**Bathrooms:** 2

Foundation: Basement standard; crawl space or slab for an additional fee

See index for more information

Images provided by designer/architect

Patio

Kit
10-4x11-8
Vaulted

Dining
10-4x11-8
Vaulted

MBr
14-0x16-0
Vaulted
Opt Coffer

Great Rm
17-8x16-3
Vaulted

Plant Shelf Above

Dn

Entry

Br 2
11-4x10-0

Garage
19-4x21-0

Porch

© Copyright by designer/architect

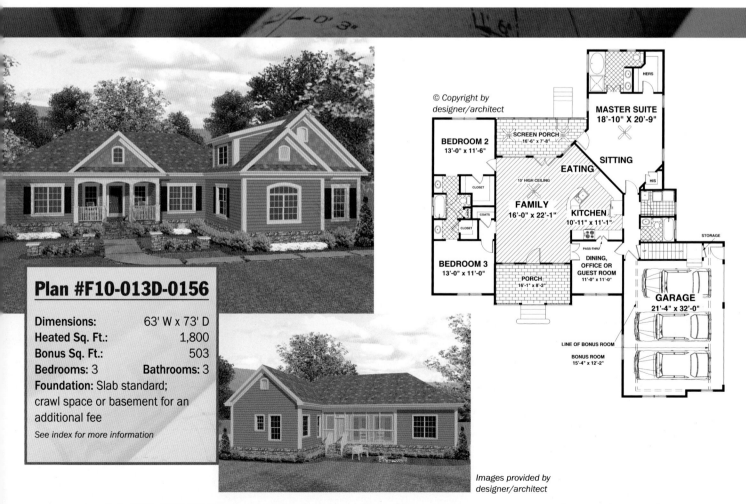

Plan #F10-013D-0156

Dimensions:	63' W x 73' D
Heated Sq. Ft.:	1,800
Bonus Sq. Ft.:	503
Bedrooms: 3	**Bathrooms:** 3

Foundation: Slab standard; crawl space or basement for an additional fee

See index for more information

© Copyright by designer/architect

MASTER SUITE
18'-10" X 20'-9"

HERS

BEDROOM 2
13'-0" x 11'-6"

SCREEN PORCH
16'-6" x 7'-8"

SITTING

CLOSET

10' HIGH CEILING

EATING

HIS

FAMILY
16'-0" x 22'-1"

KITCHEN
10'-11" x 11'-1"

STORAGE

COATS

CLOSET

PASS-THRU

BEDROOM 3
13'-0" x 11'-0"

DINING, OFFICE OR GUEST ROOM
11'-0" x 11'-0"

GARAGE
21'-4" x 32'-0"

PORCH
16'-1" x 8'-2"

LINE OF BONUS ROOM

BONUS ROOM
15'-4" x 12'-2"

Images provided by designer/architect

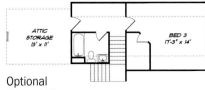

Optional
Second Floor
420 sq. ft.

Plan #F10-159D-0017

Dimensions:	44' W x 48' D
Heated Sq. Ft.:	1,200
Bonus Sq. Ft.:	1,284
Bedrooms: 2	Bathrooms: 2
Exterior Walls:	2" x 6"
Foundation:	Walk-out basement

See index for more information

Images provided by designer/architect

Optional
Lower Level
864 sq. ft.

First Floor
1,200 sq. ft.

© Copyright by designer/architect

Plan #F10-013D-0198

Dimensions:	61'9" W x 37'3" D
Heated Sq. Ft.:	1,399
Bedrooms: 3	Bathrooms: 2
Foundation:	Slab standard; crawl space or basement for an additional fee

See index for more information

Images provided by designer/architect

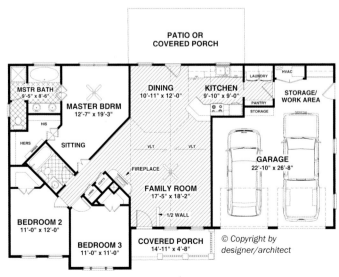

© Copyright by designer/architect

Plan #F10-032D-1142

Dimensions:	46' W x 32' D
Heated Sq. Ft.:	1,209
Bonus Sq. Ft.:	1,209
Bedrooms: 2	Bathrooms: 1
Exterior Walls:	2" x 6"

Foundation: Basement standard; crawl space, monolithic slab or floating slab for an additional fee

See index for more information

Features

- This stunning modern home has an open-concept floor plan and gathering areas
- Two bedrooms are on the opposite side of the house from one another maintaining privacy
- The open kitchen has a large island with seating for four people to dine casually
- The living room has gorgeous views of the rear porch
- The optional lower level has an additional 1,209 square feet of living area

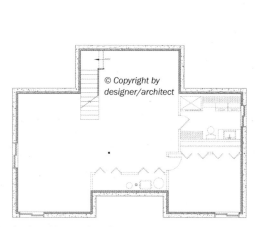

© Copyright by designer/architect

Optional Lower Level
1,209 sq. ft.

PORCH
21-0 X 11-8

LIVING ROOM
19-9 X 13-4

MASTER BEDR.
11-7 X 13-6

DINING ROOM
16-8 X 8-2

KITCHEN
15-0 X 11-4

BEDR. 2
12-3 X 11-0

WALK-IN

BATHROOM

STOOP
12-8 X 3-8

First Floor
1,209 sq. ft.

Images provided by designer/architect

Plan #F10-101D-0041

Dimensions:	103' W x 77'6" D
Heated Sq. Ft.:	4,908
Bonus Sq. Ft.:	2,207
Bedrooms: 4	**Bathrooms:** 4½
Exterior Walls:	2" x 6"
Foundation:	Walk-out basement

See index for more information

Features

- Rustic beamed ceilings take center stage in this home designed perfectly for a mountain, rustic or country locale
- The open great room flows right into the kitchen, perfect when entertaining
- The optional lower level has an additional 2,207 square feet of living area and a recreation room beyond compare with a curved wet bar and patio access
- 2-car side entry garage, and a 2-car front entry garage

Second Floor
1,872 sq. ft.

© Copyright by designer/architect

Optional
Lower Level
2,207 sq. ft.

First Floor
3,036 sq. ft.

Images provided by designer/architect

Images provided by designer/architect

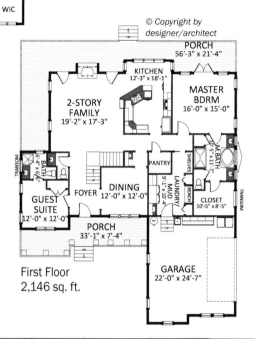

© Copyright by designer/architect

Second Floor
734 sq. ft.

First Floor
2,146 sq. ft.

Plan #F10-139D-0022

Dimensions:	56'10" W x 74' D
Heated Sq. Ft.:	2,880
Bonus Sq. Ft.:	375
Bedrooms: 4	Bathrooms: 3½
Exterior Walls:	2" x 6"

Foundation: Crawl space standard; slab, basement, daylight basement or walk-out basement for an additional fee

See index for more information

Images provided by designer/architect

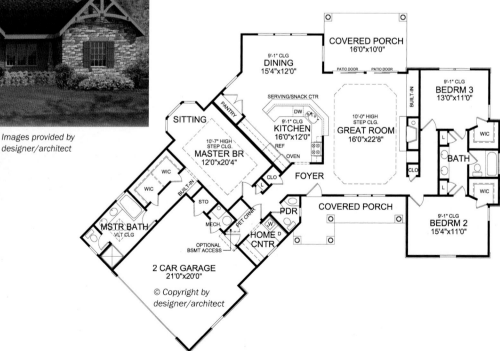

© Copyright by designer/architect

Plan #F10-016D-0105

Dimensions:	81'3" W x 63'8" D
Heated Sq. Ft.:	2,065
Bedrooms: 3	Bathrooms: 2½

Foundation: Crawl space or slab standard; basement for an additional fee

See index for more information

Plan #F10-130D-0366

Dimensions: 38' W x 52' D
Heated Sq. Ft.: 1,720
Bedrooms: 3   Bathrooms: 2½
Foundation: Slab standard; crawl space or basement for an additional fee

See index for more information

Images provided by designer/architect

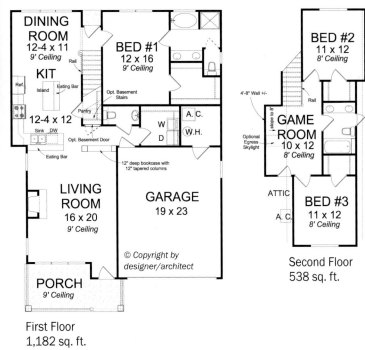

DINING ROOM
12-4 x 11
9' Ceiling

KIT
12-4 x 12

Ref.
Island   Eating Bar
Pantry
Sink   DW
Eating Bar

BED #1
12 x 16
9' Ceiling

Rail
Opt. Basement Stairs
Opt. Basement Door

A.C.
W.H.
W
D

LIVING ROOM
16 x 20
9' Ceiling

GARAGE
19 x 23

12" deep bookcase with 12" tapered columns

© Copyright by designer/architect

PORCH
9' Ceiling

First Floor
1,182 sq. ft.

BED #2
11 x 12
8' Ceiling

4'-8" Wall +/-
Rail

8' to 6' slope

GAME ROOM
10 x 12
8' Ceiling

Optional Egress Skylight

ATTIC

A.C.

BED #3
11 x 12
8' Ceiling

Second Floor
538 sq. ft.

Plan #F10-088D-0828

Dimensions: 70'10" W x 71'6" D
Heated Sq. Ft.: 2,242
Bedrooms: 3   Bathrooms: 2½
Exterior Walls: 2" x 6"
Foundation: Slab

See index for more information

Images provided by designer/architect

COV. PATIO
20' X 14'

DINING
14' X 13'

MASTER SUITE
15'4 X 13'

WIC

GREAT RM.
19'8 X 17'4

KITCHEN
14'4 X 15'4

SHOP/ STORAGE
11' X 14'6

UTILITY/MUD

PANTRY

OFFICE/ DEN
10'8 X 10'

FOYER
8' X 10'4

BDRM. #2
11'4 X 10'8

COATS/BOOTS

3 CAR GARAGE

6' COV. ENTRY PORCH

BDRM. #3
10' X 12'

WIC

© Copyright by designer/architect

Plan #F10-161D-0025

Dimensions:	80'9" W x 96'3" D
Heated Sq. Ft.:	4,964
Bonus Sq. Ft.:	438
Bedrooms: 5	Bathrooms: 5½
Exterior Walls:	2" x 6"
Foundation:	Crawl space

See index for more information

Images provided by designer/architect

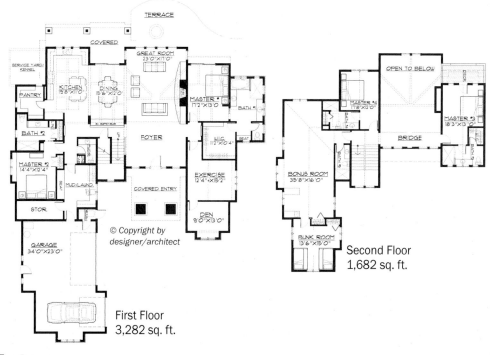

First Floor
3,282 sq. ft.

© Copyright by
designer/architect

Second Floor
1,682 sq. ft.

Features

- The ultimate Craftsman luxury home with all of the details that make Craftsman style so special
- The kitchen, dining, and great rooms flow effortlessly for a spacious interior
- There are two master suites on the first floor, and two master suites on the second floor ensuring comfort for everyone
- The second floor has a bonus room with an additional 438 square feet of living area
- 3-car side entry garage

Plan #F10-026S-0020

Dimensions:	86'9" W x 84'6" D
Heated Sq. Ft.:	4,719
Bedrooms:	4
Bathrooms:	3 full, 2 half
Foundation:	Slab

See index for more information

Images provided by designer/architect

Features

- This Spanish Mediterranean style home is truly a show stopper that is loaded with outdoor curb appeal thanks to a second floor outdoor balcony, plus the first floor front courtyard, covered porch, and loggia with a summer kitchen

- The gallery entry leads to a stunning stair hall that is a truly beautiful rotunda and it also shares a see-through fireplace with the study

- This home is designed perfectly for entertaining with a formal dining room that's connected to the kitchen via a butler's pantry

- There's a helpful planning center with a built-in desk off the kitchen for keeping family activities organized and accounted for

- The large game room attached to an octagon-shaped balcony can be found on the second floor and is bound to see many nights of family fun

- 2-car side entry garage, and a 1-car front entry garage

Second Floor
1,616 sq. ft.

© Copyright by
designer/architect

First Floor
3,103 sq. ft.

First Floor
1,032 sq. ft.

Plan #F10-032D-0834

Dimensions:	30' W x 36' D
Heated Sq. Ft.:	2,064
Bedrooms: 4	Bathrooms: 2
Exterior Walls:	2" x 6"
Foundation:	Basement

See index for more information

Images provided by designer/architect

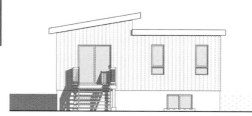

Lower Level
1,032 sq. ft.

Plan #F10-019S-0008

Dimensions:	104'3" W x 80'8" D
Heated Sq. Ft.:	4,420
Bedrooms:	4
Bathrooms:	4 full, 2 half

Foundation: Slab standard; crawl space or basement for an additional fee

See index for more information

Images provided by designer/architect

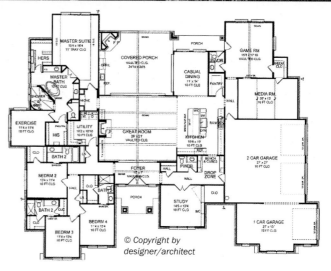

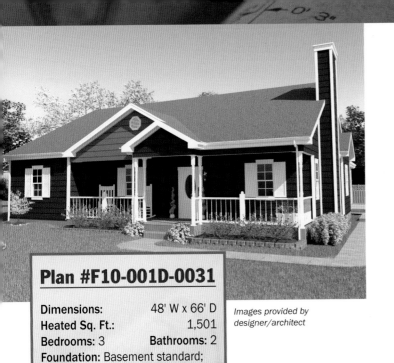

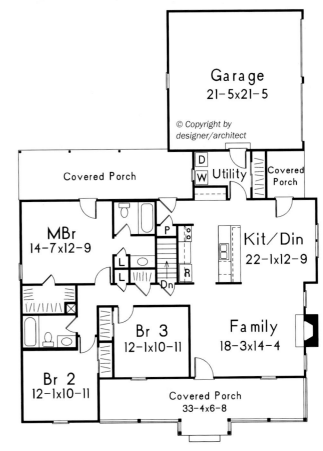

Plan #F10-001D-0031

Dimensions: 48' W x 66' D
Heated Sq. Ft.: 1,501
Bedrooms: 3   Bathrooms: 2
Foundation: Basement standard;
crawl space or slab for an
additional fee

See index for more information

*Images provided by
designer/architect*

Garage
21-5x21-5

© Copyright by
designer/architect

Covered Porch   Utility   Covered Porch
D
W

MBr
14-7x12-9   P   **Kit/Din**
22-1x12-9
L
L   R
Dn

Br 2
12-1x10-11   **Br 3**
12-1x10-11   **Family**
18-3x14-4

Covered Porch
33-4x6-8

Plan #F10-121D-0048

Dimensions: 44' W x 53'4" D
Heated Sq. Ft.: 1,615
Bedrooms: 2   Bathrooms: 2
Foundation: Basement standard;
crawl space or slab for an
additional fee

See index for more information

*Images provided by
designer/architect*

Patio

Brkfst/ Dining
12-8x14-11   **MBr**
12-8x14-6
Coffer Clg

Great Rm
16-9x21-11
12' Clg   S

DW
S

Kitchen
12-8x12-9
R
P   Dn   L

Garage
22-8x24-0   **Br 2**
12-8x11-0
Foyer

Porch

© Copyright by
designer/architect

Plan #F10-071S-0019

Dimensions:	105'4" W x 53' D
Heated Sq. Ft.:	4,300
Bedrooms: 4	Bathrooms: 3½
Exterior Walls:	2" x 6"
Foundation:	Crawl space

See index for more information

Images provided by designer/architect

Features

- Craftsman style that personifies quality, yet simplistic living, makes this home stand out
- The great room fireplace was designed to be an amazing focal point and anchor
- The home's openness will be appreciated by those grabbing a quick snack at the kitchen's breakfast bar
- Retreat to the second floor master bedroom and find a cozy fireplace, along with a private deck for stepping outdoors in privacy
- Step into the oversized whirlpool tub in the private master bath and take in the views of nature through the large window acting as a scenic tranquil backdrop
- 3-car tandem front entry garage, and a 1-car front entry garage

Second Floor
1,940 sq. ft.

© Copyright by
designer/architect

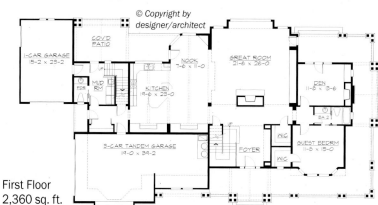

First Floor
2,360 sq. ft.

call 1-800-373-2646

houseplansandmore.com

Plan #F10-055D-0990

Dimensions: 113' W x 95'8" D
Heated Sq. Ft.: 2,555
Bonus Sq. Ft.: 509
Bedrooms: 4   **Bathrooms:** 3
Foundation: Crawl space or slab standard; basement or daylight basement for an additional fee

See index for more information

Images provided by designer/architect

Features

- Lodge-like living is perfectly achieved in this Craftsman home featuring an open split bedroom floor plan topped with a beamed ceiling
- The rear covered porch has a 10' ceiling, includes an outdoor kitchen, and leads to a remote outdoor living porch with an outdoor fireplace
- The master suite has direct access to the laundry room making this chore a lot easier to tackle
- Above the garage is a guest suite with an additional 509 square feet of living area featuring its own bath and plenty of privacy that will be appreciated when people are visiting
- 2-car attached front entry garage via a covered porch

First Floor
2,049 sq. ft.

Optional Garage
Second Floor
509 sq. ft.

Second Floor
506 sq. ft.

© Copyright by designer/architect

Plan #F10-032D-0884

Dimensions:	44' W x 24' D
Heated Sq. Ft.:	1,587
Bedrooms: 1	Bathrooms: 1½
Exterior Walls:	2" x 6"

Foundation: Basement standard; crawl space, floating slab or monolithic slab for an additional fee

See index for more information

Features

- Step inside and immediately feel as if you're in a much larger home because of the open floor plan blending the kitchen, dining and living spaces into one large area
- The bedroom is a nice size and enjoys direct access onto the large deck that spans the entire width of the home
- The second floor is an "open book" and offers that flexible space that all homeowners need allowing you to convert it to an office, art studio, playroom, a nursery, or extra guest space

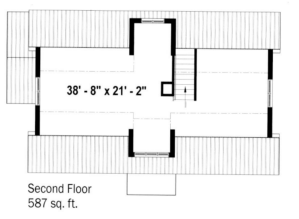

38' - 8" x 21' - 2"

Second Floor
587 sq. ft.

© Copyright by designer/architect

11' - 0" x 11' - 8"   13' - 8" x 14' - 8"   12' - 0" x 12' - 4"

11' - 2" x 11' - 0"

First Floor
1,000 sq. ft.

Images provided by designer/architect

houseplansandmore.com

Plan #F10-011S-0192

Dimensions:	60' W x 100' D
Heated Sq. Ft.:	4,106
Bedrooms:	4
Bathrooms:	3 full, 2 half
Exterior Walls:	2" x 6"

Foundation: Crawl space or slab standard; basement for an additional fee

See index for more information

Images provided by designer/architect

© Copyright by designer/architect

First Floor 2,284 sq. ft.

Second Floor 1,822 sq. ft.

Features

- This modern two-story has all of the features families want today including a large mud room
- The great room, dining area and kitchen combine to form the main gathering place within the home
- Off the dining area you'll discover a computer nook with a built-in desk
- Behind a hidden door, you'll find a home gym with direct access to a full bath and a guest bedroom
- The second floor has a fun game room with wet bar and an outdoor terrace, great for entertaining
- 3-car side entry garage

Plan #F10-101D-0045

Dimensions:	69' W x 68'3" D
Heated Sq. Ft.:	1,885
Bedrooms: 2	Bathrooms: 2½
Exterior Walls:	2" x 6"
Foundation:	Basement

See index for more information

Images provided by designer/architect

Features

- The open floor plan maximizes space creating a flowing open layout
- A dual fireplace warms the family room as well as the outdoor covered patio
- The spacious and private master suite includes its own private bath and a roomy walk-in closet
- Guests will never want to leave the guest bedroom with its own bath and large walk-in closet
- 3-car front entry garage

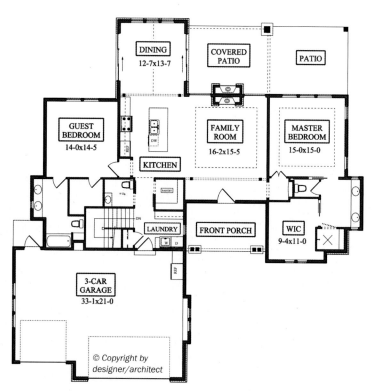

Plan #F10-055S-0115

Dimensions: 126'2" W x 110'11" D
Heated Sq. Ft.: 4,501
Bonus Sq. Ft.: 501
Bedrooms: 5   **Bathrooms:** 5½
Foundation: Crawl space or slab standard; basement or daylight basement for an additional fee

See index for more information

Features

- The two-story great room boasts double-doors that open to the rear covered porch, a fireplace, and built-in flanking shelves
- A walk-in pantry and a breakfast bar with seating for seven are some awesome features of the well-equipped kitchen
- The bonus room on the second floor has an additional 501 square feet of living area and is perfect for a home theater or game room
- 3-car front entry garage

© Copyright by designer/architect

First Floor
3,398 sq. ft.

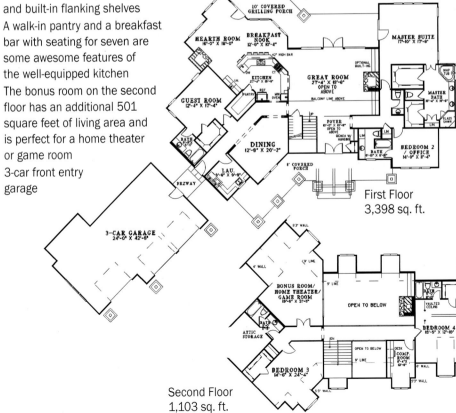

Second Floor
1,103 sq. ft.

Images provided by designer/architect

Plan #F10-077D-0184

Dimensions:	73'6" W x 62' D
Heated Sq. Ft.:	2,400
Bonus Sq. Ft.:	452
Bedrooms: 4	Bathrooms: 2½

Foundation: Slab or crawl space, please specify when ordering; for basement version, see Plan #077D-0192 at houseplansandmore.com

See index for more information

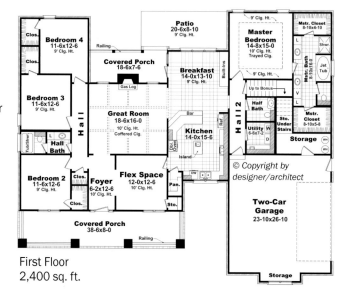

Optional Second Floor 452 sq. ft.

Attic Space

Attic Access

Down

Down

Attic Access

Attic Access

Tub/Shwr

Bonus Bath

Closet

5' Wall Height

Sloped Clg.

Sloped Clg.

5' Wall Height

Unfinished Bonus Room
14-6x18-0
8' Clg. Ht.

Attic Access

First Floor
2,400 sq. ft.

Clos.

Bedroom 4
11-6x12-6
9' Clg. Ht.

Clos.

Patio
20-6x8-10
9' Clg. Ht.

Master Bedroom
14-8x15-0
9' Clg. Ht.
Trayed Clg.

9' Clg. Ht.

Mstr. Closet
8-10x4-10

Covered Porch
18-6x7-6

Gas Log

Bedroom 3
11-6x12-6
9' Clg. Ht.

Breakfast
14-0x13-10
9' Clg. Ht.

9' Clg. Ht.

Mstr. Bath
8-10x10-0

Shwr.

Jet Tub

Built-Ins

Hall

Great Room
18-6x16-0
10' Clg. Ht.
Coffered Clg.

Bar

Up to Bonus

Hall 2

Half Bath

Mstr. Closet
8-10x5-8

Tub/Shwr

Hall Bath

Kitchen
14-0x15-6

Island

Dbl. Oven

Ref.

Utility
6-6x7-2

Sto. Under Stairs

Storage

Bedroom 2
11-6x12-6
9' Clg. Ht.

Clos.

Foyer
6-2x12-6
10' Clg. Ht.

Flex Space
12-0x12-6
10' Clg. Ht.

Pan.

DW

Sto.

© Copyright by designer/architect

Two-Car Garage
23-10x26-10

Clos.

Covered Porch
38-6x8-0

Railing

Storage

Plan #F10-026D-1999

Dimensions:	68' W x 57' D
Heated Sq. Ft.:	2,292
Bedrooms: 1	Bathrooms: 1½

Foundation: Slab standard; crawl space, basement or walk-out basement for an additional fee

See index for more information

Images provided by designer/architect

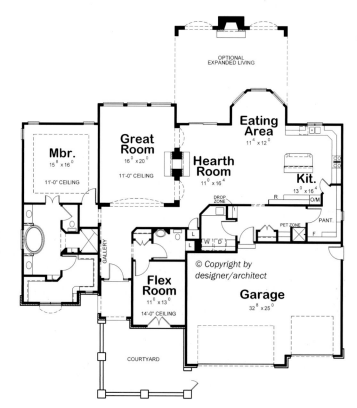

OPTIONAL EXPANDED LIVING

Mbr.
15⁸ x 16⁰
11'-0" CEILING

Great Room
16⁰ x 20⁰
11'-0" CEILING

Eating Area
11⁴ x 12⁰

Hearth Room
11⁰ x 16⁴

Kit.
13⁰ x 16⁴

DROP ZONE

R

O/M

GALLERY

PET ZONE

PANT.

L

W D

L

FL

Flex Room
11⁰ x 13⁰
14'-0" CEILING

Garage
32⁸ x 25⁰

© Copyright by designer/architect

COURTYARD

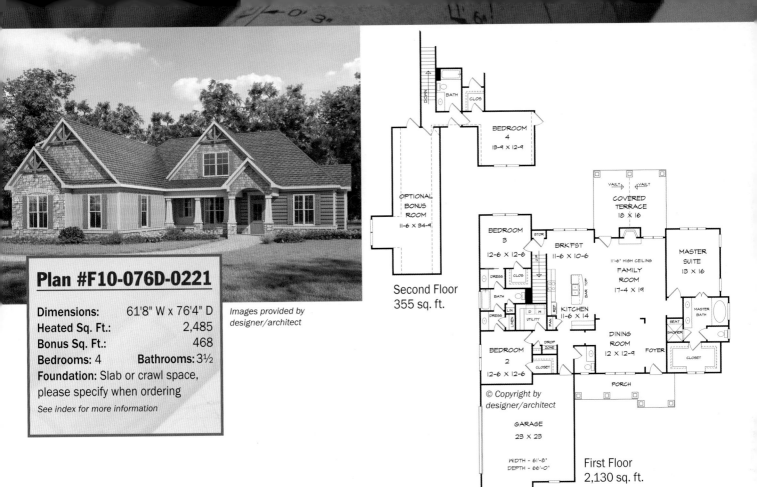

Plan #F10-076D-0221

Dimensions: 61'8" W x 76'4" D
Heated Sq. Ft.: 2,485
Bonus Sq. Ft.: 468
Bedrooms: 4   **Bathrooms:** 3½
Foundation: Slab or crawl space, please specify when ordering

See index for more information

Images provided by designer/architect

Second Floor
355 sq. ft.

First Floor
2,130 sq. ft.

BEDROOM 4
13-9 X 12-9

BATH

CLOS

OPTIONAL BONUS ROOM
11-6 X 34-9

BEDROOM 3
12-6 X 12-6

STOR

DRESS   CLOS

BATH

DRESS   LIN

UTILITY

BEDROOM 2
12-6 X 12-6

CLOSET

DROP ZONE

BRK'FST
11-6 X 10-6

KITCHEN
11-6 X 14

PAN

VAULT   VAULT

COVERED TERRACE
18 X 16

11'-6" HIGH CEILING

FAMILY ROOM
17-4 X 19

DINING ROOM
12 X 12-9

MASTER SUITE
13 X 16

MASTER BATH

SEAT

SHOWER

FOYER

CLOSET

© Copyright by designer/architect

PORCH

GARAGE
23 X 23

WIDTH - 61'-8"
DEPTH - 66'-0"

Plan #F10-106D-0036

Dimensions: 61'8" W x 74'6" D
Heated Sq. Ft.: 2,762
Bedrooms: 4   **Bathrooms:** 3½
Exterior Walls: Concrete block
Foundation: Monolithic slab

See index for more information

Images provided by designer/architect

BEDROOM 3
11'-0" X 12'-0"
10'-0" CLG.

BEDROOM 3
11'-0" X 12'-0"
10'-0" CLG.

BATH
5' X 12'

W.I.C.
3'3"X4'4"

CL.

CLOSET

CLOSET

COVERED PORCH
32'-8" X 12'-0"

CABANA
6'-0" X 11'-0"

CL.

AHU

AHU

BEDROOM 4
13'-0" X 11'-0"
10'-0" CLG.

CAFE
13'-6" X 7'-0"
10'-0" CLG.

FAMLIY ROOM
20'-6" X 16'-0"
TRAY CLG.

MASTER BEDROOM
12'-1" X 19'-0"
11'-0" CLG.

LIVING ROOM
13'-8" X 14'-0"
10'-0" CLG.

RANGE   DW

KITCHEN
13'-2" X 9'-10"
10'-0" CLG.

REF

FIREPLACE

PWDR
5' X 5'6"

UTILITY
10'-10" X 5'-6"

WH

CL.

W.I.C.
7'-0" X 6'-0"

CL.

FOYER
6'-8" X 6'-0"

CL.

DINING ROOM
11'-0" X 12'-0"
10'-0" CLG.

2-CAR GARAGE
22'-8" X 21'-0"
8'-0" CLG.

STUDY ROOM
10'-0" X 12'-0"
10'-0" CLG.

COV'D ENTRY
6' X 7'-10"

BATH
8'-8" X 12'-6"

© Copyright by designer/architect

DRIVEWAY

Plan #F10-106S-0062

Dimensions:	76'8" W x 93' D
Heated Sq. Ft.:	6,175
Bedrooms: 7	Bathrooms: 7½
Exterior Walls:	Concrete block
Foundation:	Monolithic slab

See index for more information

Images provided by designer/architect

Features

- This traditional Mediterranean style home features a large rear covered patio with a storage area and summer kitchen

- A gourmet kitchen features an eating bar, a huge center island, and a large pantry for convenience

- The master bedroom enjoys a private terrace and two large walk-in closets as well as a master bath with a beautiful walk-through shower and a corner spa tub

- Two 2-car side entry garages

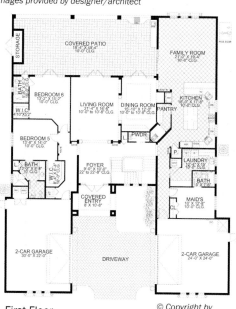

First Floor
3,251 sq. ft.

© Copyright by
designer/architect

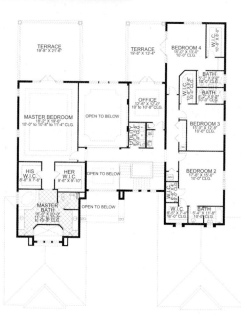

Second Floor
2,924 sq. ft.

Plan #F10-011S-0195

Dimensions:	61'8" W x 103'6" D
Heated Sq. Ft.:	4,455
Bedrooms: 4	**Bathrooms:** 4½
Exterior Walls:	2" x 6"

Foundation: Crawl space or slab standard; basement for an additional fee

See index for more information

Images provided by designer/architect

First Floor
2,551 sq. ft.

Second Floor
1,904 sq. ft.

© Copyright by designer/architect

Features

- Luxury European home has an innovative floor plan that maximizes the first floor square footage to the fullest by combining the great room, kitchen and dining room into one large gathering space
- The second floor features a gym, a wet bar, and a recreation room
- The cozy den includes built-ins and a safe
- 3-car side entry garage

Plan #F10-076D-0237

Dimensions: 91'5" W x 79' D
Heated Sq. Ft.: 2,780
Bonus Sq. Ft.: 432
Bedrooms: 4 **Bathrooms:** 2½
Foundation: Crawl space or slab, please specify when ordering

See index for more information

Images provided by designer/architect

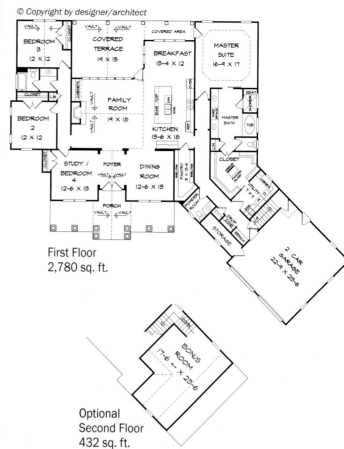

© Copyright by designer/architect

First Floor
2,780 sq. ft.

Optional
Second Floor
432 sq. ft.

Plan #F10-007D-0244

Dimensions: 59' W x 52' D
Heated Sq. Ft.: 1,605
Bedrooms: 2 **Bathrooms:** 2
Foundation: Walk-out basement

See index for more information

First Floor
1,437 sq. ft.

© Copyright by designer/architect

Lower Level
168 sq. ft.

Images provided by designer/architect

Plan #F10-007D-0008

Dimensions: 70'8" W x 70'4" D
Heated Sq. Ft.:   2,452
Bedrooms: 3   **Bathrooms:** 2½
Foundation: Basement standard;
crawl space or slab for an
additional fee

See index for more information

*Images provided by
designer/architect*

© Copyright by
designer/architect

Deck

MBr
13-6x19-8
vaulted

Brk'ft Rm
13-4x12-0

Great Rm
19-5x18-0
vaulted

Br 2
13-6x11-0

Kitchen

13-6x12-0

Hall

Dining
13-0x11-10

Br 3
11-8x11-0

Entry

P

W
D   LAUN.

L

Porch

Garage
29-4x21-4

Home Office
17-4x11-10
vaulted

Plan #F10-130D-0396

Dimensions: 31' W x 57' D
Heated Sq. Ft.:   1,420
Bedrooms: 3   **Bathrooms:** 2
Exterior Walls: 2" x 6"
Foundation: Slab standard;
basement or crawl space for an
additional fee

See index for more information

*Images provided by
designer/architect*

© Copyright by
designer/architect

Storage

BED #1
12 x 15-4
9' Ceiling

DINING
ROOM
12-4 x 11
9' Ceiling

Hers

His

Pantry   KIT
         Island   Ref.
12-4 x 10-3
     DW Sink

BED #2
12 x 10
9' Ceiling

D
W

Slope 9' to 11'   Eating Bar

BED #3
12 x 10
9' Ceiling

Opt. Basement
Stairs

LIVING
ROOM
16 x 18
11' Ceiling

Slope 9' to 11'

STUDY
12 x 11
9' Ceiling

PORCH
12-8 x 8
9' Ceiling

Seat

Plan #F10-172D-0011

Dimensions:	67' W x 50' D
Heated Sq. Ft.:	1,667
Bonus Sq. Ft.:	1,620
Bedrooms: 3	Bathrooms: 2½
Exterior Walls:	2" x 6"
Foundation:	Basement

See index for more information

Images provided by designer/architect

Features

- This country ranch has a timeless style, but with today's fantastic open layout
- The kitchen, large dining area and family room are all completely open to one another
- The master bedroom is spacious and has a private bath and sunny bay window
- The optional lower level has an additional 1,620 square feet of living area and includes three additional bedrooms, a family room and a bath
- 3-car front entry garage

First Floor
1,667 sq. ft.

Optional
Lower Level
1,620 sq. ft.

© Copyright by designer/architect

Plan #F10-169D-0004

Dimensions:	37' W x 15' D
Heated Sq. Ft.:	520
Bedrooms: 1	**Bathrooms:** 1

Foundation: Slab standard; crawl space for an additional fee

See index for more information

Features

- Enjoy ADU style living in this compact one bedroom home with an open floor plan
- The dining/living area has a galley style kitchen on one wall making this multi-tasking space highly efficient and comfortable
- The kitchen enjoys all the comforts and includes a dishwasher, full-size cooktop and refrigerator
- The full bath features an oversized walk-in shower making it easily accessible for all ages and abilities
- The master bedroom has ample closetspace and also includes an area for a stackable washer and dryer

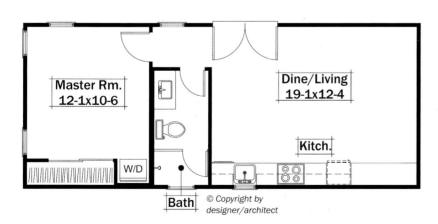

Master Rm.
12-1x10-6

Dine/Living
19-1x12-4

Kitch.

W/D

Bath   © Copyright by designer/architect

Images provided by designer/architect

Plan #F10-007D-0134

Dimensions:	73'8" W x 32' D
Heated Sq. Ft.:	1,310
Bedrooms: 3	Bathrooms: 2

Foundation: Basement standard; crawl space or slab for an additional fee

See index for more information

Images provided by designer/architect

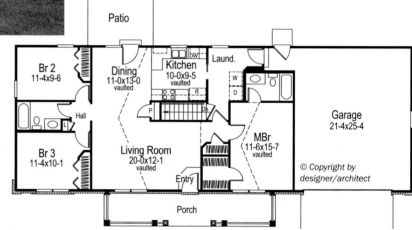

© Copyright by designer/architect

Plan #F10-130D-0335

Images provided by designer/architect

Dimensions:	84' W x 59' D
Heated Sq. Ft.:	2,796
Bonus Sq. Ft.:	316
Bedrooms: 4	Bathrooms: 4

Foundation: Slab standard; basement or crawl space for an additional fee

See index for more information

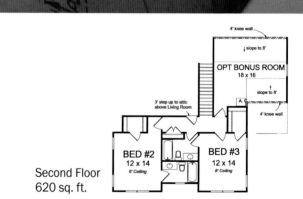

Second Floor
620 sq. ft.

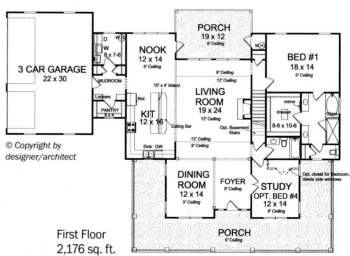

© Copyright by designer/architect

First Floor
2,176 sq. ft.

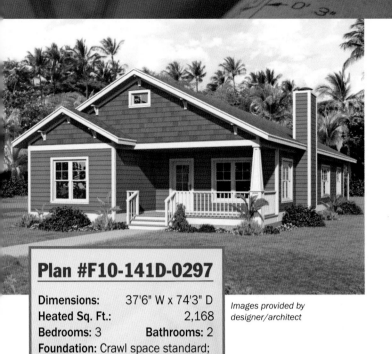

Plan #F10-141D-0297

Dimensions: 37'6" W x 74'3" D
Heated Sq. Ft.: 2,168
Bedrooms: 3 **Bathrooms:** 2
Foundation: Crawl space standard; slab, basement or walk-out basement for an additional fee

See index for more information

Images provided by designer/architect

© Copyright by designer/architect

Plan #F10-076D-0209

Dimensions: 94' W x 81' D
Heated Sq. Ft.: 3,033
Bonus Sq. Ft.: 3,492
Bedrooms: 3 **Bathrooms:** 3½
Foundation: Basement, slab or crawl space, please specify when ordering

See index for more information

Images provided by designer/architect

© Copyright by designer/architect

First Floor
3,033 sq. ft.

Optional Second Floor
656 sq. ft.

Optional Lower Level
2,836 sq. ft.

Plan #F10-155D-0153

Dimensions:	72'10" W x 65' D
Heated Sq. Ft.:	1,967
Bonus Sq. Ft.:	429
Bedrooms: 4	**Bathrooms:** 2
Exterior Walls:	2" x 6"

Foundation: Crawl space or slab standard; basement or daylight basement for an additional fee

See index for more information

Images provided by designer/architect

© Copyright by designer/architect

First Floor
1,967 sq. ft.

Optional Second Floor
429 sq. ft.

Plan #F10-007D-0192

Dimensions:	75'8" W x 32' D
Heated Sq. Ft.:	1,420
Bedrooms: 3	**Bathrooms:** 2

Foundation: Basement standard; crawl space or slab for an additional fee

See index for more information

Images provided by designer/architect

© Copyright by designer/architect

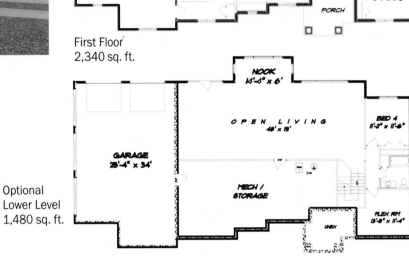

© Copyright by designer/architect

First Floor
2,340 sq. ft.

DECK 13' x 14'
COVERED DECK 15'-8" x 14'
DINING 14'-4" x 10'
M BED 15' x 16'
KITCHEN 14'-4" x 14'
GREAT RM 18'-5" x 22'-3"
BED 3 11'-7" x 11'-6"
3-CAR GARAGE 25' x 34'
W.I.C. 11'-4" x 6'-3"
LAUNDRY 7'-6" x 9'-3"
STUDY 11' x 11'-4"
FOYER
BED 2 11'-7" x 11'-6"
PORCH

Optional Lower Level 1,480 sq. ft.

NOOK 13'-4" x 6'
OPEN LIVING 48' x 19'
BED 4 11'-3" x 11'-6"
GARAGE 25'-4" x 34'
MECH / STORAGE
FLEX RM 13'-8" x 11'-4"
UNEX

Plan #F10-159D-0014

Dimensions:	87'8" W x 56'8" D
Heated Sq. Ft.:	2,340
Bonus Sq. Ft.:	1,480
Bedrooms: 3	Bathrooms: 2½
Exterior Walls:	2" x 6"
Foundation:	Walk-out basement

See index for more information

Images provided by designer/architect

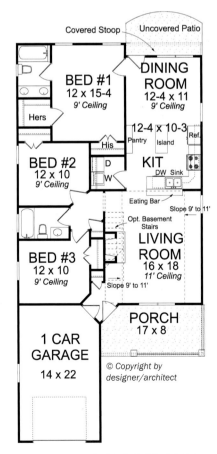

Covered Stoop
Uncovered Patio
BED #1 12 x 15-4 9' Ceiling
DINING ROOM 12-4 x 11 9' Ceiling
Hers
12-4 x 10-3
His
Pantry
Island
Ref.
BED #2 12 x 10 9' Ceiling
D
W
KIT
DW
Sink
Eating Bar
Slope 9' to 11'
Opt. Basement Stairs
LIVING ROOM 16 x 18 11' Ceiling
BED #3 12 x 10 9' Ceiling
Slope 9' to 11'
1 CAR GARAGE 14 x 22
PORCH 17 x 8

© Copyright by designer/architect

Plan #F10-130D-0377

Dimensions:	31' W x 64' D
Heated Sq. Ft.:	1,284
Bedrooms: 3	Bathrooms: 2

Foundation: Slab standard; crawl space or basement for an additional fee

See index for more information

Images provided by designer/architect

Plan #F10-123D-0150

Dimensions:	57' W x 64'8" D
Heated Sq. Ft.:	2,076
Bonus Sq. Ft.:	1,984
Bedrooms: 3	**Bathrooms:** 2½
Foundation:	Basement

standard; crawl space, slab or walk-out basement for an additional fee

See index for more information

Images provided by designer/architect

Features

- This home has a great open layout, a classic farmhouse look with a wrap-around porch and room for expansion if needed
- The open kitchen enjoys a square island with plenty of space for buffet style meals or prepping meals for the week
- The optional second floor has an additional 389 square feet of living area; while the optional lower level has an additional 1,595 square feet and has a rec area with a bar, a family room, an exercise room, two bedrooms, a built-in desk and a bath
- 2-car side entry garage

Optional
Second Floor
389 sq. ft.

Bonus
11 x 26

© Copyright by
designer/architect

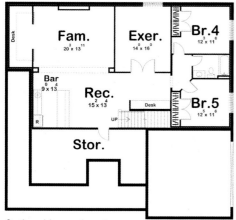

Optional Lower Level
1,595 sq. ft.

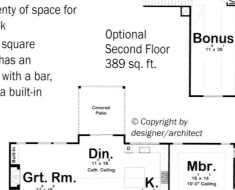

First Floor
2,076 sq. ft.

houseplansandmore.com

Plan #F10-032D-0965

Dimensions:	36' W x 32' D
Heated Sq. Ft.:	1,024
Bonus Sq. Ft.:	1,024
Bedrooms: 3	Bathrooms: 1
Exterior Walls:	2" x 6"

Foundation: Basement standard; crawl space, floating slab or monolithic slab for an additional fee

See index for more information

Features

- This Modern Craftsman has tons of personality inside and out thanks to rustic beams spanning the main gathering spaces
- The kitchen and living area are open to one another
- The bedrooms are positioned close to the full bath
- The optional lower level has an additional 1,024 square feet of living area and shows space for additional bedrooms, a bath and a laundry room

Images provided by designer/architect

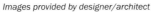

First Floor
1,024 sq. ft.

© Copyright by designer/architect

Optional
Lower Level
1,024 sq. ft.

Plan #F10-166D-0005

Dimensions:	90'10" W x 57'5" D
Heated Sq. Ft.:	2,628
Bedrooms: 4	Bathrooms: 3
Exterior Walls:	2" x 6"
Foundation:	Slab

See index for more information

Images provided by designer/architect

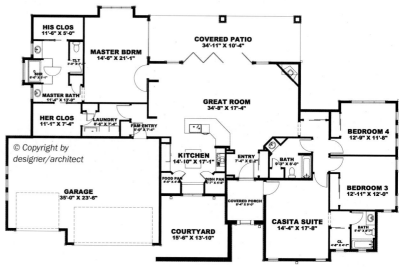

© Copyright by designer/architect

HIS CLOS 11'-6" X 5'-0"
MASTER BDRM 14'-6" X 21'-1"
COVERED PATIO 34'-11" X 10'-4"
MASTER BATH 11'-4" X 13'-9"
HER CLOS 11'-1" X 7'-4"
LAUNDRY 8'-6" X 7'-4"
FAM ENTRY 8'-6" X 7'-4"
GREAT ROOM 34'-8" X 17'-4"
BEDROOM 4 12'-9" X 11'-8"
KITCHEN 14'-10" X 17'-1"
ENTRY 7'-4" X 6'-2"
BATH 9'-3" X 6'-0"
BEDROOM 3 12'-11" X 12'-0"
FOOD PAN
DISH PAN
GARAGE 35'-0" X 23'-6"
COVERED PORCH 6'-4" X 9'-0"
CASITA SUITE 14'-4" X 17'-8"
BATH
COURTYARD 15'-6" X 13'-10"
CL

Plan #F10-007D-0088

Dimensions:	28' W x 40' D
Heated Sq. Ft.:	1,299
Bedrooms: 3	Bathrooms: 2½
Foundation:	Basement

See index for more information

Images provided by designer/architect

© Copyright by designer/architect

Br 2 12-0x12-6
Br 3 11-0x12-6
Balcony/Hall
Living Rm. below
Attic
Second Floor 465 sq. ft.

Patio
Kit 12-0x14-10
MBr 13-0x13-6
Living Rm 12-1x18-3 vaulted
Dn
Up
Entry
Porch
First Floor 834 sq. ft.

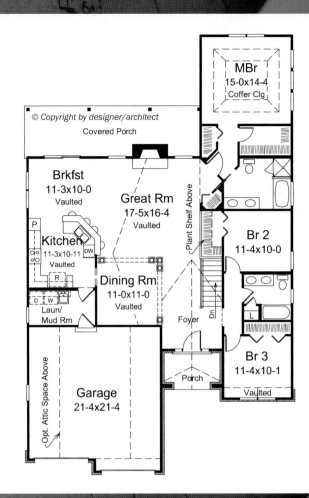

Covered Porch

MBr
15-0x14-4
Coffer Clg

Brkfst
11-3x10-0
Vaulted

Great Rm
17-5x16-4
Vaulted

Kitchen
11-3x10-11
Vaulted

Br 2
11-4x10-0

Dining Rm
11-0x11-0
Vaulted

Plant Shelf Above

Laun/
Mud Rm

Foyer

Br 3
11-4x10-1
Vaulted

Porch

Opt. Attic Space Above

Garage
21-4x21-4

Plan #F10-121D-0035

Dimensions: 45'8" W x 72'4" D
Heated Sq. Ft.: 1,759
Bedrooms: 3 **Bathrooms:** 2
Foundation: Basement standard;
crawl space or slab for an
additional fee

See index for more information

*Images provided by
designer/architect*

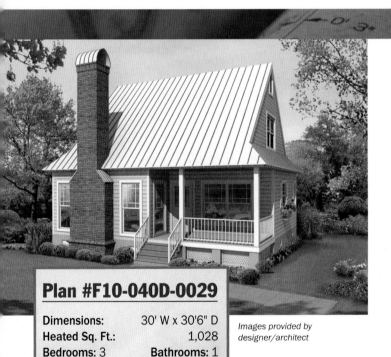

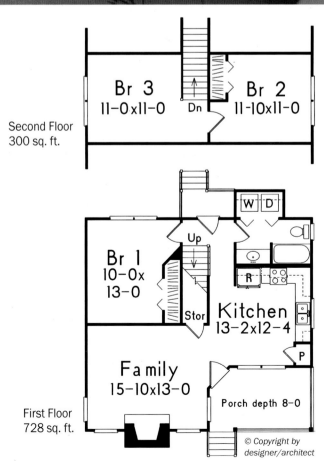

Second Floor
300 sq. ft.

Br 3
11-0x11-0

Dn

Br 2
11-10x11-0

Br 1
10-0x
13-0

Up

Stor

W D

Kitchen
13-2x12-4

Family
15-10x13-0

Porch depth 8-0

First Floor
728 sq. ft.

Plan #F10-040D-0029

Dimensions: 30' W x 30'6" D
Heated Sq. Ft.: 1,028
Bedrooms: 3 **Bathrooms:** 1
Foundation: Crawl space

See index for more information

*Images provided by
designer/architect*

Plan #F10-056S-0049

Dimensions:	104'3" W x 84' D
Heated Sq. Ft.:	5,780
Bonus Sq. Ft.:	753
Bedrooms:	4
Bathrooms:	4 full, 2 half
Foundation:	Basement standard; crawl space or slab for an additional fee

See index for more information

Images provided by designer/architect

Features

- This Craftsman masterpiece is reminiscent of Old World style thanks to the wood details in the gables
- A beautiful lodge room with a beamed ceiling is a beautiful place to relax after a long day
- The kitchen with island has an open view of the beautiful circular breakfast area with views of the covered porch and open deck
- The optional second floor has an additional 753 square feet of living area
- 2-car front entry garage

First Floor
3,463 sq. ft.

Optional
Second Floor
753 sq. ft.

Lower Level
2,317 sq. ft.

© Copyright by designer/architect

houseplansandmore.com

Plan #F10-024S-0021

Dimensions: 80' W x 66' D
Heated Sq. Ft.: 5,862
Bedrooms: 6 **Bathrooms:** 5
Foundation: Basement or pier, please specify when ordering

See index for more information

Images provided by designer/architect

Features

- Decorative columns line the perimeter of the formal dining room for an elegant feel
- The master bedroom features a private sitting area that leads to the covered porch
- One of the second floor bedrooms has direct access to a private balcony
- This plan features an above ground basement option
- 3-car drive under side entry garage

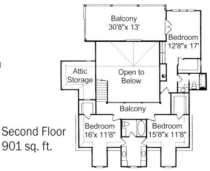

Second Floor
901 sq. ft.

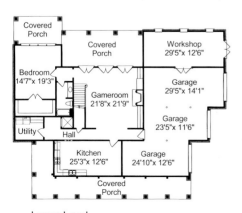

Lower Level
1,818 sq. ft.

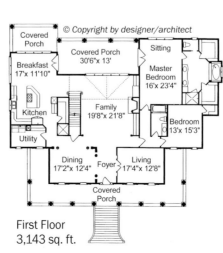

© Copyright by designer/architect

First Floor
3,143 sq. ft.

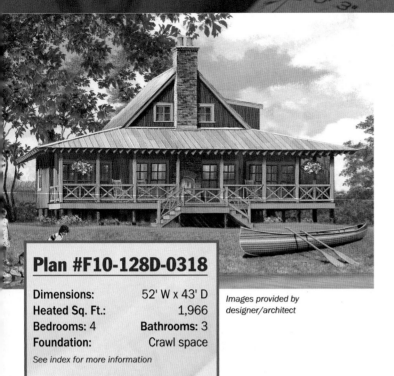

Plan #F10-128D-0318

Dimensions:	52' W x 43' D
Heated Sq. Ft.:	1,966
Bedrooms: 4	Bathrooms: 3
Foundation:	Crawl space

See index for more information

Images provided by designer/architect

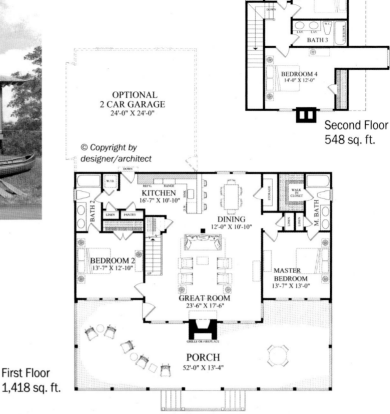

OPTIONAL
2 CAR GARAGE
24'-0" X 24'-0"

© Copyright by
designer/architect

Second Floor
548 sq. ft.

BEDROOM 3
11'-0" X 11'-4"

WALK IN CLOSET

LINEN

BATH 3

LAV LAV W.C.

DOWN

BEDROOM 4
14'-0" X 12'-0"

First Floor
1,418 sq. ft.

KITCHEN
16'-7" X 10'-10"

DINING
12'-0" X 10'-10"

BATH 2

LINEN PANTRY

BEDROOM 2
13'-7" X 12'-10"

GREAT ROOM
23'-6" X 17'-6"

WALK IN CLOSET

M. BATH

MASTER BEDROOM
13'-7" X 13'-0"

GRILLE OR FIREPLACE

PORCH
52'-0" X 13'-4"

Plan #F10-122D-0001

Dimensions:	33' W x 35' D
Heated Sq. Ft.:	1,105
Bedrooms: 2	Bathrooms: 1½
Foundation:	Slab

See index for more information

Images provided by designer/architect

Second Floor
225 sq. ft.

Bath

Bedroom 1
11-10x14-2

Open

Dn

© Copyright by
designer/architect

Bedroom 2
11-9x11-4

P

Dining
9-4x7-8

Kitchen
9-0x9-0

R

DW

Hall

Bath

Up

Lndry

W

D

Living Rm
17-8x14-11

Sloped Clg.

Foyer

Patio

First Floor
880 sq. ft.

Images provided by designer/architect

© Copyright by designer/architect

Plan #F10-003D-0005

Dimensions:	80' W x 42' D
Heated Sq. Ft.:	1,708
Bedrooms: 3	**Bathrooms:** 2

Foundation: Basement standard; crawl space or slab for an additional fee

See index for more information

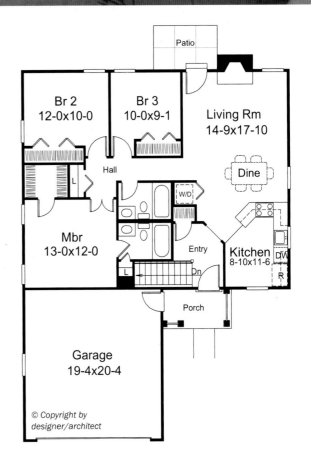

Plan #F10-007D-0181

Images provided by designer/architect

Dimensions:	38' W x 52'8" D
Heated Sq. Ft.:	1,140
Bedrooms: 3	**Bathrooms:** 2

Foundation: Basement standard; crawl space or slab for an additional fee

See index for more information

© Copyright by designer/architect

Plan #F10-106D-0051

Dimensions:	100'4" W x 70' D
Heated Sq. Ft.:	6,488
Bedrooms: 6	**Bathrooms:** 6
Exterior Walls:	Concrete block
Foundation:	Monolithic slab

See index for more information

Features

- This Industrial Modern masterpiece takes sleek living to a whole new level
- The kitchen and family room join forces for a casual relaxation place
- There's a formal living room for entertaining as well as a VIP guest suite with its own bath
- The master suite has a terrace, a sitting room, and posh bath
- 3-car front entry garage

© Copyright by designer/architect

First Floor
3,764 sq. ft.

Second Floor
2,724 sq. ft.

Images provided by designer/architect

Plan #F10-011D-0266

Dimensions:	40' W x 75' D
Heated Sq. Ft.:	2,190
Bedrooms: 3	**Bathrooms:** 2½
Exterior Walls:	2" x 6"

Foundation: Crawl space or slab standard; basement for an additional fee

See index for more information

Images provided by designer/architect

Features

- This Modern style home has personality thanks to its slanted roof lines and various exterior textures, materials and color choices
- Perfect for an urban lot because of its narrow width, this home utilizes living to the fullest and even offers a courtyard scenario that wraps around the home in an L-shape to offer that outdoor living everyone loves
- The dining and living areas are wide open to the kitchen creating a central hub in this home for eating, relaxing and entertaining
- The master suite is tucked away on the first floor for privacy, and the same goes for an office near the front foyer
- Two bedrooms can be found on the second floor along with a shared bath
- 2-car front entry garage

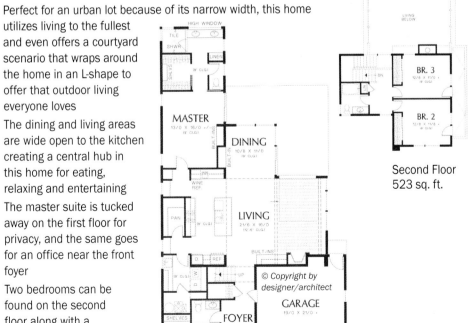

Second Floor
523 sq. ft.

© Copyright by designer/architect

First Floor
1,667 sq. ft.

call 1-800-373-2646

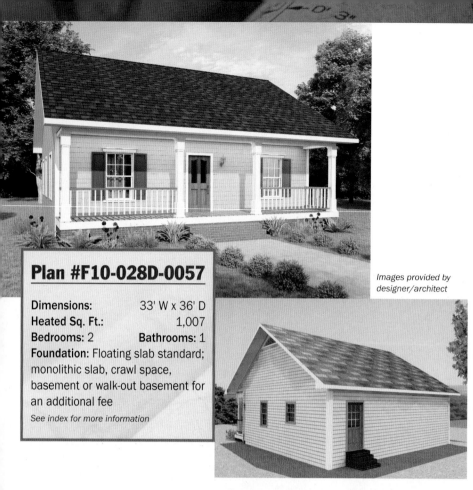

MASTER BEDROOM
13'-0" X 16'-6"

CLO.
8'-0" X 6'-6"

LAUNDRY
9'-8" X 6'-6"

STOR

WH

KITCHEN
12'-0" X 10'-0"

LINEN

LINEN

SNACK BAR

BEDROOM 2
13'-0" X 10'-0"

GREAT ROOM
20'-0" X 14'-0"

© Copyright by designer/architect

COVERED PORCH

Plan #F10-028D-0057

Dimensions: 33' W x 36' D
Heated Sq. Ft.:   1,007
Bedrooms: 2   Bathrooms: 1
Foundation: Floating slab standard; monolithic slab, crawl space, basement or walk-out basement for an additional fee

See index for more information

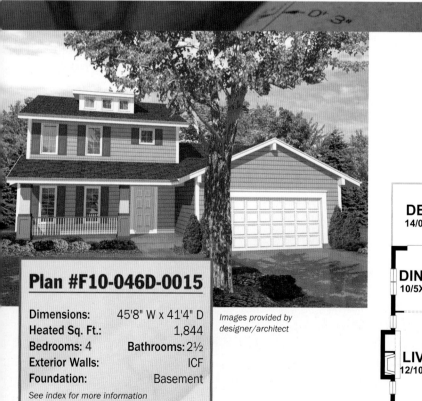

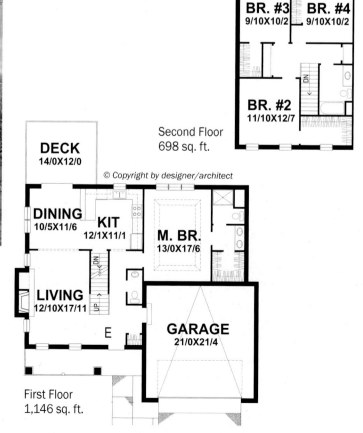

BR. #3
9/10X10/2

BR. #4
9/10X10/2

BR. #2
11/10X12/7

DN

Second Floor
698 sq. ft.

© Copyright by designer/architect

DECK
14/0X12/0

DINING
10/5X11/6

KIT
12/1X11/1

M. BR.
13/0X17/6

LIVING
12/10X17/11

UP

DN

E

GARAGE
21/0X21/4

First Floor
1,146 sq. ft.

Plan #F10-046D-0015

Dimensions: 45'8" W x 41'4" D
Heated Sq. Ft.:   1,844
Bedrooms: 4   Bathrooms: 2½
Exterior Walls: ICF
Foundation: Basement

See index for more information

Plan #F10-013D-0201

Dimensions: 71'2" W x 64'6" D
Heated Sq. Ft.: 2,294
Bonus Sq. Ft.: 1,562
Bedrooms: 3   Bathrooms: 3½
Foundation: Crawl space standard; basement or slab for an additional fee

See index for more information

Images provided by designer/architect

Optional Second Floor
1,562 sq. ft.

© Copyright by designer/architect

First Floor
2,294 sq. ft.

Plan #F10-130D-0344

Dimensions: 32' W x 70' D
Heated Sq. Ft.: 2,062
Bedrooms: 4   Bathrooms: 3
Foundation: Slab standard; crawl space or basement for an additional fee

See index for more information

Images provided by designer/architect

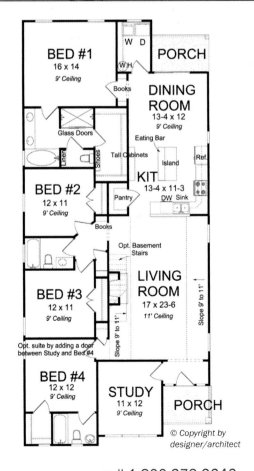

© Copyright by designer/architect

Plan #F10-091D-0021

Dimensions:	98'4" W x 55'8" D
Heated Sq. Ft.:	3,289
Bedrooms: 3	Bathrooms: 2½
Exterior Walls:	2" x 6"
Foundation:	Walk-out basement

See index for more information

Images provided by designer/architect

Second Floor
1,609 sq. ft.

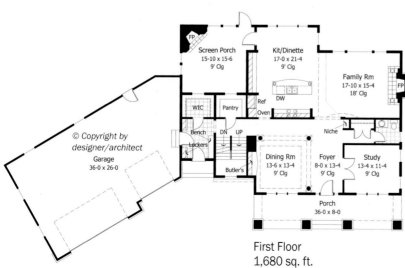

First Floor
1,680 sq. ft.

Features

- Decorative columns define the dining room and provide an elegant first impression upon entering the home
- Double doors to the right of the foyer open to a private study, perfect as a home office
- A screen porch off the kitchen includes a corner fireplace creating a cozy atmosphere
- The kitchen is open and provides a huge center island with dining space that intersects both the dinette and the family room
- At the garage entrance, a bench, lockers, and a walk-in closet keep everything organized
- The second floor owner's suite is luxurious
- 3-car front entry garage

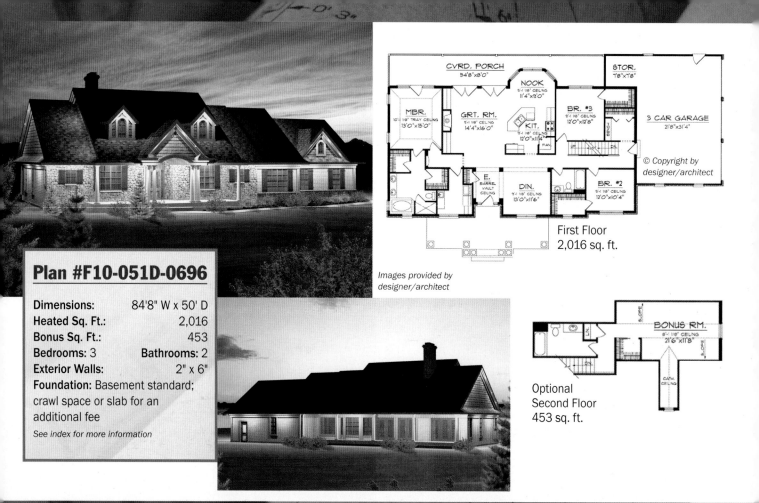

First Floor
2,016 sq. ft.

Images provided by
designer/architect

Optional
Second Floor
453 sq. ft.

BONUS RM.

Plan #F10-051D-0696

Dimensions:	84'8" W x 50' D
Heated Sq. Ft.:	2,016
Bonus Sq. Ft.:	453
Bedrooms: 3	Bathrooms: 2
Exterior Walls:	2" x 6"

Foundation: Basement standard;
crawl space or slab for an
additional fee

See index for more information

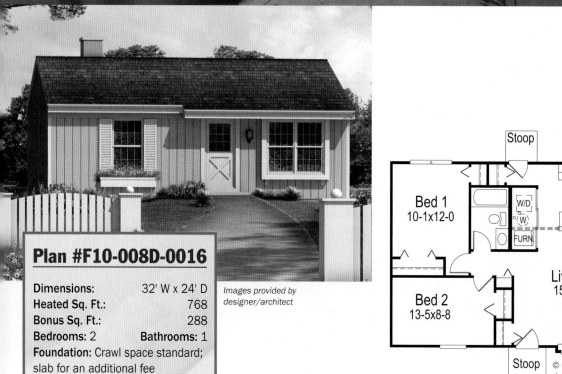

Plan #F10-008D-0016

Dimensions:	32' W x 24' D
Heated Sq. Ft.:	768
Bonus Sq. Ft.:	288
Bedrooms: 2	Bathrooms: 1

Foundation: Crawl space standard;
slab for an additional fee

See index for more information

Images provided by
designer/architect

Stoop

Stoop

Storage

Kitchen
12-0x8-1

Bed 1
10-1x12-0

W/D

FURN.

Living Rm
15-2x14-11

Opt Bed
11-8x14-7

Bed 2
13-5x8-8

Stoop

Plan #F10-001D-0036

Dimensions: 30' W x 50' D
Heated Sq. Ft.: 1,320
Bedrooms: 3   **Bathrooms:** 2
Foundation: Crawl space standard;
slab for an additional fee

See index for more information

Images provided by designer/architect

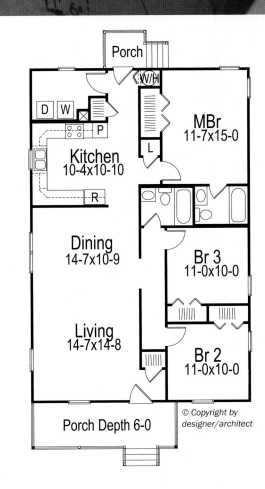

© Copyright by designer/architect

Plan #F10-007D-0075

Dimensions: 55'8" W x 46'4" D
Heated Sq. Ft.: 2,194
Bedrooms: 3   **Bathrooms:** 2
Foundation: Walk-out basement

See index for more information

Images provided by designer/architect

Plan #F10-011S-0143

Dimensions:	56' W x 70' D
Heated Sq. Ft.:	3,926
Bedrooms: 5	**Bathrooms:** 4½
Exterior Walls:	2" x 6"
Foundation:	Daylight basement

See index for more information

Images provided by designer/architect

Second Floor
1,207 sq. ft.

Lower Level
984 sq. ft.

First Floor
1,735 sq. ft.

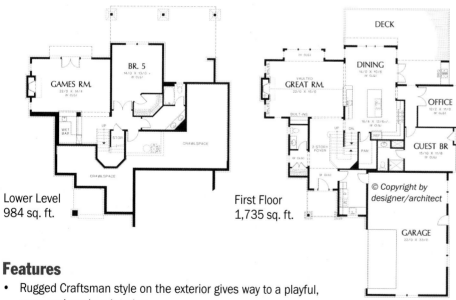

© Copyright by designer/architect

Features

- Rugged Craftsman style on the exterior gives way to a playful, open and modern interior
- The first floor has a vaulted great room that intermingles with the nearby dining area and kitchen
- The kitchen island is large enough for dining and food prep
- A private guest bedroom promises to be comfortable for guests tucked back near the office
- The lower level game room with wet bar will be a favorite when entertaining
- 2-car side entry garage

Plan #F10-128D-0010

Dimensions: 56'4" W x 35'4" D
Heated Sq. Ft.: 2,069
Bonus Sq. Ft.: 382
Bedrooms: 3   **Bathrooms:** 2½
Foundation: Crawl space or basement, please specify when ordering

See index for more information

Images provided by designer/architect

Features

- Old Key West charm with covered porches offers abundant curb appeal and outdoor living space
- Enter the foyer near the dining room, great when entertaining
- The spacious great room with a fireplace also has direct access to a rear screen porch
- The kitchen is near the breakfast area for convenience and has a center island for work prep space and a walk-in pantry
- The master bedroom offers a luxury private bath with a whirlpool tub, a double-bowl vanity, and a huge his and her wardrobe closet
- The future recreation room on the second floor has an additional 382 square feet of living area
- 2-car side entry garage

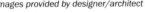

Second Floor
994 sq. ft.

© Copyright by designer/architect

First Floor
1,075 sq. ft.

call 1-800-373-2646

Plan #F10-148D-0040

Dimensions:	44' W x 42' D
Heated Sq. Ft.:	2,181
Bedrooms: 3	**Bathrooms:** 2½
Exterior Walls:	2" x 6"
Foundation:	Basement

See index for more information

Images provided by designer/architect

Second Floor
1,206 sq. ft.

First Floor
975 sq. ft.

© Copyright by designer/architect

Plan #F10-077D-0187

Images provided by designer/architect

Dimensions:	65' W x 60'8" D
Heated Sq. Ft.:	1,816
Bonus Sq. Ft.:	326
Bedrooms: 3	**Bathrooms:** 2

Foundation: Basement or walk-out basement, please specify when ordering; for slab or crawl space versions, see Plan #077D-0140 at houseplansandmore.com

See index for more information

Optional
Second Floor
326 sq. ft.

First Floor
1,816 sq. ft.

© Copyright by designer/architect

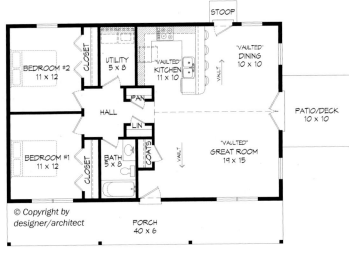

Plan #F10-141D-0207

Dimensions:	40' W x 25' D
Heated Sq. Ft.:	1,000
Bedrooms: 2	**Bathrooms:** 1

Foundation: Slab standard; crawl space, basement or walk-out basement for an additional fee

See index for more information

Images provided by designer/architect

© Copyright by designer/architect

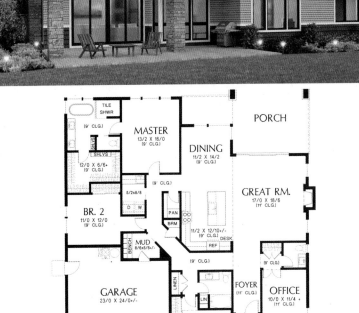

Plan #F10-011D-0685

Dimensions:	55' W x 61' D
Heated Sq. Ft.:	2,179
Bedrooms: 3	**Bathrooms:** 2½
Exterior Walls:	2" x 6"

Foundation: Crawl space or slab standard; basement for an additional fee

See index for more information

Images provided by designer/architect

© Copyright by designer/architect

Plan #F10-167D-0009

Dimensions:	67'11" W x 65'10" D
Heated Sq. Ft.:	3,363
Bedrooms: 4	Bathrooms: 3½
Exterior Walls:	2" x 6"

Foundation: Crawl space standard; slab for an additional fee

See index for more information

Images provided by designer/architect

Features

- A country farmhouse for today's family with lots of great spaces throughout the first floor including an office/study, a dining area, a vaulted great room, and a quiet rear den
- A first floor bedroom with bath is ideal as a guest suite and a master suite with a bath featuring a huge walk-through shower and two big walk-in closets can also be found on the first floor
- The kitchen has plenty of storage with a walk-in pantry
- The second floor has two additional bedrooms that share a full bath
- 2-car front entry detached garage

Second Floor
690 sq. ft.

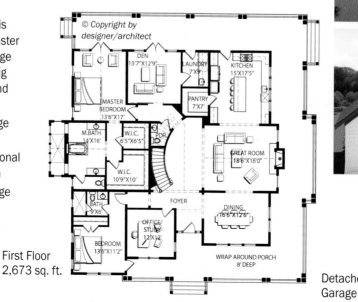

First Floor
2,673 sq. ft.

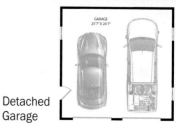

Detached Garage

houseplansandmore.com

Plan #F10-172D-0028

Dimensions:	75'1" W x 42' D
Heated Sq. Ft.:	1,555
Bonus Sq. Ft.:	1,518
Bedrooms: 3	**Bathrooms:** 2
Exterior Walls:	2" x 6"

Foundation: Basement standard; crawl space, monolithic slab, stem wall slab, daylight basement or walk-out basement for an additional fee

See index for more information

Images provided by designer/architect

Features

- This one-story home offers formal and informal spaces
- The kitchen has a breakfast bar for casual dining
- The living room could easily be converted to a home office area
- The bayed master suite includes a walk-in closet and a private bath
- The optional lower level has an additional 1,518 square feet of living area and includes a huge family room, two bedrooms and a bath
- 3-car front entry garage

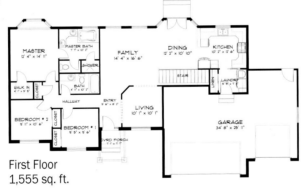

First Floor
1,555 sq. ft.

© Copyright by designer/architect

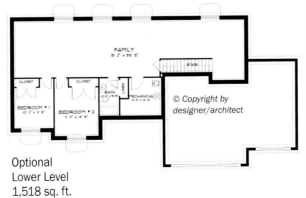

Optional
Lower Level
1,518 sq. ft.

Plan #F10-013D-0155

Dimensions:	63' W x 73' D
Heated Sq. Ft.:	1,800
Bonus Sq. Ft.:	503
Bedrooms: 3	Bathrooms: 3

Foundation: Slab standard; crawl space or basement for an additional fee

See index for more information

© Copyright by designer/architect

Images provided by designer/architect

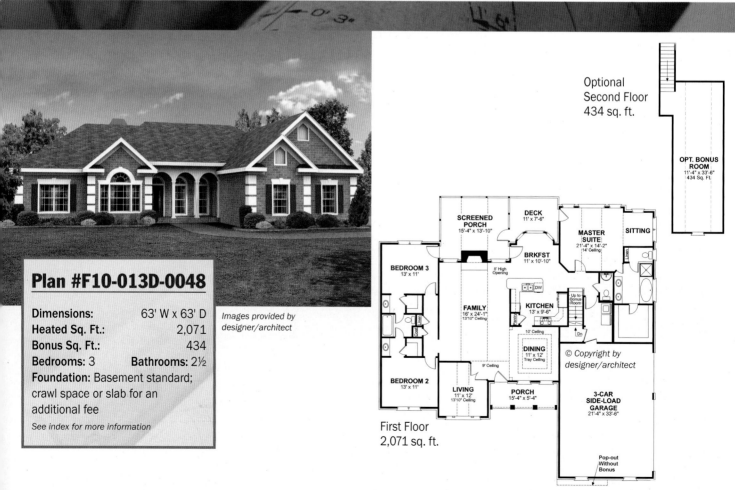

Plan #F10-013D-0048

Dimensions:	63' W x 63' D
Heated Sq. Ft.:	2,071
Bonus Sq. Ft.:	434
Bedrooms: 3	Bathrooms: 2½

Foundation: Basement standard; crawl space or slab for an additional fee

See index for more information

Images provided by designer/architect

© Copyright by designer/architect

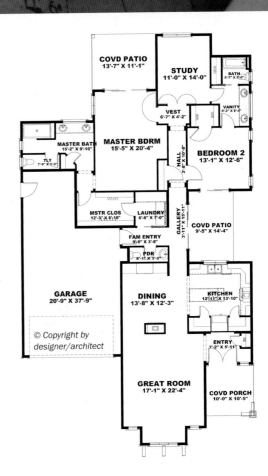

Plan #F10-166D-0001

Images provided by designer/architect

Dimensions:	49'5" W x 84'9" D
Heated Sq. Ft.:	2,232
Bedrooms: 2	Bathrooms: 2½
Exterior Walls:	2" x 6"
Foundation:	Slab

See index for more information

© Copyright by designer/architect

Plan #F10-130D-0372

Images provided by designer/architect

Dimensions:	53' W x 41' D
Heated Sq. Ft.:	1,597
Bedrooms: 3	Bathrooms: 2½
Foundation:	Slab standard; crawl space or basement for an additional fee

See index for more information

© Copyright by designer/architect

Second Floor
447 sq. ft.

First Floor
1,150 sq. ft.

Plan #F10-051S-0054

Dimensions: 89'4" W x 67' D
Heated Sq. Ft.: 4,579
Bedrooms: 4 **Bathrooms:** 3
Exterior Walls: 2" x 6"
Foundation: Walk-out basement standard; crawl space or slab for an additional fee

See index for more information

Images provided by designer/architect

Features

- The wood beam ceiling treatment in the great room adds spectacular dimension to the interior especially with the cathedral style ceiling
- The open kitchen is a chef's dream with a nearby walk-in pantry and utility room with a built-in locker system
- A cathedral ceiling adds spaciousness and elegance to the master bedroom that also enjoys a private covered porch
- Retreat to the lower level and find an amazing recreation room with a wet bar and a nearby media room
- 3-car side entry garage

© Copyright by designer/architect

First Floor
2,551 sq. ft.

Lower Level
2,028 sq. ft.

Plan #F10-147D-0003

Dimensions:	63' W x 40'4" D
Heated Sq. Ft.:	1,773
Bedrooms: 3	**Bathrooms:** 2

Foundation: Basement standard; crawl space or slab for an additional fee

See index for more information

Images provided by designer/architect

Features

- Spectacular country style that blends with Modern farmhouse details to create a modernized family home
- Enter at the entry and to the right is the spacious great room surrounded in windows and adorned with a cozy fireplace
- To the left of the entry are all of the bedrooms
- The wrap-around porch leads to a covered patio off the sunny dining area
- The kitchen includes a breakfast bar with seating for four
- 2-car detached front entry garage

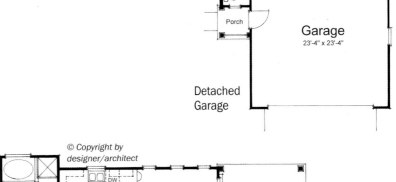

Detached Garage

First Floor
1,773 sq. ft.

Plan #F10-172D-0008

Dimensions:	78' W x 47' D
Heated Sq. Ft.:	3,016
Bonus Sq. Ft.:	1,515
Bedrooms: 4	Bathrooms: 2½
Exterior Walls:	2" x 6"

Foundation: Basement standard; crawl space, monolithic slab, stem wall slab, daylight basement or walk-out basement for an additional fee

See index for more information

Features

- This two-story country home enjoys an open first floor layout that also includes a cozy den and a home office
- The second floor has all of the bedrooms as well as a centrally located laundry room for making this chore much easier
- The mud room includes a long bench creating a drop zone
- The optional lower level has an additional 1,515 square feet of living area and includes a large family room, a bedroom and a full bath
- 3-car front entry garage

Second Floor
1,484 sq. ft.

Images provided by designer/architect

Optional Lower Level
1,515 sq. ft.

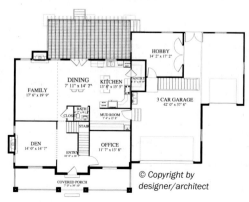

© Copyright by designer/architect

First Floor
1,532 sq. ft.

Plan #F10-026D-1856

Dimensions:	117'4" W x 155'6" D
Heated Sq. Ft.:	9,360
Bonus Sq. Ft.:	168
Bedrooms:	6
Bathrooms:	6 full, 2 half
Foundation:	Slab

See index for more information

Images provided by designer/architect

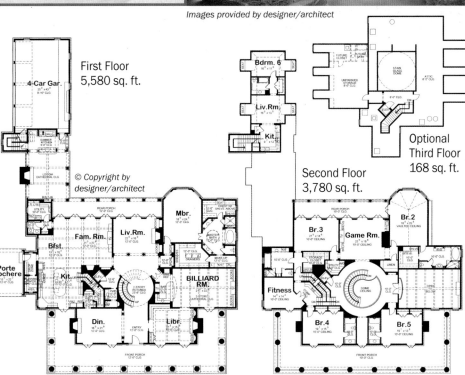

First Floor
5,580 sq. ft.

© Copyright by
designer/architect

Second Floor
3,780 sq. ft.

Optional
Third Floor
168 sq. ft.

Features

- Live in luxury in your own Lowcountry Plantation style dream home
- Amenities abound in this amazing home with a fitness room, billiard room, library, game room, summer kitchen, and elevator
- There's six bedrooms with the apartment above the garage, ideal for guests
- 4-car side entry garage

Plan #F10-071S-0032

Dimensions:	71' W x 70' D
Heated Sq. Ft.:	4,725
Bedrooms: 4	Bathrooms: 4½
Exterior Walls:	2" x 6"
Foundation:	Crawl space

See index for more information

Images provided by designer/architect

Features

- Step into the foyer and let it lead you to the stunning rotunda with an angled staircase to the second floor
- The family room is full of warmth thanks to the corner fireplace
- The kitchen is perfectly positioned between the formal dining room and the casual breakfast nook
- The second floor loft is a great hideaway perfect for studying, or relaxing
- 4-car side entry garage

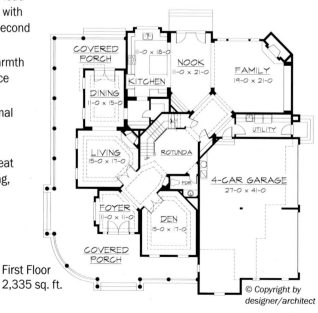

First Floor
2,335 sq. ft.

© Copyright by
designer/architect

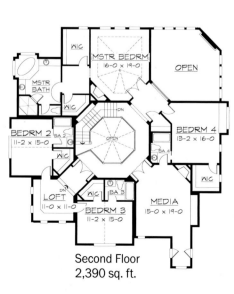

Second Floor
2,390 sq. ft.

houseplansandmore.com

Plan #F10-024S-0037

Dimensions:	57' W x 82' D
Heated Sq. Ft.:	4,380
Bonus Sq. Ft.:	1,275
Bedrooms: 4	Bathrooms: 3½
Foundation:	Pier

See index for more information

Images provided by designer/architect

Features

- 11' ceilings on the first floor, and 9' ceilings on the second floor create a spacious interior
- Intricate porch details display one-of-a-kind craftsmanship
- The impressive foyer has a curved staircase creating a grand entry
- One second floor bedroom accesses a private balcony
- The optional lower level has an additional 1,275 square feet of living area
- 3-car drive under side entry garage

Optional
Lower Level
1,275 sq. ft.

First Floor
2,974 sq. ft.

© Copyright by
designer/architect

Second Floor
1,406 sq. ft.

Images provided by designer/architect

© Copyright by designer/architect

Plan #F10-148D-0404
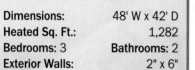

Dimensions:	48' W x 42' D
Heated Sq. Ft.:	1,282
Bedrooms: 3	**Bathrooms:** 2
Exterior Walls:	2" x 6"
Foundation:	Basement

See index for more information

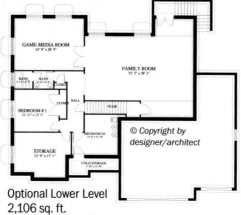

Images provided by designer/architect

Plan #F10-172D-0021

Dimensions:	67'4" W x 53' D
Heated Sq. Ft.:	2,050
Bonus Sq. Ft.:	2,106
Bedrooms: 3	**Bathrooms:** 2½
Exterior Walls:	2" x 6"

Foundation: Walk-out basement standard; crawl space, monolithic slab, stem wall slab, basement or daylight basement for an additional fee

See index for more information

© Copyright by designer/architect

Optional Lower Level
2,106 sq. ft.

First Floor
2,050 sq. ft.

Second Floor
849 sq. ft.

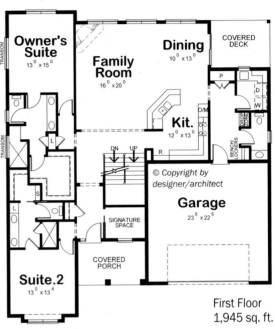

First Floor
1,945 sq. ft.

© Copyright by designer/architect

Plan #F10-026D-1930

Images provided by designer/architect

Dimensions: 52' W x 59' D
Heated Sq. Ft.: 2,794
Bedrooms: 4   Bathrooms: 4½
Exterior Walls: 2" x 6"
Foundation: Basement standard; slab, crawl space or walk-out basement for an additional fee

See index for more information

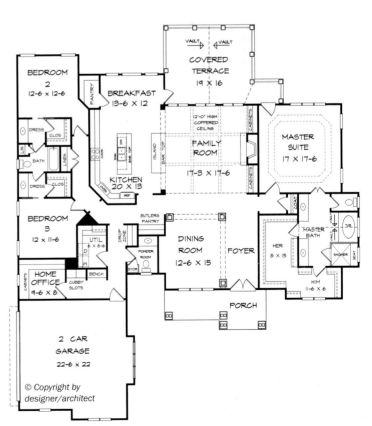

© Copyright by designer/architect

Plan #F10-076D-0213

Images provided by designer/architect

Dimensions: 71'8" W x 79'7" D
Heated Sq. Ft.: 2,896
Bedrooms: 3   Bathrooms: 2½
Foundation: Crawl space or slab, please specify when ordering

See index for more information

Plan #F10-024S-0026

Dimensions:	87' W x 103' D
Heated Sq. Ft.:	4,957
Bonus Sq. Ft.:	1,047
Bedrooms: 5	Bathrooms: 5½
Foundation:	Floating slab

See index for more information

© Copyright by designer/architect

First Floor
4,421 sq. ft.

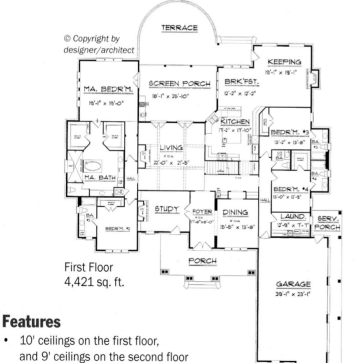

Second Floor
536 sq. ft.

Images provided by designer/architect

Features

- 10' ceilings on the first floor, and 9' ceilings on the second floor
- A terrific screen porch can be accessed from the living room and master bedroom
- A peninsula style spa whirlpool tub is the main focal point of the luxurious private master bath
- The future second floor media room, game room and den have an additional 1,047 square feet of living area
- 3-car side entry garage

Plan #F10-056D-0134

Dimensions:	76'2" W x 92'2" D
Heated Sq. Ft.:	4,917
Bonus Sq. Ft.:	275
Bedrooms:	5
Bathrooms:	4 full, 2 half
Foundation:	Basement standard; crawl space or slab for an additional fee

See index for more information

Images provided by designer/architect

Features

- This rustic Craftsman home has several levels of great space for entertaining
- The lodge room is stunning with its centered vault, stone fireplace and views of the outdoor screened porch with fireplace
- The lower level has many places to have fun including a wet bar, billiards area, and a social room with a wine cellar
- The optional bonus room on the second floor has an additional 275 square feet of living area
- 1-car side entry porte-cochere, a 1-car side entry garage, and a golf cart garage

Second Floor
826 sq. ft.

Lower Level
1,912 sq. ft.

© Copyright by
designer/architect

First Floor
2,179 sq. ft.

the wow factor:

The "It" Features
home buyers want

The features found in homes today are being included for a reason; these are the things homeowners are asking for to make their lives easier! Home buyers' attitudes have shifted in recent years and today's homeowners are very practical. They are content with a smaller home featuring an open floor plan, which requires less maintenance, all while ideally being built with affordable green materials. Their need for the bells and whistles has waned, and they seek a modern, less cluttered style. Homes of yesteryear can't compete with the amazing new home designs that incorporate so many automated features and sleek open floor plans. Let's take a closer look at many of the most demanded features sought in new homes today.

go with the flow

Today's floor plans have less square footage, which means they must maximize every last square foot to the fullest. Today's homes have fewer rooms, but the rooms they do have serve many purposes. Open floor plans remain all the rage and offer the potential for a smaller home to feel larger and more functional. However, since the pandemic, the need for more compartmentalized spaces has increased with many family members working and learning from home. So, the seamless flow from the dining area, kitchen, and even the great room often seen with an open floor plan has created some issues with functionality for many families in the past year. But, many homeowners do want the interior to flow freely visually into the outdoor areas. Similar flooring color and furniture outdoors tends to visually extend the home even farther making a smaller home feel comfortably roomy and less confined. Homeowners desire outdoor spaces that mimic their home's interior and include a dedicated area for sitting and dining space. Many of these spaces include outdoor fireplaces, or calming fountains. Today's homeowners had been looking for less yard space in recent years; just enough to have an oasis to retreat to, but not enough to create additional chores and maintenance. And if there is a patio or deck, Millennials especially want exterior finishes to be as maintenance free as possible. But, many homeowners since the pandemic have moved out of more densely populated suburban areas and are seeking more yard space.

An open flow is even more important than size. So more windows and doors, and fewer walls are optimal features that add a feeling of spaciousness and volume. Formal dining and living rooms are considered spaces of the past, and in their place are flex spaces that can be converted to home offices, a guest room, or kid's playroom. With today's family, flexibility is key. Higher ceilings throughout are more popular now than attention-seeking dramatic two-story foyers.

clean living

With open, airy spaces also comes the desire for sleek interior spaces and furnishings especially in the kitchen where clutter can easily occur. Architecturally, today's homes are using simpler lines. Think less trimwork and moldings, and more streamline Craftsman and Prairie style woodwork. Cabinet styles are less rounded and Traditional now, and sleek angled cabinets are popular.

Quartz countertops are being chosen more often than granite since they have more subtle surfaces. Wider plank style flooring designs are still the most popular, but the dark colors have been toned down a bit more. With the sleeker cabinets and counters, homeowners love the look of matte appliances rather than their shiny steel counterparts. Definitely a more subdued look, these appliances tend to hide scratches and fingerprints much better.

Unless noted, copyright by designer/architect; Page 458 top: Small, compact kitchen utilizes space to the fullest, istockphoto.com; middle: A great open kitchen layout, Plan #F10-011S-0189 on page 12; bottom: Sleek surfaces and cabinets are the trend, Plan #101D-0108; Page 459, top, left clockwise: Sleek and modern sink, Kohler Indio Sink, us.kohler. com; Quartz countertops look clean and fresh, Plan #F10-101D-0052 on page 231, Damon Searles, photographer; A huge kitchen island is where its at, Plan #F10-101D-0121; Matte appliances keep surfaces looking clean and free of fingerprints, kitchenaid. com. See additional photos and purchase plans at houseplansandmore.com.

i am an island

Kitchen islands are a must-have since they offer additional prep space, storage, casual dining space, and are often steps from the dining area. Their open shelving can offer an open feel and easy access for frequently used items. Pantry sizes have increased, while the amount of cabinets has decreased. This gives the illusion of a sleeker kitchen overall.

Kitchens have become larger and more open with less clutter. Basically, today's best features in the kitchen are popular because they make it appear simpler.

peace out

Sleek, clean living continues into the bathroom, too. No longer are homeowners requesting large garden style tubs that often featured multiple steps and ornate columns. Oversized garden tubs simply take up too much bathroom real estate in today's smaller scaled homes. Instead, open walk-in showers often with practically invisible glass surrounds are trending. If the home is larger and there is space for a tub, then homeowners are requesting free-standing modern style tubs. Large floor tiles and sleek fixtures complement this Zen-like space to create a feeling of tranquility.

lite brite

When many think clean, they think bright. So, white is becoming the color of choice for both kitchen and baths. And, incorporating larger and extra windows, glass doors and skylights helps to carry out the bright theme to the fullest. If a new home is being painted a color, then it's a color being called, "greige". This hybrid combines beige and gray and is a great neutral. Sleek, classic subway tile is being used everywhere. If there's anything that isn't minimalist in home design, then it's a homeowners desire for statement lighting, which are unique, often oversized fixtures that add drama to the space.

go green

Homeowners today are interested in value, environmentally sound material choices, and products that will provide lasting durability and comfort. Those building a new home realize that it's worth paying a little more for certain materials because it will result in bigger savings over the lifespan of the home. From low-E windows to high efficiency air conditioners, there are countless ways to include green building materials, and all provide an opportunity to save money on your utility bills.

Home buyers are also more interested than ever in maintaining good indoor air quality. So, green products that use zero VOCs or low VOCs are extremely popular. Practically every item in your home emits chemicals into the air. From paint and varnishes to carpeting fibers and drapery textiles, all of these things fill the air with allergens that can be harmful. Green products typically contain chemicals less harsh to our environment and offer a gentler solution overall.

smart solutions

The fastest growing trend in home design is automation. In the last few years and since the creation of smart phones, the number of products available to automate your home has flooded the market. Products that act as a "hub" can be activated with the touch of a button, and they can control and manage multiple apps devoted to maintaining your home. From monitoring your home's security, efficiency, comfort level, and inhabitants, you can virtually manage your home and everything in it all with the touch of your fingertip on your smart phone. Home buyers are also seeking more electrical outlets throughout a home in addition to high quality Wi-Fi access for every room. And, builders are hearing frequent requests for docking stations, or car charging stations in garages as the popularity of electronic cars continues to grow.

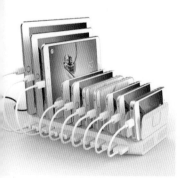

just drop it

Also, in line with making life easier is the popular feature of a drop zone. A drop zone is typically an area near the garage entrance that features lockers, cubbies, a bench, and possibly a desk with a charging station for hand held devices and smart phones. It's another practical and smart storage solution homeowners are deeming a necessity especially with families.

we are family

Our pets are becoming more a part of the family than ever before and it's dictating features being seen in home design. Built-in bowls; integrated crates and gates, and beds all make the home feel like all attention to detail was considered throughout the design process instead of these necessities appearing like an after-thought.

Thoughtful, practical, and purposeful. Today's homeowners are a unique group who want a home to feel like it was entirely designed for them. Everything in it should serve a purpose, while offering ease with life's everyday challenges for every person who dwells there right down to the family pet.

Plan #F10-013S-0014

Dimensions:	88'6" W x 62' D
Heated Sq. Ft.:	7,434
Bedrooms: 4	**Bathrooms:** 4½
Exterior Walls:	2" x 6"

Foundation: Walk-out basement standard; crawl space or slab for an additional fee

See index for more information

Images provided by designer/architect

Features

- A circular sitting room invites the owners into their lovely master bedroom, which also features a private bath and a screen porch
- The great room has a fireplace, a window wall and direct access to the outdoors onto the porch/deck
- Entertaining is easy on the lower level, which has rec and music rooms, a game area, a wet bar, and a sport court
- 2-car front entry garage, and a 1-car side entry garage

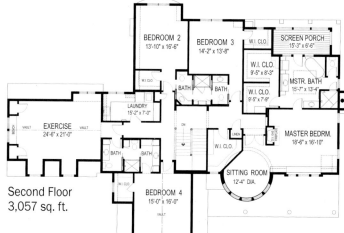

Second Floor
3,057 sq. ft.

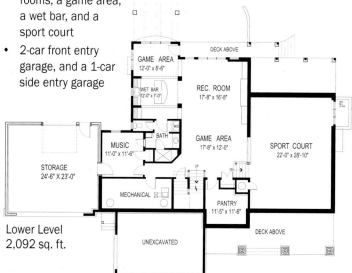

Lower Level
2,092 sq. ft.

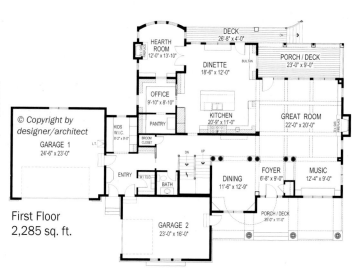

First Floor
2,285 sq. ft.

Plan #F10-143D-0003

Images provided by designer/architect

Dimensions:	70'6" W x 27'4" D
Heated Sq. Ft.:	1,324
Bedrooms: 3	Bathrooms: 2
Exterior Walls:	2" x 6"

Foundation: Basement, crawl space or slab, please specify when ordering

See index for more information

Plan #F10-013D-0200

Dimensions:	71'2" W x 64'6" D
Heated Sq. Ft.:	4,508
Bonus Sq. Ft.:	1,535
Bedrooms: 4	Bathrooms: 5

Foundation: Walk-out basement standard; crawl space or slab for an additional fee

See index for more information

Images provided by designer/architect

Optional Second Floor
1,535 sq. ft.

© Copyright by designer/architect

Lower Level
2,352 sq. ft.

First Floor
2,156 sq. ft.

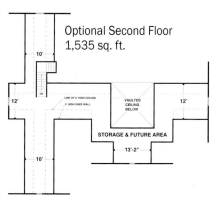

houseplansandmore.com

Plan #F10-058D-0240

Dimensions:	55' W x 46' D
Heated Sq. Ft.:	1,594
Bedrooms: 3	Bathrooms: 2
Foundation:	Basement

See index for more information

Images provided by designer/architect

© Copyright by designer/architect

Plan #F10-065D-0320

Dimensions:	62'2" W x 53'4" D
Heated Sq. Ft.:	2,234
Bedrooms: 4	Bathrooms: 2½
Foundation:	Basement

See index for more information

Images provided by designer/architect

Second Floor
610 sq. ft.

First Floor
1,624 sq. ft.

© Copyright by designer/architect

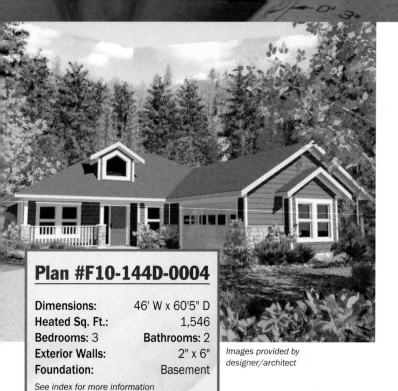

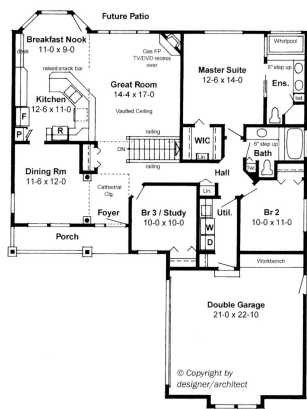

Plan #F10-144D-0004

Dimensions:	46' W x 60'5" D
Heated Sq. Ft.:	1,546
Bedrooms: 3	Bathrooms: 2
Exterior Walls:	2" x 6"
Foundation:	Basement

See index for more information

Images provided by designer/architect

© Copyright by designer/architect

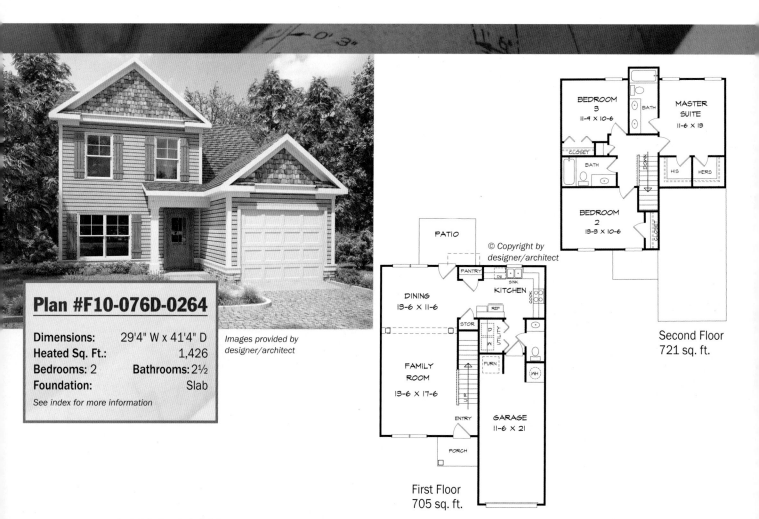

Plan #F10-076D-0264

Dimensions:	29'4" W x 41'4" D
Heated Sq. Ft.:	1,426
Bedrooms: 2	Bathrooms: 2½
Foundation:	Slab

See index for more information

Images provided by designer/architect

Second Floor
721 sq. ft.

First Floor
705 sq. ft.

© Copyright by designer/architect

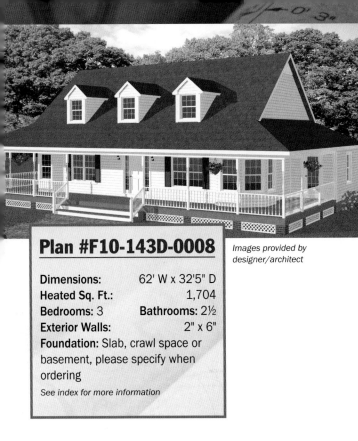

Plan #F10-143D-0008

Images provided by designer/architect

Dimensions: 62' W x 32'5" D
Heated Sq. Ft.: 1,704
Bedrooms: 3   **Bathrooms:** 2½
Exterior Walls: 2" x 6"
Foundation: Slab, crawl space or basement, please specify when ordering

See index for more information

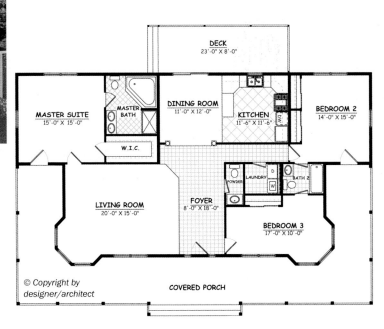

DECK
23'-0" X 8'-0"

MASTER SUITE
15'-0" X 15'-0"

MASTER BATH

W.I.C.

DINING ROOM
11'-0" X 12'-0"

KITCHEN
11'-6" X 11'-6"

BEDROOM 2
14'-0" X 15'-0"

POWDER

LAUNDRY

BATH 2

LIVING ROOM
20'-0" X 15'-0"

FOYER
8'-0" X 18'-0"

BEDROOM 3
17'-0" X 10'-0"

COVERED PORCH

© Copyright by designer/architect

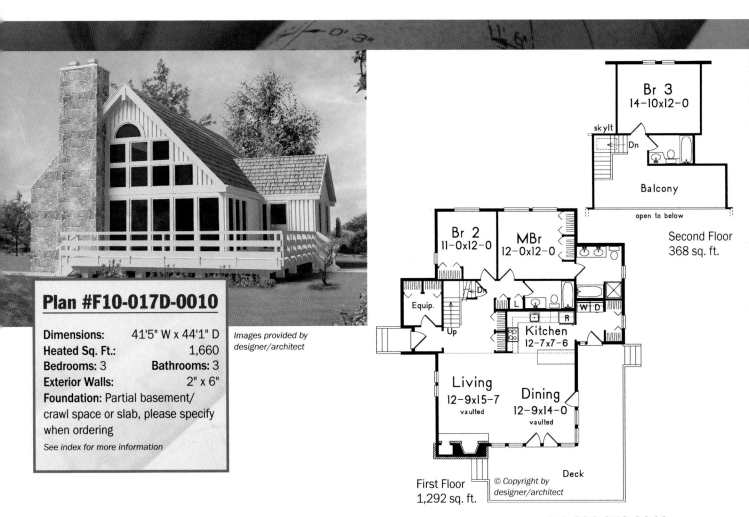

Plan #F10-017D-0010

Images provided by designer/architect

Dimensions: 41'5" W x 44'1" D
Heated Sq. Ft.: 1,660
Bedrooms: 3   **Bathrooms:** 3
Exterior Walls: 2" x 6"
Foundation: Partial basement/ crawl space or slab, please specify when ordering

See index for more information

Br 3
14-10x12-0

skylt

Dn

Balcony

open to below

Second Floor
368 sq. ft.

Br 2
11-0x12-0

MBr
12-0x12-0

Equip.

Up

Kitchen
12-7x7-6

Living
12-9x15-7
vaulted

Dining
12-9x14-0
vaulted

Deck

First Floor
1,292 sq. ft.

© Copyright by designer/architect

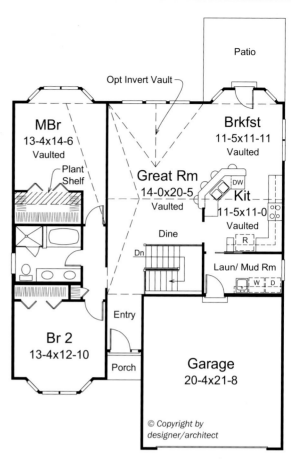

Plan #F10-121D-0017

Dimensions: 40' W x 52' D
Heated Sq. Ft.: 1,379
Bedrooms: 2   **Bathrooms:** 1
Foundation: Basement standard; crawl space or slab for an additional fee

See index for more information

Images provided by designer/architect

MBr
13-4x14-6
Vaulted

Plant Shelf

Opt Invert Vault

Great Rm
14-0x20-5
Vaulted

Brkfst
11-5x11-11
Vaulted

Patio

Kit
11-5x11-0
Vaulted

DW

R

Dine

Laun/ Mud Rm

W D

Dn

Br 2
13-4x12-10

Entry

Porch

Garage
20-4x21-8

© Copyright by designer/architect

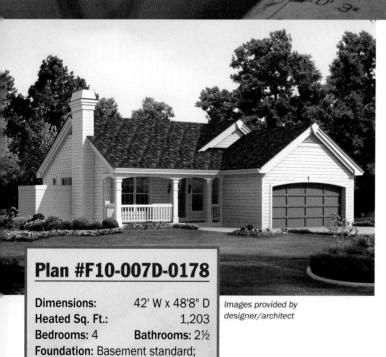

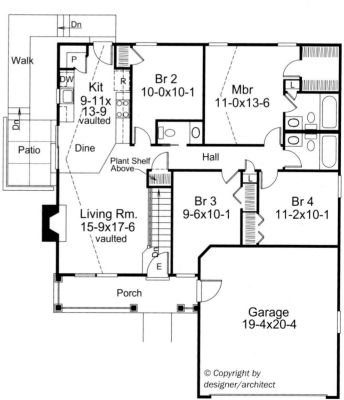

Plan #F10-007D-0178

Dimensions: 42' W x 48'8" D
Heated Sq. Ft.: 1,203
Bedrooms: 4   **Bathrooms:** 2½
Foundation: Basement standard; crawl space or slab for an additional fee

See index for more information

Images provided by designer/architect

Walk

Dn

Patio

Dn

P

DW

Kit
9-11x
13-9
vaulted

R

Br 2
10-0x10-1

Mbr
11-0x13-6

L

Dine

L

Hall

Plant Shelf Above

Living Rm.
15-9x17-6
vaulted

Br 3
9-6x10-1

Br 4
11-2x10-1

L

E

Porch

Garage
19-4x20-4

© Copyright by designer/architect

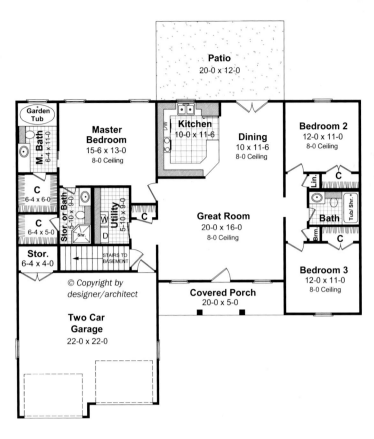

Patio
20-0 x 12-0

Garden Tub

M. Bath
6-4 x 11-0

Master Bedroom
15-6 x 13-0
8-0 Ceiling

Kitchen
10-0 x 11-6

Dining
10 x 11-6
8-0 Ceiling

Bedroom 2
12-0 x 11-0
8-0 Ceiling

C
6-4 x 6-0

C
6-4 x 5-0

Stor. or Bath
5-10 x 9-0

Utility
5-10 x 9-0

Great Room
20-0 x 16-0
8-0 Ceiling

Lin.

Bath

Tub/ Shr.

Stor.
6-4 x 4-0

STAIRS TO BASEMENT

Bedroom 3
12-0 x 11-0
8-0 Ceiling

© Copyright by designer/architect

Covered Porch
20-0 x 5-0

Two Car Garage
22-0 x 22-0

Plan #F10-077D-0024

Images provided by designer/architect

Dimensions: 54' W x 48' D
Heated Sq. Ft.: 1,488
Bedrooms: 3   Bathrooms: 2
Foundation: Basement or daylight basement, please specify when ordering; for crawl space or slab versions, see Plan #077D-0023 at houseplansandmore.com

See index for more information

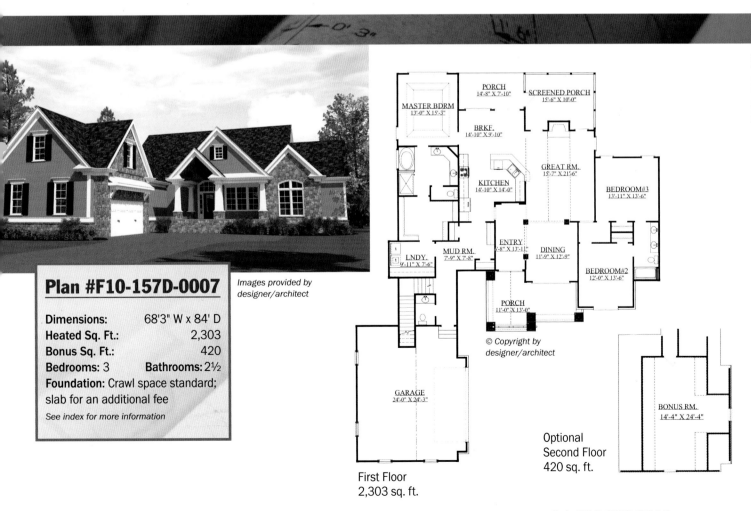

PORCH
14'-8" X 7'-10"

SCREENED PORCH
15'-6" X 10'-0"

MASTER BDRM
13'-0" X 15'-3"

BRKF.
14'-10" X 9'-10"

GREAT RM.
15'-7" X 21'-6"

BEDROOM#3
13'-11" X 13'-6"

KITCHEN
14'-10" X 14'-0"

ENTRY
5'-8" X 13'-11"

DINING
11'-9" X 12'-9"

BEDROOM#2
12'-0" X 13'-6"

LNDY.
9'-11" X 7'-6"

MUD RM.
7'-9" X 7'-8"

PORCH
11'-0" X 13'-0"

© Copyright by designer/architect

GARAGE
24'-0" X 24'-3"

BONUS RM.
14'-4" X 24'-4"

Optional Second Floor
420 sq. ft.

First Floor
2,303 sq. ft.

Plan #F10-157D-0007

Images provided by designer/architect

Dimensions: 68'3" W x 84' D
Heated Sq. Ft.: 2,303
Bonus Sq. Ft.: 420
Bedrooms: 3   Bathrooms: 2½
Foundation: Crawl space standard; slab for an additional fee

See index for more information

Plan #F10-126D-0883

Dimensions:	24'10" W x 38' D
Heated Sq. Ft.:	1,377
Bedrooms: 3	Bathrooms: 1½
Exterior Walls:	2" x 6"
Foundation:	Basement

See index for more information

Images provided by designer/architect

© Copyright by designer/architect

Second Floor
776 sq. ft.

12'-0"x13'-6"
3,66x4,12

10'-8"x11'-2"
3,25x3,40

12'-0"x9'-6"
3,66x2,90

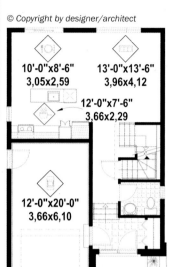

10'-0"x8'-6"
3,05x2,59

13'-0"x13'-6"
3,96x4,12

12'-0"x7'-6"
3,66x2,29

12'-0"x20'-0"
3,66x6,10

First Floor
601 sq. ft.

Plan #F10-144D-0005

Dimensions:	48' W x 58' D
Heated Sq. Ft.:	1,506
Bedrooms: 3	Bathrooms: 2
Exterior Walls:	2" x 6"

Foundation: Daylight basement standard; slab, crawl space, basement or walk-out basement for an additional fee

See index for more information

Images provided by designer/architect

Covered Deck

Whirlpool

Ens

Master Suite
16-0 x 12-0

French Doors

Dining
10-0 x 14-4

Kitchen
10-8 x 14-0

lin

WIC

Br 2
10-0 x 10-0

raised snack bar

F

P

Bath

3-sided Gas FP

1/2 wall

DN

railing

lin

Great Room
18-0 x 17-6

Hall

niche

Br 3
10-0 x 10-0

French Doors

Foyer

Util.

W
D

Gazebo

Porch

Double Garage
19-4 x 21-8

© Copyright by designer/architect

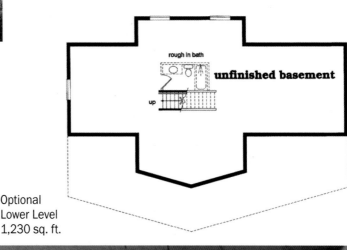

First Floor
1,230 sq. ft.

**Optional
Lower Level**
1,230 sq. ft.

Plan #F10-062D-0047

Images provided by designer/architect

Dimensions:	55'6" W x 30' D
Heated Sq. Ft.:	1,230
Bonus Sq. Ft.:	1,230
Bedrooms: 3	**Bathrooms:** 2
Exterior Walls:	2" x 6"

Foundation: Crawl space standard; basement for an additional fee

See index for more information

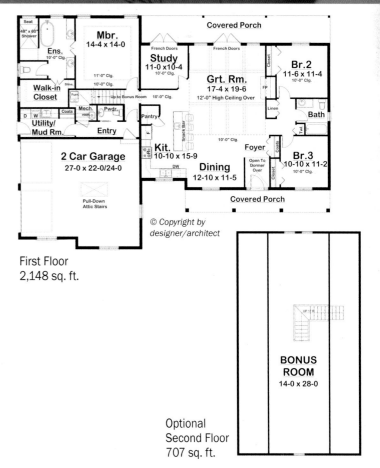

First Floor
2,148 sq. ft.

**Optional
Second Floor**
707 sq. ft.

Plan #F10-144D-0039

Images provided by designer/architect

Dimensions:	71' W x 49' D
Heated Sq. Ft.:	2,148
Bonus Sq. Ft.:	707
Bedrooms: 3	**Bathrooms:** 2½
Exterior Walls:	2" x 6"

Foundation: Crawl space standard; slab, basement, daylight basement or walk-out basement for an additional fee

See index for more information

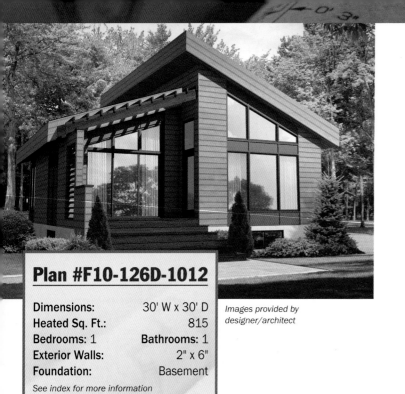

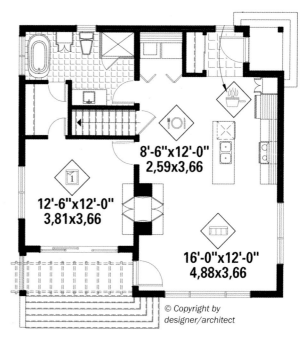

Plan #F10-126D-1012

Dimensions:	30' W x 30' D
Heated Sq. Ft.:	815
Bedrooms: 1	Bathrooms: 1
Exterior Walls:	2" x 6"
Foundation:	Basement

See index for more information

Images provided by designer/architect

8'-6"x12'-0"
2,59x3,66

12'-6"x12'-0"
3,81x3,66

16'-0"x12'-0"
4,88x3,66

© Copyright by designer/architect

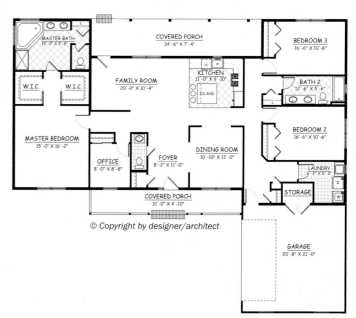

Plan #F10-143D-0001

Images provided by designer/architect

Dimensions:	67'10" W x 58'2" D
Heated Sq. Ft.:	1,975
Bedrooms: 3	Bathrooms: 2½
Exterior Walls:	2" x 6"

Foundation: Slab, crawl space or basement, please specify when ordering

Pricing subject to change

© Copyright by designer/architect

Plan #F10-007D-0235

Dimensions: 75' W x 39' D
Heated Sq. Ft.: 2,213
Bedrooms: 3   Bathrooms: 2
Foundation: Walk-out basement

See index for more information

Images provided by designer/architect

© Copyright by designer/architect

First Floor
2,213 sq. ft.

Lower Level

Plan #F10-139D-0009

Dimensions: 73' W x 80' D
Heated Sq. Ft.: 2,954
Bonus Sq. Ft.: 492
Bedrooms: 4   Bathrooms: 3
Exterior Walls: 2" x 6"
Foundation: Crawl space standard;
slab, basement, daylight basement
or walk-out basement for an
additional fee

See index for more information

Images provided by designer/architect

© Copyright by designer/architect

First Floor
2,954 sq. ft.

Optional
Second Floor
492 sq. ft.

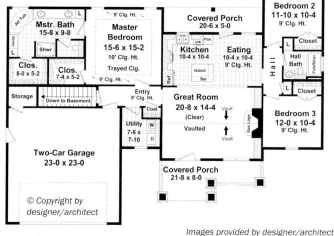

© Copyright by designer/architect

Plan #F10-077D-0250

Dimensions:	65'10" W x 49' D
Heated Sq. Ft.:	1,627
Bedrooms: 3	**Bathrooms:** 2
Exterior Walls:	2" x 6"

Foundation: Basement; for crawl space or slab foundation, see Plan #077D-0222 at houseplansandmore.com

See index for more information

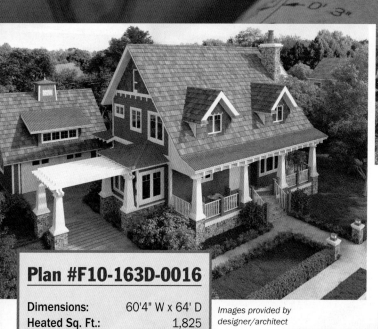

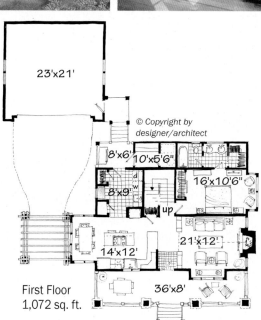

© Copyright by designer/architect

Plan #F10-163D-0016

Dimensions:	60'4" W x 64' D
Heated Sq. Ft.:	1,825
Bonus Sq. Ft.:	24
Bedrooms: 3	**Bathrooms:** 3
Exterior Walls:	2" x 6"
Foundation:	Crawl space

See index for more information

Second Floor
753 sq. ft.

First Floor
1,072 sq. ft.

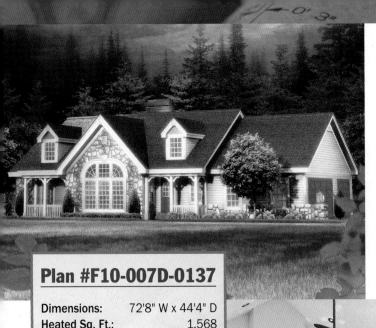

Patio

Screened Porch
19-3x17-4
vaulted

MBr
14-5x13-3
vaulted

Dining
12-1x12-0

Boat/Jet Ski
Garage
21-4x12-8

DW

Kit
12-1x15-0

Garage
21-4x20-4

Hall

Br 2
14-1x11-0

Great Room
19-4x25-8
vaulted

Raised
Entry

Laund
W D

© Copyright by
designer/architect

Porch

Porch

Images provided by designer/architect

Plan #F10-007D-0137

Dimensions: 72'8" W x 44'4" D
Heated Sq. Ft.: 1,568
Bedrooms: 2   **Bathrooms:** 2
Foundation: Crawl space standard;
slab for an additional fee

See index for more information

BR. #2
13'8"x14'8"

OPEN TO
BELOW

PLAY RM.
13'0"x26'4"

BR. #4
12'0"x13'4"

BR. #3
13'8"x14'8"

Second Floor
1,625 sq. ft.

Plan #F10-051D-0879

Images provided by designer/architect

Dimensions: 75'4" W x 59' D
Heated Sq. Ft.: 3,651
Bedrooms: 4   **Bathrooms:** 3½
Exterior Walls: 2" x 6"
Foundation: Basement standard;
slab or crawl space for an additional fee

See index for more information

DECK

GRT. RM.
23'6"x15'8"

DIN. RM.
13'0"x14'6"

2 CAR GARAGE
23'4"x22'4"

MBR.
13'8"x15'6"

KIT.
18'0"x12'0"

DEN
13'8"x12'0"

COMPUTER
NOOK

2 CAR GARAGE
23'8"x25'4"

© Copyright by
designer/architect

First Floor
2,026 sq. ft.

Plan #F10-071S-0051

Dimensions:	82' W x 86' D
Heated Sq. Ft.:	4,309
Bonus Sq. Ft.:	375
Bedrooms: 4	Bathrooms: 3½
Exterior Walls:	2" x 6"
Foundation:	Crawl space

See index for more information

Images provided by designer/architect

Features

- The two-story family room has a beautiful view and a double-door entry to the rear covered patio with an outdoor fireplace
- A separate kitchen, living, and dining area on the second floor is perfect for live-in relatives, or house guests
- The master bedroom suite includes a bay window sitting area, a grand walk-in closet, and a whirlpool tub in the exquisite master bath
- The optional lower level has an additional 375 square feet of living area
- 3-car side entry garage

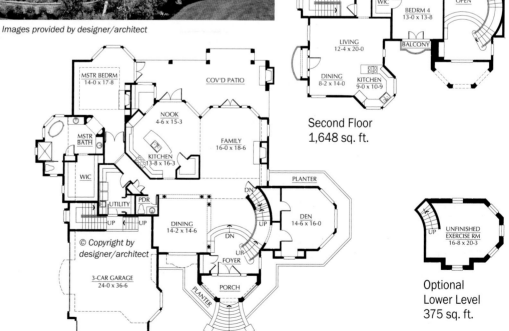

Second Floor
1,648 sq. ft.

First Floor
2,661 sq. ft.

Optional
Lower Level
375 sq. ft.

Optional
Second Floor
480 sq. ft.

Bonus Room
14' × 30'

First Floor
1,999 sq. ft.

Plan #F10-172D-0025

Dimensions:	63'1" W x 51' D
Heated Sq. Ft.:	1,999
Bonus Sq. Ft.:	2,437
Bedrooms: 3	Bathrooms: 2½
Exterior Walls:	2" x 6"

Foundation: Walk-out basement standard; crawl space, monolithic slab, stem wall slab, basement or daylight basement for an additional fee

See index for more information

Images provided by designer/architect

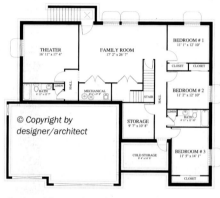

© Copyright by designer/architect

Optional Lower Level
1,957 sq. ft.

Plan #F10-007D-0168

Dimensions:	89'10" W x 40'2" D
Heated Sq. Ft.:	1,814
Bedrooms: 3	Bathrooms: 2
Foundation:	Basement

See index for more information

Images provided by designer/architect

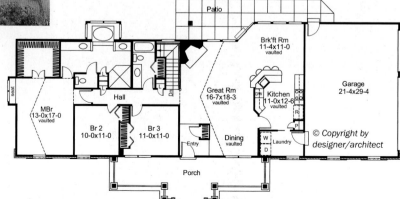

© Copyright by designer/architect

Covered Porch
23-0 x 5-0

Bedroom 2
12-0 x 12-0
9-0 Ceiling

M. Bath
15-0 x 10-0

Master
Bedroom
14-6 x 16-0

Garden
Tub

VAULT

Kitchen
12-0 x 11-0

Eating
11-0 x 11-0
9-0 Ceiling

S

VAULT

Island

BAR

C
8-0 x 6-0

C
7-0 x 6-0

Hall
Bath

Hall

C

Stor.
8-0 x 7-0

Utility
9-6 x 8-0

Entry

Trayed
Ceiling

9-0 Ceiling

10-0 Ceiling

F

C

Great
Room
23-0 x 16-0

Gas Logs

Cabs

Bedroom 3
12-0 x 12-0
9-0 Ceiling

Media/
Hobby
9-0 x 8-0

OPTIONAL STAIRS
TO BASEMENT

Cabs

2 Car
Garage
21-0 x 22-0

Covered Porch
23-0 x 4-0

© Copyright by designer/architect

OPTIONAL EXTENSION OF GARAGE
IF BASEMENT OPTION IS CHOSEN.

Plan #F10-077D-0043

Dimensions: 64' W x 45'10" D
Heated Sq. Ft.: 1,752
Bedrooms: 3   **Bathrooms:** 2
Foundation: Slab, crawl space, basement, daylight basement or walk-out basement, please specify when ordering

See index for more information

Second Floor
708 sq. ft.

Sloped Clg

Br 2
10-8x12-0

Dn

L

Br 3
10-8x12-0

Sloped Clg

Detached Garage
23-4x23-4

© Copyright by
designer/architect

Patio

Kitchen
12-10x11-9

Dining
12-3x11-9

DW

P

R

MBr
16-8x15-8

Dn

Great Rm
18-8x19-3

Up

First Floor
1,280 sq. ft.

Porch

Plan #F10-121D-0050

Dimensions: 40' W x 38' D
Heated Sq. Ft.: 1,988
Bedrooms: 3   **Bathrooms:** 2½
Foundation: Basement standard; crawl space or slab for an additional fee

See index for more information

Images provided by designer/architect

Plan #F10-101D-0101

Dimensions:	59'2" W x 94'9" D
Heated Sq. Ft.:	3,307
Bonus Sq. Ft.:	1,023
Bedrooms: 4	Bathrooms: 3½
Exterior Walls:	2" x 6"
Foundation:	Basement

See index for more information

Features

- Formal and informal spaces for dining are available
- The master bedroom has covered patio access, a grand bath and a wardrobe-sized closet to die for
- The second floor overlooks the two-story great room and entry, and has three bedrooms and two baths
- The optional lower level has an additional 1,023 square feet of living area with a rec room with wet bar, a fifth bedroom and a full bath, great for guests
- 3-car side entry garage

First Floor
2,208 sq. ft.

Optional Lower Level
1,023 sq. ft.

Second Floor
1,099 sq. ft.

Images provided by designer/architect

Plan #F10-155D-0062

Dimensions:	174'8" W x 143'3" D
Heated Sq. Ft.:	6,554
Bedrooms:	4
Bathrooms:	4 full, 2 half
Exterior Walls:	2" x 6"

Foundation: Crawl space or slab, please specify when ordering

See index for more information

Images provided by designer/architect

Features

- This spacious sprawling one-story offers so many amenities around every corner
- The kitchen has multiple islands for prep and dining and enjoys lovely views of the nearby hearth room
- A home theater promises family nights will be exciting and fun
- A remote outdoor covered porch is topped with a steep vaulted ceiling and has an outdoor kitchen, and a fireplace
- The master suite with fireplace has its own private wing including a posh private bath, a huge walk-in closet, and access to an outdoor covered porch with a whirlpool tub
- 3-car rear entry garage

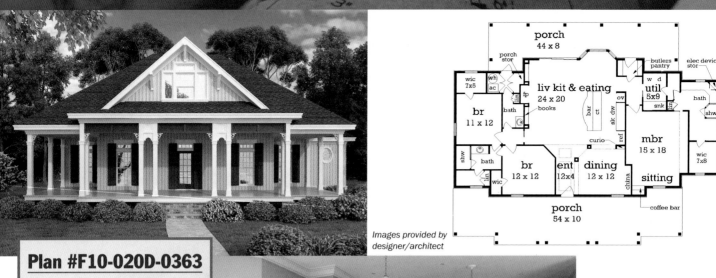

porch
44 x 8

porch stor

wic 7x5

wh

ac

liv kit & eating
24 x 20

books

fp

bath

butlers pantry

elec devices stor

br
11 x 12

bar
ct

slc dw

ov

util
5x9

w d

snk

bath

shw

shw

bath

br
12 x 12

ent
12x4

curio

dining
12 x 12

ref

china

mbr
15 x 18

sitting

wic
7x8

wic

porch
54 x 10

coffee bar

Images provided by designer/architect

Plan #F10-020D-0363

Dimensions:	63' W x 51' D
Heated Sq. Ft.:	1,832
Bedrooms: 3	Bathrooms: 2½
Exterior Walls:	2" x 6"

Foundation: Crawl space standard; slab for an additional fee

See index for more information

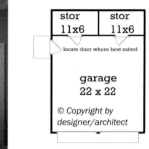

stor 11x6 | stor 11x6

locate door where best suited

garage
22 x 22

© Copyright by designer/architect

Detached Garage

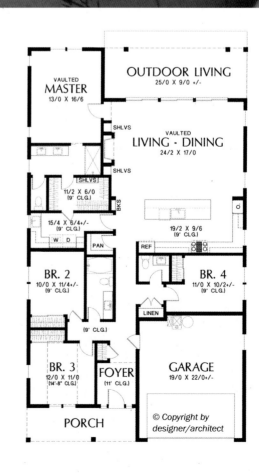

OUTDOOR LIVING
25/0 X 9/0 +/-

VAULTED
MASTER
13/0 X 16/6

SHLVS

SHLVS

VAULTED
LIVING · DINING
24/2 X 17/0

11/2 X 6/0
(9' CLG.)

SHLVS

BKS

15/4 X 6/4+/-
(9' CLG.)

19/2 X 9/6
(9' CLG.)

W D

PAN

REF

BR. 2
10/0 X 11/4+/-
(9' CLG.)

BR. 4
11/0 X 10/2+/-
(9' CLG.)

LINEN

BR. 3
12/0 X 11/0
(14'-8" CLG.)

(9' CLG.)

FOYER
(11' CLG.)

GARAGE
19/0 X 22/0+/-

PORCH

© Copyright by designer/architect

Plan #F10-011D-0686

Dimensions:	40' W x 70' D
Heated Sq. Ft.:	2,009
Bedrooms: 4	Bathrooms: 2½
Exterior Walls:	2" x 6"

Foundation: Crawl space or slab standard; basement for an additional fee

See index for more information

Images provided by designer/architect

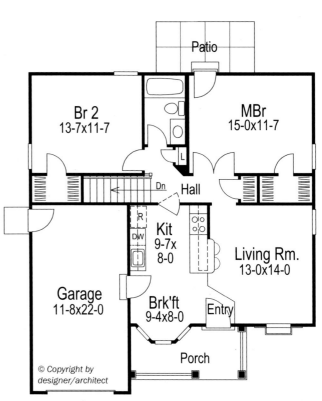

Patio

Br 2
13-7x11-7

MBr
15-0x11-7

Dn   Hall

R

DW

Kit
9-7x
8-0

Living Rm.
13-0x14-0

Garage
11-8x22-0

Brk'ft
9-4x8-0

Entry

Porch

© Copyright by
designer/architect

*Images provided by
designer/architect*

Plan #F10-007D-0109

Dimensions: 35' W x 38' D
Heated Sq. Ft.:   888
Bedrooms: 2   **Bathrooms:** 1
Foundation: Basement standard;
crawl space or slab for an
additional fee

See index for more information

VAULTED
MASTER
19/0 X 13/4

VAULTED
LIVING / DINING
19/0 X 25/0

COURTYARD
24/0 X 26/0

(9' CLG)

LINEN

W / D

VAULTED
13/6 X 9/6

PORCH
19/0 X 11/6

(9' CLG)

BR. 2
12/4 X 13/0
(9' CLG)

PANTRY
7/4x8/8

FOYER
(HIGH CLG)

GARAGE
21/0 X 27/0+/-

PORCH

LINEN
SHLVS

BR. 3
13/0 X 12/8
(9' CLG)

© Copyright by
designer/architect

*Images provided by
designer/architect*

Plan #F10-011D-0682

Dimensions: 69' W x 68' D
Heated Sq. Ft.:   2,451
Bedrooms: 3   **Bathrooms:** 3½
Exterior Walls: 2" x 6"
Foundation: Crawl space or slab
standard; basement for an
additional fee

See index for more information

Plan #F10-011S-0103

Dimensions:	60' W x 59' D
Heated Sq. Ft.:	3,558
Bedrooms: 4	Bathrooms: 4
Exterior Walls:	2" x 6"
Foundation:	Daylight basement

See index for more information

Features

- This stylish ranch home has a popular floor plan that eliminates wasted formal spaces and has one main gathering space with a central great room
- The kitchen has a breakfast bar that overlooks the great room as well as the sunny breakfast nook
- There's a lovely outdoor living space with a fireplace and a built-in grill around the corner for enjoying the outdoors to the fullest year-round
- The master suite and the den/bedroom 4 are located on the first floor, while bedrooms 2 and 3 can be found on the lower level
- The lower level enjoys a fun game room with a fireplace, a snack bar, a wine cellar and access to a covered patio
- 2-car front entry garage

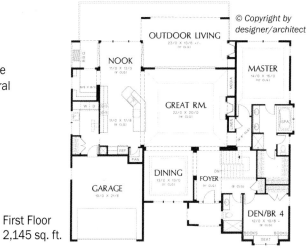

© Copyright by designer/architect

First Floor
2,145 sq. ft.

Lower Level
1,413 sq. ft.

Images provided by designer/architect

Plan #F10-076D-0281

Dimensions: 103'5" W x 100'10" D
Heated Sq. Ft.: 3,204
Bonus Sq. Ft.: 3,596
Bedrooms: 4   Bathrooms: 3½
Foundation: Basement

See index for more information

Optional
Second Floor
545 sq. ft.

Features

- The terrace is perfect for grilling season since it connects to the breakfast area
- The kitchen has a view of the fireplace in the family room
- The master suite has a walk-in closet, and a bath leading to the laundry room
- The optional lower level has an additional 3,051 square feet of living area, while the second floor has an additional 545 square feet of living area
- 3-car front entry garage

First Floor
3,204 sq. ft.

© Copyright by
designer/architect

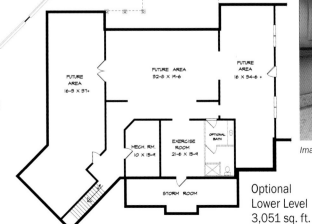

Optional
Lower Level
3,051 sq. ft.

Images provided by designer/architect

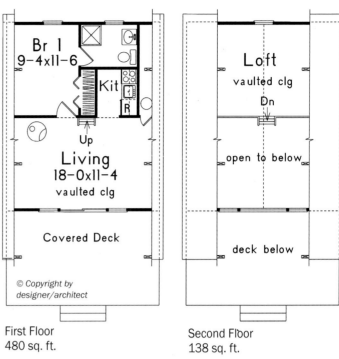

First Floor
480 sq. ft.

Second Floor
138 sq. ft.

Plan #F10-008D-0161

Dimensions:	20' W x 30' D
Heated Sq. Ft.:	618
Bedrooms: 1	Bathrooms: 1
Foundation:	Pier

Images provided by designer/architect

See index for more information

© Copyright by designer/architect

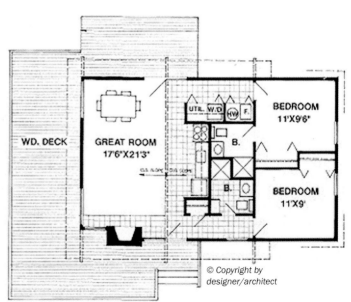

Plan #F10-145D-0001

Dimensions:	36' W x 22' D
Heated Sq. Ft.:	786
Bedrooms: 2	Bathrooms: 2
Foundation:	Crawl space or slab, please specify when ordering

Images provided by designer/architect

See index for more information

© Copyright by designer/architect

Plan #F10-026D-1923

Dimensions:	52'4" W x 67'6" D
Heated Sq. Ft.:	2,721
Bedrooms: 4	Bathrooms: 2½
Exterior Walls:	2" x 6"

Foundation: Basement standard; walk-out basement for an additional fee

See index for more information

Images provided by designer/architect

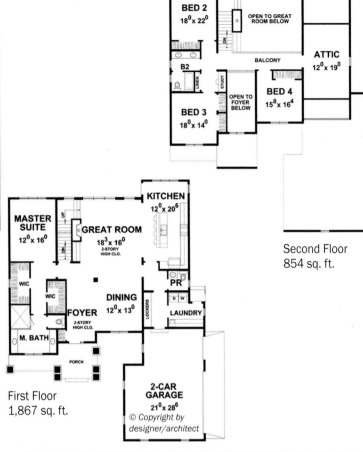

Second Floor
854 sq. ft.

First Floor
1,867 sq. ft.

© Copyright by designer/architect

Plan #F10-076D-0260

Dimensions:	54'5" W x 51'6" D
Heated Sq. Ft.:	1,949
Bonus Sq. Ft.:	306
Bedrooms: 4	Bathrooms: 3
Foundation:	Slab

See index for more information

Images provided by designer/architect

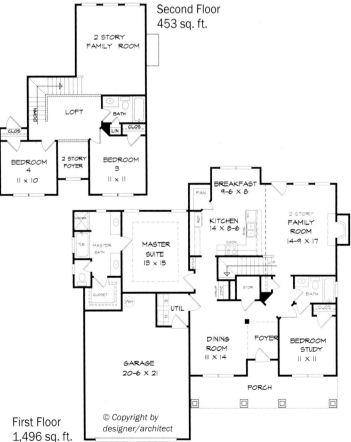

Second Floor
453 sq. ft.

First Floor
1,496 sq. ft.

© Copyright by designer/architect

Plan #F10-055D-0214

Dimensions: 76'10" W x 53'4" D
Heated Sq. Ft.: 2,373
Bonus Sq. Ft.: 1,672
Bedrooms: 4   **Bathrooms:** 3
Foundation: Crawl space or slab standard; basement or daylight basement for an additional fee
See index for more information

Images provided by designer/architect

Features

- The grilling porch extends dining opportunities to the outdoors
- The fireplace in the great room also warms the adjoining kitchen and the breakfast room
- The relaxing master suite enjoys a deluxe bath with a whirlpool tub and a walk-in closet
- The optional second floor has an additional 1,672 square feet of living area
- 2-car side entry garage

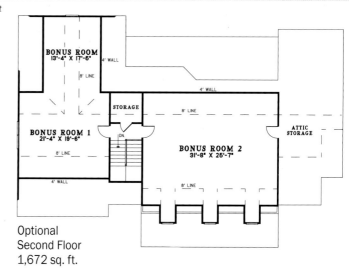

Optional
Second Floor
1,672 sq. ft.

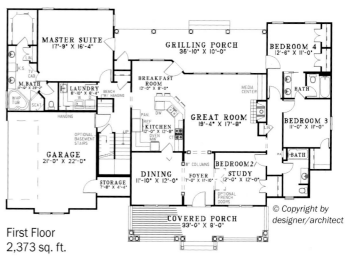

First Floor
2,373 sq. ft.

© Copyright by designer/architect

Plan #F10-101D-0065

Dimensions:	65' W x 76'6" D
Heated Sq. Ft.:	2,269
Bonus Sq. Ft.:	1,563
Bedrooms: 2	Bathrooms: 2½
Exterior Walls:	2" x 6"
Foundation:	Basement

See index for more information

Images provided by designer/architect

Features

- The great room enjoys a freestanding fireplace as the main focal point
- The first floor master bedroom pampers the homeowner with its luxurious dressing area and large walk-in closet
- The other bedroom on the first floor would make an ideal in-law suite
- The covered deck enjoys the warmth of a fireplace
- The optional lower level has an additional 1,563 square feet of living area
- 3-car front entry garage

Optional
Lower Level
1,563 sq. ft.

First Floor
2,269 sq. ft.

© Copyright by
designer/architect

Plan #F10-071S-0007

Dimensions:	71' W x 91'6" D
Heated Sq. Ft.:	5,250
Bedrooms: 4	Bathrooms: 4½
Exterior Walls:	2" x 6"
Foundation:	Crawl space

See index for more information

Images provided by designer/architect

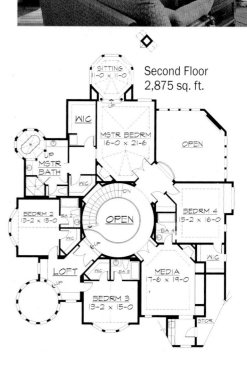

Features

- The spacious wrap-around covered porch features an outdoor fireplace and built-in barbecue grill, perfect for entertaining
- Each bedroom has its own bath and walk-in closet
- The dramatic circular staircase is highlighted in a rotunda with a 27' ceiling above
- The master bath showcases an octagon-shaped space featuring a whirlpool tub
- The rear covered porch extends living to the outdoors with its cozy built-in fireplace
- 4-car side entry garage

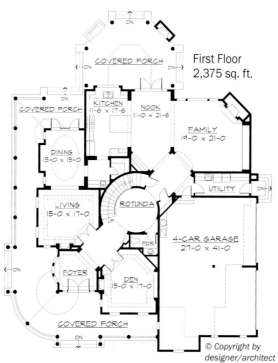

First Floor
2,375 sq. ft.

Second Floor
2,875 sq. ft.

© Copyright by designer/architect

Plan #F10-076D-0226

Dimensions:	121' W x 61' D
Heated Sq. Ft.:	3,277
Bonus Sq. Ft.:	3,271
Bedrooms: 4	Bathrooms: 4½
Exterior Walls:	2" x 6"

Foundation: Basement, slab or crawl space, please specify when ordering

See index for more information

Images provided by designer/architect

Features

- Country Craftsman style takes precedence with this home's inviting exterior

- The first floor urges guests to relax in the family room with its cozy fireplace

- The screen porch offers pest-free dining, and connects to the outdoor kitchen for easy grill access

- The guest suite has its own bath, which will be appreciated by visitors

- The optional lower level has an additional 2,230 square feet of living area and has a gathering room, rec room, theater, and wet bar; and is always ready for the party

- The optional bonus room above the garage has an additional 691 square feet of living area, and the optional media room has an additional 325 square feet of living area

- 3-car front entry garage

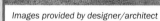

Second Floor
770 sq. ft.

First Floor
2,507 sq. ft.

© Copyright by designer/architect

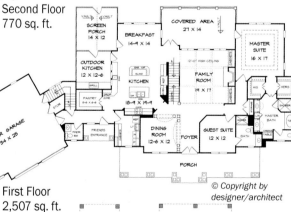

Optional
Lower Level
2,230 sq. ft.

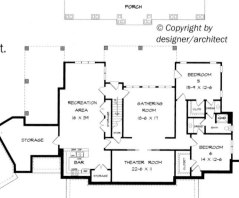

Plan #F10-055S-0105

Dimensions:	95' W x 47'9" D
Heated Sq. Ft.:	3,374
Bonus Sq. Ft.:	250
Bedrooms: 3	**Bathrooms:** 2½

Foundation: Crawl space or slab standard; basement or daylight basement for an additional fee

See index for more information

Features

- An enchanting courtyard surrounding the garage leads to a patio area that has access to the breakfast room
- Relax in the master bath that has an oversized tub, two large walk-in closets and a lovely vaulted ceiling
- The vaulted foyer leads to an open and airy first floor
- A functional space saving wet bar is tucked into a closet-like corner near the great room
- A private office can be accessed from the master suite or the foyer
- The bonus room on the second floor has an additional 250 square feet of living area
- 3-car side entry garage

Second Floor
714 sq. ft.

Images provided by designer/architect

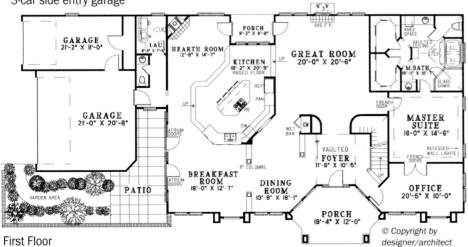

First Floor
2,660 sq. ft.

© Copyright by designer/architect

call 1-800-373-2646

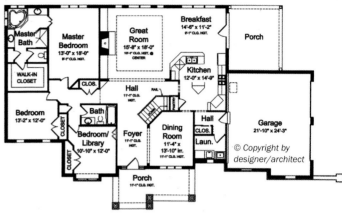

Plan #F10-065D-0307

Dimensions:	80'2" W x 44'6" D
Heated Sq. Ft.:	2,246
Bedrooms: 3	Bathrooms: 2

Foundation: Basement standard; crawl space or slab for an additional fee

See index for more information

Images provided by designer/architect

© Copyright by designer/architect

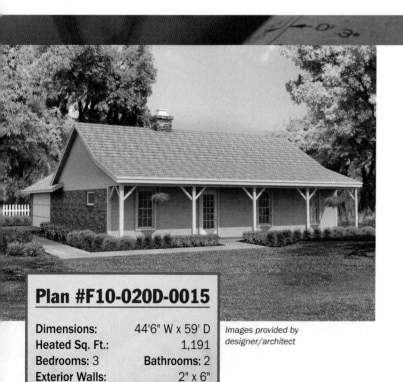

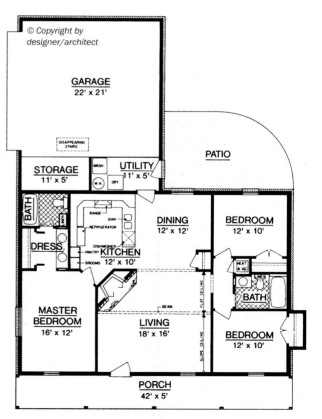

Plan #F10-020D-0015

Dimensions:	44'6" W x 59' D
Heated Sq. Ft.:	1,191
Bedrooms: 3	Bathrooms: 2
Exterior Walls:	2" x 6"

Foundation: Slab standard; crawl space or basement for an additional fee

See index for more information

Images provided by designer/architect

© Copyright by designer/architect

Plan #F10-091D-0507

Dimensions:	82'6" W x 69' D
Heated Sq. Ft.:	2,486
Bonus Sq. Ft.:	448
Bedrooms: 3	Bathrooms: 2½
Exterior Walls:	2" x 6"

Foundation: Crawl space standard; slab, basement, daylight basement or walk-out basement for an additional fee

See index for more information

Images provided by designer/architect

Optional
Second Floor
448 sq. ft.

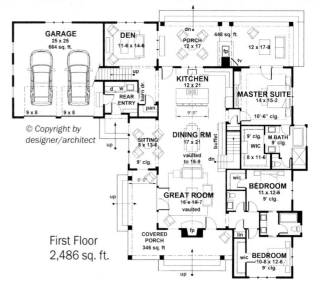

First Floor
2,486 sq. ft.

Plan #F10-170D-0018

Dimensions:	80' W x 85'2" D
Heated Sq. Ft.:	2,621
Bedrooms: 3	Bathrooms: 2

Foundation: Slab or monolithic slab, please specify when ordering

See index for more information

Images provided by designer/architect

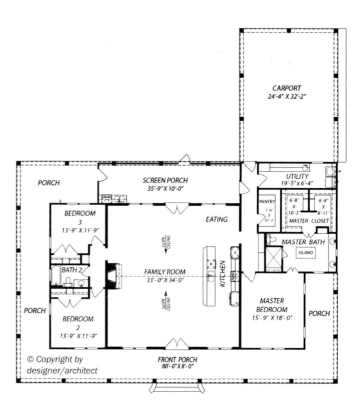

BONUS ROOM
ABOVE
GARAGE
12'-0" X 24'-0"

Optional
Second Floor
288 sq. ft.

© Copyright by
designer/architect

2 CAR GARAGE
24'-0" X 24'-0"

MUD ROOM
10'-0" X 6'-0"

STORAGE
10'-0" X 10'-0"

PORCH NO. 2
46'-0" X 6'-0"

DINING AREA
14'-0" X 17'-0"

LAUNDRY

WALK-IN
CLO.

BEDROOM NO. 3
14'-0" X 15'-0"

VENTLESS
GAS FIREPLACE

GREAT ROOM
24'-0" X 24'-0"
11' TRAY CEILING

PANTRY

MASTER
BATH
14'-0" X 7'-0"

BATH
2

KITCHEN
14'-0" X 18'-0"

MASTER BEDROOM
18'-0" X 20'-0"

BEDROOM NO. 2
14'-0" X 15'-0"

BEDROOM NO. 4
14'-0" X 10'-0"

BATH 3

FOYER

SITTING
ROOM
14'-0" X 8'-0"

PORCH NO. 1
70'-0" X 6'-0"

First Floor
3,029 sq. ft.

Plan #F10-028D-0022

Dimensions: 70' W x 80' D
Heated Sq. Ft.: 3,029
Bonus Sq. Ft.: 288
Bedrooms: 4   Bathrooms: 3
Foundation: Floating slab standard; monolithic slab, crawl space, basement or walk-out basement for an additional fee

See index for more information

Images provided by designer/architect

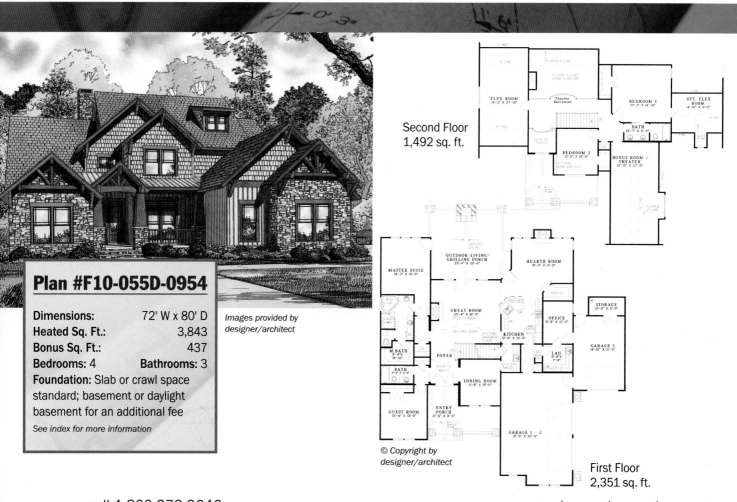

Second Floor
1,492 sq. ft.

FLEX ROOM
14'-2" X 27'-0"

Theater
Balconies

BEDROOM 3
17'-2" X 14'-0"

OPT. FLEX
ROOM
14'-0" X 10'-0"

BATH

BEDROOM 2

BONUS ROOM /
THEATER
12'-10" X 27'-0"

MASTER SUITE
14'-7" X 16'-0"

OUTDOOR LIVING/
GRILLING PORCH
29'-4" X 20'-0"

HEARTH ROOM
18'-0" X 12'-8"

M. BATH
9'-4"

GREAT ROOM
20'-4" X 18'-0"
OPEN TO ABOVE

KITCHEN
12'-0" X 13'-0"

OFFICE
8'-8" X 12'-0"

STORAGE
10'-4" X 5'-0"

BATH
9'-4" X 5'-0"

FOYER

LAU.
8'-8" X
7'-8"

GARAGE 3
14'-10" X 21'-0"

GUEST ROOM
13'-4" X 12'-0"

ENTRY
PORCH
9'-6" X 6'-0"

DINING ROOM
11'-8" X 13'-0"

GARAGE 1 - 2
21'-0" X 32'-0"

© Copyright by
designer/architect

First Floor
2,351 sq. ft.

Plan #F10-055D-0954

Dimensions: 72' W x 80' D
Heated Sq. Ft.: 3,843
Bonus Sq. Ft.: 437
Bedrooms: 4   Bathrooms: 3
Foundation: Slab or crawl space standard; basement or daylight basement for an additional fee

See index for more information

Images provided by designer/architect

Plan #F10-155D-0016

Dimensions: 41'8" W x 61'8" D
Heated Sq. Ft.: 3,307
Bedrooms: 3   **Bathrooms:** 4½
Foundation: Walk-out basement or basement, please specify when ordering

See index for more information

Images provided by designer/architect

Second Floor 709 sq. ft.

Lower Level 1,299 sq. ft.

First Floor 1,299 sq. ft.

© Copyright by designer/architect

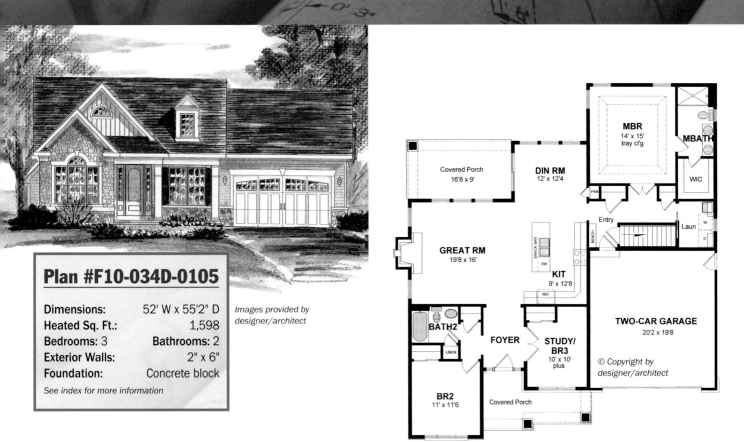

Plan #F10-034D-0105

Dimensions: 52' W x 55'2" D
Heated Sq. Ft.: 1,598
Bedrooms: 3   **Bathrooms:** 2
Exterior Walls: 2" x 6"
Foundation: Concrete block

See index for more information

Images provided by designer/architect

© Copyright by designer/architect

First Floor
1,764 sq. ft.

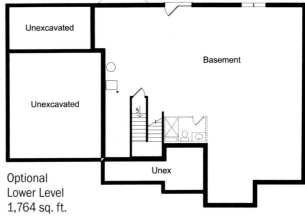

Optional Lower Level
1,764 sq. ft.

Plan #F10-065D-0458

Dimensions:	67' W x 46'4" D
Heated Sq. Ft.:	1,764
Bonus Sq. Ft.:	1,764
Bedrooms: 3	**Bathrooms:** 2
Foundation:	Walk-out basement

See index for more information

Images provided by designer/architect

Plan #F10-065D-0460

Dimensions:	68'3" W x 45'9" D
Heated Sq. Ft.:	1,706
Bonus Sq. Ft.:	1,706
Bedrooms: 3	**Bathrooms:** 2
Foundation:	Walk-out basement

See index for more information

Images provided by designer/architect

First Floor
1,706 sq. ft.

Optional Lower Level
1,706 sq. ft.

Plan #F10-155D-0039

Dimensions: 52'6" W x 57'10" D
Heated Sq. Ft.: 1,640
Bonus Sq. Ft.: 281
Bedrooms: 3 **Bathrooms:** 2
Foundation: Slab or crawl space, please specify when ordering

See index for more information

Images provided by designer/architect

First Floor
1,640 sq. ft.

© Copyright by designer/architect

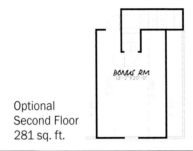

Optional
Second Floor
281 sq. ft.

Plan #F10-155D-0051

Dimensions: 39'4" W x 44'10" D
Heated Sq. Ft.: 1,806
Bedrooms: 3 **Bathrooms:** 3
Foundation: Slab or crawl space standard; basement or daylight basement for an additional fee

See index for more information

Images provided by designer/architect

Second Floor
620 sq. ft.

© Copyright by designer/architect

First Floor
1,186 sq. ft.

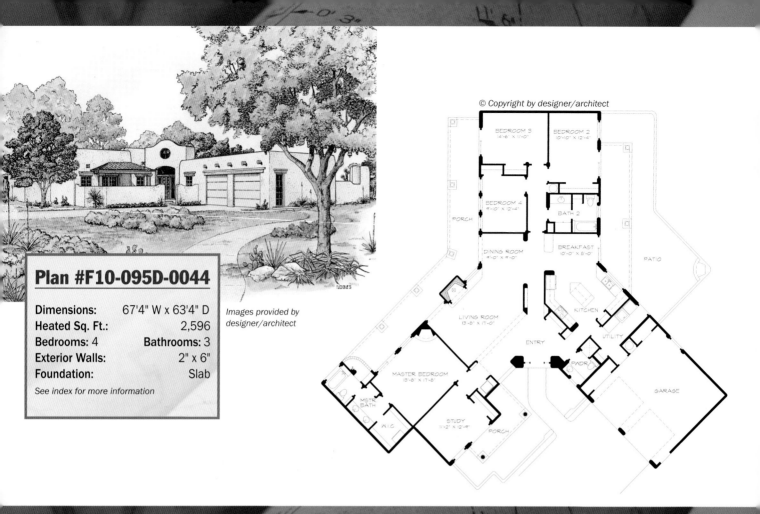

© Copyright by designer/architect

Images provided by designer/architect

Plan #F10-095D-0044

Dimensions:	67'4" W x 63'4" D
Heated Sq. Ft.:	2,596
Bedrooms: 4	Bathrooms: 3
Exterior Walls:	2" x 6"
Foundation:	Slab

See index for more information

Images provided by designer/architect

© Copyright by designer/architect

Plan #F10-036D-0208

Dimensions:	75' W x 71'10" D
Heated Sq. Ft.:	2,487
Bonus Sq. Ft.:	628
Bedrooms: 3	Bathrooms: 2½
Foundation:	Slab

See index for more information

Optional
Second Floor
628 sq. ft.

First Floor
2,487 sq. ft.

Optional
Second Floor
812 sq. ft.

Plan #F10-055D-0213

Dimensions:	84' W x 55'6" D
Heated Sq. Ft.:	1,921
Bonus Sq. Ft.:	812
Bedrooms: 3	Bathrooms: 2

Foundation: Slab or crawl space
standard; basement or daylight
basement for an additional fee

See index for more information

Images provided by designer/architect

© Copyright by
designer/architect

First Floor
1,921 sq. ft.

Plan #F10-034D-0109

Dimensions:	62' W x 49'4" D
Heated Sq. Ft.:	1,917
Bonus Sq. Ft.:	462
Bedrooms: 2	Bathrooms: 2½
Exterior Walls:	2" x 6"
Foundation:	Concrete block

See index for more information

Images provided by designer/architect

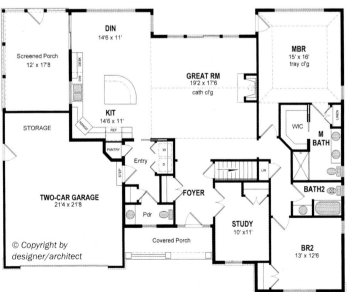

© Copyright by
designer/architect

Plan #F10-155D-0053

Dimensions:	69' W x 62'10" D
Heated Sq. Ft.:	2,506
Bedrooms: 4	**Bathrooms:** 3

Foundation: Slab or crawl space, please specify when ordering

See index for more information

Images provided by designer/architect

© Copyright by designer/architect

Plan #F10-155D-0030

Dimensions:	64'8" W x 62' D
Heated Sq. Ft.:	2,119
Bedrooms: 4	**Bathrooms:** 2½

Foundation: Slab or crawl space standard; basement or daylight basement for an additional fee

See index for more information

Images provided by designer/architect

© Copyright by designer/architect

First Floor
1,330 sq. ft.

© Copyright by designer/architect

Lower Level
591 sq. ft.

Plan #F10-155D-0033

Dimensions:	72' W x 37'10" D
Heated Sq. Ft.:	1,921
Bedrooms: 2	**Bathrooms:** 3
Foundation:	Walk-out basement

See index for more information

Images provided by designer/architect

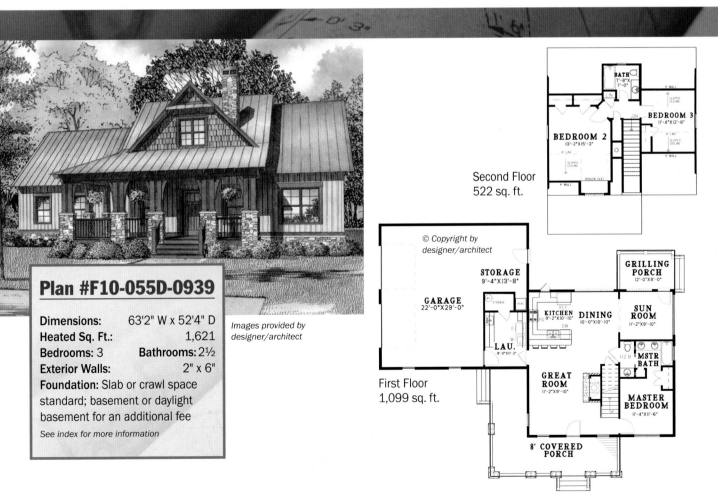

Second Floor
522 sq. ft.

© Copyright by designer/architect

First Floor
1,099 sq. ft.

Plan #F10-055D-0939

Dimensions:	63'2" W x 52'4" D
Heated Sq. Ft.:	1,621
Bedrooms: 3	**Bathrooms:** 2½
Exterior Walls:	2" x 6"

Foundation: Slab or crawl space standard; basement or daylight basement for an additional fee

See index for more information

Images provided by designer/architect

Plan #F10-032D-0482

Dimensions:	45' W x 68'6" D
Heated Sq. Ft.:	3,513
Bonus Sq. Ft.:	517
Bedrooms: 4	**Bathrooms:** 2½
Exterior Walls:	2" x 6"

Foundation: Basement standard; crawl space, floating slab or monolithic slab for an additional fee

See index for more information

Images provided by designer/architect

© Copyright by designer/architect

Features

- A charming wrap-around porch extends the living space to the outdoors
- The master suite includes a private bath with a dramatic curved walled walk-in closet
- The garage enters the home to find an expansive utility area that houses a pantry, sink and space for a washer and dryer
- The optional bonus room on the second floor has an additional 517 square feet of living area
- 2-car side entry garage

First Floor
2,376 sq. ft.

Second Floor
1,137 sq. ft.

Plan #F10-172D-0004

Dimensions:	53' W x 52'2" D
Heated Sq. Ft.:	2,710
Bedrooms: 4	**Bathrooms:** 3
Exterior Walls:	2" x 6"

Foundation: Crawl space standard; monolithic slab, stem wall slab, basement, daylight basement or walk-out basement for an additional fee

See index for more information

Features

- This home has the appearance of a one-story from the front, but in reality it is a two-story with two bedrooms, a full bath, and a roomy loft on the second floor
- The kitchen has an angled island with seating for five people, and a walk-in pantry
- The open family room merges with the dining area
- The master bedroom has a large bath and a walk-in closet
- 3-car front entry garage

First Floor
1,670 sq. ft.

Second Floor
1,040 sq. ft.

Images provided by designer/architect

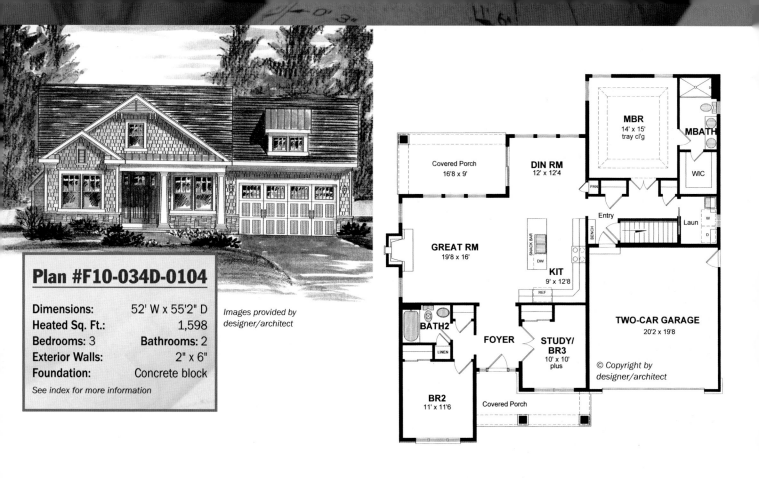

Plan #F10-034D-0104

Dimensions:	52' W x 55'2" D
Heated Sq. Ft.:	1,598
Bedrooms: 3	Bathrooms: 2
Exterior Walls:	2" x 6"
Foundation:	Concrete block

See index for more information

Images provided by designer/architect

© Copyright by designer/architect

Plan #F10-065D-0459

Dimensions:	55'4" W x 42' D
Heated Sq. Ft.:	2,700
Bonus Sq. Ft.:	1,400
Bedrooms: 4	Bathrooms: 2½
Foundation:	Basement

See index for more information

Images provided by designer/architect

© Copyright by designer/architect

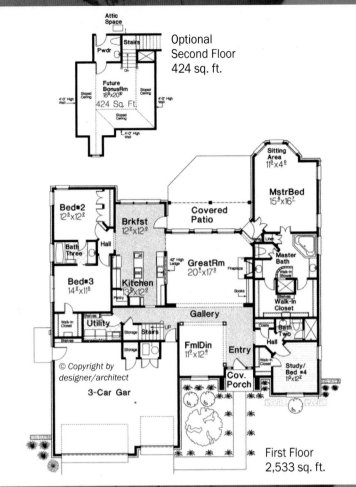

Optional
Second Floor
424 sq. ft.

Future BonusRm
18⁸x20¹⁰
424 Sq. Ft.

First Floor
2,533 sq. ft.

© Copyright by designer/architect

Plan #F10-036D-0205

Images provided by designer/architect

Dimensions:	64'5" W x 72'9" D
Heated Sq. Ft.:	2,533
Bonus Sq. Ft.:	424
Bedrooms: 4	Bathrooms: 3
Foundation:	Slab

See index for more information

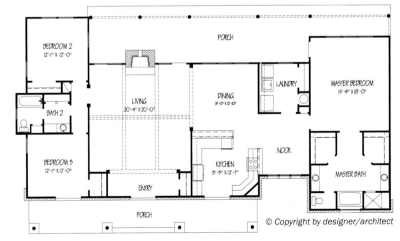

© Copyright by designer/architect

Plan #F10-095D-0049

Images provided by designer/architect

Dimensions:	75'4" W x 43'10" D
Heated Sq. Ft.:	2,136
Bedrooms: 3	Bathrooms: 2
Foundation:	Slab

See index for more information

Plan #F10-037D-0015

Dimensions:	43'6" W x 65'8" D
Heated Sq. Ft.:	2,772
Bedrooms: 4	Bathrooms: 3½
Foundation:	Slab

See index for more information

Features

- 10' ceilings on the first floor and 9' ceilings on the second floor create a spacious atmosphere
- Large bay windows accent the study and master bath
- The breakfast room features a dramatic curved window wall with a direct view and access onto the covered wrap-around porch
- 2-car side entry garage

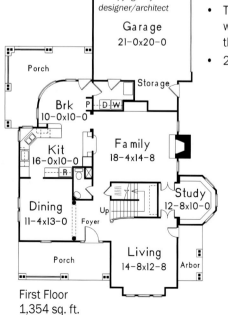

© Copyright by designer/architect

Garage
21-0x20-0

Porch

Storage

Brk
10-0x10-0

Kit
16-0x10-0

Family
18-4x14-8

Study
12-8x10-0

Dining
11-4x13-0

Foyer

Up

Living
14-8x12-8

Porch

Arbor

First Floor
1,354 sq. ft.

Br 4
12-0x11-0

Br 3
13-0x11-0

Br 2
12-0x13-0

Dn

MBr
20-4x14-4

Alcove
10-0x7-0

Second Floor
1,418 sq. ft.

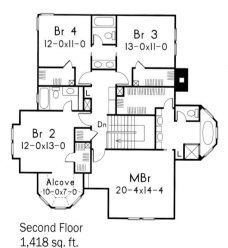

Images provided by designer/architect

Plan #F10-065S-0033

Dimensions:	85' W x 99'7" D
Heated Sq. Ft.:	8,292
Bedrooms: 4	Bathrooms: 5½
Foundation:	Basement

See index for more information

Features

- Amazing Country French home has the style of a European chateau
- A stylish pub is near the cozy sitting room with a corner fireplace that has access to a covered porch with an outdoor fireplace
- A stunning dome ceiling graces the luxurious master bedroom featuring a private bath and a huge walk-in closet
- Hours of fun and relaxation is the intent of the finished lower level with a large recreation room, a wet bar, and a unique soccer room
- 3-car side entry garage

Second Floor
1,684 sq. ft.

© Copyright by
designer/architect

Lower Level
2,513 sq. ft.

First Floor
4,095 sq. ft.

Images provided by designer/architect

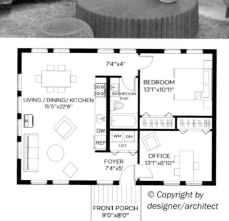

Plan #F10-181D-0005

Dimensions:	36' W x 24' D
Heated Sq. Ft.:	777
Bedrooms: 1	**Bathrooms:** 1
Exterior Walls:	2" x 6"

Foundation: Slab standard; crawl space or basement for an additional fee

See index for more information

Images provided by designer/architect

© Copyright by designer/architect

7'4"x4'

BEDROOM
13'1"x10'11"

LIVING / DINING/ KITCHEN
15'5"x22'6"

BATHROOM
5'x9'

DW

REF | WM DM
LDY

FOYER
7'4"x5'

OFFICE
13'1"x8'10"

FRONT PORCH
9'0"x8'0"

© Copyright by designer/architect

Plan #F10-180D-0025

Dimensions:	28' W x 36' D
Heated Sq. Ft.:	784
Bedrooms: 2	**Bathrooms:** 1
Exterior Walls:	2" x 6"

Foundation: Crawl space or slab, please specify when ordering

See index for more information

Images provided by designer/architect

BED-1
10'6 X 10'6

QUEEN

DESK

5'0 TUB / SHOWER

BATH
5 X 12

TOWELS

DRESSER

DESK

BED-2
10'6 X 10'6

QUEEN

4 FT CLOSET | SHELVES

LINEN

4 FT CLOSET

FURN.

PANTRY | H/W | W/D

HALL

(9FT CEILING)

BENCH & HOOKS

30 FR

ISLAND
72" X 42"

LIVING RM.
15'3 X 13'8

FURNITURE

KITCHEN
11'8 X 13'8

DW

BBQ

OPEN DECK
11'6 X 8'0

COVERED PORCH
16'6 X 8'0

2 STEPS

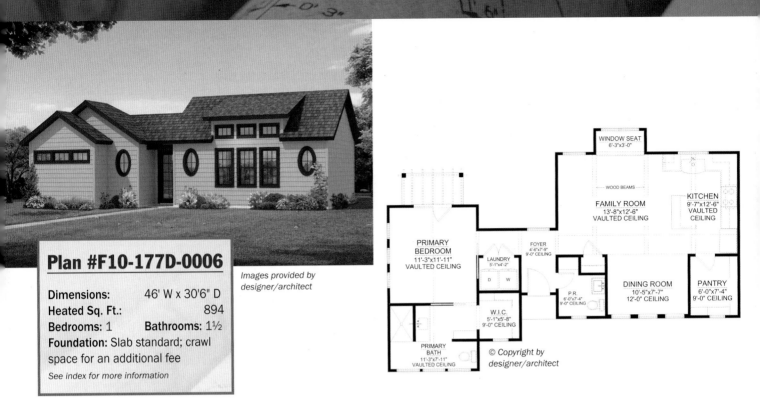

Plan #F10-177D-0006

Dimensions:	46' W x 30'6" D
Heated Sq. Ft.:	894
Bedrooms: 1	**Bathrooms:** 1½

Foundation: Slab standard; crawl space for an additional fee

See index for more information

Images provided by designer/architect

© Copyright by designer/architect

Plan #F10-180D-0060

Dimensions:	42' W x 52'8" D
Heated Sq. Ft.:	2,421
Bedrooms: 6	**Bathrooms:** 3
Exterior Walls:	2" x 6"

Foundation: Crawl space or slab, please specify when ordering

See index for more information

Images provided by designer/architect

Second Floor
1,194 sq. ft.

First Floor
1,227 sq. ft.

Plan #F10-167D-0003

Dimensions:	50'6" W x 50'5" D
Heated Sq. Ft.:	2,569
Bonus Sq. Ft.:	508
Bedrooms:	4
Bathrooms:	3 full, 2 half
Exterior Walls:	2" x 6"

Foundation: Crawl space standard; slab or basement for an additional fee

See index for more information

Images provided by designer/architect

Features

- Two stories of great family living can be found inside this Craftsman home
- Double doors off the foyer lead to an office
- The vaulted living room with fireplace is open to a dining area and the kitchen
- The awesome mudroom has a walk-in pantry, coat closet, and locker space
- The first floor owner's suite has a lovely bath with a huge walk-in shower and walk-in closet
- The second floor has three additional bedrooms and two baths
- The detached garage has a pool bath and an optional loft space above that has 508 square feet that could be finished into a game room or play area
- 2-car detached garage

Second Floor
848 sq. ft.

First Floor
1,721 sq. ft.

© Copyright by designer/architect

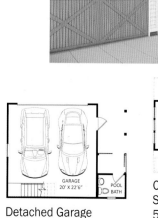

Detached Garage

Optional Second Floor
508 sq. ft.

514   call 1-800-373-2646   houseplansandmore.com

Home Plans Index

Plan Number	Square Feet	PDF File	Page	Plan Number	Square Feet	PDF File	Page	Plan Number	Square Feet	PDF File	Page
F10-001D-0013	1,882	$1,049	322	F10-007D-0168	1,814	$1,049	480	F10-011D-0657	1,394	$1,263	135
F10-001D-0024	1,360	$949	342	F10-007D-0172	1,646	$1,049	386	F10-011D-0660	1,704	$1,423	245
F10-001D-0031	1,501	$1,049	403	F10-007D-0178	1,203	$949	470	F10-011D-0662	2,460	$1,701	254
F10-001D-0036	1,320	$949	437	F10-007D-0181	1,140	$949	429	F10-011D-0664	2,576	$1,888	112
F10-001D-0040	864	$849	385	F10-007D-0192	1,420	$949	420	F10-011D-0674	1,552	$1,321	190
F10-001D-0041	1,000	$849	338	F10-007D-0199	496	$449	293	F10-011D-0676	1,196	$1,184	195
F10-001D-0067	1,285	$949	272	F10-007D-0207	2,884	$1,249	106	F10-011D-0681	2,577	$1,738	348
F10-001D-0085	720	$649	341	F10-007D-0235	2,213	$1,149	475	F10-011D-0682	2,451	$1,638	485
F10-001D-0086	1,154	$949	336	F10-007D-0244	1,605	$1,049	414	F10-011D-0683	944	$1,080	181
F10-001D-0088	800	$649	339	F10-007D-0252	2,593	$1,249	343	F10-011D-0685	2,179	$1,544	441
F10-003D-0005	1,708	$1,049	429	F10-007D-5060	1,344	$949	341	F10-011D-0686	2,009	$1,472	484
F10-005D-0001	1,400	$949	320	F10-008D-0016	768	$649	436	F10-011D-0687	1,975	$1,501	256
F10-007D-0008	2,452	$1,149	415	F10-008D-0133	624	$649	387	F10-011D-0692	1,855	$1,429	350
F10-007D-0010	1,845	$1,049	311	F10-008D-0134	1,275	$949	257	F10-011D-0738	2,117	$1,556	332
F10-007D-0029	576	$649	340	F10-008D-0148	784	$649	265	F10-011D-0757	2,456	$1,575	330
F10-007D-0040	632	$600	316	F10-008D-0153	792	$649	335	F10-011D-0770	2,588	$1,846	319
F10-007D-0042	914	$849	391	F10-008D-0161	618	$649	488	F10-011S-0018	4,600	$2,502	167
F10-007D-0043	647	$649	342	F10-011D-0006	1,873	$1,482	165	F10-011S-0066	4,270	$2,471	258
F10-007D-0049	1,791	$1,049	71	F10-011D-0007	1,580	$1,323	334	F10-011S-0085	6,658	$3,267	43
F10-007D-0055	2,029	$1,149	315	F10-011D-0008	1,728	$1,390	122	F10-011S-0087	4,372	$2,562	35
F10-007D-0060	1,268	$949	309	F10-011D-0013	2,001	$1,513	87	F10-011S-0088	4,352	$2,443	19
F10-007D-0062	2,483	$1,149	94	F10-011D-0037	2,262	$1,741	186	F10-011S-0090	4,887	$2,729	44
F10-007D-0070	929	$700	390	F10-011D-0069	1,999	$1,468	215	F10-011S-0103	3,558	$2,088	486
F10-007D-0075	2,194	$1,149	437	F10-011D-0091	2,650	$1,763	93	F10-011S-0112	5,155	$2,755	358
F10-007D-0077	1,978	$1,049	321	F10-011D-0225	1,891	$1,431	54	F10-011S-0130	3,623	$2,112	47
F10-007D-0085	1,787	$1,049	302	F10-011D-0246	2,080	$1,520	145	F10-011S-0143	3,926	$2,226	438
F10-007D-0088	1,299	$949	424	F10-011D-0266	2,190	$1,635	431	F10-011S-0184	5,266	$2,739	270
F10-007D-0102	1,452	$949	386	F10-011D-0272	1,899	$1,512	259	F10-011S-0187	4,142	$2,425	33
F10-007D-0104	1,207	$949	361	F10-011D-0311	1,988	$1,497	172	F10-011S-0189	4,903	$2,821	12
F10-007D-0105	1,084	$849	326	F10-011D-0335	2,557	$1,718	177	F10-011S-0191	6,349	$3,181	88
F10-007D-0108	983	$849	329	F10-011D-0342	2,368	$1,674	262	F10-011S-0192	4,106	$2,339	407
F10-007D-0109	888	$849	485	F10-011D-0347	2,910	$1,889	183	F10-011S-0195	4,455	$2,446	413
F10-007D-0110	1,169	$949	369	F10-011D-0351	3,242	$1,984	84	F10-011S-0196	7,149	$3,449	28
F10-007D-0113	2,547	$1,249	336	F10-011D-0417	3,084	$1,963	9	F10-011S-0210	3,504	$2,074	170
F10-007D-0114	1,671	$1,049	317	F10-011D-0440	2,002	$1,520	213	F10-013D-0015	1,787	$1,295	137
F10-007D-0117	2,695	$1,249	334	F10-011D-0507	2,074	$1,534	70	F10-013D-0022	1,992	$1,295	110
F10-007D-0124	1,944	$1,049	323	F10-011D-0526	2,735	$1,943	218	F10-013D-0025	2,097	$1,395	71
F10-007D-0128	1,072	$849	323	F10-011D-0527	2,373	$1,753	139	F10-013D-0027	2,184	$1,395	388
F10-007D-0134	1,310	$949	418	F10-011D-0542	2,217	$1,551	77	F10-013D-0039	2,972	$1,495	75
F10-007D-0135	801	$849	211	F10-011D-0586	2,988	$1,878	226	F10-013D-0048	2,071	$1,395	444
F10-007D-0136	1,532	$1,049	310	F10-011D-0588	3,026	$1,932	76	F10-013D-0053	2,461	$1,395	98
F10-007D-0137	1,568	$1,049	477	F10-011D-0617	2,104	$1,663	215	F10-013D-0133	953	$1,045	338
F10-007D-0140	1,591	$1,049	312	F10-011D-0627	1,878	$1,475	27	F10-013D-0134	1,496	$1,195	329
F10-007D-0146	1,929	$1,049	351	F10-011D-0640	1,834	$1,456	236	F10-013D-0154	953	$1,045	80
F10-007D-0161	1,480	$949	206	F10-011D-0642	2,608	$1,704	191	F10-013D-0155	1,800	$1,295	444
F10-007D-0162	1,519	$1,049	334	F10-011D-0650	2,213	$1,757	213	F10-013D-0156	1,800	$1,295	394
F10-007D-0164	1,741	$1,049	352	F10-011D-0652	2,448	$1,677	207				

515

Home Plans Index

Plan Number	Square Feet	PDF File	Page	Plan Number	Square Feet	PDF File	Page	Plan Number	Square Feet	PDF File	Page
F10-013D-0159	1,992	$1,295	385	F10-024S-0008	3,366	$3,328	152	F10-028D-0120	2,096	$1,050	244
F10-013D-0168	2,000	$1,395	210	F10-024S-0011	3,493	$3,328	121	F10-028D-0122	2,352	$1,050	272
F10-013D-0198	1,399	$1,195	395	F10-024S-0021	5,862	$3,328	427	F10-028D-0141	1,334	$850	150
F10-013D-0199	1,666	$1,295	294	F10-024S-0024	3,610	$3,328	93	F10-032D-0040	1,480	$1,395	41
F10-013D-0200	4,508	$1,395	466	F10-024S-0025	4,099	$3,328	238	F10-032D-0368	1,625	$1,555	176
F10-013D-0201	2,294	$1,395	433	F10-024S-0026	4,957	$3,328	454	F10-032D-0482	3,513	$2,290	506
F10-013D-0204	1,671	$1,295	214	F10-024S-0030	4,424	$3,328	157	F10-032D-0513	1,832	$1,605	83
F10-013D-0229	1,800	$1,295	368	F10-024S-0037	4,380	$3,328	451	F10-032D-0709	480	$1,125	176
F10-013D-0236	2,183	$1,395	217	F10-026D-0175	3,094	$1,255	40	F10-032D-0808	900	$1,180	327
F10-013D-0253	2,943	$1,495	212	F10-026D-1856	9,360	$7,490	449	F10-032D-0809	924	$1,180	303
F10-013D-0256	3,630	$1,495	228	F10-026D-1870	2,255	$1,155	40	F10-032D-0825	1,313	$1,395	125
F10-013D-0257	1,059	$1,195	301	F10-026D-1871	1,945	$1,105	368	F10-032D-0834	2,064	$1,605	402
F10-013S-0009	3,799	$2,150	203	F10-026D-1872	2,495	$1,155	267	F10-032D-0880	1,944	$1,605	359
F10-013S-0010	6,342	$2,150	307	F10-026D-1876	1,995	$1,105	172	F10-032D-0884	1,587	$1,555	406
F10-013S-0011	5,565	$2,150	235	F10-026D-1890	2,449	$1,155	54	F10-032D-0885	2,808	$2,230	255
F10-013S-0013	4,689	$2,150	169	F10-026D-1891	2,407	$1,155	60	F10-032D-0887	1,212	$1,395	223
F10-013S-0014	7,434	$2,150	464	F10-026D-1901	1,973	$1,105	384	F10-032D-0919	2,021	$1,605	242
F10-013S-0015	5,085	$1,695	174	F10-026D-1913	3,322	$1,255	290	F10-032D-0963	1,178	$1,340	239
F10-016D-0005	2,347	$1,125	39	F10-026D-1923	2,721	$1,205	489	F10-032D-0965	1,024	$1,340	423
F10-016D-0029	1,635	$940	164	F10-026D-1930	2,794	$1,205	453	F10-032D-1023	1,556	$1,555	349
F10-016D-0048	2,567	$1,155	31	F10-026D-1939	1,635	$1,105	146	F10-032D-1067	3,599	$2,290	154
F10-016D-0049	1,793	$995	49	F10-026D-1997	1,356	$1,055	346	F10-032D-1068	1,816	$1,605	62
F10-016D-0062	1,380	$870	179	F10-026D-1999	2,292	$1,155	410	F10-032D-1071	3,170	$2,035	185
F10-016D-0105	2,065	$1,040	398	F10-026D-2007	2,506	$1,205	288	F10-032D-1104	1,920	$1,605	271
F10-017D-0006	3,006	$1,205	157	F10-026D-2072	1,619	$1,105	249	F10-032D-1108	1,188	$1,340	309
F10-017D-0010	1,660	$940	469	F10-026D-2079	1,600	$1,105	299	F10-032D-1112	2,380	$1,715	134
F10-019D-0046	2,413	$1,995	57	F10-026D-2092	2,448	$1,155	273	F10-032D-1122	1,583	$1,555	240
F10-019S-0004	3,381	$1,995	32	F10-026D-2102	2,155	$1,155	131	F10-032D-1123	2,496	$1,715	166
F10-019S-0007	3,886	$1,995	190	F10-026D-2113	1,390	$1,055	194	F10-032D-1124	2,117	$1,605	216
F10-019S-0008	4,420	$1,995	402	F10-026D-2117	1,511	$1,105	364	F10-032D-1135	1,788	$1,555	42
F10-020D-0015	1,191	$900	496	F10-026D-2134	1,387	$1,005	264	F10-032D-1142	1,209	$1,395	396
F10-020D-0250	2,020	$1,100	47	F10-026S-0018	4,629	$3,215	90	F10-032D-1143	1,891	$1,605	299
F10-020D-0305	2,791	$1,200	102	F10-026S-0020	4,719	$3,215	401	F10-032D-1145	2,814	$2,035	182
F10-020D-0317	3,119	$1,250	111	F10-027D-0005	2,135	$1,149	169	F10-032D-1151	2,113	$1,605	243
F10-020D-0348	2,342	$1,100	45	F10-028D-0001	864	$795	129	F10-032D-1212	1,940	$1,605	333
F10-020D-0363	1,832	$1,000	484	F10-028D-0022	3,029	$1,250	498	F10-033D-0012	1,546	$1,510	337
F10-020D-0365	1,976	$1,000	153	F10-028D-0054	2,123	$1,050	103	F10-034D-0104	1,598	$1,210	508
F10-020S-0014	3,568	$1,350	46	F10-028D-0057	1,007	$850	432	F10-034D-0105	1,598	$1,210	499
F10-022D-0026	1,993	$1,049	23	F10-028D-0064	1,292	$850	173	F10-034D-0109	1,917	$1,210	503
F10-024D-0008	1,650	$1,953*	55	F10-028D-0097	1,908	$1,050	38	F10-036D-0205	2,533	$1,485	509
F10-024D-0011	1,819	$1,309	127	F10-028D-0099	1,320	$850	234	F10-036D-0208	2,487	$1,335	502
F10-024D-0013	1,863	$1,309	136	F10-028D-0100	1,311	$850	195	F10-036D-0242	3,341	$1,685	14
F10-024D-0062	4,257	$2,261	41	F10-028D-0103	1,520	$1,050	228	F10-037D-0005	3,050	$1,349	129
F10-024D-0624	3,223	$3,328	142	F10-028D-0106	2,525	$1,150	303	F10-037D-0015	2,772	$1,249	510
F10-024D-0795	3,076	$3,328	392	F10-028D-0109	890	$795	353	F10-038D-0086	3,526	$1,180	165
F10-024D-0797	2,780	$3,328	280	F10-028D-0115	1,035	$850	337	F10-040D-0016	3,013	$1,349	158
				F10-028D-0116	1,120	$850	251	F10-040D-0029	1,028	$849	425

Home Plans Index

Plan Number	Square Feet	PDF File	Page	Plan Number	Square Feet	PDF File	Page	Plan Number	Square Feet	PDF File	Page
F10-041D-0006	1,189	$949	152	F10-055D-0990	2,555	$2,050	405	F10-076D-0209	3,033	$1,995	419
F10-046D-0015	1,844	$1,049	432	F10-055D-1039	2,661	$1,550	97	F10-076D-0210	2,650	$1,800	292
F10-047D-0022	1,768	$950	50	F10-055D-1049	2,470	$1,550	78	F10-076D-0213	2,896	$1,800	453
F10-047D-0083	2,293	$1,050	193	F10-055D-1070	2,498	$1,550	149	F10-076D-0219	3,060	$1,995	224
F10-051D-0246	3,099	$1,478	325	F10-055D-1077	1,516	$800	265	F10-076D-0220	3,061	$1,995	56
F10-051D-0670	3,109	$1,478	38	F10-055S-0036	4,121	$2,250	204	F10-076D-0221	2,485	$1,800	411
F10-051D-0696	2,016	$1,305	436	F10-055S-0105	3,374	$2,050	495	F10-076D-0223	2,818	$1,800	36
F10-051D-0736	1,662	$1,215	269	F10-055S-0115	4,501	$2,050	409	F10-076D-0226	3,277	$1,995	494
F10-051D-0757	1,501	$1,215	340	F10-055S-0127	3,766	$1,650	263	F10-076D-0230	2,298	$1,800	22
F10-051D-0847	1,047	$1,130	369	F10-056D-0094	3,104	$1,445	13	F10-076D-0237	2,780	$1,800	414
F10-051D-0849	1,170	$1,130	365	F10-056D-0098	3,123	$2,195	15	F10-076D-0238	2,925	$1,800	86
F10-051D-0850	1,334	$1,172	217	F10-056D-0104	1,925	$1,245	220	F10-076D-0239	2,772	$1,800	246
F10-051D-0852	1,432	$1,172	250	F10-056D-0134	4,917	$2,495	455	F10-076D-0249	2,488	$1,800	344
F10-051D-0879	3,651	$2,118	477	F10-056D-0137	2,342	$1,495	207	F10-076D-0255	2,435	$1,800	180
F10-051D-0886	4,540	$2,633	64	F10-056S-0021	3,314	$1,443	363	F10-076D-0259	1,730	$1,400	221
F10-051D-0960	2,784	$1,433	144	F10-056S-0049	5,780	$2,895	426	F10-076D-0260	1,949	$1,400	489
F10-051D-0963	3,485	$1,518	147	F10-057D-0013	1,117	$949	354	F10-076D-0264	1,426	$1,200	468
F10-051D-0964	4,206	$2,439	100	F10-058D-0016	1,558	$700	23	F10-076D-0265	1,276	$1,200	352
F10-051D-0970	1,354	$1,172	138	F10-058D-0020	1,428	$700	314	F10-076D-0280	2,585	$1,800	188
F10-051D-0972	1,490	$1,172	131	F10-058D-0171	1,635	$700	229	F10-076D-0281	3,204	$1,995	487
F10-051D-0977	1,837	$1,257	39	F10-058D-0240	1,594	$700	467	F10-076D-0287	2,159	$1,800	348
F10-051D-0991	3,583	$2,078	155	F10-058D-0241	1,330	$700	360	F10-076D-0290	2,535	$1,800	212
F10-051D-0993	4,210	$2,442	72	F10-058D-0249	1,699	$700	269	F10-076D-0304	2,162	$1,800	244
F10-051D-1009	4,388	$2,545	162	F10-060D-0229	1,944	$1,049	92	F10-077D-0002	1,855	$1,595	82
F10-051S-0054	4,579	$2,656	446	F10-060D-0233	1,962	$1,049	75	F10-077D-0019	1,400	$1,455	326
F10-052D-0073	2,389	$1,200	48	F10-060D-0400	2,871	$1,349	123	F10-077D-0024	1,488	$1,455	471
F10-052D-0147	2,706	$1,400	94	F10-062D-0047	1,230	$855	473	F10-077D-0039	1,654	$1,595	312
F10-052D-0157	2,067	$1,200	351	F10-065D-0002	2,101	$1,050	124	F10-077D-0042	1,752	$1,595	308
F10-053D-0002	1,668	$1,100	122	F10-065D-0062	1,390	$925	339	F10-077D-0043	1,752	$1,595	481
F10-055D-0030	2,107	$1,100	126	F10-065D-0166	1,698	$925	95	F10-077D-0052	1,802	$1,595	295
F10-055D-0031	2,133	$1,000	130	F10-065D-0307	2,246	$1,050	496	F10-077D-0058	2,002	$1,645	143
F10-055D-0162	1,921	$1,100	316	F10-065D-0315	1,597	$925	384	F10-077D-0088	800	$1,315	241
F10-055D-0192	2,096	$1,200	95	F10-065D-0320	2,234	$1,050	467	F10-077D-0131	2,021	$1,645	237
F10-055D-0193	2,129	$1,100	328	F10-065D-0372	2,479	$1,050	268	F10-077D-0138	1,509	$1,595	256
F10-055D-0194	1,379	$800	30	F10-065D-0458	1,764	$925	500	F10-077D-0142	2,067	$1,645	194
F10-055D-0196	2,039	$1,100	214	F10-065D-0459	2,700	$1,050	508	F10-077D-0165	1,800	$1,595	345
F10-055D-0199	2,951	$1,350	99	F10-065D-0460	1,706	$925	500	F10-077D-0184	2,400	$1,645	410
F10-055D-0205	1,989	$1,100	353	F10-065S-0033	8,292	$1,500	511	F10-077D-0187	1,816	$1,595	440
F10-055D-0213	1,921	$1,100	503	F10-065S-0034	6,465	$1,500	141	F10-077D-0250	1,627	$1,595	476
F10-055D-0214	2,373	$1,200	490	F10-071S-0001	7,900	$4,600	274	F10-077D-0291	2,149	$1,645	349
F10-055D-0215	2,470	$1,200	160	F10-071S-0007	5,250	$3,100	492	F10-077D-0293	1,800	$1,645	177
F10-055D-0677	3,167	$1,550	121	F10-071S-0019	4,300	$3,400	404	F10-077D-0294	1,600	$1,595	252
F10-055D-0748	2,525	$1,100	109	F10-071S-0030	4,336	$2,700	171	F10-077D-0295	1,416	$1,595	185
F10-055D-0790	2,075	$1,200	98	F10-071S-0032	4,725	$2,700	450	F10-077D-0297	904	$1,315	301
F10-055D-0939	1,621	$1,100	505	F10-071S-0051	4,309	$2,700	478	F10-080D-0004	1,154	$945	83
F10-055D-0954	3,843	$1,650	498	F10-072D-1108	2,445	$1,149	101	F10-080D-0012	1,370	$945	202
F10-055D-0976	2,180	$1,550	328	F10-072D-1121	3,718	$1,349	120				

Home Plans Index

Plan Number	Square Feet	PDF File	Page	Plan Number	Square Feet	PDF File	Page	Plan Number	Square Feet	PDF File	Page
F10-080D-0014	1,923	$945	168	F10-101D-0077	2,422	$1,750	281	F10-121D-0025	1,368	$949	327
F10-082D-0030	3,962	$4,735	48	F10-101D-0080	2,682	$1,750	279	F10-121D-0028	1,433	$949	394
F10-082D-0066	1,833	$1,275	11	F10-101D-0086	3,587	$2,200	164	F10-121D-0035	1,759	$1,049	425
F10-082S-0001	6,816	$5,500	24	F10-101D-0093	2,615	$1,750	156	F10-121D-0036	1,820	$1,049	333
F10-084D-0016	1,492	$1,060	178	F10-101D-0094	2,650	$1,750	148	F10-121D-0037	2,240	$1,149	350
F10-084D-0063	2,280	$1,260	365	F10-101D-0101	3,307	$2,200	482	F10-121D-0040	1,863	$1,049	288
F10-084D-0085	2,252	$1,260	381	F10-101D-0107	2,861	$1,950	34	F10-121D-0046	1,983	$1,049	245
F10-084D-0086	1,725	$1,160	151	F10-101D-0113	3,082	$1,950	163	F10-121D-0047	1,983	$1,049	294
F10-084D-0087	3,507	$1,460	241	F10-101D-0118	2,775	$1,950	192	F10-121D-0048	1,615	$1,049	403
F10-084D-0089	1,769	$1,160	191	F10-101D-0121	3,380	$2,200	227	F10-121D-0050	1,988	$1,049	481
F10-084D-0090	2,221	$1,260	248	F10-101D-0122	4,966	$3,850	128	F10-122D-0001	1,105	$949	428
F10-084D-0091	1,936	$1,160	26	F10-101D-0123	3,456	$2,200	61	F10-123D-0006	1,343	$1,200	82
F10-084D-0092	2,366	$1,260	313	F10-101D-0125	2,970	$1,950	232	F10-123D-0056	1,701	$1,400	306
F10-088D-0141	3,304	$1,495	324	F10-101D-0131	2,889	$1,950	37	F10-123D-0060	1,185	$1,200	388
F10-088D-0242	2,281	$1,295	343	F10-101D-0228	2,730	$1,950	318	F10-123D-0112	1,797	$1,400	158
F10-088D-0594	2,264	$1,295	211	F10-101D-0230	2,439	$1,750	65	F10-123D-0150	2,076	$1,500	422
F10-088D-0608	4,234	$2,295	297	F10-106D-0036	2,762	$1,400	411	F10-123D-0156	2,015	$1,500	236
F10-088D-0731	3,643	$1,895	381	F10-106D-0051	6,488	$2,100	430	F10-123D-0171	1,030	$1,100	252
F10-088D-0736	2,910	$1,345	361	F10-106S-0062	6,175	$2,500	412	F10-126D-0832	2,453	$1,070	20
F10-088D-0828	2,242	$1,295	399	F10-106S-0070	7,100	$2,600	378	F10-126D-0883	1,377	$920	472
F10-091D-0017	2,982	$2,050	89	F10-111D-0005	1,940	$995	55	F10-126D-0903	2,145	$1,070	187
F10-091D-0021	3,289	$2,050	434	F10-111D-0009	2,112	$1,445	123	F10-126D-1012	815	$730	474
F10-091D-0023	3,253	$2,050	125	F10-111D-0029	3,162	$1,995	31	F10-126D-1174	1,318	$920	206
F10-091D-0449	3,207	$2,050	21	F10-111D-0031	3,236	$1,995	49	F10-126D-1175	910	$760	345
F10-091D-0478	1,598	$1,725	111	F10-111D-0035	1,338	$995	70	F10-128D-0010	2,069	$1,100	439
F10-091D-0485	1,918	$1,725	73	F10-111D-0036	1,391	$995	50	F10-128D-0065	2,441	$1,100	201
F10-091D-0506	2,241	$2,050	296	F10-111D-0037	1,466	$995	221	F10-128D-0097	2,479	$1,100	159
F10-091D-0507	2,486	$2,050	497	F10-111D-0039	1,846	$995	366	F10-128D-0108	3,480	$1,200	159
F10-091D-0520	2,751	$2,050	355	F10-111D-0040	2,154	$1,445	273	F10-128D-0318	1,966	$1,000	428
F10-091D-0523	2,514	$2,050	380	F10-111D-0050	2,090	$1,445	143	F10-129S-0021	3,359	$1,550	74
F10-091D-0525	2,453	$2,050	80	F10-111D-0060	1,768	$995	107	F10-130D-0135	2,252	$1,055	78
F10-095D-0044	2,596	$1,249	502	F10-111D-0066	1,933	$995	102	F10-130D-0335	2,796	$1,085	418
F10-095D-0049	2,136	$1,149	509	F10-111D-0081	2,137	$1,445	237	F10-130D-0344	2,062	$1,025	433
F10-101D-0002	1,612	$1,450	120	F10-111D-0095	2,458	$1,445	300	F10-130D-0366	1,720	$985	399
F10-101D-0027	5,002	$3,850	96	F10-111D-0101	2,662	$1,445	173	F10-130D-0372	1,597	$965	445
F10-101D-0041	4,908	$3,850	397	F10-111D-0113	3,132	$1,995	168	F10-130D-0377	1,284	$945	421
F10-101D-0044	3,897	$2,400	260	F10-111D-0117	3,228	$1,995	383	F10-130D-0391	1,558	$965	391
F10-101D-0045	1,885	$1,550	408	F10-111S-0005	3,937	$1,995	222	F10-130D-0395	1,420	$965	383
F10-101D-0047	2,478	$1,750	304	F10-116D-0045	2,313	$1,250	51	F10-130D-0396	1,420	$965	415
F10-101D-0050	4,784	$3,400	16	F10-121D-0006	2,241	$1,149	277	F10-137D-0065	2,361	$1,149	22
F10-101D-0052	2,611	$1,750	231	F10-121D-0010	1,281	$949	308	F10-137D-0082	1,442	$949	142
F10-101D-0056	2,593	$1,750	140	F10-121D-0011	2,241	$1,149	81	F10-137D-0271	1,094	$849	124
F10-101D-0057	2,037	$1,550	8	F10-121D-0015	1,983	$1,049	295	F10-139D-0009	2,954	$1,595	475
F10-101D-0061	6,563	$4,500	53	F10-121D-0016	1,582	$1,049	322	F10-139D-0022	2,880	$1,595	398
F10-101D-0062	2,648	$1,750	104	F10-121D-0017	1,379	$949	470	F10-139D-0038	2,368	$1,595	209
F10-101D-0065	2,269	$1,550	491	F10-121D-0020	2,037	$1,149	249	F10-139D-0041	2,073	$1,595	389
				F10-121D-0023	1,762	$1,049	268	F10-139D-0047	4,086	$1,595	278

Home Plans Index

Plan Number	Square Feet	PDF File	Page	Plan Number	Square Feet	PDF File	Page	Plan Number	Square Feet	PDF File	Page
F10-140D-0002	1,553	$1,049	137	F10-155D-0053	2,506	$1,650	504	F10-167D-0006	2,939	$1,249	257
F10-140D-0006	1,765	$1,049	46	F10-155D-0062	6,554	$3,250	483	F10-167D-0008	3,328	$1,349	230
F10-141D-0011	1,843	$1,715	132	F10-155D-0065	1,897	$1,200	313	F10-167D-0009	3,363	$1,349	442
F10-141D-0013	1,200	$1,435	389	F10-155D-0079	2,381	$1,650	30	F10-167D-0010	3,409	$1,349	208
F10-141D-0014	1,973	$1,715	179	F10-155D-0111	4,575	$2,050	367	F10-169D-0001	1,400	$949	184
F10-141D-0016	1,990	$1,715	229	F10-155D-0134	2,031	$1,200	184	F10-169D-0002	1,762	$1,049	180
F10-141D-0018	1,979	$1,715	253	F10-155D-0153	1,967	$1,200	420	F10-169D-0003	1,762	$1,049	99
F10-141D-0021	1,267	$1,505	300	F10-155D-0162	2,294	$1,100	317	F10-169D-0004	520	$649	417
F10-141D-0027	2,272	$2,135	79	F10-155D-0170	1,897	$1,200	81	F10-169D-0005	809	$849	63
F10-141D-0036	3,500	$2,795	382	F10-155D-0171	1,131	$1,000	298	F10-170D-0001	1,768	$845	106
F10-141D-0037	2,697	$2,135	51	F10-155D-0179	2,382	$1,100	302	F10-170D-0003	2,672	$945	15
F10-141D-0088	3,036	$2,835	126	F10-156D-0007	528	$675	277	F10-170D-0004	1,581	$845	85
F10-141D-0207	1,000	$1,435	441	F10-156D-0011	710	$675	347	F10-170D-0005	1,422	$745	63
F10-141D-0223	2,095	$1,855	248	F10-157D-0001	2,182	$966	354	F10-170D-0006	2,176	$1,045	110
F10-141D-0297	2,168	$1,855	419	F10-157D-0006	2,883	$1,029	209	F10-170D-0010	1,824	$845	62
F10-141D-0315	750	$1,295	289	F10-157D-0007	2,303	$966	471	F10-170D-0012	2,605	$945	79
F10-141D-0328	2,100	$1,855	224	F10-157D-0015	2,620	$1,029	220	F10-170D-0015	2,694	$945	14
F10-143D-0001	1,975	$1,250	474	F10-157D-0023	2,873	$1,029	390	F10-170D-0016	3,013	$1,045	156
F10-143D-0003	1,324	$1,175	466	F10-159D-0004	1,655	$1,150	107	F10-170D-0018	2,621	$945	497
F10-143D-0005	1,381	$1,175	296	F10-159D-0010	2,900	$1,200	225	F10-170D-0019	2,648	$945	247
F10-143D-0006	1,400	$1,175	380	F10-159D-0014	2,340	$1,250	421	F10-170D-0022	2,303	$945	181
F10-143D-0007	1,380	$1,175	360	F10-159D-0017	1,200	$1,050	395	F10-172D-0004	2,710	$1,350	507
F10-143D-0008	1,704	$1,200	469	F10-159D-0018	1,818	$1,150	276	F10-172D-0008	3,016	$1,450	448
F10-144D-0001	1,677	$1,150	225	F10-161D-0001	4,036	$2,095	58	F10-172D-0011	1,667	$1,050	416
F10-144D-0004	1,546	$1,150	468	F10-161D-0002	3,959	$1,995	393	F10-172D-0021	2,050	$1,250	452
F10-144D-0005	1,506	$1,150	472	F10-161D-0016	3,275	$1,995	356	F10-172D-0023	1,069	$950	297
F10-144D-0023	928	$1,040	18	F10-161D-0025	4,964	$2,095	400	F10-172D-0024	3,054	$1,450	52
F10-144D-0024	1,024	$1,090	355	F10-161D-0028	4,021	$2,095	266	F10-172D-0025	1,999	$1,250	480
F10-144D-0039	2,148	$1,270	473	F10-163D-0001	3,922	$3,650	216	F10-172D-0028	1,555	$1,050	443
F10-145D-0001	786	$649*	488	F10-163D-0004	681	$1,375	148	F10-172D-0031	1,493	$950	347
F10-147D-0001	1,472	$949	387	F10-163D-0006	1,362	$1,575	136	F10-172D-0040	2,438	$1,250	113
F10-147D-0003	1,773	$1,049	447	F10-163D-0008	3,480	$3,375	130	F10-172D-0041	2,313	$1,250	208
F10-147D-0008	2,136	$1,149	87	F10-163D-0013	1,676	$1,850	293	F10-172D-0051	1,635	$1,050	362
F10-147D-0012	1,500	$949	382	F10-163D-0016	1,825	$1,850	476	F10-177D-0006	894	$995	513
F10-148D-0040	2,181	$1,805	440	F10-164D-0028	4,587	$2,982	149	F10-180D-0022	897	$849	128
F10-148D-0404	1,282	$1,273	452	F10-164D-0030	4,295	$2,792	364	F10-180D-0025	784	$799	512
F10-149D-0004	2,234	$1,160	86	F10-164D-0031	4,522	$2,940	10	F10-180D-0043	1,627	$949	240
F10-149D-0005	2,885	$1,360	92	F10-164D-0036	5,303	$3,447	357	F10-180D-0060	2,421	$999	513
F10-155D-0016	3,307	$2,050	499	F10-164D-0037	4,083	$3,879	74	F10-181D-0001	1,020	$1,249	127
F10-155D-0023	2,470	$1,550	344	F10-164D-0044	3,287	$2,137	346	F10-181D-0002	1,578	$1,249	298
F10-155D-0027	2,513	$1,550	103	F10-166D-0001	2,232	$1,149	445	F10-181D-0005	777	$1,249	512
F10-155D-0030	2,119	$1,350	504	F10-166D-0004	2,512	$1,249	253	F10-185D-0026	1,365	$800	264
F10-155D-0033	1,921	$1,350	505	F10-166D-0005	2,628	$1,249	424	F10-185S-0002	7,519	$4,000	108
F10-155D-0035	5,054	$2,850	153	F10-167D-0001	2,017	$1,149	292				
F10-155D-0039	1,640	$1,100	501	F10-167D-0002	2,063	$1,149	289	*F10-024D-0008 - CAD Package price only			
F10-155D-0048	2,071	$1,350	210	F10-167D-0003	2,569	$1,249	514	*F10-145D-0001 - 5-Set Package price only			
F10-155D-0051	1,806	$1,350	501	F10-167D-0004	2,589	$1,249	276				

why buy
stock plans?

Building a home yourself presents many opportunities to showcase your creativity, individuality, and dreams turned into reality. With these opportunities, many challenges and questions will crop up. Location, size, and budget are all important to consider, as well as special features and amenities. When you begin to examine everything, it can become overwhelming to search for your dream home. But, before you get too anxious, start the search process an easier way and choose a home design that's a stock home plan.

Custom home plans, as well as stock home plans, offer positives and negatives; what is "best" can only be determined by your lifestyle, budget, and time. A customized home plan is one that a homeowner and designer or architect work together to develop from scratch, taking ideas and putting them down on paper. These plans require extra patience, as it may be months before the architect has them drawn and ready. A stock plan is a pre-developed plan that fits the needs and desires of a group of people, or the general population. These are often available within days of purchasing and typically cost up to one-tenth of the price of customized home plans. They still have all of the amenities you were looking for in a home, and usually at a much more affordable price than having custom plans drawn for you.

When compared to a customized plan, some homeowners fear that a stock home will be a carbon copy home, taking away the opportunity for individualism and creating a unique design. This is a common misconception that can waste a lot of money and time!

As you can see from the home designs throughout this book, the variety of stock plans available is truly impressive, encompassing the most up-to-date features and amenities. With a little patience, browse the numerous available stock plans available throughout this book, and easily purchase a plan and be ready to build almost immediately.

Plus, stock plans can be customized. For example, perhaps you see a stock plan that is just about perfect, but you wish the mud room was a tad larger. Rather than go through the cost and time of having a custom home design drawn, you could have our customizing service modify the stock home plan and have your new dream plan ready to go in no time. Also, stock home plans often have a material list available, helping to eliminate unknown costs from developing during construction.

It's often a good idea to speak with someone who has recently built. Did they use stock or custom plans? What would they recommend you do, or do not undertake? Can they recommend professionals that will help you narrow down your options? As you take a look at plans throughout this publication, don't hesitate to take notes, or write down questions. Also, take advantage of our website, houseplansandmore.com. This website is very user-friendly, allowing you to search for the perfect house design by style, size, budget, and a home's features. With all of these tools readily available to you, you'll find the home design of your dreams in no time at all, thanks to the innovative stock plans readily available today that take into account your wishes in a floor plan as well as your wallet.

how can I find out if I can **afford** to build a home?

GET AN ACCURATE ESTIMATED COST-TO-BUILD REPORT

The most important question for someone wanting to build a new home is, "How much is it going to cost?" Obviously, you must have an accurate budget set before ordering house plans and beginning construction, or your dream home will quickly turn into a nightmare. We make building your dream home a much simpler reality thanks to the estimated cost-to-build report available for all of the home plans in this book and on our website, houseplansandmore.com. Price is always the number one factor when choosing a new home. Price dictates the size and the quality of materials you will use. So, it comes as no surprise that having an accurate building estimate prior to making your final decision on a home plan quite possibly is the most important step. If you feel you've found "the" home, then before buying the plans, order a cost-to-build report for the zip code where you want to build. This report is created specifically for you when ordered, and it will educate you on all costs associated with building the home. Simply order the cost-to-build report on houseplansandmore.com for the home design you want to build and gain knowledge of the material and labor cost. Not only does the report allow you to choose the quality of the materials, you can also select from various options from lot condition to contractor fees. Successfully manage your construction budget in all areas, clearly see where the majority of the costs lie, and save money from start to finish. Listed to the right are the categories included in a cost-to-build report. Each category breaks down labor cost, material cost, funds needed, and the report offers the ability to manipulate over/under adjustments if necessary.

BASIC INFORMATION includes your contact information, the state and zip code where you intend to build and material class. This section also includes: square footage, number of windows, fireplaces, balconies, baths, garage location and size, decks, foundation type, and bonus room square footage.

GENERAL SOFT COSTS include cost for plans, customizing (if applicable), building permits, pre-construction services, and planning expenses.

SITE WORK & UTILITIES include water, sewer, electric, and gas. Choose the type of site work and if you'll need a driveway.

FOUNDATION includes a menu that lists the most common types.

FRAMING ROUGH SHELL calculates rough framing costs including framing for fireplaces, balconies, decks, porches, basements and bonus rooms.

ROOFING includes several common options.

DRY OUT SHELL allows you to select doors, windows, and siding.

ELECTRICAL includes wiring and the quality of the light fixtures.

PLUMBING includes labor costs, plumbing materials, plumbing fixtures, and fire proofing materials.

HVAC includes costs for both labor and materials.

INSULATION includes costs for both labor and materials.

FINISH SHELL includes drywall, interior doors and trim, stairs, shower doors, mirrors, bath accessories, and labor costs.

CABINETS & VANITIES select the grade of your cabinets, vanities, kitchen countertops, and bathroom vanity materials, as well as appliances.

PAINTING includes all painting materials, paint quality, and labor.

FLOORING includes over a dozen flooring material options.

SPECIAL EQUIPMENT NEEDS calculate cost for unforeseen expenses.

CONTRACTOR FEE / PROJECT MANAGER includes the cost of your cost-to-build report, project manager and/or general contractor fees. If you're doing the managing yourself, your costs will be tremendously lower in this section.

LAND PAYOFF includes the cost of your land.

RESERVES / CLOSING COSTS includes interest, contingency reserves, and closing costs.

We've taken the guesswork out of figuring out what your new home is going to cost. Take control of construction, determine the major expenses, and save money. Supervise all costs, from labor to materials and manage construction with confidence, which allows you to avoid costly mistakes and unforeseen expenses. To order a Cost-To-Build Report, visit houseplansandmore.com and search for the specific plan. Then, look for the button that says, "Request Your Report" and get started.

what kind of
plan package do I need?

PLEASE NOTE: *Please visit houseplansandmore.com for a plan's options and pricing, or call 1-800-373-2646 for all current options available. The plan pricing shown in this book is subject to change without notice.*

5-SET PLAN PACKAGE includes five complete sets of construction drawings. Besides one set for yourself, additional sets of blueprints will be required for your lender, your local building department, your contractor, and any other tradespeople working on your project.

Please note: These 5 sets of plans are copyrighted, so they can't be altered or copied.

8-SET PLAN PACKAGE includes eight complete sets of construction drawings. Besides one set for yourself, additional sets of blueprints will be required for your lender, your local building department, your contractor, and any other tradespeople working on your project.

Please note: These 8 sets of plans are copyrighted, so they can't be altered or copied.

PDF FILE FORMAT is our most popular plan package option because of how fast you can receive them your blueprints (usually within 24 to 48 hours Monday-Friday), and their ability to be easily shared via email with your contractor, subcontractors, and local building officials. The PDF file format is a complete set of construction drawings in an electronic file format. It includes a one-time build copyright release that allows you to make changes and copies of the plans. Typically you will receive a PDF file via email within 24-48 hours (Monday-Friday, 7:30am-4:30pm CST) allowing you to save money on shipping. Upon receiving, visit a local copy or print shop and print the number of plans you need to build your home, or print one and alter the plan by using correction fluid and drawing in your modifications.

Please note: These are flat image files and cannot be altered electronically. PDF files are non-refundable and not returnable.

CAD FILE FORMAT is the actual computer files for a plan directly from AutoCAD, or another computer aided design program. CAD files are the best option if you have a significant amount of changes to make to the plan, or if you need to make the plan fit your local codes. If you purchase a CAD File, it allows you, or a local design professional the ability to modify the plans electronically in a CAD program, so making changes to the plan is easier and less expensive than using a paper set of plans when modifying. A CAD package also includes a one-time build copyright release that allows you to legally make your changes, and print multiple copies of the plan. See the index for availability and pricing.

Please note: CAD files are non-refundable and not returnable.

MIRROR REVERSE SETS Sometimes a home fits a site better if it is flipped left to right. A mirror reverse set of plans is simply a mirror image of the original drawings causing the lettering and dimensions to read backwards. Therefore, when ordering a mirror reverse set of plans, you must purchase at least one set of the original plans to read from, and use the mirror reverse set for construction. Some plans offer right reading reverse for an additional fee. This means the plan has been redrawn by the designer as the mirrored version and can easily be read.

ADDITIONAL SETS You can order extra plan sets of a plan for an additional fee. A 5-set or 8-set plan package must have been previously purchased.

Please note: Only available within 90 days after purchase of a plan package.

2" X 6" EXTERIOR WALLS 2" x 6" exterior walls can be purchased for some plans for an additional fee (see houseplansandmore.com for availability and pricing).

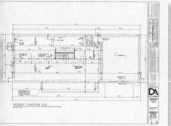

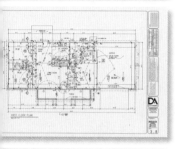

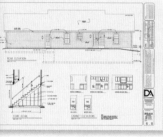

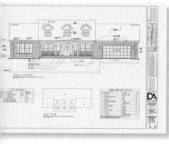

our plan packages include...

Quality plans for building your future, with extras that provide unsurpassed value, ensure good construction and long-term enjoyment. A quality home - one that looks good, functions well, and provides years of enjoyment - is a product of many things - design, materials, and craftsmanship. But it's also the result of outstanding blueprints - the actual plans and specifications that tell the builder exactly how to build your home.

And with our BLUEPRINT PACKAGES you get the absolute best. A complete set of blueprints is available for every design in this book. These "working drawings" are highly detailed, resulting in two key benefits:

- **BETTER UNDERSTANDING BY THE CONTRACTOR OF HOW TO BUILD YOUR HOME AND...**
- **MORE ACCURATE CONSTRUCTION ESTIMATES THAT WILL SAVE YOU TIME AND MONEY.**

Below is a sample of the plan information included for most of the designs in this book. Specific details may vary with each designer's plan. While this information is typical for most plans, we cannot assure the inclusion of all the following referenced items. Please contact us at 1-800-373-2646 for a plan's specific information, including which of the following items are included.

1 cover sheet
is included with many of the plans, the cover sheet is the artist's rendering of the exterior of the home. It will give you an idea of how your home will look when completed and landscaped.

2 foundation
plan shows the layout of the basement, walk-out basement, crawl space, slab or pier foundation. All necessary notations and dimensions are included. See plan page for the foundation types included. If the home plan you choose does not have your desired foundation type, our Customer Service Representatives can advise you on how to customize your foundation to suit your specific needs or site conditions.

3 floor plans
show the placement of walls, doors, closets, plumbing fixtures, electrical outlets, columns, and beams for each level of the home.

4 interior elevations
provide views of special interior elements such as fireplaces, kitchen cabinets, built-in units and other features of the home.

5 exterior elevations
illustrate the front, rear and both sides of the house, with all details of exterior materials and the required dimensions.

6 sections
show detail views of the home or portions of the home as if it were sliced from the roof to the foundation. This sheet shows important areas such as load-bearing walls, stairs, joists, trusses and other structural elements, which are critical for proper construction.

7 details
show how to construct certain components of your home, such as the roof system, stairs, deck, etc.

do you want to make changes to your plan?

We understand that sometimes it is difficult to find blueprints that meet all of your specific needs.
That is why we offer home plan modification services so you can build a home exactly the way you want it!

ARE YOU THINKING ABOUT CUSTOMIZING A PLAN?

If you're like many customers, you may want to make changes to your home plan to make it the dream home you've always wanted. That's where our expert design and modification partners come in. You won't find a more efficient and economic way to get your changes done than by using our home plan customizing services.

Whether it's enlarging a kitchen, adding a porch, or converting a crawl space to a basement, we can customize any plan and make it perfect for your needs. Simply create your wish list and let us go to work. Soon you'll have the blueprints for your new home, and at a fraction of the cost of hiring a local architect!

IT'S EASY!

- We can customize any of the plans in this book, or on houseplansandmore.com.
- We provide a FREE cost estimate for your home plan modifications within 24-48 hours (Monday-Friday, 7:30am-4:30pm CST).
- Average turn-around time to complete the modifications is typically 4-5 weeks.
- You will receive one-on-one design consultations.

CUSTOMIZING FACTS

- The average cost to have a house plan customized is typically less than 1 percent of the building costs — compare that to the national average of 7 percent of building costs.
- The average modification cost for a home is typically $800 to $1,500. This does not include the cost of purchasing the PDF file format of the blueprints, which is required to legally make plan changes.

OTHER HELPFUL INFORMATION

- Sketch, or make a specific list of changes you'd like to make on the Home Plan Modification Request Form.
- A home plan modification specialist will contact you within 24-48 hours with your free estimate.
- Upon accepting the estimate, you will need to purchase the PDF or CAD file format.
- A contract, which includes a specific list of changes and fees will be sent to you prior for your approval.
- Upon approving the contract, our design partners will keep you up to date by emailing sketches throughout the project.
- Plans can be converted to metric, or to a Barrier-free layout (also referred to as a universal home design, which allows easy mobility for an individual with limitations of any kind).

 easy steps

1 visit

houseplansandmore.com and click on the Resources tab at the top of the home page, then click "How to Customize Your House Plan," or scan the QR code here to download the Home Plan Modification Request Form.

2 email

your completed form to: customizehpm@designamerica.com, or fax it to: 651-602-5050.

If you are not able to access the Internet, please call 1-800-373-2646 (Monday-Friday, 7:30am - 4:30pm CST).

helpful **building aids**

Your Blueprint Package will contain all of the necessary construction information you need to build your home. But, we also offer the following products and services to save you time and money during the building process.

MATERIAL LIST

Many of the home plans in this book have a material list available for purchase that gives you the quantity, dimensions, and description of the building materials needed to construct the home (see the index for availability and pricing). Keep in mind, due to variations in local building code requirements, exact material quantities cannot be guaranteed. Note: Material lists are created with the standard foundation type only. Please review the material list and the construction drawings with your material supplier to verify measurements and quantities of the materials listed before ordering supplies.

THE LEGAL KIT

Avoid many legal pitfalls and build your home with confidence using the forms and contracts featured in this kit. Included are request for proposal documents, various fixed price and cost plus contracts, instructions on how and when to use each form, warranty statements and more. Save time and money before you break ground on your new home or start a remodeling project. All forms are reproducible. This kit is ideal for homebuilders and contractors. Cost: $35.00

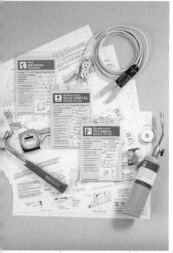

DETAIL PLAN PACKAGES - ELECTRICAL, FRAMING & PLUMBING

Three separate packages offer homebuilders details for constructing various foundations; numerous floor, wall and roof framing techniques; simple to complex residential wiring; sump and water softener hookups; plumbing connection methods; installation of septic systems, and more. Each package includes three dimensional illustrations and a glossary of terms. Purchase one or all three. Please note: These drawings do not pertain to a specific home plan, but they include general guidelines and tips for construction in all 3 of these trades. Cost: $30 each or all three for $60

EXPRESS DELIVERY

Most orders are processed within 24 hours of receipt. Please allow 7-10 business days for standard delivery. If you need to place a rush order, please call us by 11:00am Monday-Friday CST and ask for express service (allow 1-2 business days). Please see page 527 for all shipping and handling charges.

TECHNICAL ASSISTANCE

If you have questions about your blueprints, we offer technical assistance by calling 1-314-770-2228 between 7:30am and 4:30pm Monday-Friday CST. Whether it involves design modifications or field assistance, our home plans team is extremely familiar with all of our home designs and will be happy to help. We want your home to be everything you expect it to be.

before you **order**

Please note: Plan pricing is subject to change without notice. For current pricing, visit houseplansandmore.com, or call us at 1-800-373-2646.

BUILDING CODE REQUIREMENTS At the time the construction drawings were prepared, every effort was made to ensure that these plans and specifications met nationally recognized codes. These plans conform to most national building codes. Because building codes vary from area to area, some drawing modifications and/or the assistance of a professional designer or architect may be necessary to comply with your local codes, or to accommodate your specific building site conditions. We advise you to consult with your local building official, or a local builder for information regarding codes governing your area prior to ordering blueprints.

COPYRIGHT Plans are protected under Copyright Law. Reproduction by any means is strictly prohibited. The right of building only one structure from all plan packages is licensed exclusively to the buyer and the plans may not be resold unless by express written authorization from the home designer, or architect. You may not use this plan to build a second or multiple structure(s) without purchasing a multi-build license. Each violation of the Copyright Law is punishable in a fine.

LICENSE TO BUILD When you purchase a "full set of construction drawings" from Design America, Inc., you are purchasing an exclusive one-time "License to Build," not the rights to the design. Design America, Inc. is granting you permission on behalf of the plan's designer or architect to use the construction drawings one-time for the building of the home. The construction drawings (also referred to as blueprints/plans and any derivative of that plan whether extensive or minor) are still owned and protected under copyright laws by the original designer. The blueprints/plans cannot be resold, transferred, rented, loaned or used by anyone other than the original purchaser of the "License to Build" without written consent from Design America, Inc., or the plan designer. If you are interested in building the plan more than once, please call 1-800-373-2646 and inquire about purchasing a Multi-Build License that will allow you to build a home design more than one time. Please note: A multi-build license can only be purchased if a CAD file or PDF file were initially purchased.

EXCHANGE POLICY Since blueprints are printed in response to your order, we cannot honor requests for refunds.

SHIPPING & HANDLING CHARGES

U.S. SHIPPING -
(AK and HI express only)
Regular (allow 7-10 business days)	$35.00
Priority (allow 3-5 business days)	$55.00
Express* (allow 1-2 business days)	$75.00

CANADA SHIPPING*
Regular (allow 8-12 business days)	$50.00
Express* (allow 3-5 business days)	$100.00

OVERSEAS SHIPPING/INTERNATIONAL
Call, fax, or e-mail (customerservice@designamerica.com) for shipping costs.

*   For express delivery please call us by 11:00am Monday-Friday CST

**   Orders may be subject to custom's fees and or duties/taxes.

Note: Shipping and handling does not apply on PDF and CAD File orders. PDF and CAD File orders will be emailed within 24-48 hours (Monday-Friday, 7:30am-4:30pm CST) of purchase.

Order Form

Please send me the following:

Plan Number: F10-_____

Select Foundation Type: (Select ONE- see plan page for available options).

❏ Slab   ❏ Crawl space   ❏ Basement

❏ Walk-out basement   ❏ Pier

❏ Optional Foundation for an additional fee

    Enter foundation cost here $ _____

Plan Package   Cost

❏ CAD File $ _____

❏ PDF File Format (recommended) $ _____

❏ 8-Set Plan Package $ _____

❏ 5-Set Plan Package $ _____

Visit houseplansandmore.com to see current pricing and all plan package options available, or call 1-800-373-2646.

Important Extras

❏ Additional plan sets*:

    _____ set(s) at $_____ per set $ _____

❏ Print in right-reading reverse:

    one-time additional fee of $_____ $ _____

❏ Print in mirror reverse:

    _____ set(s) at $_____ per set $ _____
    (where right reading reverse is not available)

❏ Material list (see houseplansandmore.com) $ _____

❏ Legal Kit (001D-9991, see page 526) $ _____

Detail Plan Packages: (see page 526)

    ❏ Framing   ❏ Electrical   ❏ Plumbing $ _____
    (001D-9992)   (001D-9993)   (001D-9994)

Shipping (see page 527) $ _____

SUBTOTAL $ _____

Sales Tax (MO residents only, add 8.24%) $ _____

TOTAL $ _____

*Available only within 90 days after purchase of plan.

HELPFUL TIPS

- You can upgrade to a different plan package within 90 days of your plan purchase.
- Additional sets cannot be ordered without purchasing a 5-Set or 8-Set plan package.

Name _____
            (Please print or type)

Street _____
         (Please do not use a P.O. Box)

City _____ State _____

Country _____ Zip _____

Daytime telephone   (_____) _____

E-Mail _____
      (For invoice and tracking information)

Payment   ❏ Bank check/money order. No personal checks.
           Make checks payable to Design America, Inc.

❏ MasterCard   ❏ VISA   ❏ Discover   ❏ American Express Cards

Credit card number _____

Expiration date (mm/yy) _____ CID _____

Signature _____

❏ I hereby authorize Design America, Inc. to charge this purchase to my credit card.

Please check the appropriate box:
❏ Building home for myself
❏ Building home for someone else

ORDER ONLINE

houseplansandmore.com

ORDER BY PHONE

1-800-373-2646
Fax: 314-770-2226

ORDER BY MAIL

Design America, Inc.
734 West Port Plaza, Suite #208
St. Louis, MO 63146

EXPRESS DELIVERY

Most orders are processed within 24 hours of receipt. If you need to place a rush order, please call us by 11:00am CST and ask for express service.

Business Hours: Monday-Friday (7:30am - 4:30pm CST)

Ultimate Book of Home Plans

SOURCE CODE F10